As a Reincarnated ARISTOCRAT, I'll Use My Appraisal Skill to Rise in the World

1

[Story] **Miraijin A**
[Art] **Natsumi Inoue**
[Character Design] **jimmy**

☆☆☆☆☆

CONTENTS

Chapter 1:	Reincarnation and Appraisal	003
Chapter 2:	The Test	051
Chapter 3:	Victory or Defeat	085
Chapter 4:	On the Brink	105
Chapter 5:	Inequality and Change	119
Chapter 6:	Charlotte Lace	135
Chapter 7:	Haves and Have-Nots	153
Chapter 8:	Anger	171

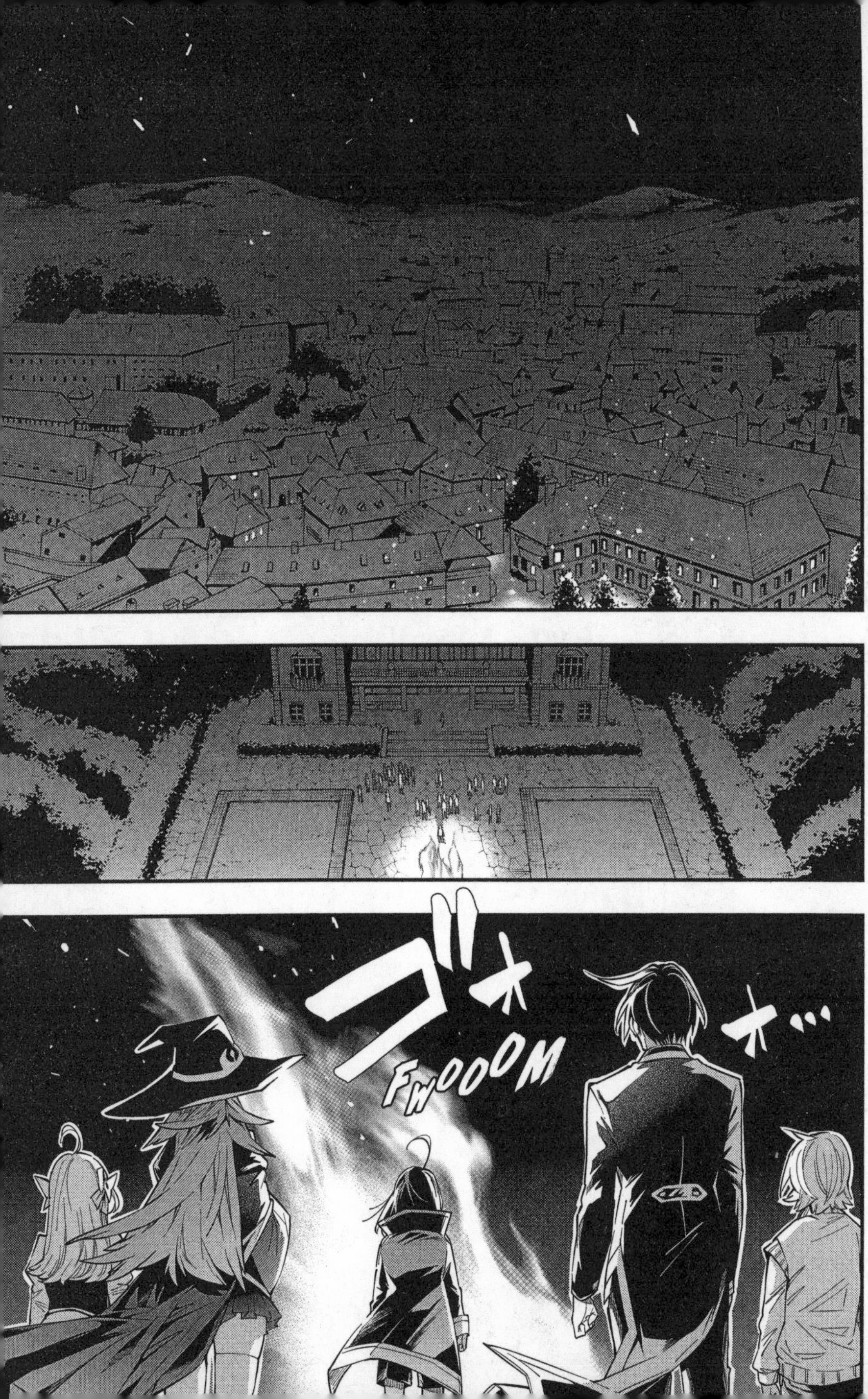
ゴォ
FWOOOM
ォ…

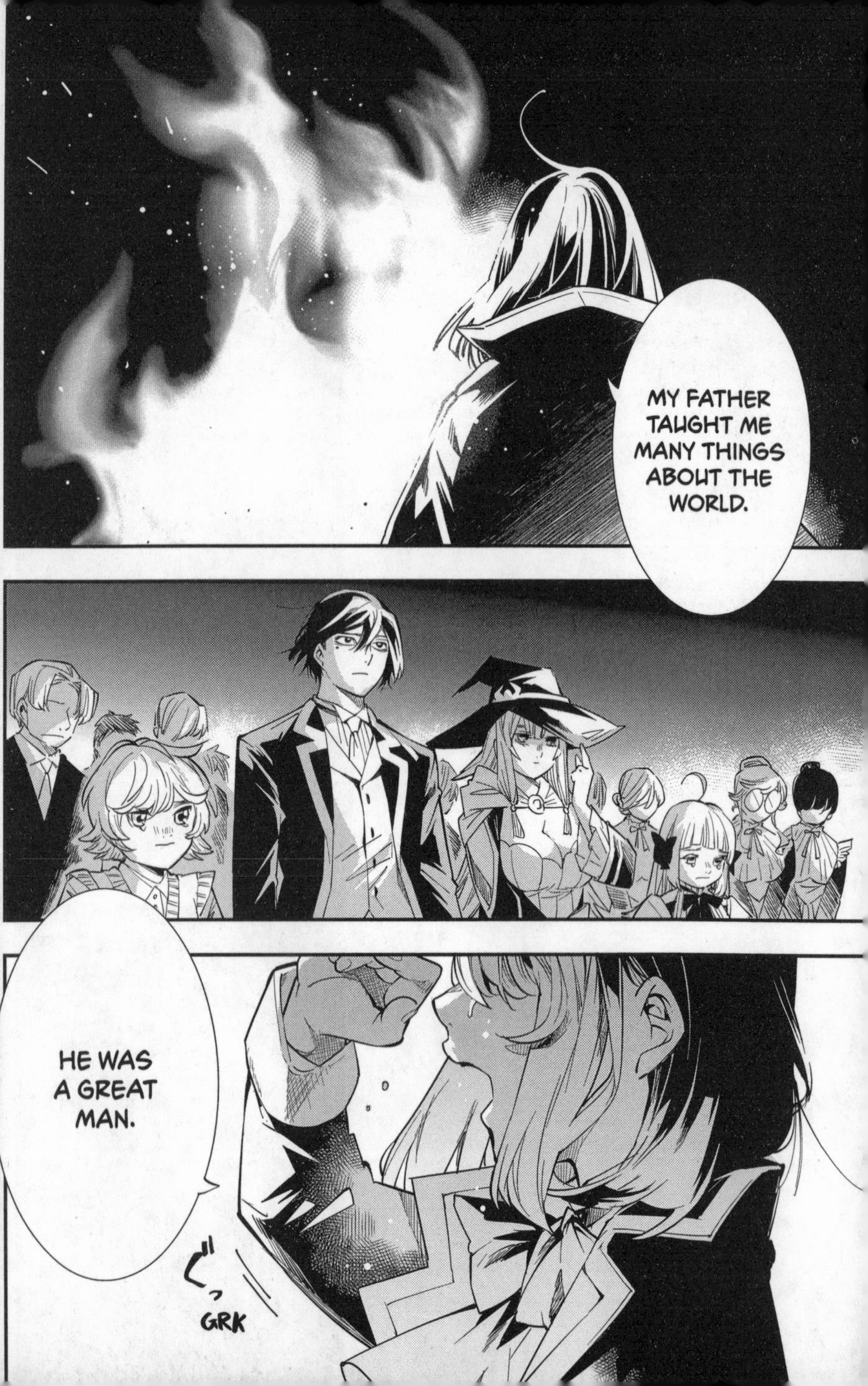
MY FATHER TAUGHT ME MANY THINGS ABOUT THE WORLD.
HE WAS A GREAT MAN.
GRK

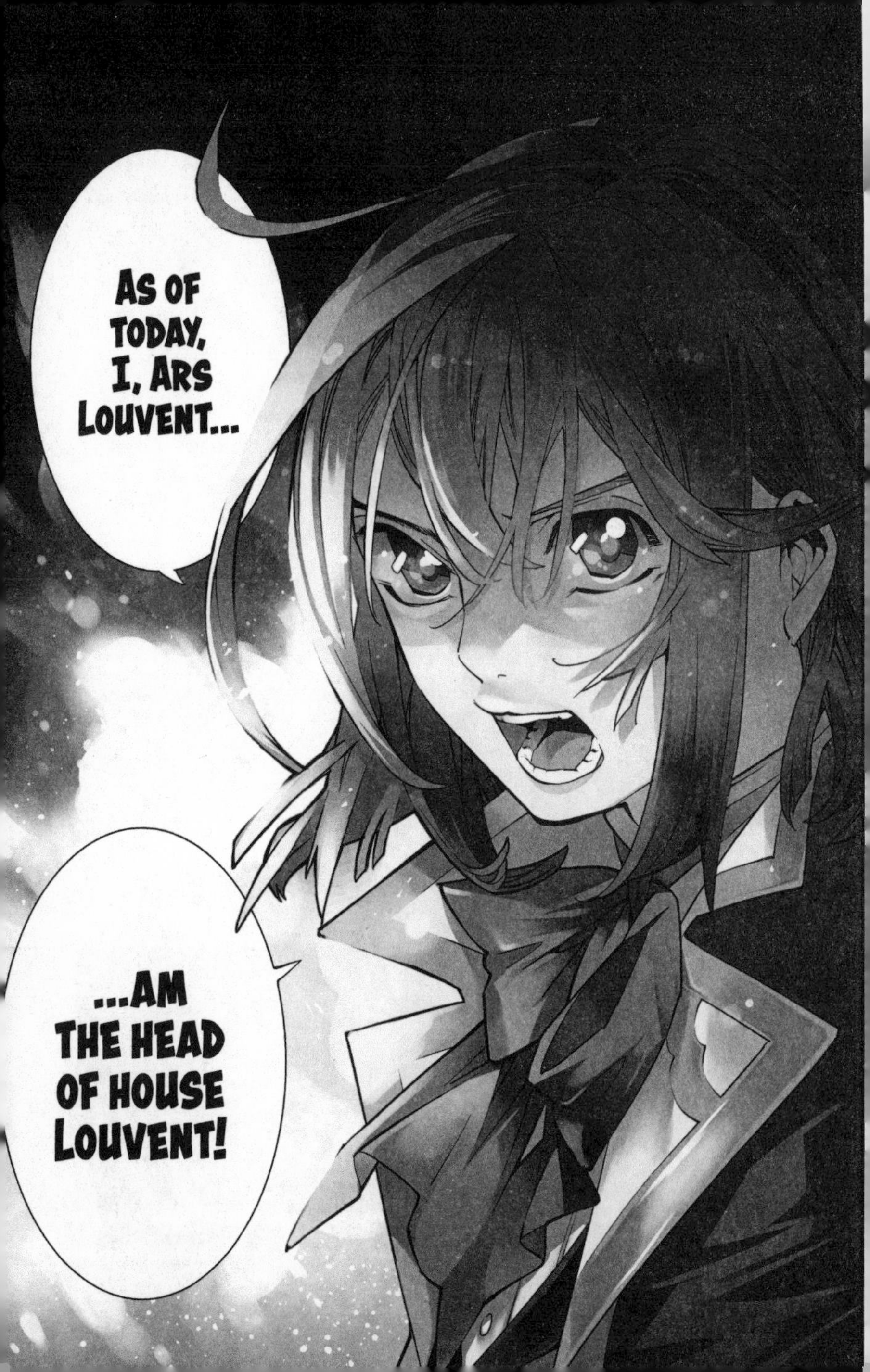
AS OF TODAY, I, ARS LOUVENT...
...AM THE HEAD OF HOUSE LOUVENT!

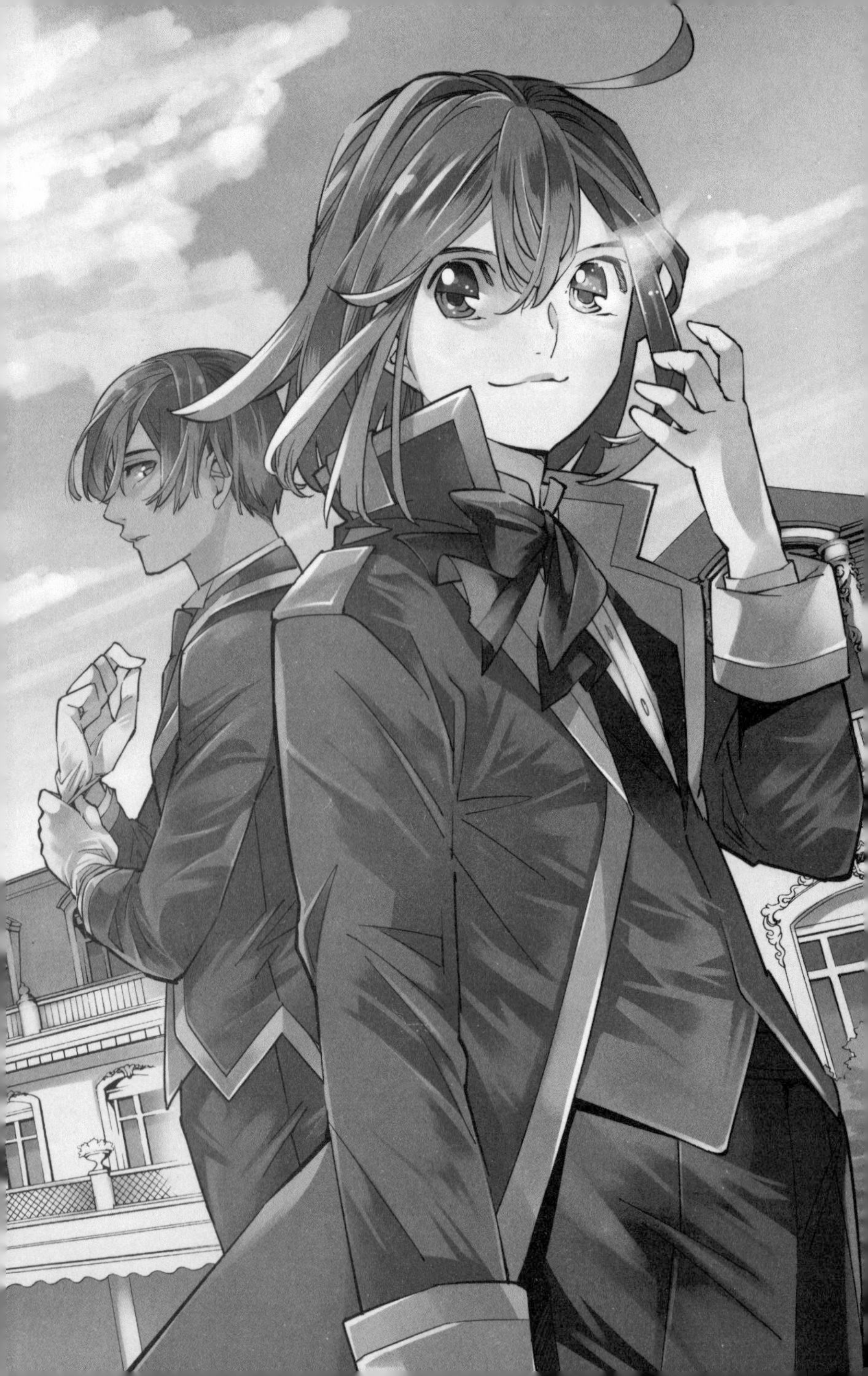

Chapter 1: Reincarnation and Appraisal

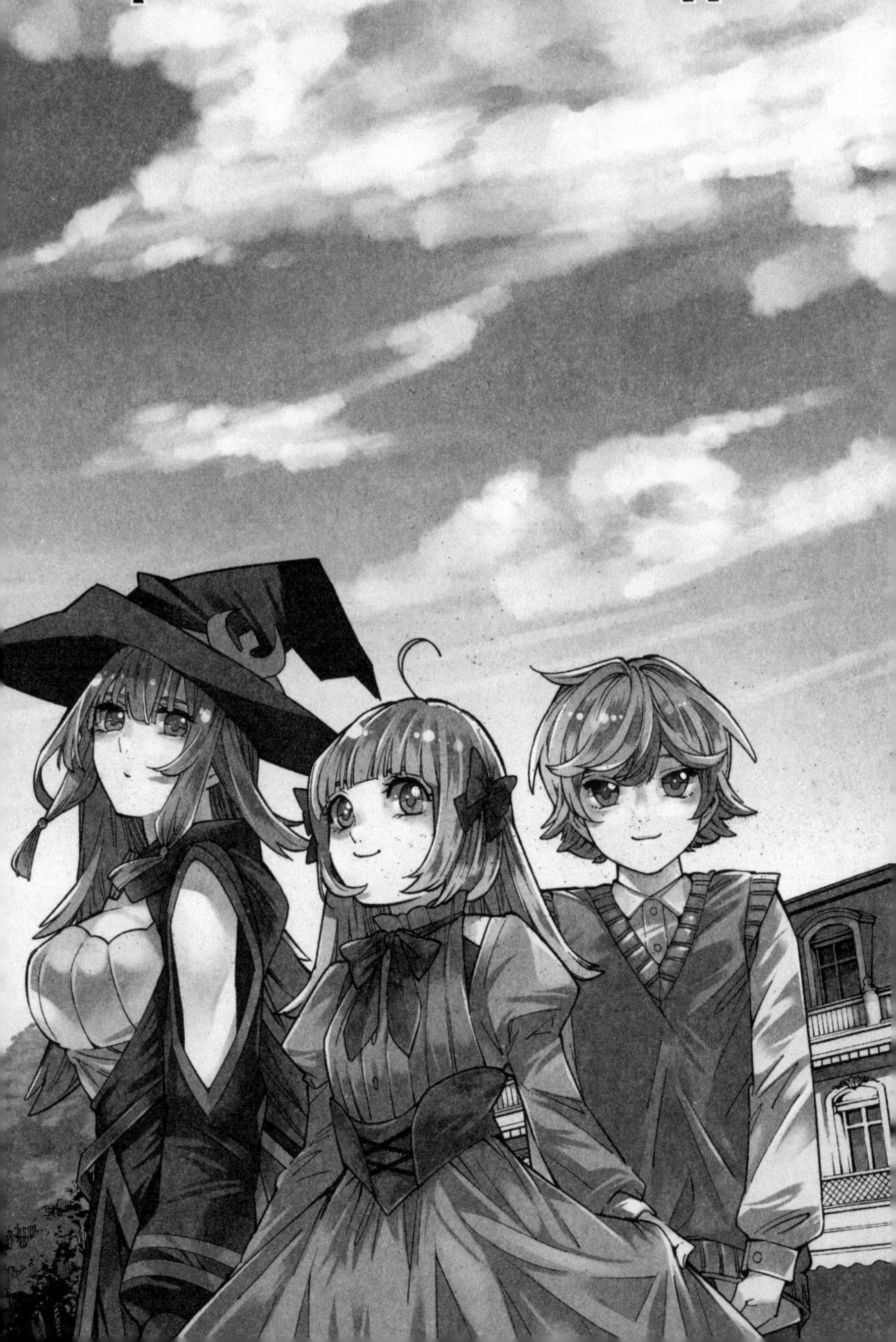

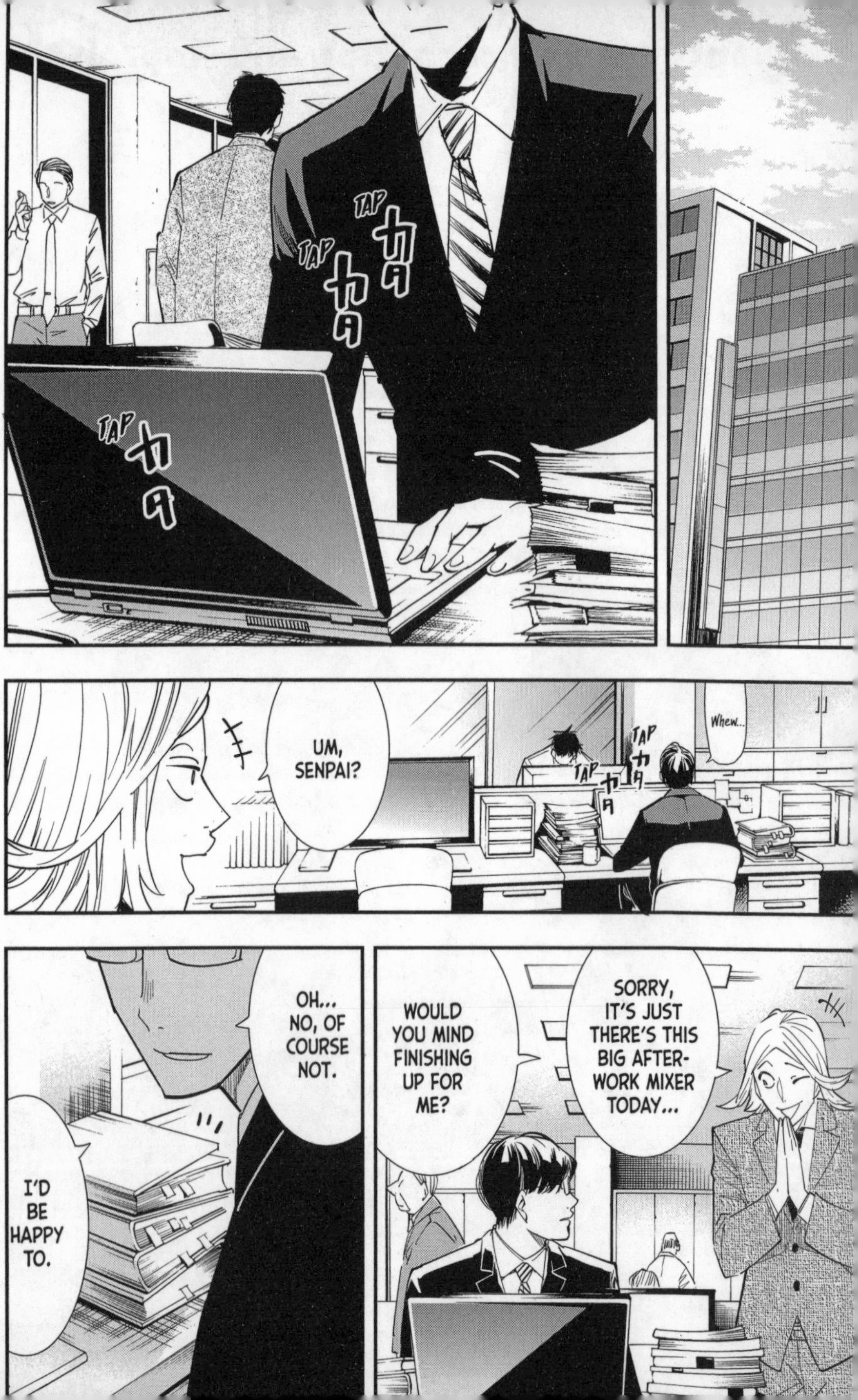
TAP カタ
TAP カタ
TAP カタ
Whew...
TAP カタ
TAP カタ
UM, SENPAI?
SORRY, IT'S JUST THERE'S THIS BIG AFTER-WORK MIXER TODAY...
WOULD YOU MIND FINISHING UP FOR ME?
OH... NO, OF COURSE NOT.
I'D BE HAPPY TO.

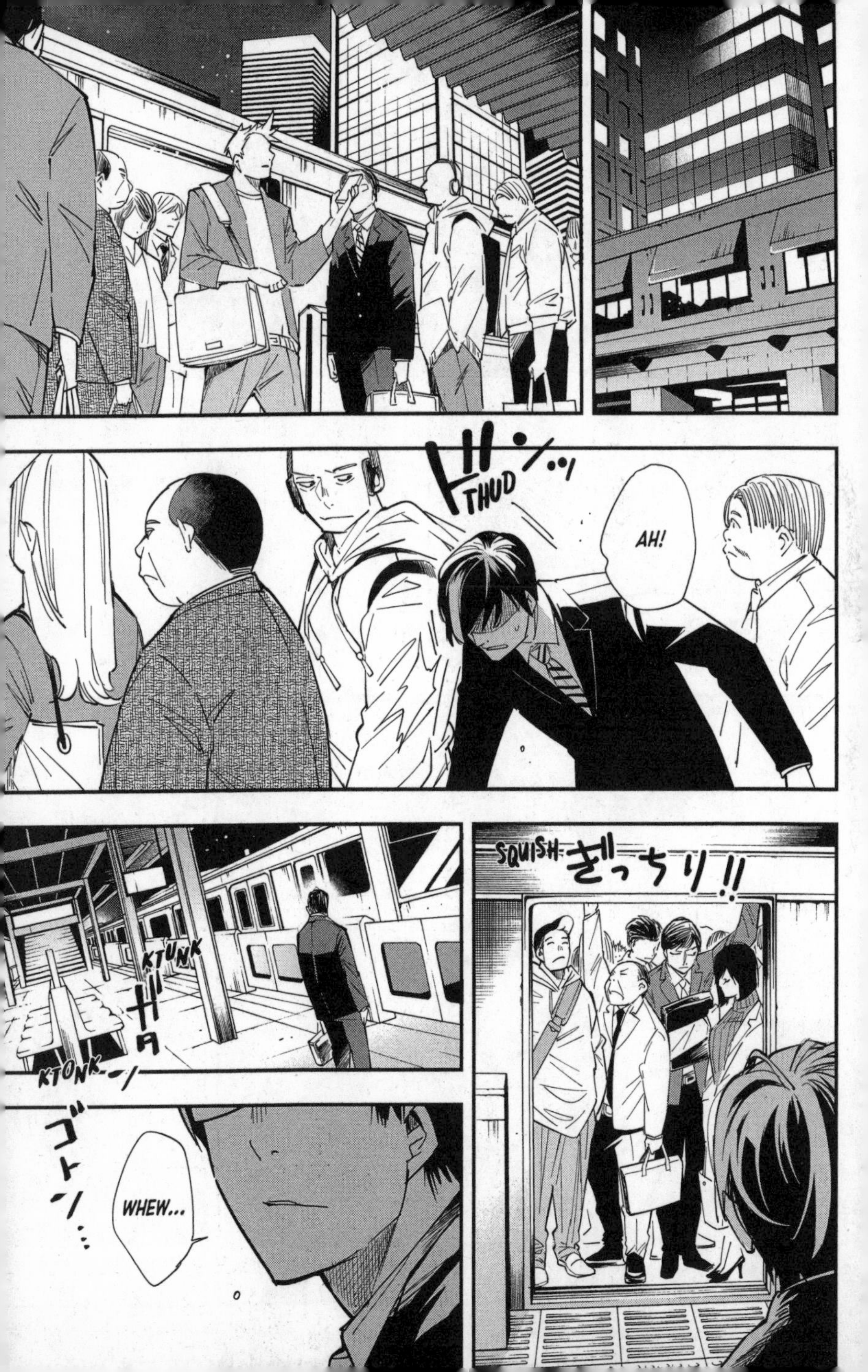
AH!
THUD
ドンッ
SQUISH
ぎっちり!!
KTUNK
ガタ
KTONK
ゴトン…
WHEW...

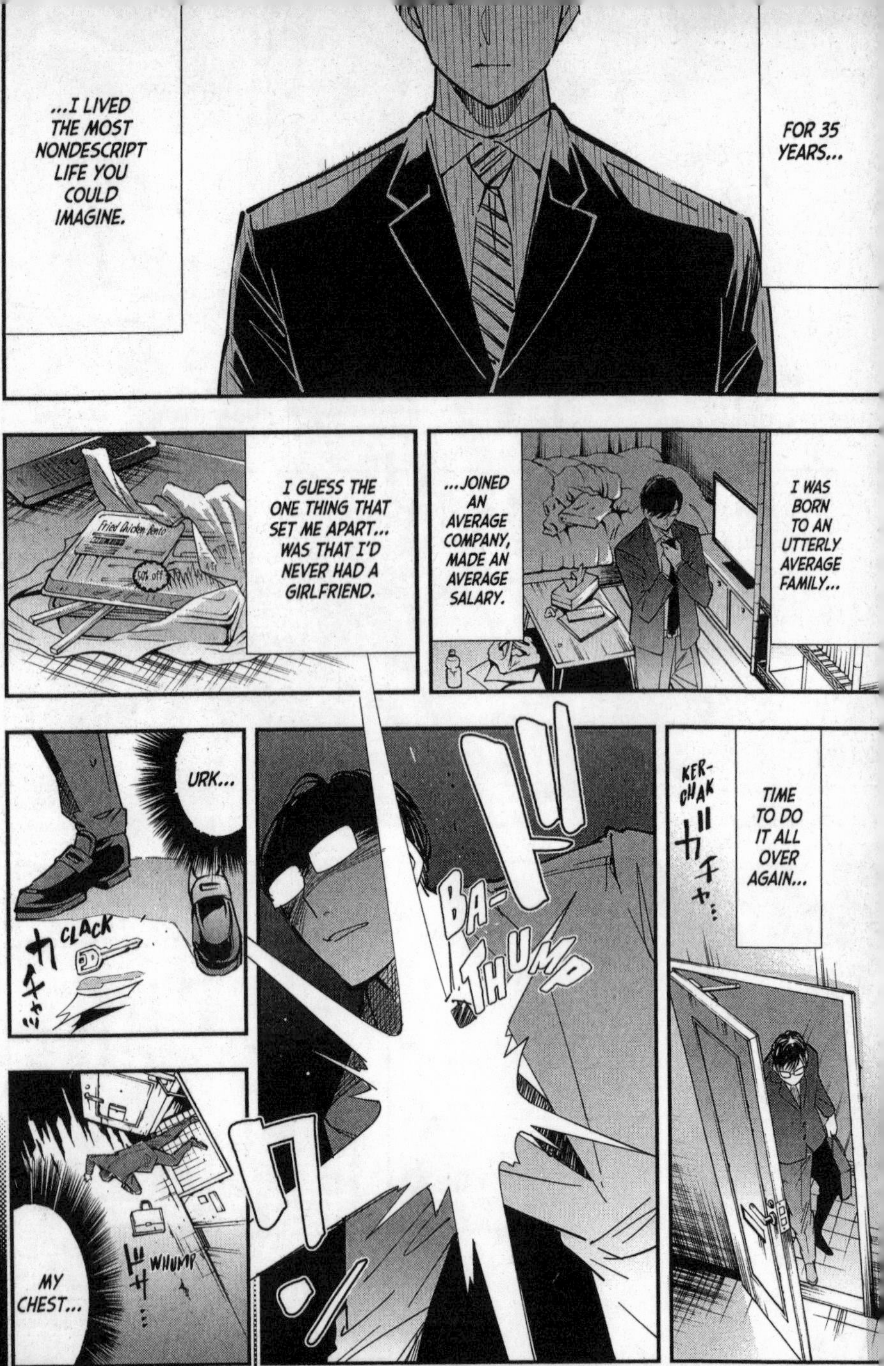

FOR 35 YEARS...
...I LIVED THE MOST NONDESCRIPT LIFE YOU COULD IMAGINE.
I WAS BORN TO AN UTTERLY AVERAGE FAMILY...
...JOINED AN AVERAGE COMPANY, MADE AN AVERAGE SALARY.
I GUESS THE ONE THING THAT SET ME APART... WAS THAT I'D NEVER HAD A GIRLFRIEND.
50% off
TIME TO DO IT ALL OVER AGAIN...
KER-CHAK
ガチャ…
BA-THUMP
URK...
CLACK
カチャッ
MY CHEST...
WHUMP
ドサ…

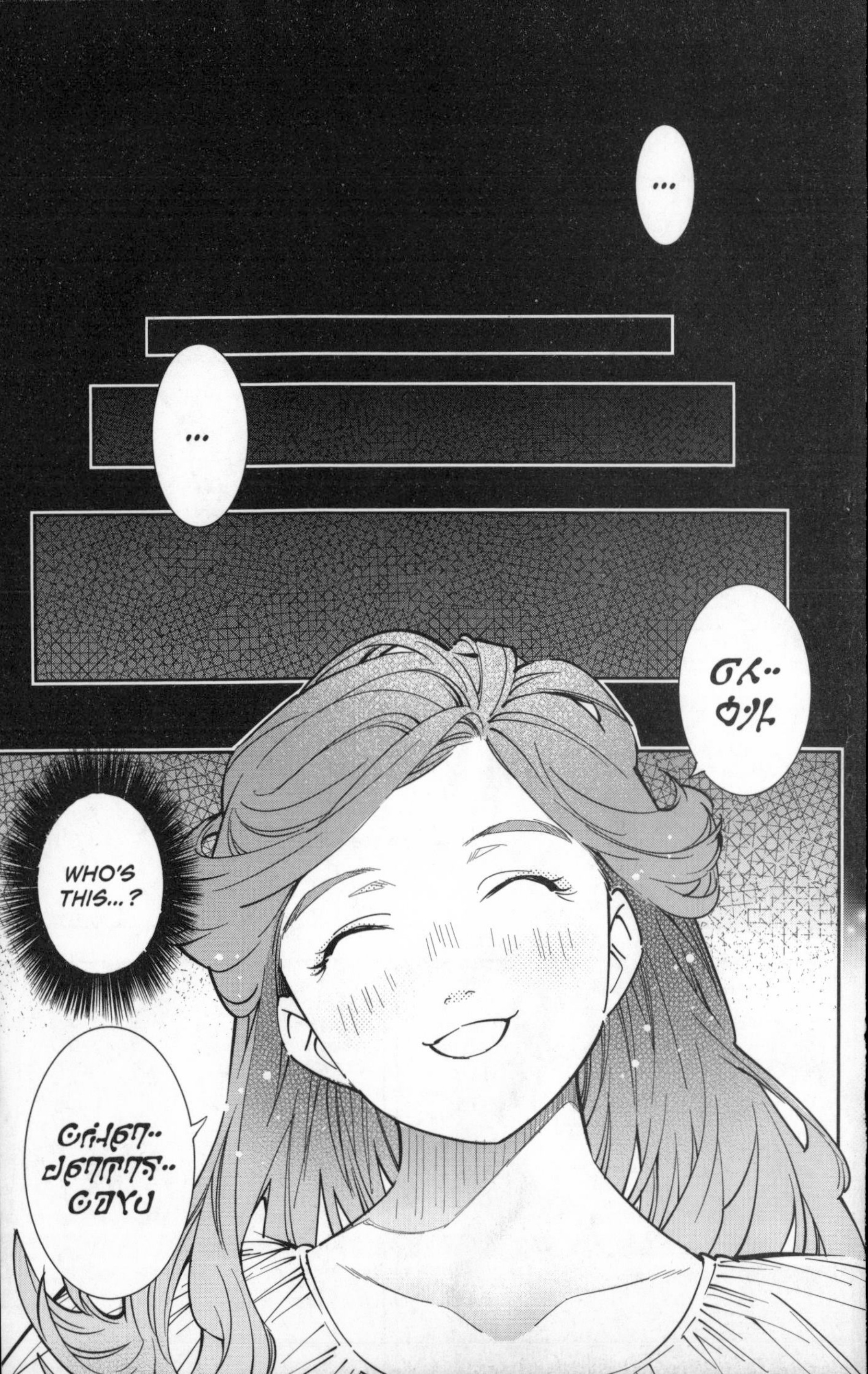
...
...
WHO'S THIS...?

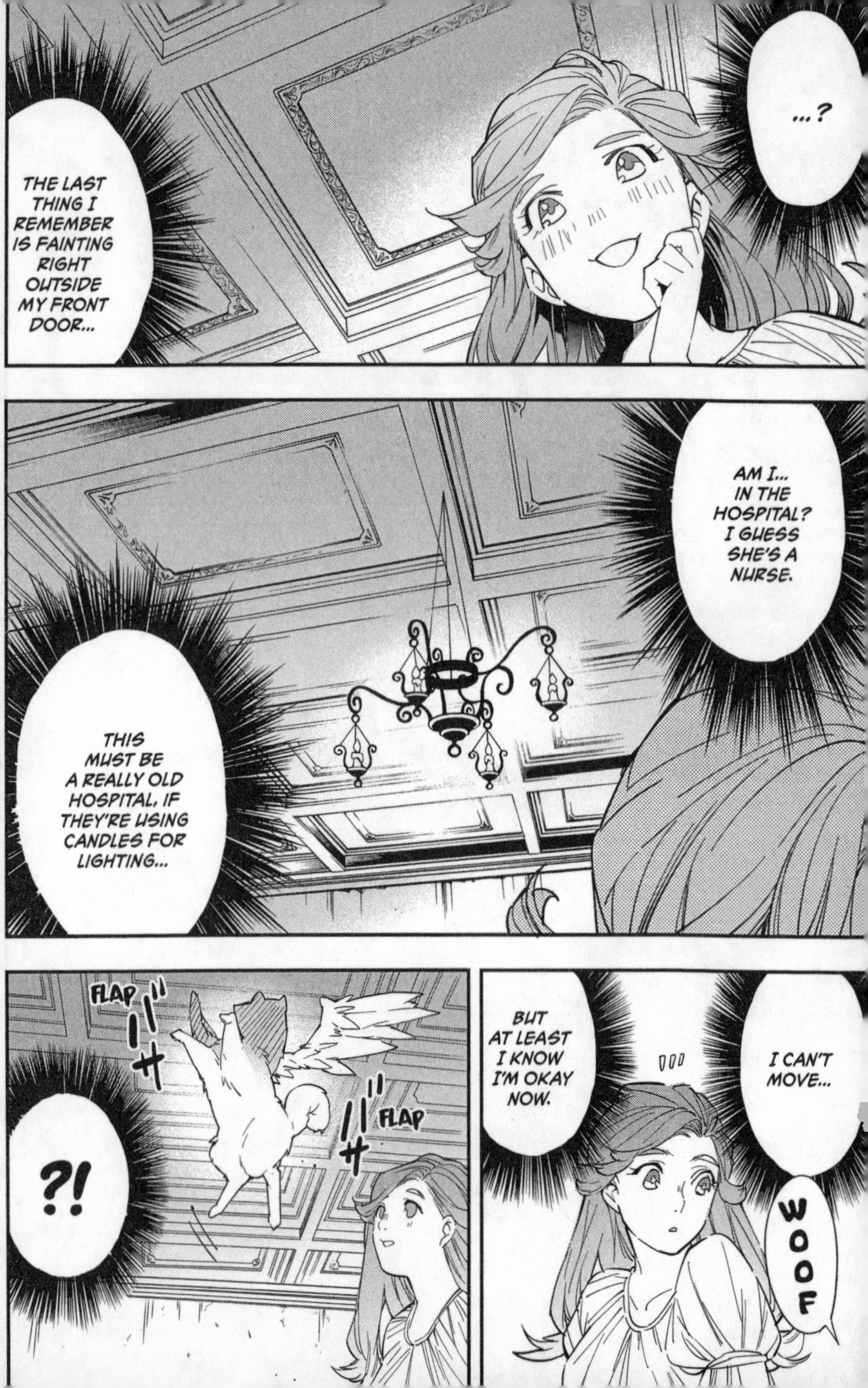
...?
THE LAST THING I REMEMBER IS FAINTING RIGHT OUTSIDE MY FRONT DOOR...
AM I... IN THE HOSPITAL? I GUESS SHE'S A NURSE.
THIS MUST BE A REALLY OLD HOSPITAL, IF THEY'RE USING CANDLES FOR LIGHTING...
I CAN'T MOVE...
BUT AT LEAST I KNOW I'M OKAY NOW.
WOOF
FLAP
FLAP
?!

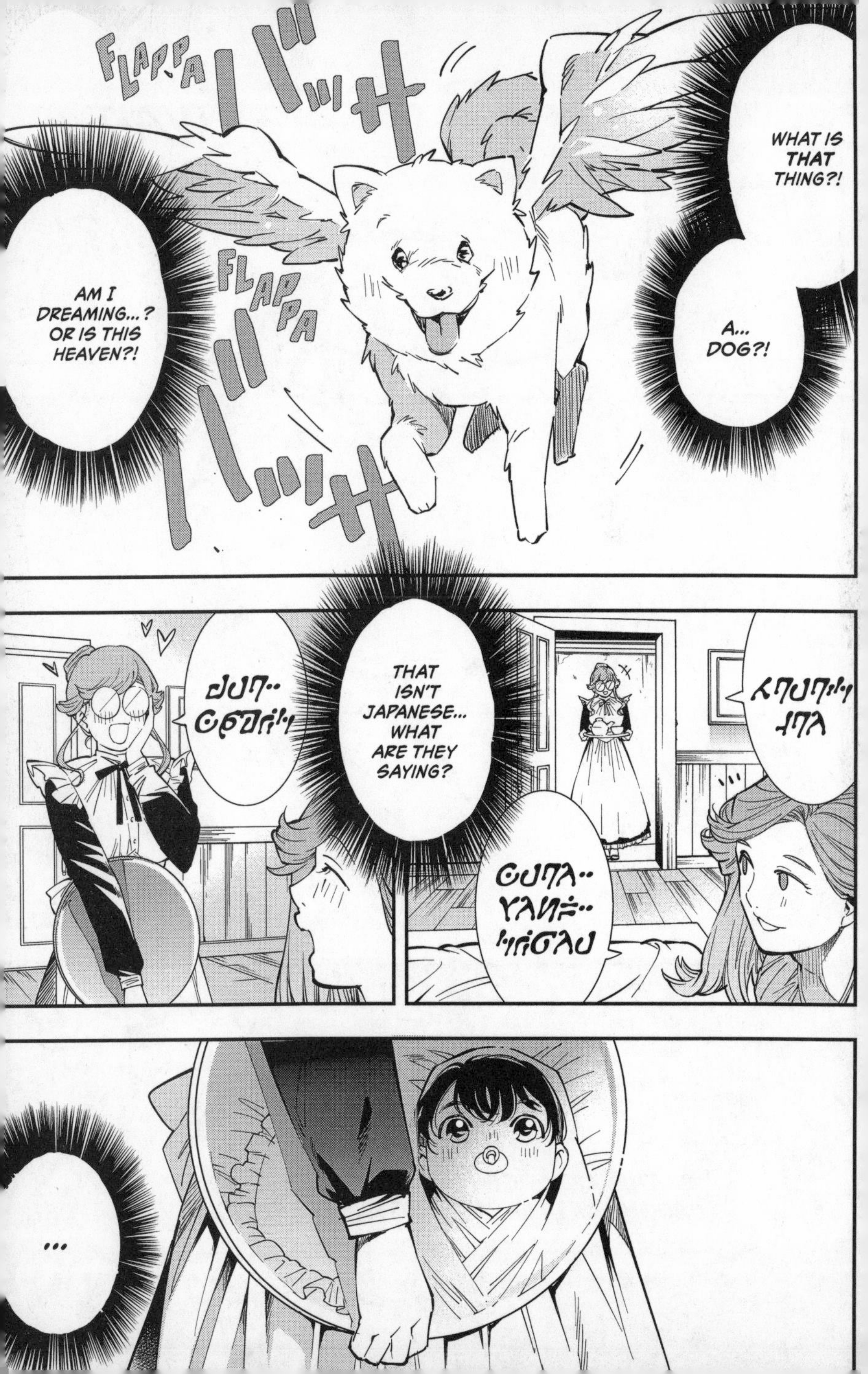
WHAT IS THAT THING?!
A... DOG?!
FLAPPA
FLAPPA
AM I DREAMING...? OR IS THIS HEAVEN?!
THAT ISN'T JAPANESE... WHAT ARE THEY SAYING?
...

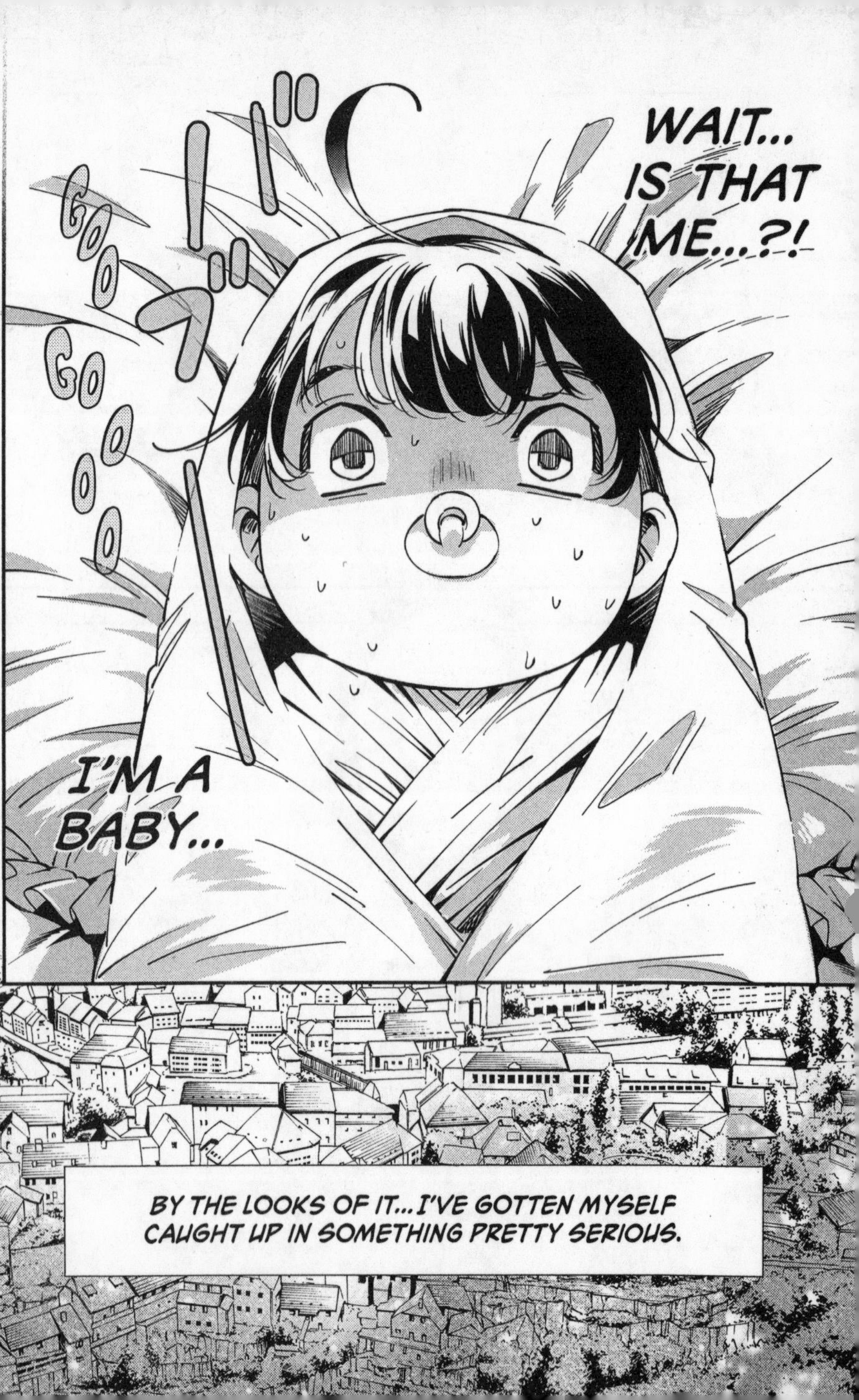
WAIT... IS THAT ME...?!
GOOO
GOOOO
I'M A BABY...
BY THE LOOKS OF IT... I'VE GOTTEN MYSELF CAUGHT UP IN SOMETHING PRETTY SERIOUS.

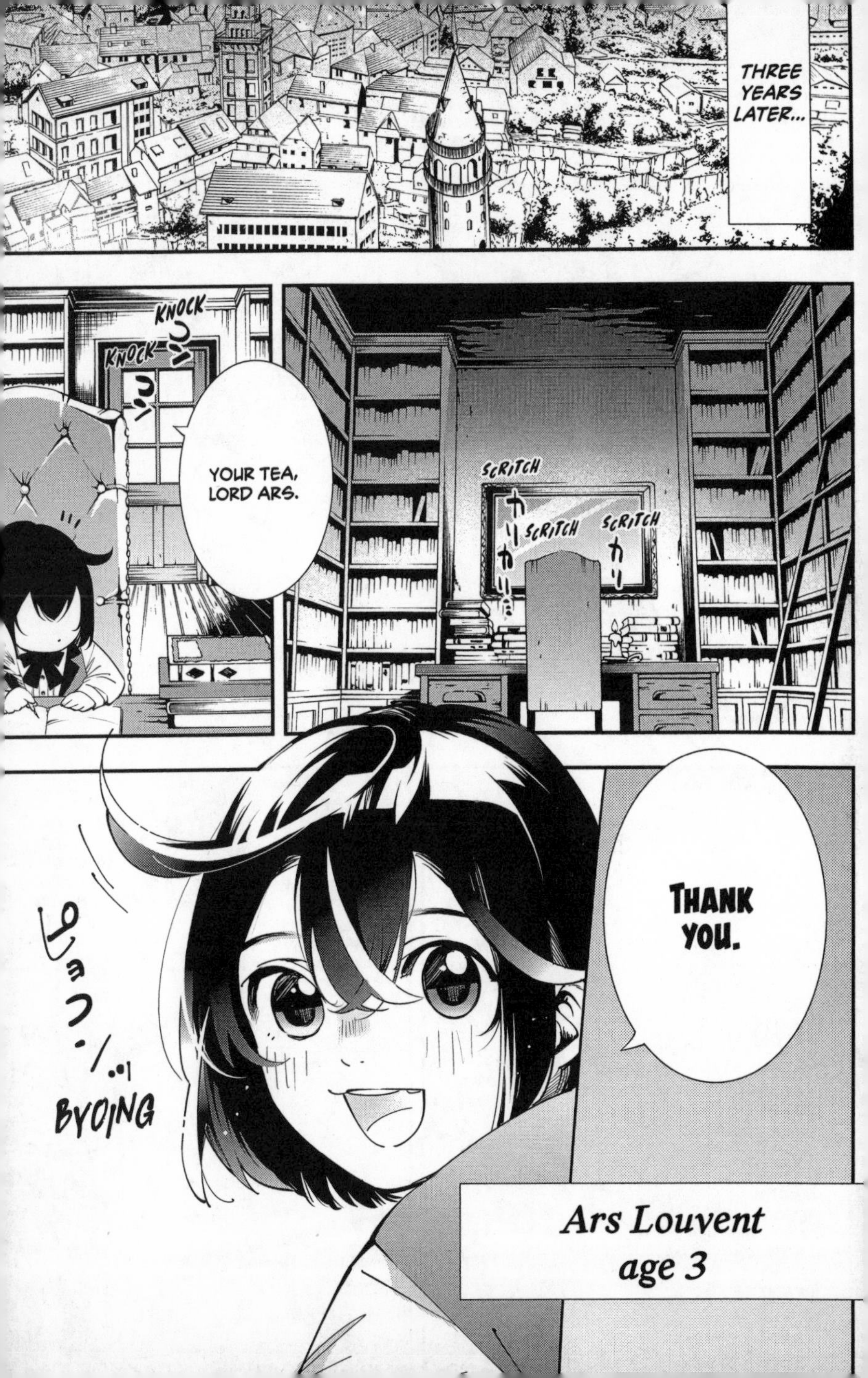
THREE YEARS LATER...
SCRITCH
SCRITCH
SCRITCH
KNOCK
KNOCK
YOUR TEA, LORD ARS.
THANK YOU.
BYOING
Ars Louvent
age 3

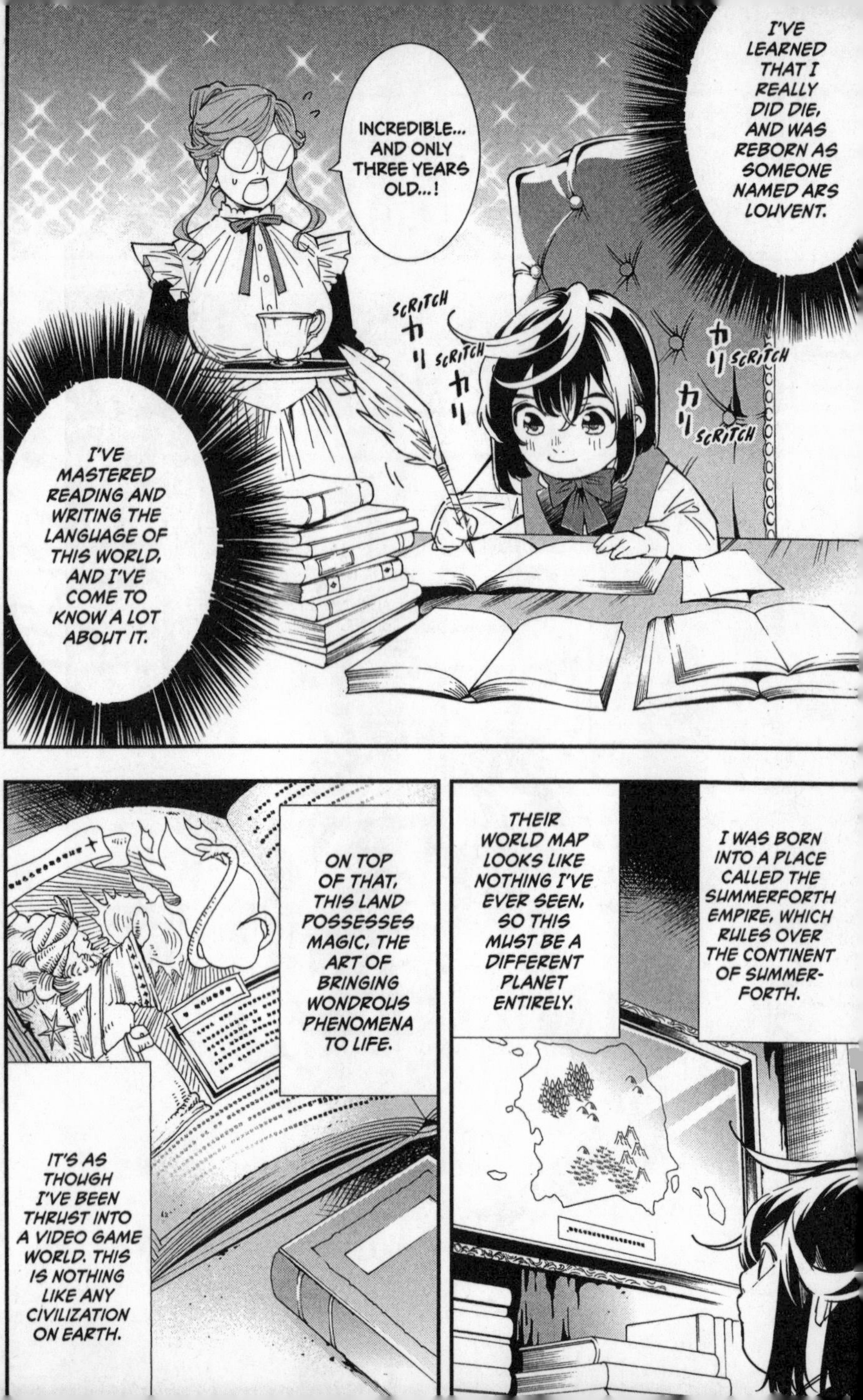
I'VE LEARNED THAT I REALLY DID DIE, AND WAS REBORN AS SOMEONE NAMED ARS LOUVENT.
INCREDIBLE... AND ONLY THREE YEARS OLD...!
カリ SCRITCH
カリ SCRITCH
カリ SCRITCH
カリ SCRITCH
I'VE MASTERED READING AND WRITING THE LANGUAGE OF THIS WORLD, AND I'VE COME TO KNOW A LOT ABOUT IT.
I WAS BORN INTO A PLACE CALLED THE SUMMERFORTH EMPIRE, WHICH RULES OVER THE CONTINENT OF SUMMER-FORTH.
THEIR WORLD MAP LOOKS LIKE NOTHING I'VE EVER SEEN, SO THIS MUST BE A DIFFERENT PLANET ENTIRELY.
ON TOP OF THAT, THIS LAND POSSESSES MAGIC, THE ART OF BRINGING WONDROUS PHENOMENA TO LIFE.
IT'S AS THOUGH I'VE BEEN THRUST INTO A VIDEO GAME WORLD. THIS IS NOTHING LIKE ANY CIVILIZATION ON EARTH.

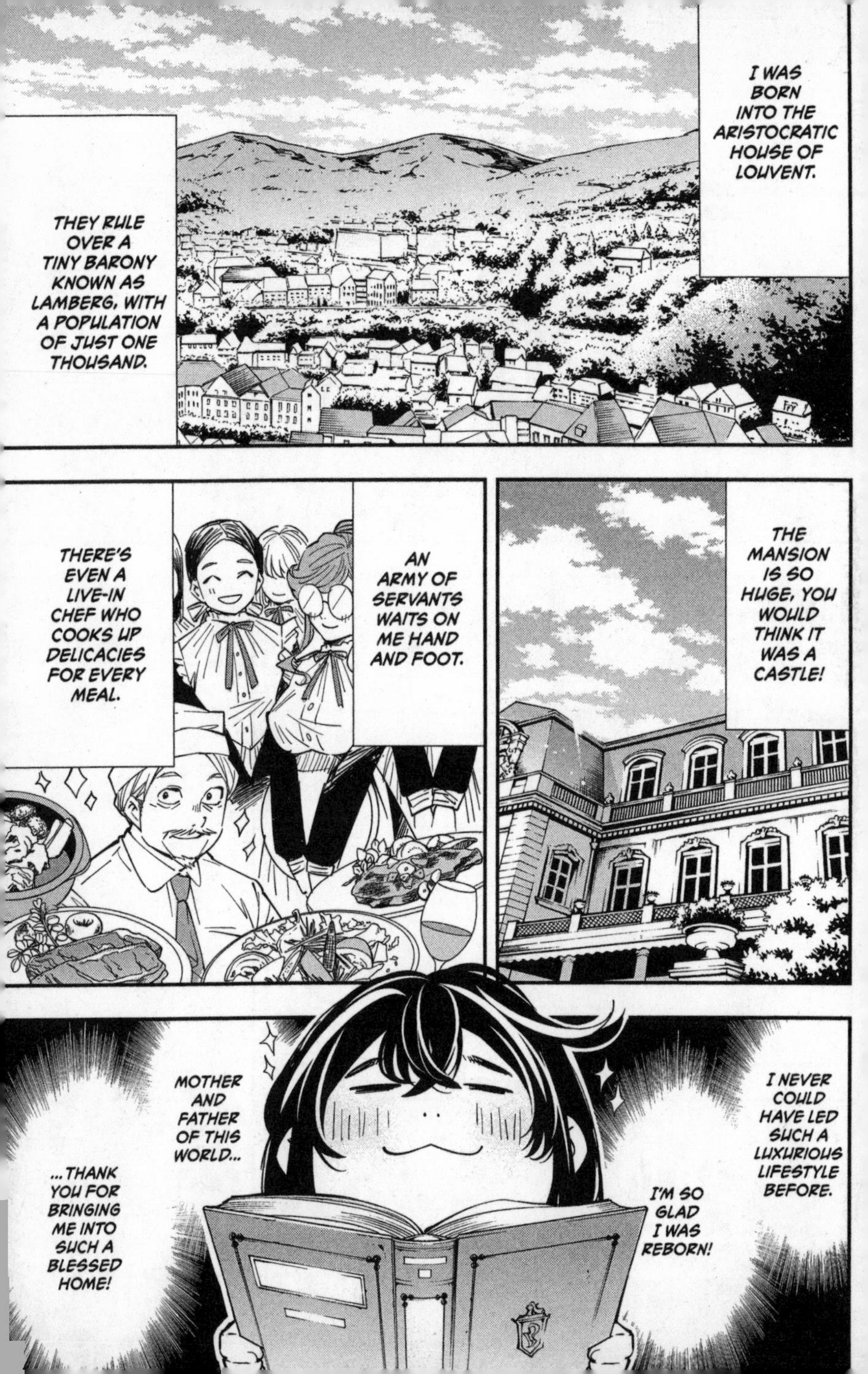
I WAS BORN INTO THE ARISTOCRATIC HOUSE OF LOUVENT.
THEY RULE OVER A TINY BARONY KNOWN AS LAMBERG, WITH A POPULATION OF JUST ONE THOUSAND.
THE MANSION IS SO HUGE, YOU WOULD THINK IT WAS A CASTLE!
AN ARMY OF SERVANTS WAITS ON ME HAND AND FOOT.
THERE'S EVEN A LIVE-IN CHEF WHO COOKS UP DELICACIES FOR EVERY MEAL.
I NEVER COULD HAVE LED SUCH A LUXURIOUS LIFESTYLE BEFORE.
I'M SO GLAD I WAS REBORN!
MOTHER AND FATHER OF THIS WORLD...
...THANK YOU FOR BRINGING ME INTO SUCH A BLESSED HOME!

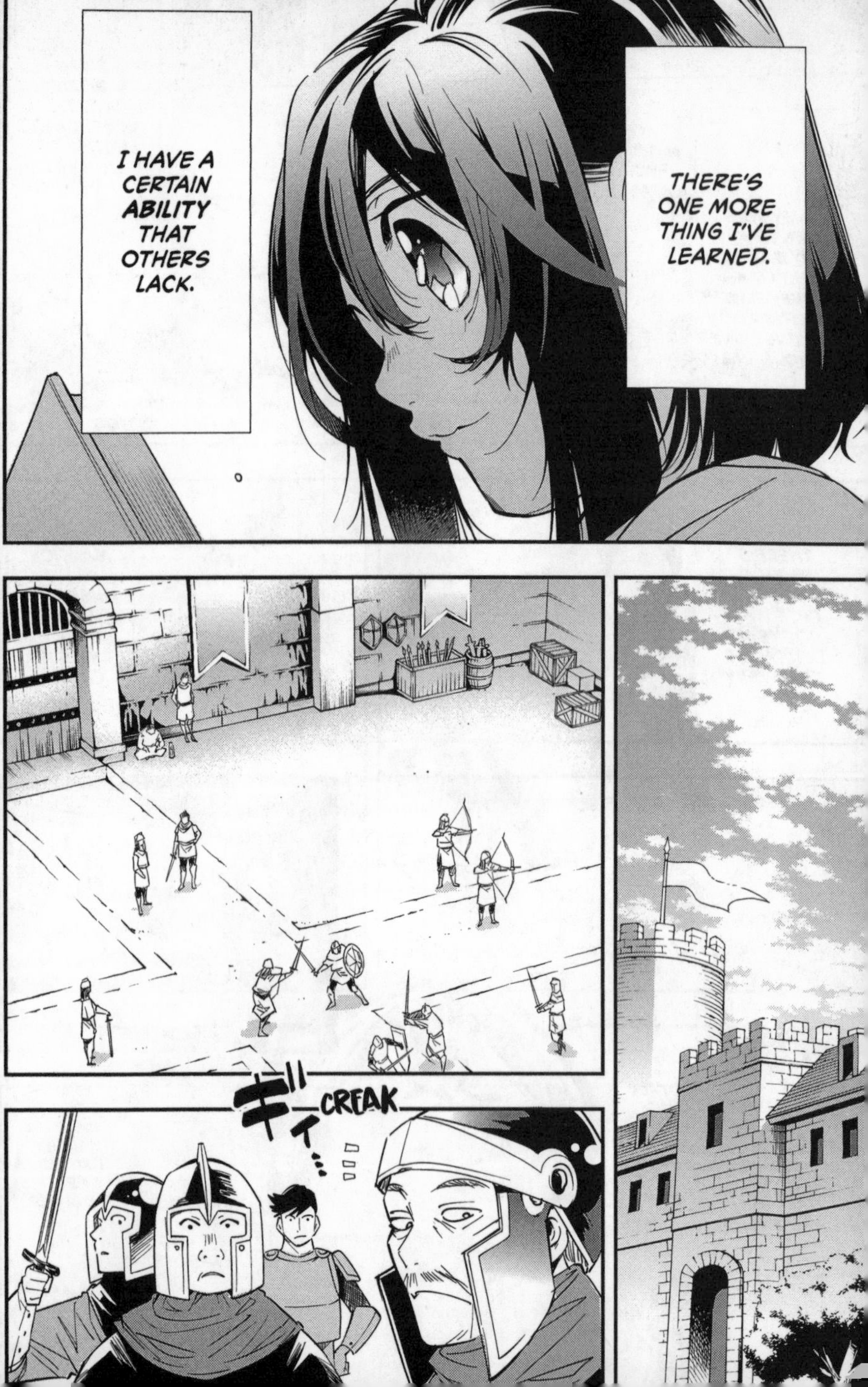

THERE'S ONE MORE THING I'VE LEARNED.
I HAVE A CERTAIN ABILITY THAT OTHERS LACK.
CREAK

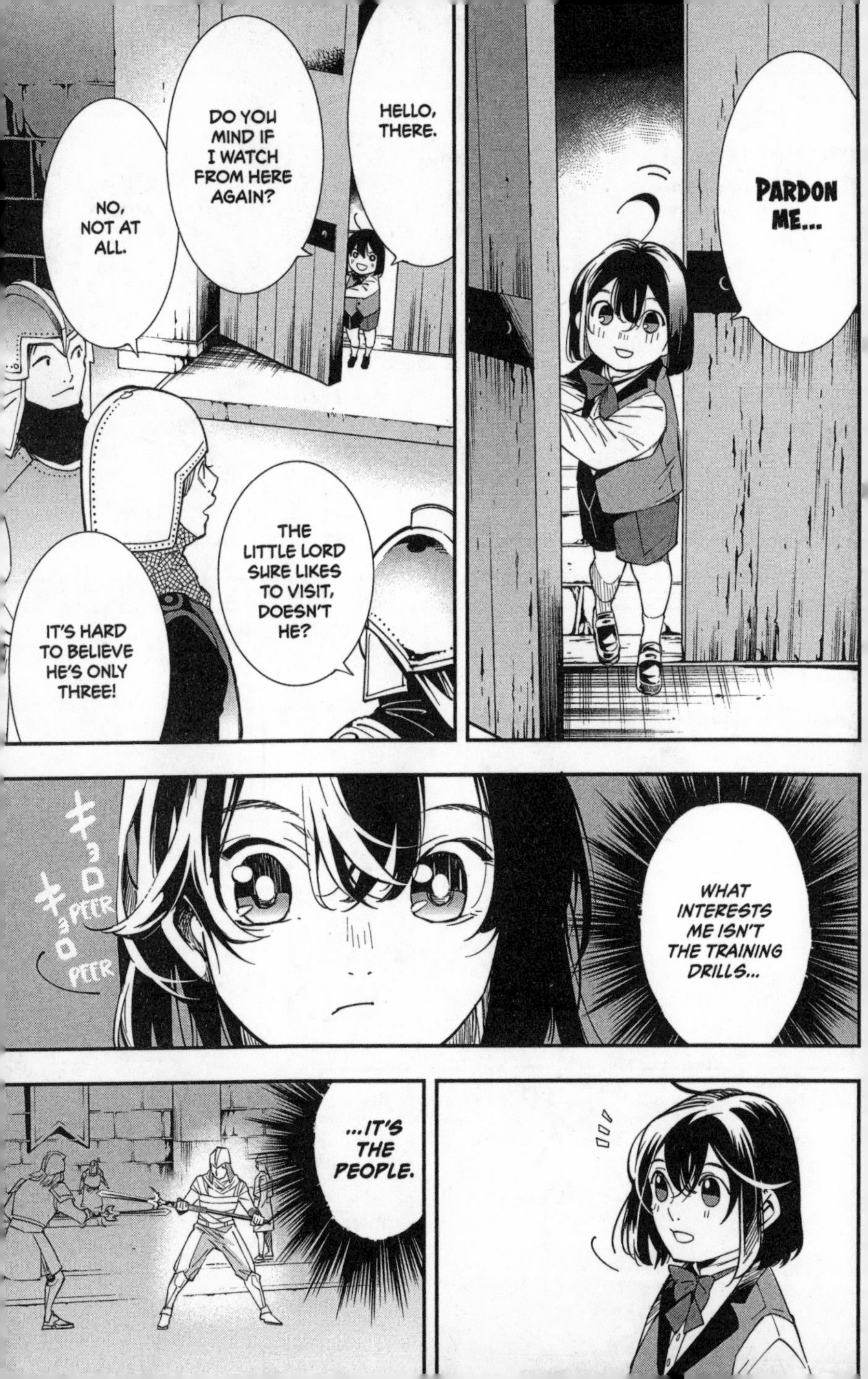
PARDON ME...
HELLO, THERE.
DO YOU MIND IF I WATCH FROM HERE AGAIN?
NO, NOT AT ALL.
THE LITTLE LORD SURE LIKES TO VISIT, DOESN'T HE?
IT'S HARD TO BELIEVE HE'S ONLY THREE!
WHAT INTERESTS ME ISN'T THE TRAINING DRILLS...
キョロ キョロ
PEER PEER
...IT'S THE PEOPLE.

MY UNIQUE ABILITY...

...IS SOMETHING I LIKE TO CALL...

STARE

"...APPRAISAL."

★★★★
Millais Cristal - Age 21 ♂

Stats

	CURRENT	MAX
Command	2 1	3 5
Prowess	6 0	6 2
Intellect	2 2	3 2
Diplomacy	1 5	3 1
Ambition	3	

Aptitude

Fighter	D	Cavalier	D	Archer	B
Mage	D	Engineer	D	Armorer	D
Mariner	D	Pilot	D	Tactician	D

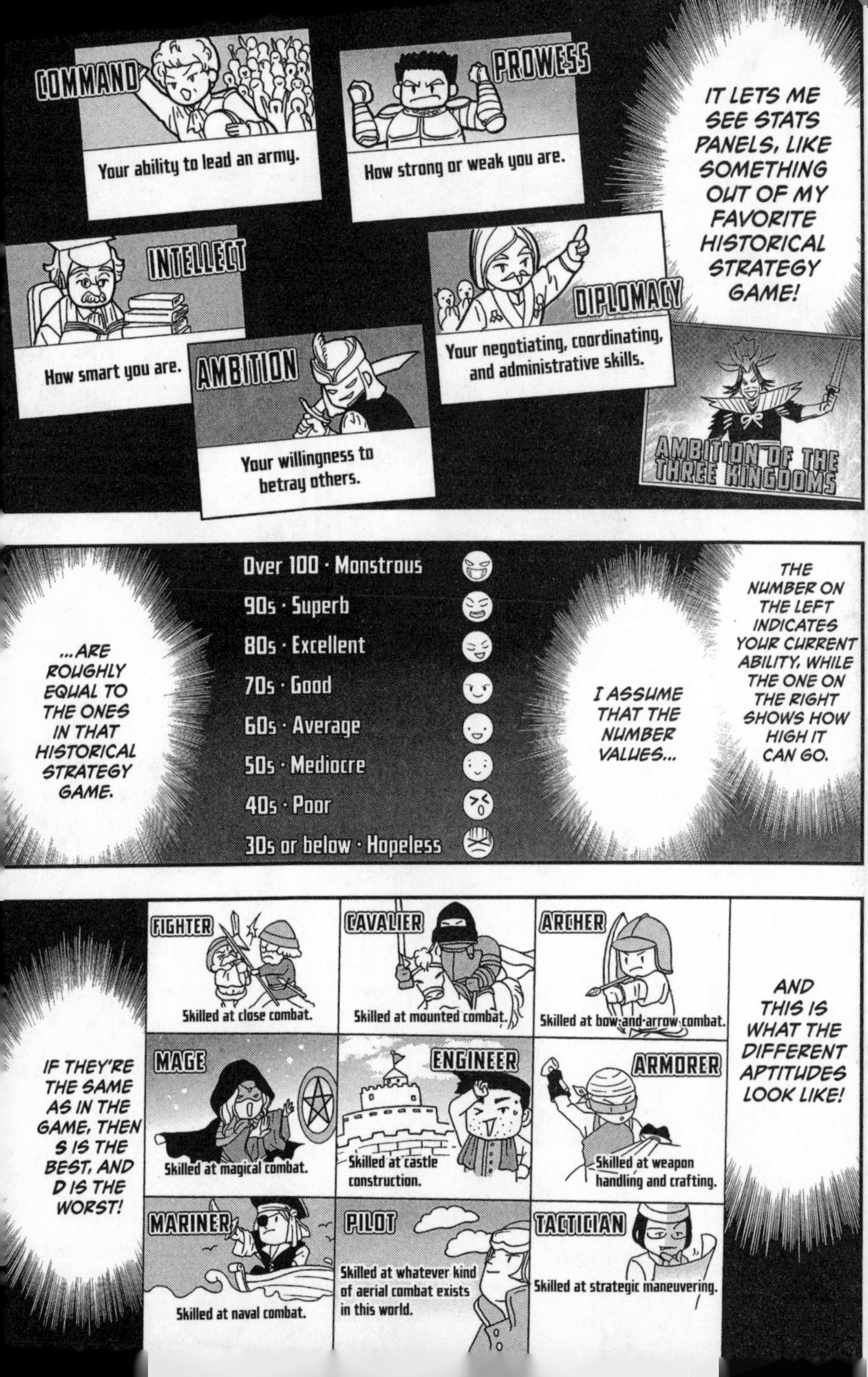
IT LETS ME SEE STATS PANELS, LIKE SOMETHING OUT OF MY FAVORITE HISTORICAL STRATEGY GAME!
AMBITION OF THE THREE KINGDOMS
PROWESS
How strong or weak you are.
COMMAND
Your ability to lead an army.
DIPLOMACY
Your negotiating, coordinating, and administrative skills.
INTELLECT
How smart you are.
AMBITION
Your willingness to betray others.
THE NUMBER ON THE LEFT INDICATES YOUR CURRENT ABILITY, WHILE THE ONE ON THE RIGHT SHOWS HOW HIGH IT CAN GO.
I ASSUME THAT THE NUMBER VALUES...
Over 100 · Monstrous
90s · Superb
80s · Excellent
70s · Good
60s · Average
50s · Mediocre
40s · Poor
30s or below · Hopeless
...ARE ROUGHLY EQUAL TO THE ONES IN THAT HISTORICAL STRATEGY GAME.
AND THIS IS WHAT THE DIFFERENT APTITUDES LOOK LIKE!
ARCHER
Skilled at bow-and-arrow combat.
CAVALIER
Skilled at mounted combat.
FIGHTER
Skilled at close combat.
ARMORER
Skilled at weapon handling and crafting.
ENGINEER
Skilled at castle construction.
MAGE
Skilled at magical combat.
TACTICIAN
Skilled at strategic maneuvering.
PILOT
Skilled at whatever kind of aerial combat exists in this world.
MARINER
Skilled at naval combat.
IF THEY'RE THE SAME AS IN THE GAME, THEN S IS THE BEST, AND D IS THE WORST!

IT'S A SHAME... BUT THEN AGAIN, I'D BE SCARED TO LOOK AT MY OWN STATS.

FOR SOME REASON, I CAN'T APPRAISE MYSELF.

I'LL TAKE A LOOK AT MILLAIS'S STATS WHILE HE'S BUSY TRAINING...

HE HAS A HIGH APTITUDE FOR ARCHERY, SO HE'D BE BETTER SERVED USING A BOW.

Millais Cristal · Age 21

Stats

	Current	Max
Command	2 1	3 5
Prowess	6 0	6 2
Intellect	2 2	3 2
Diplomacy	1 5	3 1
Ambition	3	

Aptitude

Fighter D	Cavalier D	Archer B
Mage D	Engineer D	Armorer D
Mariner D	Pilot D	Tactician D

I WISH HE WOULD.

WHY DOESN'T HE TRY A BOW AND ARROW...?

FIDGET
FIDGET

BUT HE'S TRAINING WITH A SPEAR RIGHT NOW.

...IT DOESN'T REALLY SEEM TO SUIT HIM.

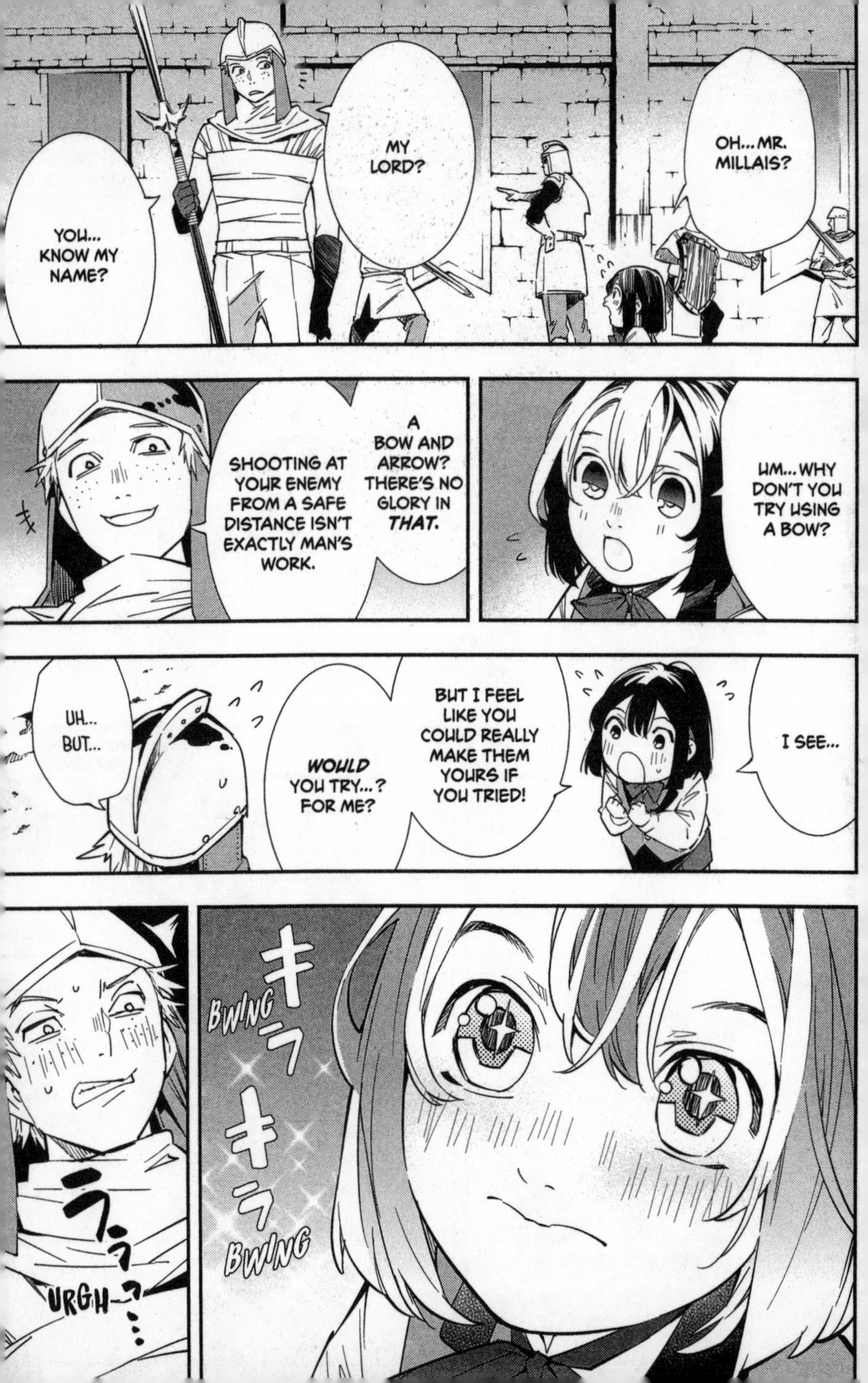
OH... MR. MILLAIS?
MY LORD?
YOU... KNOW MY NAME?
UM... WHY DON'T YOU TRY USING A BOW?
A BOW AND ARROW? THERE'S NO GLORY IN *THAT.*
SHOOTING AT YOUR ENEMY FROM A SAFE DISTANCE ISN'T EXACTLY MAN'S WORK.
I SEE...
BUT I FEEL LIKE YOU COULD REALLY MAKE THEM YOURS IF YOU TRIED!
WOULD YOU TRY...? FOR ME?
UH... BUT...
キラ
BWING
キラ
BWING
ううっ…
URGH

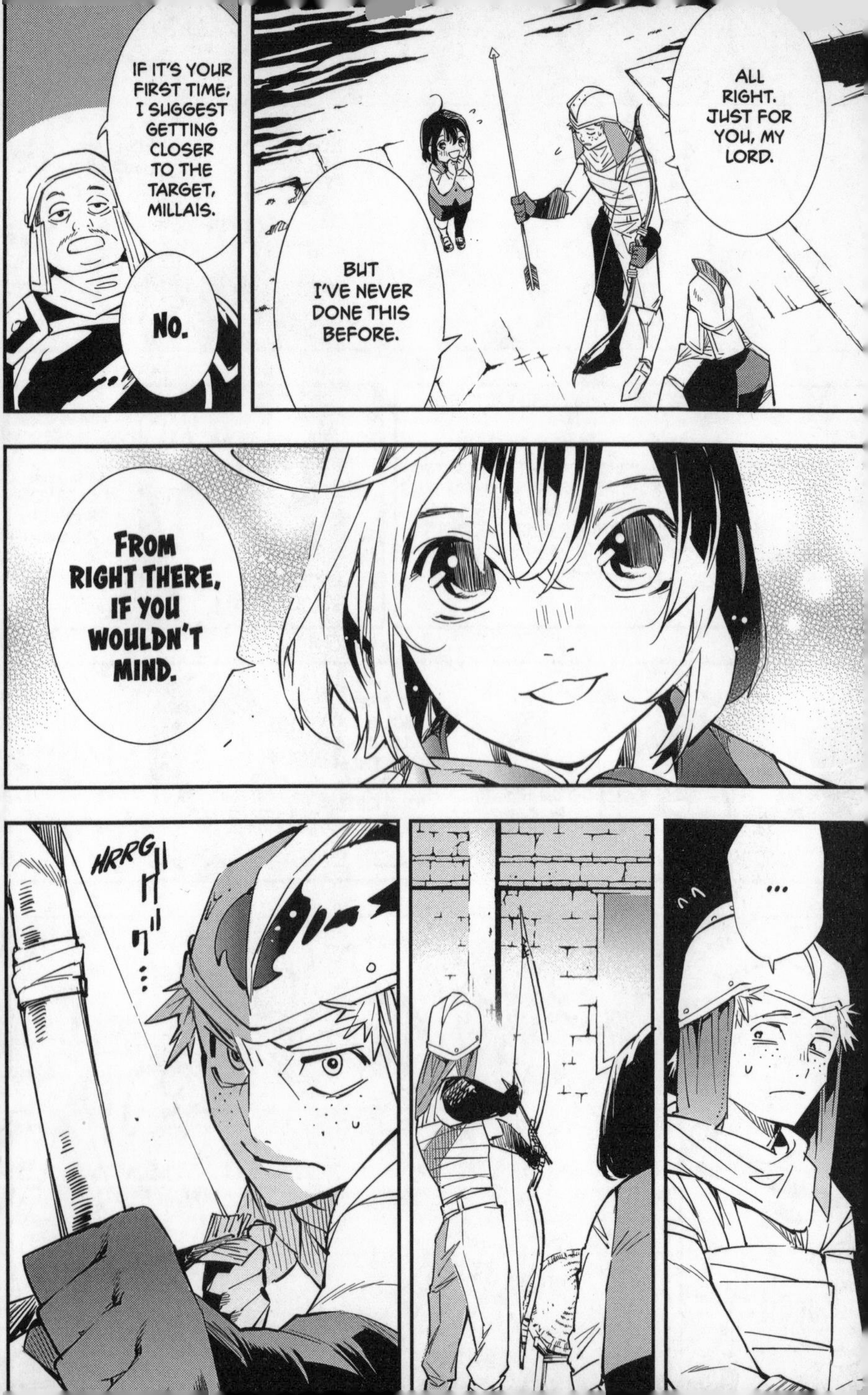
ALL RIGHT. JUST FOR YOU, MY LORD.
BUT I'VE NEVER DONE THIS BEFORE.
IF IT'S YOUR FIRST TIME, I SUGGEST GETTING CLOSER TO THE TARGET, MILLAIS.
No.
FROM RIGHT THERE, IF YOU WOULDN'T MIND.
...
HRRG

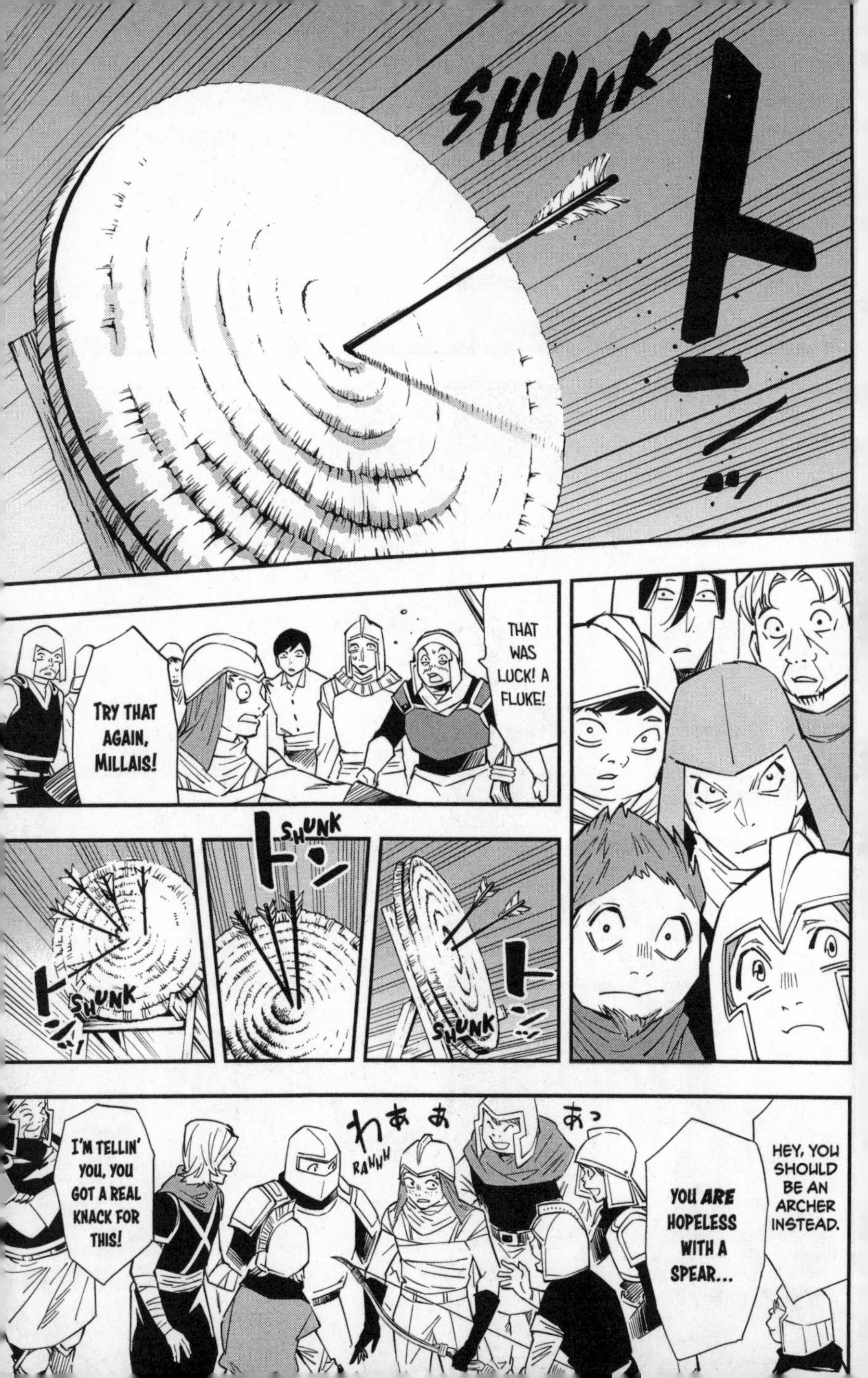
SHUNK
ト
THAT WAS LUCK! A FLUKE!
TRY THAT AGAIN, MILLAIS!
SHUNK
ト
SHUNK
トン
SHUNK
ト
HEY, YOU SHOULD BE AN ARCHER INSTEAD.
YOU **ARE** HOPELESS WITH A SPEAR...
わああ あっ
RAHHH
I'M TELLIN' YOU, YOU GOT A REAL KNACK FOR THIS!

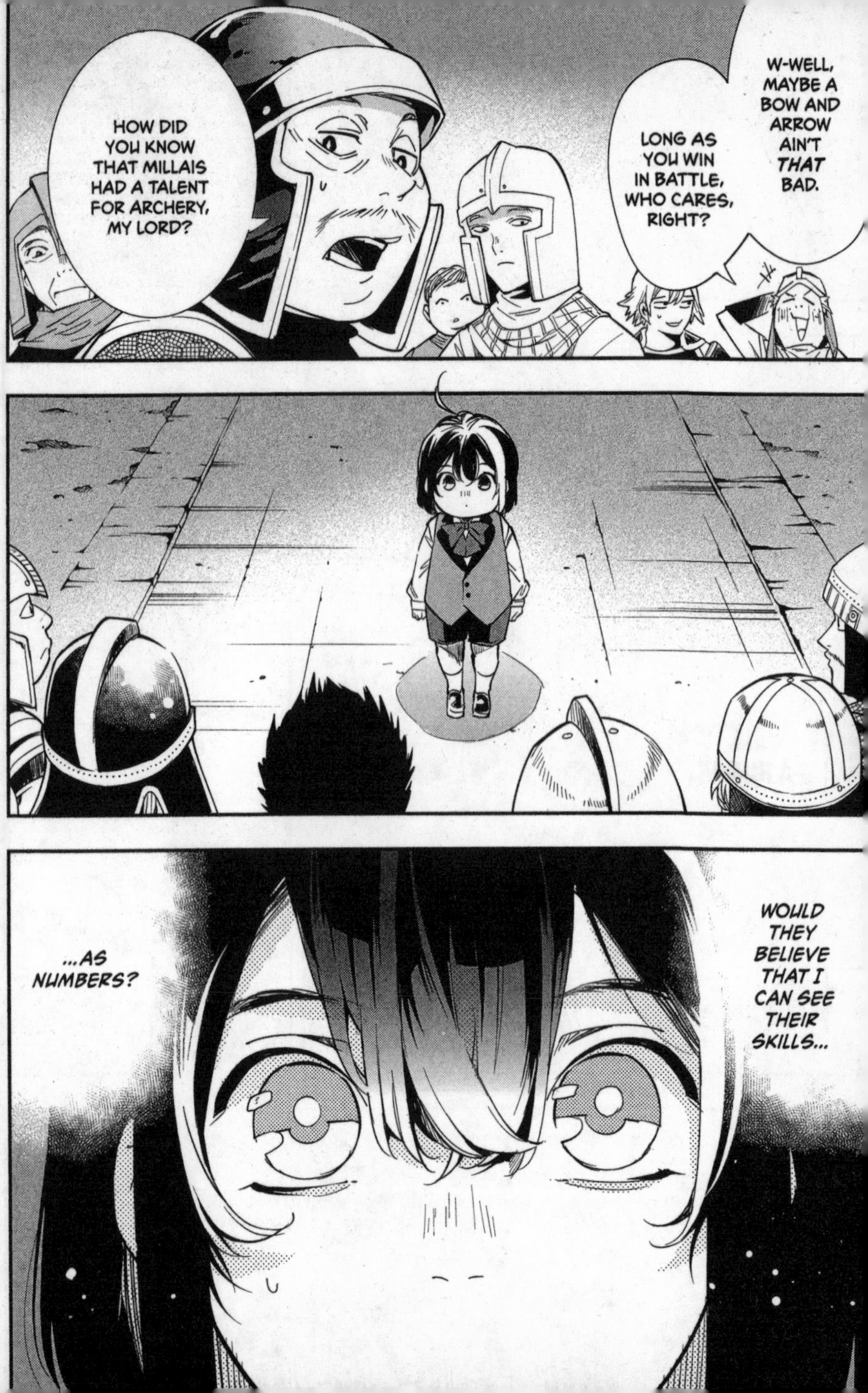
W-WELL, MAYBE A BOW AND ARROW AIN'T *THAT* BAD.
LONG AS YOU WIN IN BATTLE, WHO CARES, RIGHT?
HOW DID YOU KNOW THAT MILLAIS HAD A TALENT FOR ARCHERY, MY LORD?
WOULD THEY BELIEVE THAT I CAN SEE THEIR SKILLS...
...AS NUMBERS?

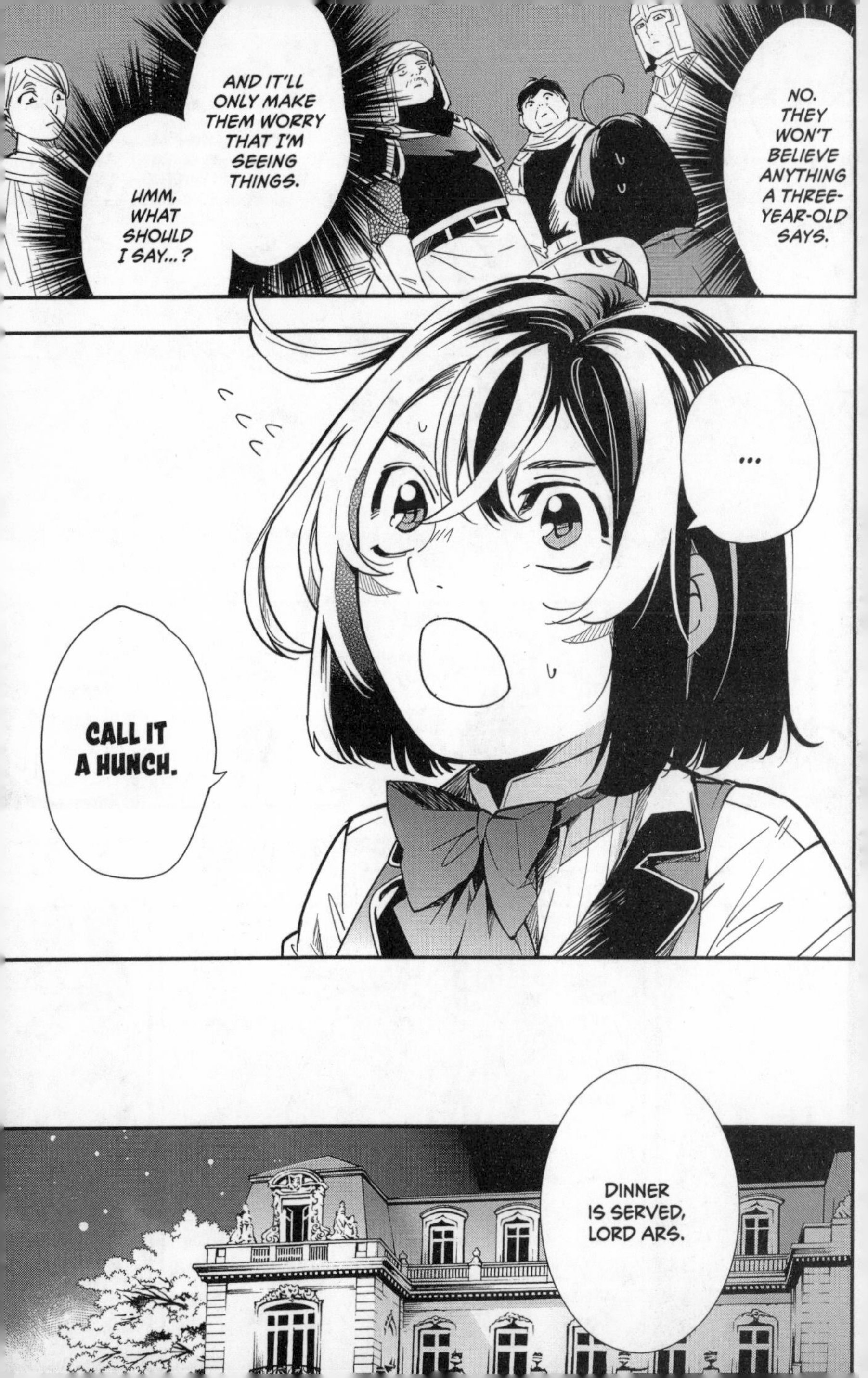
NO. THEY WON'T BELIEVE ANYTHING A THREE-YEAR-OLD SAYS.
AND IT'LL ONLY MAKE THEM WORRY THAT I'M SEEING THINGS.
UMM, WHAT SHOULD I SAY...?
...
CALL IT A HUNCH.
DINNER IS SERVED, LORD ARS.

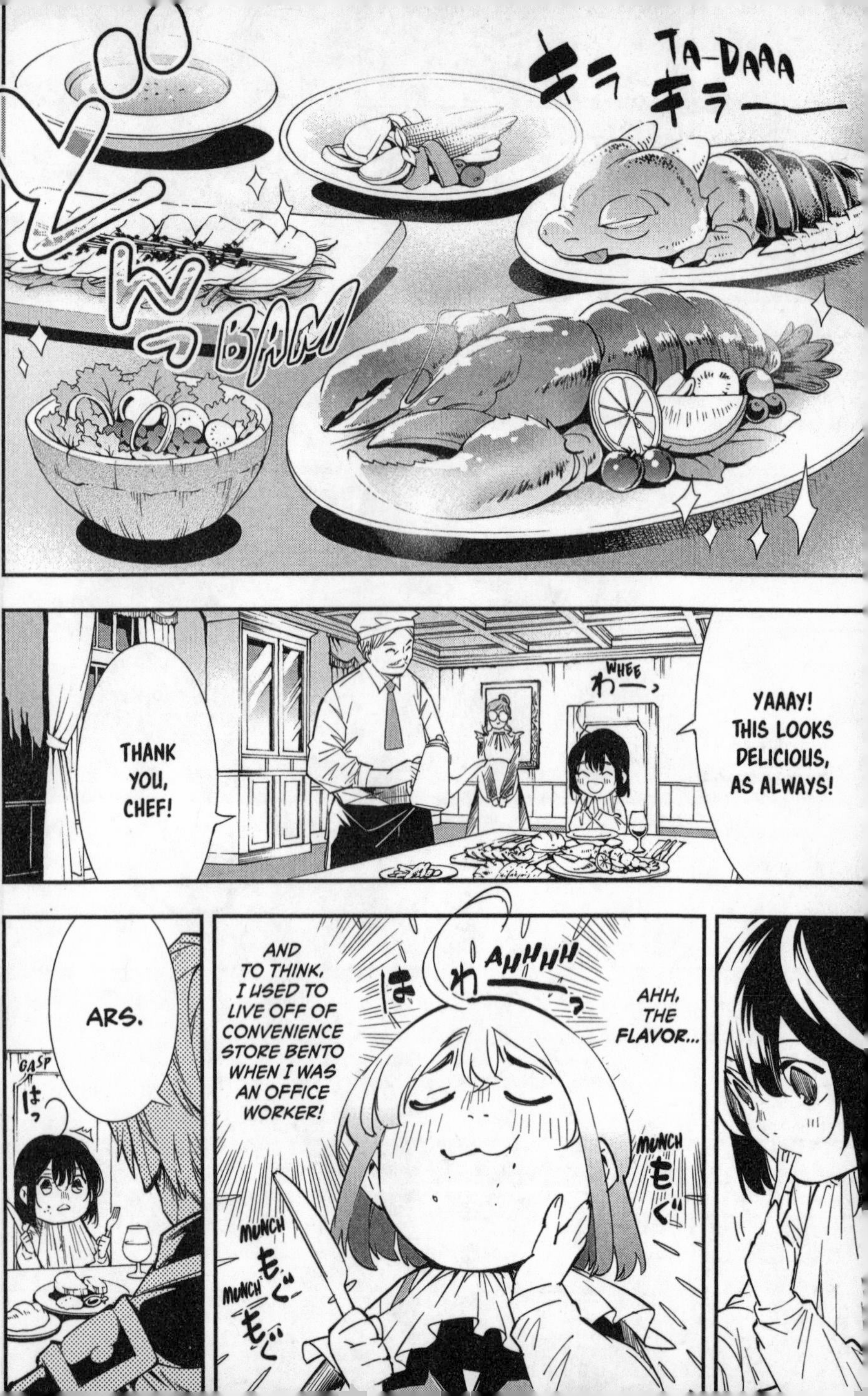
TA-DAAA
キラ キラー
BAM
YAAAY! THIS LOOKS DELICIOUS, AS ALWAYS!
WHEE
わーっ
THANK YOU, CHEF!
AHH, THE FLAVOR...
AHHHH
はわーっ
AND TO THINK, I USED TO LIVE OFF OF CONVENIENCE STORE BENTO WHEN I WAS AN OFFICE WORKER!
MUNCH
もぐ
MUNCH
もぐ
MUNCH
もぐ
ARS.
GASP
はっ

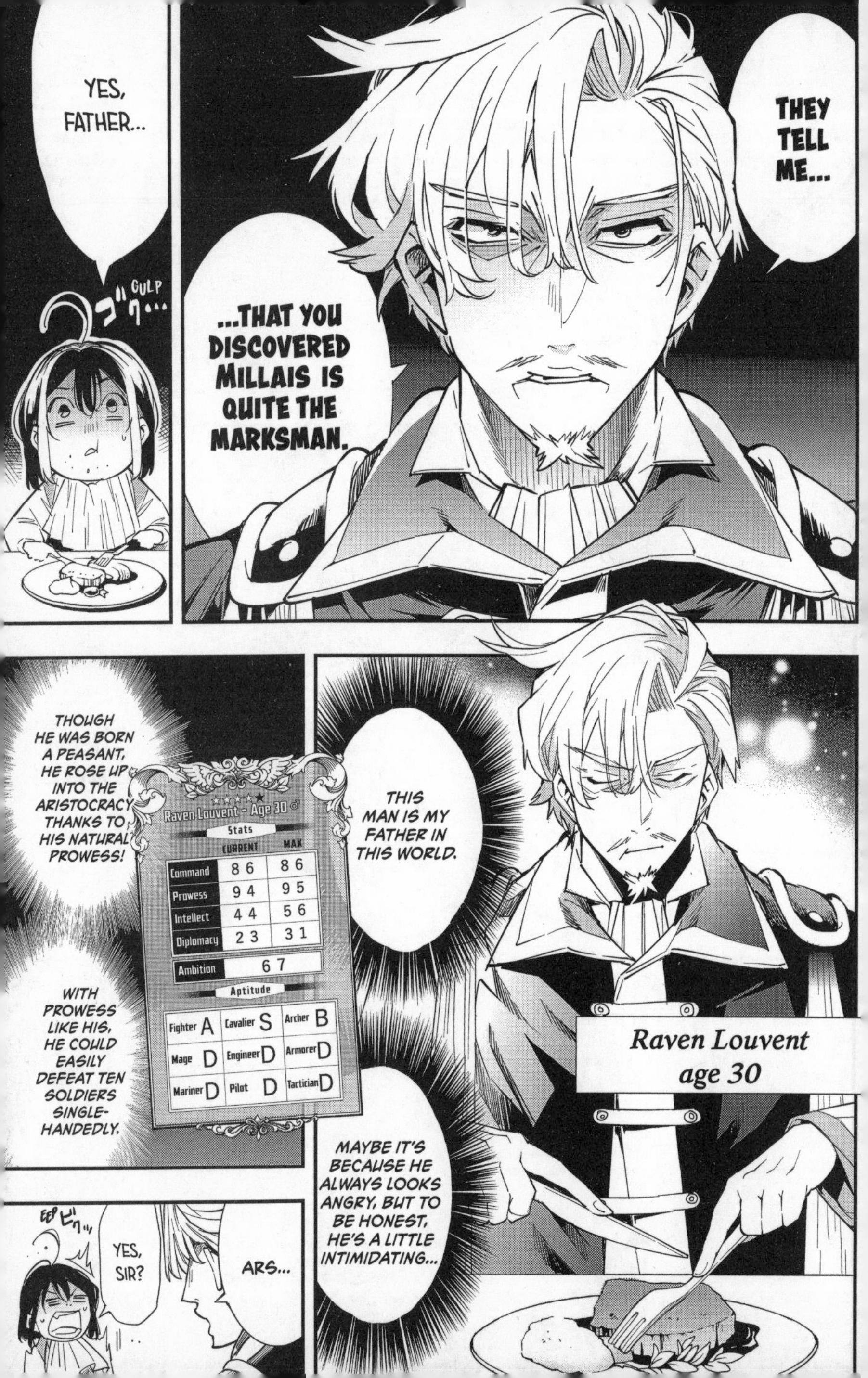
THEY TELL ME...
...THAT YOU DISCOVERED MILLAIS IS QUITE THE MARKSMAN.
YES, FATHER...
GULP
THIS MAN IS MY FATHER IN THIS WORLD.
Raven Louvent age 30
MAYBE IT'S BECAUSE HE ALWAYS LOOKS ANGRY, BUT TO BE HONEST, HE'S A LITTLE INTIMIDATING...
THOUGH HE WAS BORN A PEASANT, HE ROSE UP INTO THE ARISTOCRACY THANKS TO HIS NATURAL PROWESS!
Raven Louvent - Age 30 ♂
Stats
CURRENT MAX
Command 86 86
Prowess 94 95
Intellect 44 56
Diplomacy 23 31
Ambition 67
Aptitude
Fighter A Cavalier S Archer B
Mage D Engineer D Armorer D
Mariner D Pilot D Tactician D
WITH PROWESS LIKE HIS, HE COULD EASILY DEFEAT TEN SOLDIERS SINGLE-HANDEDLY.
ARS...
YES, SIR?
EEP

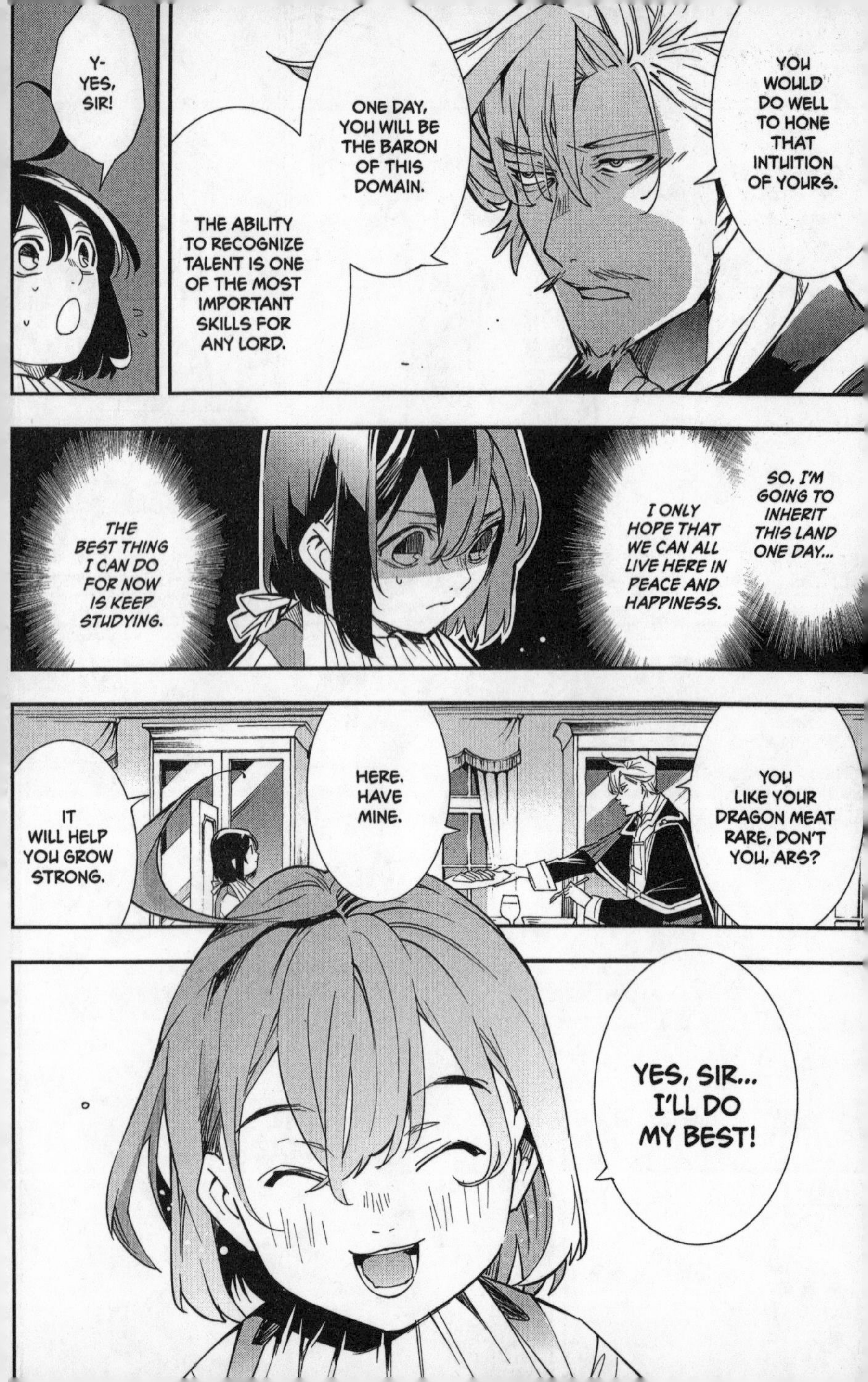
YOU WOULD DO WELL TO HONE THAT INTUITION OF YOURS.
ONE DAY, YOU WILL BE THE BARON OF THIS DOMAIN.
THE ABILITY TO RECOGNIZE TALENT IS ONE OF THE MOST IMPORTANT SKILLS FOR ANY LORD.
Y- YES, SIR!
SO, I'M GOING TO INHERIT THIS LAND ONE DAY...
I ONLY HOPE THAT WE CAN ALL LIVE HERE IN PEACE AND HAPPINESS.
THE BEST THING I CAN DO FOR NOW IS KEEP STUDYING.
YOU LIKE YOUR DRAGON MEAT RARE, DON'T YOU, ARS?
HERE. HAVE MINE.
IT WILL HELP YOU GROW STRONG.
YES, SIR... I'LL DO MY BEST!

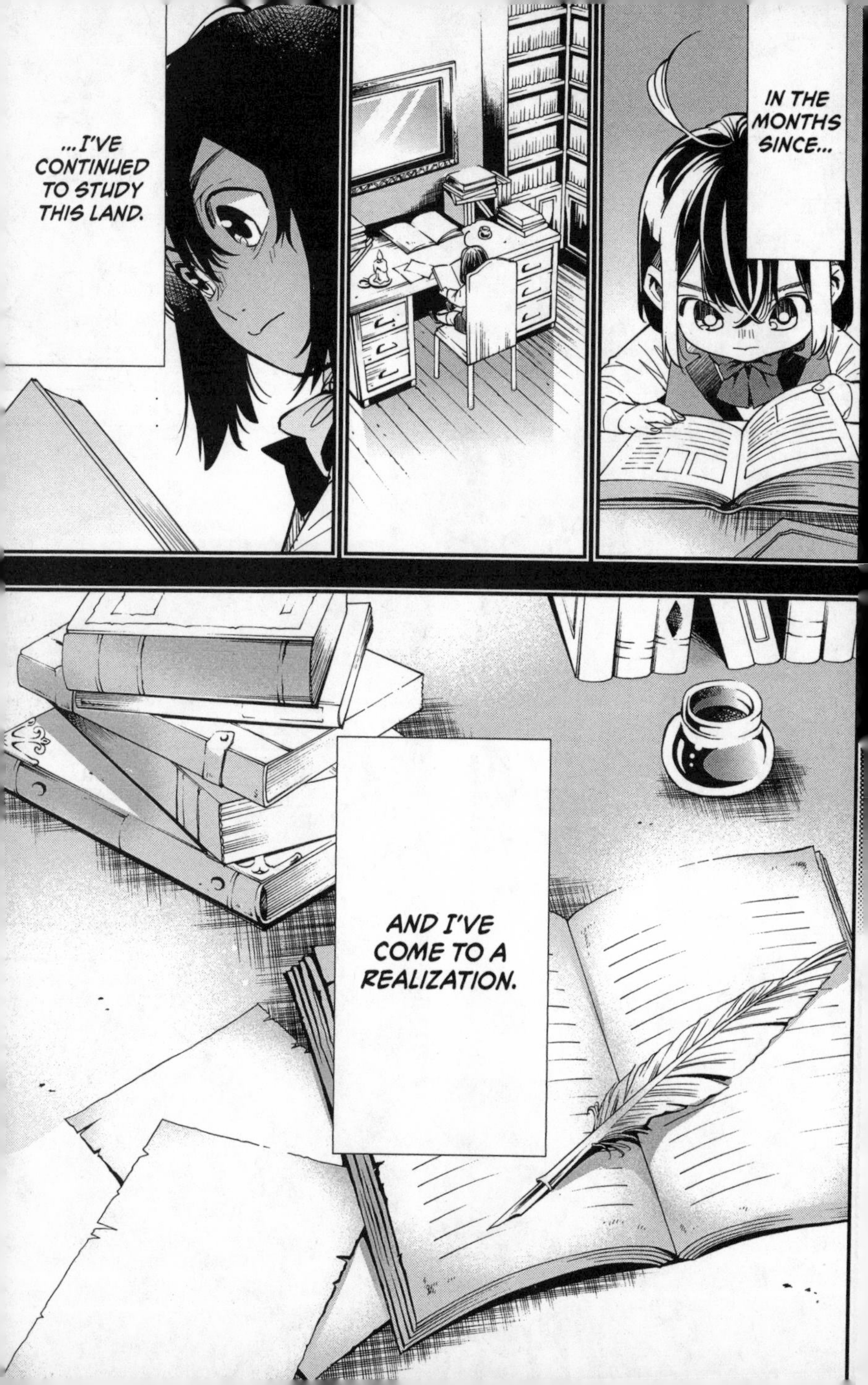
IN THE MONTHS SINCE...
...I'VE CONTINUED TO STUDY THIS LAND.
AND I'VE COME TO A REALIZATION.

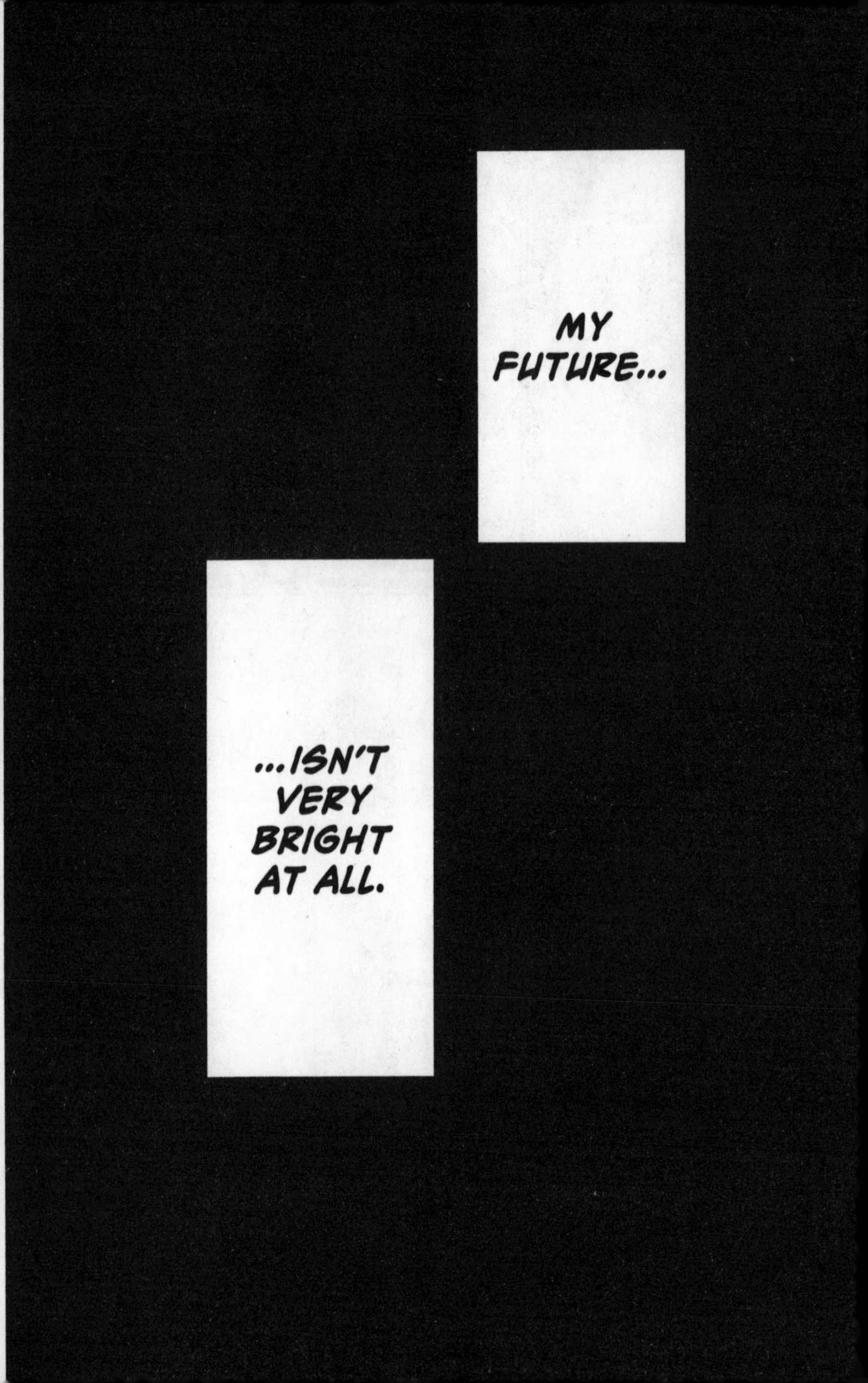
MY FUTURE...
...ISN'T VERY BRIGHT AT ALL.

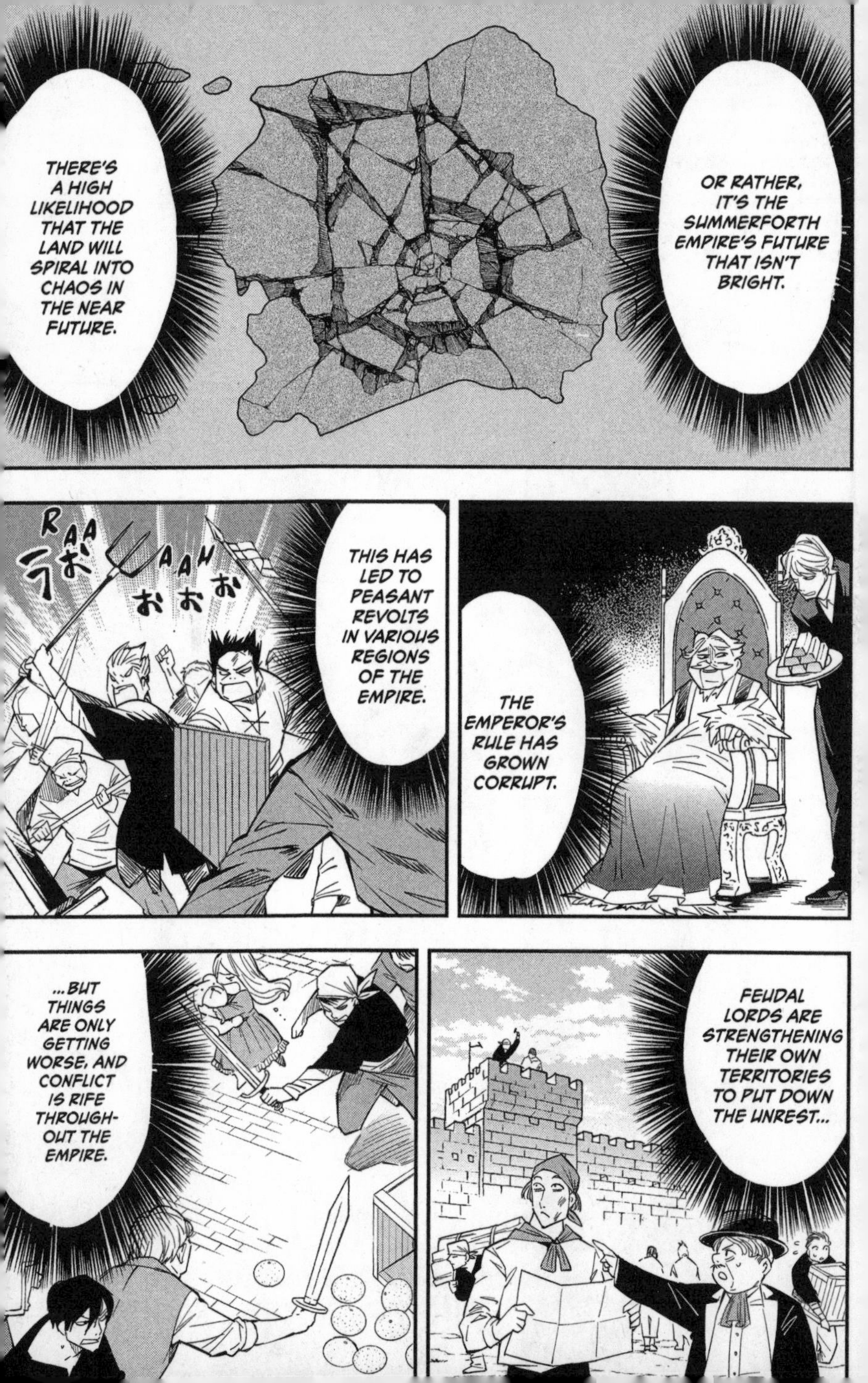
OR RATHER, IT'S THE SUMMERFORTH EMPIRE'S FUTURE THAT ISN'T BRIGHT.
THERE'S A HIGH LIKELIHOOD THAT THE LAND WILL SPIRAL INTO CHAOS IN THE NEAR FUTURE.
THE EMPEROR'S RULE HAS GROWN CORRUPT.
THIS HAS LED TO PEASANT REVOLTS IN VARIOUS REGIONS OF THE EMPIRE.
RAAAAH
うおおおお
FEUDAL LORDS ARE STRENGTHENING THEIR OWN TERRITORIES TO PUT DOWN THE UNREST...
...BUT THINGS ARE ONLY GETTING WORSE, AND CONFLICT IS RIFE THROUGH-OUT THE EMPIRE.

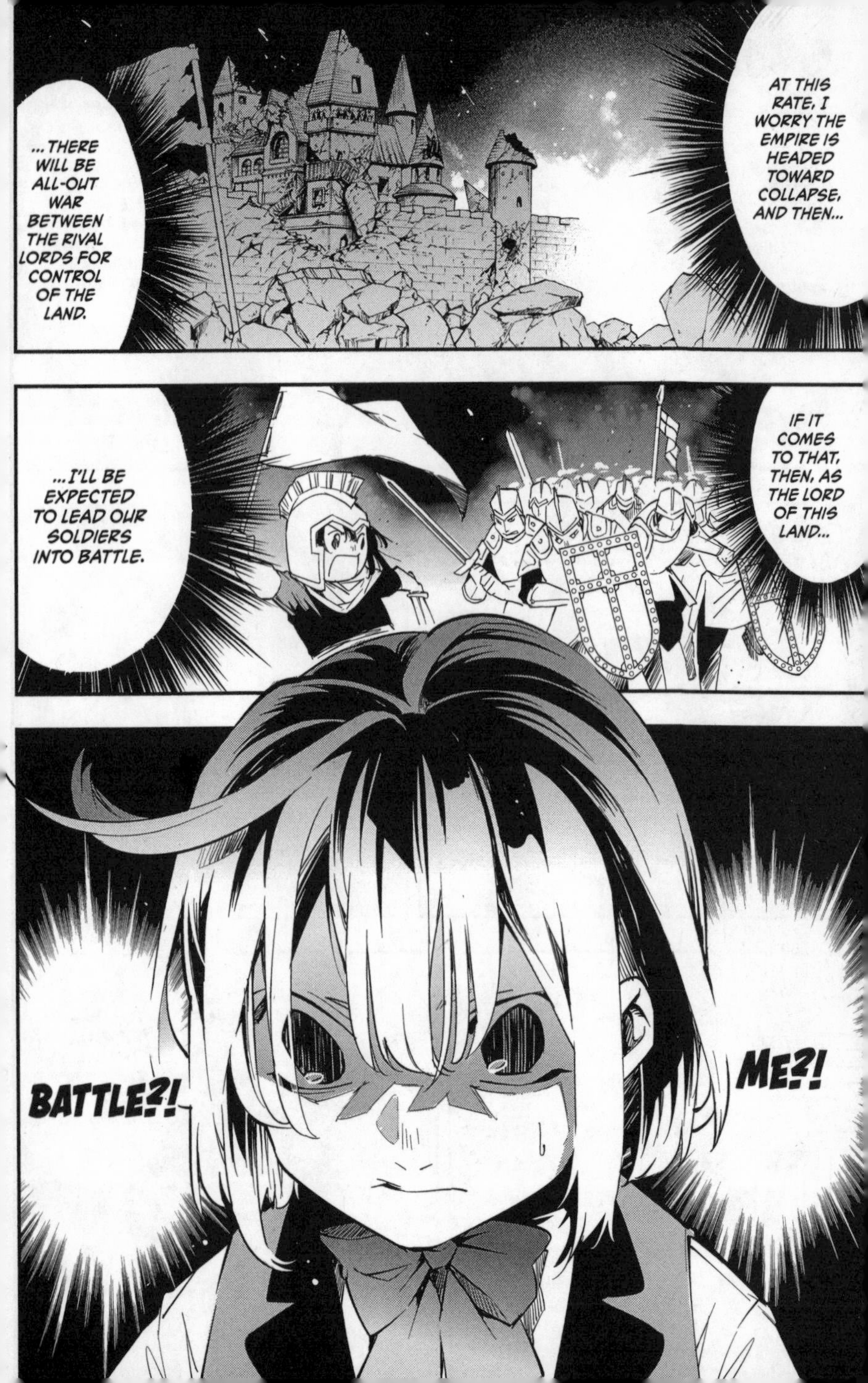
AT THIS RATE, I WORRY THE EMPIRE IS HEADED TOWARD COLLAPSE, AND THEN...
...THERE WILL BE ALL-OUT WAR BETWEEN THE RIVAL LORDS FOR CONTROL OF THE LAND.
IF IT COMES TO THAT, THEN, AS THE LORD OF THIS LAND...
...I'LL BE EXPECTED TO LEAD OUR SOLDIERS INTO BATTLE.
ME?!
BATTLE?!

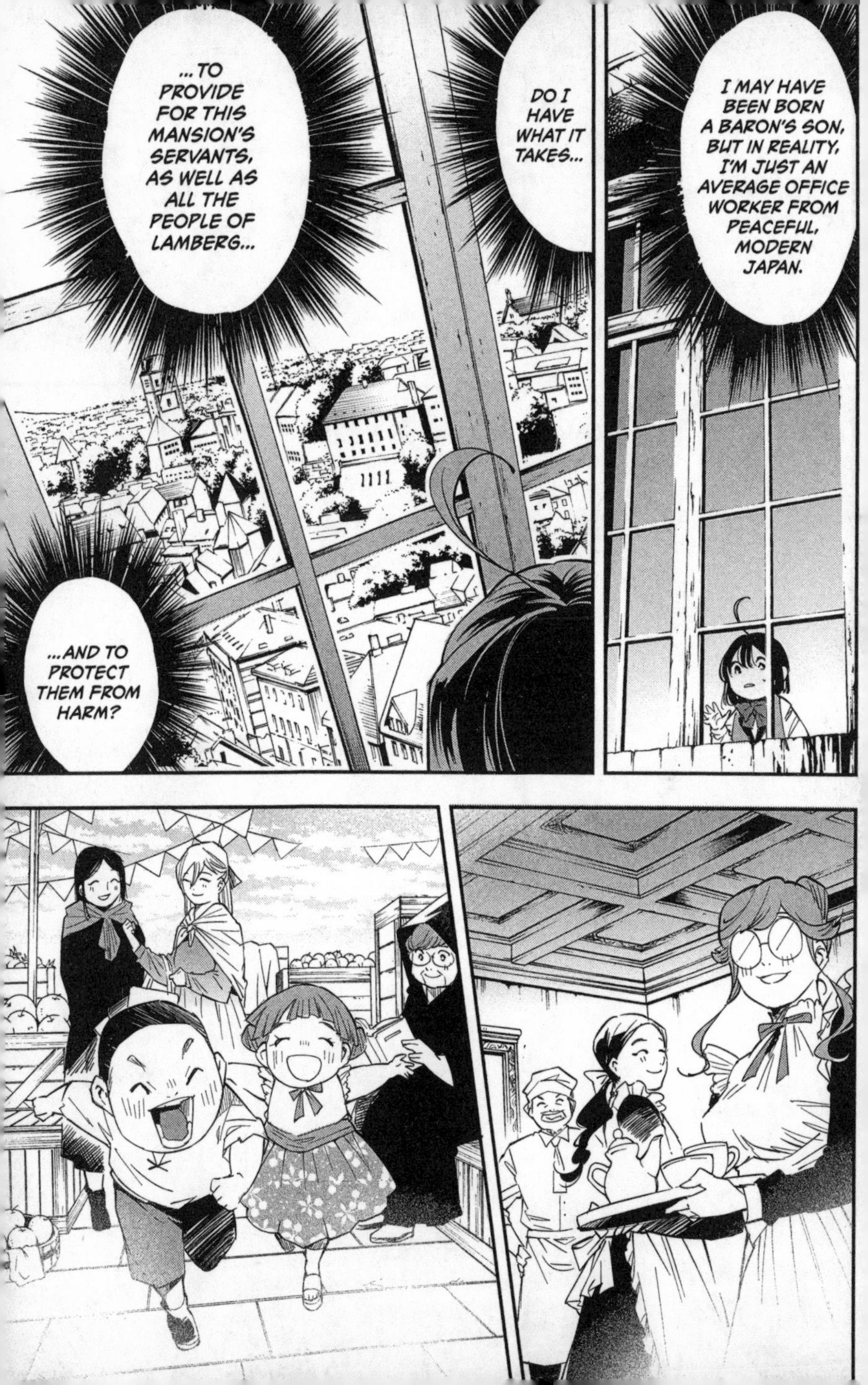
I MAY HAVE BEEN BORN A BARON'S SON, BUT IN REALITY, I'M JUST AN AVERAGE OFFICE WORKER FROM PEACEFUL, MODERN JAPAN.
DO I HAVE WHAT IT TAKES...
...TO PROVIDE FOR THIS MANSION'S SERVANTS, AS WELL AS ALL THE PEOPLE OF LAMBERG...
...AND TO PROTECT THEM FROM HARM?

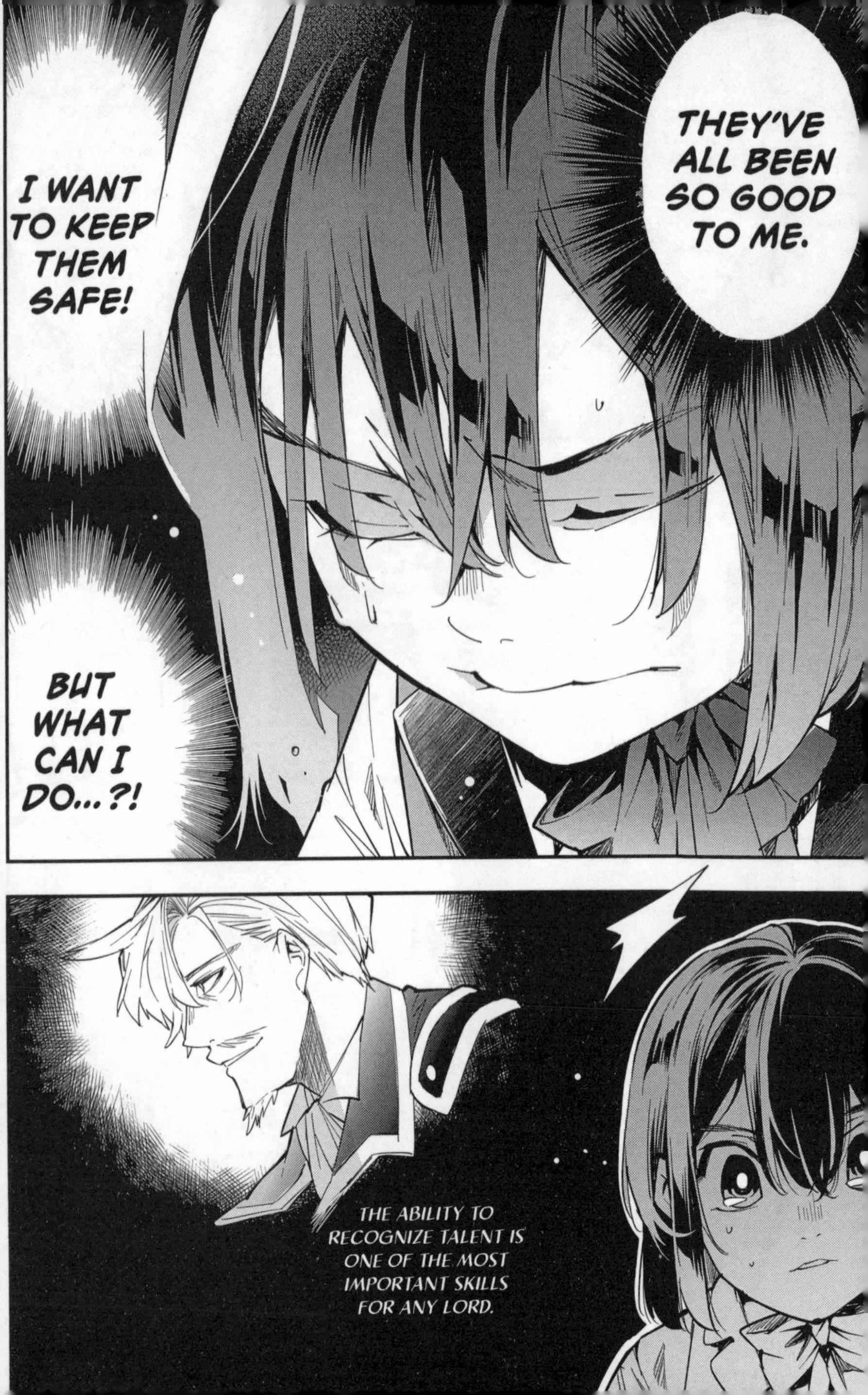
THEY'VE ALL BEEN SO GOOD TO ME.
I WANT TO KEEP THEM SAFE!
BUT WHAT CAN I DO...?!
THE ABILITY TO RECOGNIZE TALENT IS ONE OF THE MOST IMPORTANT SKILLS FOR ANY LORD.

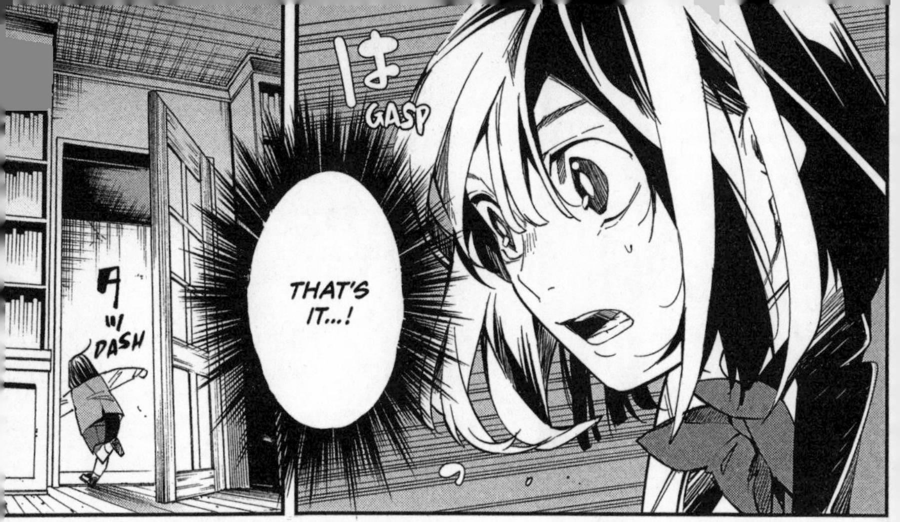
は
GASP
THAT'S IT...!
タッ
DASH

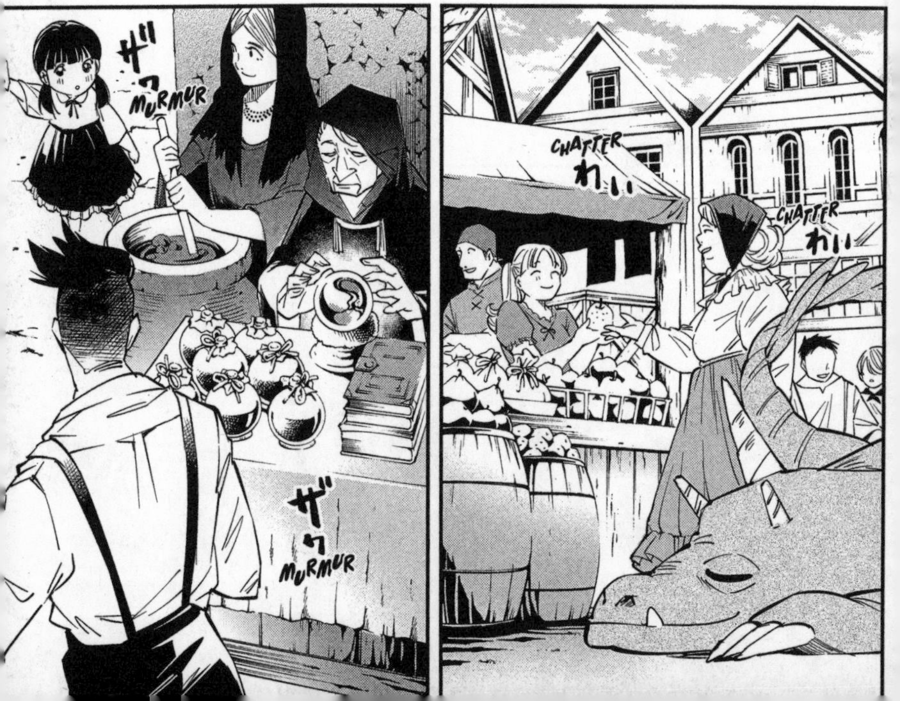
CHATTER
わい
CHATTER
わい
ザワ
MURMUR
ザワ
MURMUR

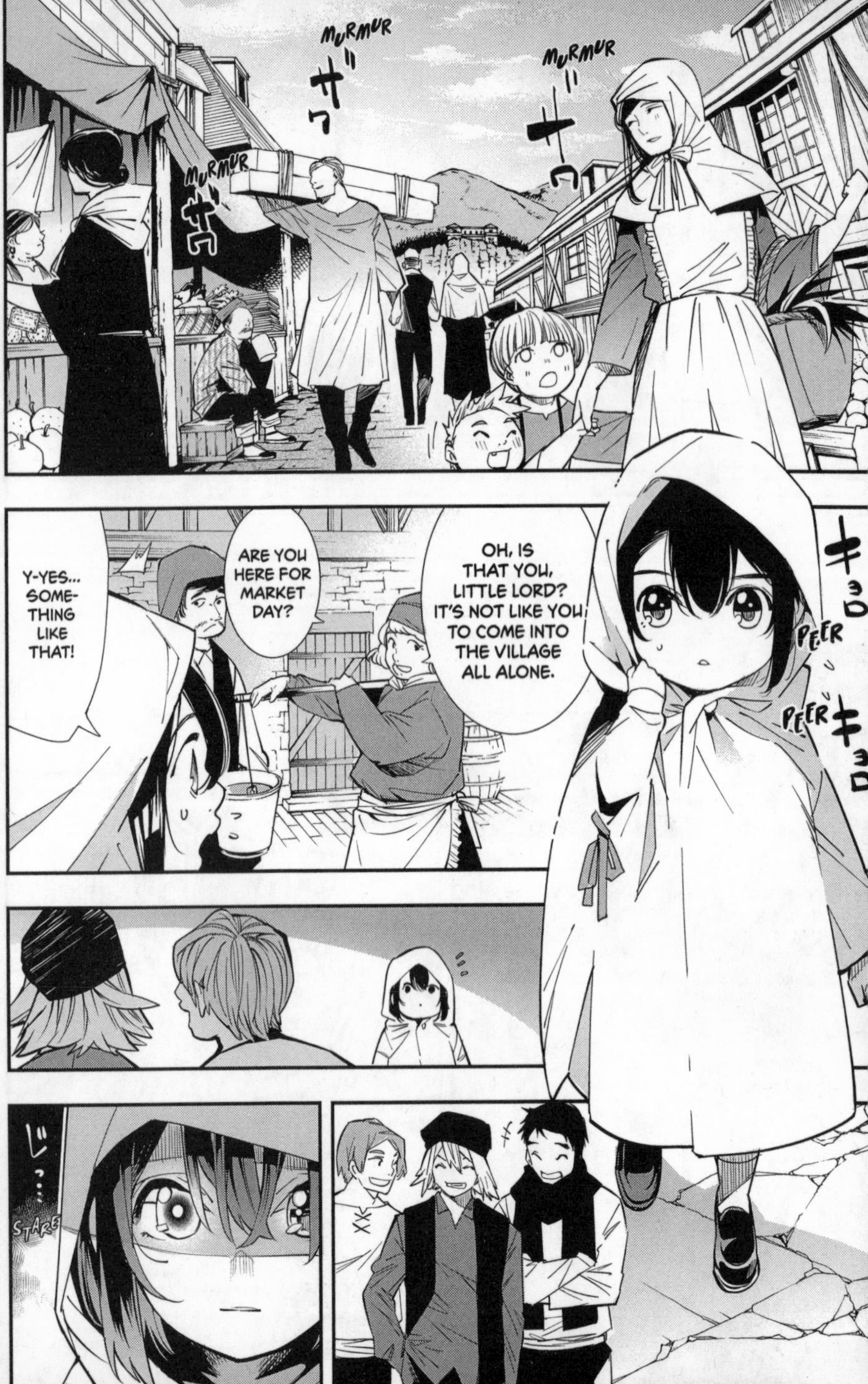
MURMUR
ザワ
MURMUR
ザワ
MURMUR
ザワ
PEER
キョロ
PEER
キョロ
OH, IS THAT YOU, LITTLE LORD? IT'S NOT LIKE YOU TO COME INTO THE VILLAGE ALL ALONE.
ARE YOU HERE FOR MARKET DAY?
Y-YES... SOMETHING LIKE THAT!
じっ…
STARE

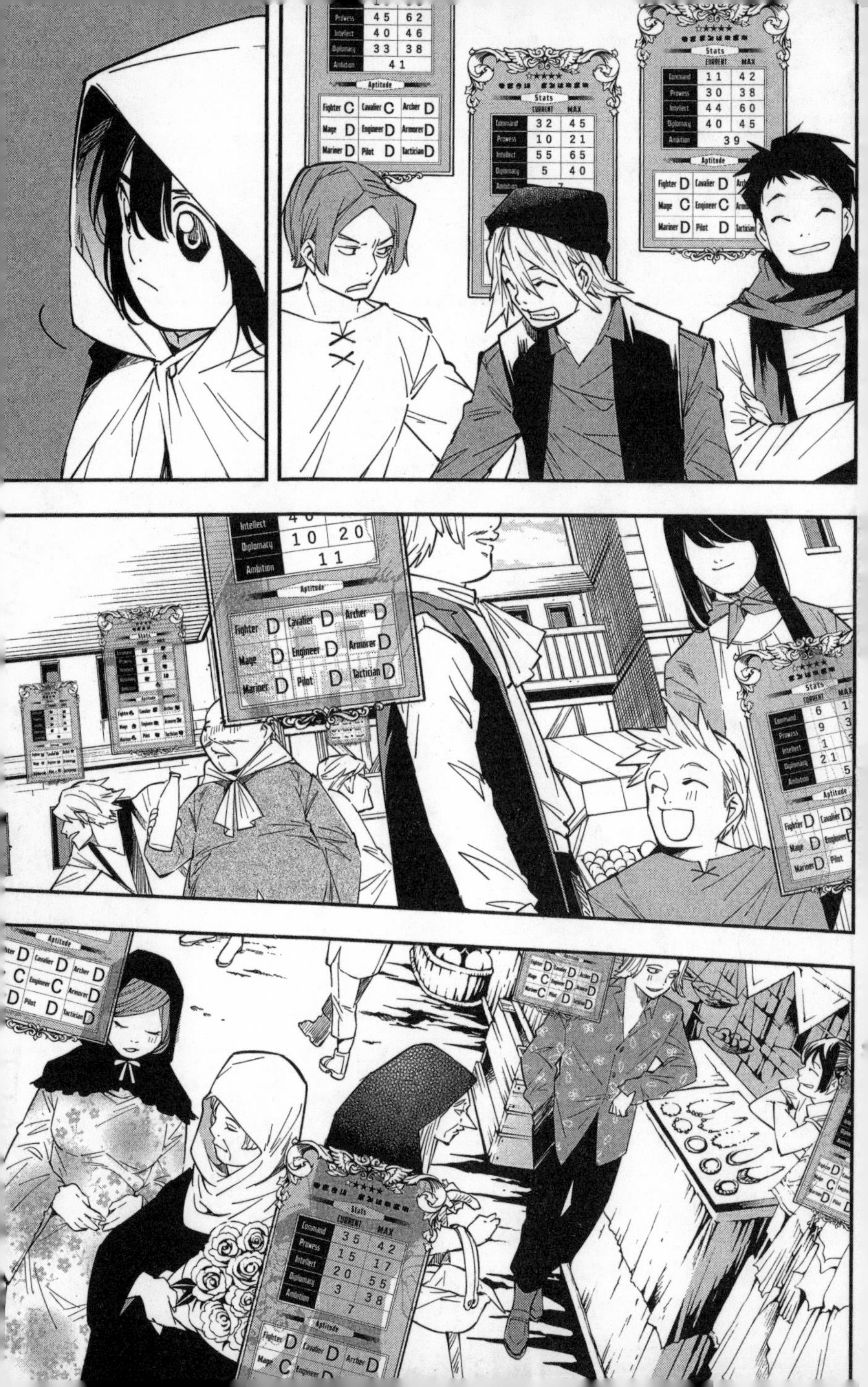
Stats
CURRENT MAX
Command 11 42
Prowess 30 38
Intellect 44 60
Diplomacy 40 45
Ambition 39
Aptitude
Fighter D Cavalier D
Mage C Engineer C
Mariner D Pilot D
Stats
CURRENT MAX
Command 32 45
Prowess 10 21
Intellect 55 65
Diplomacy 5 40
Prowess 45 62
Intellect 40 46
Diplomacy 33 38
Ambition 41
Aptitude
Fighter C Cavalier C Archer D
Mage D Engineer D Armorer D
Mariner D Pilot D Tactician D
Stats
CURRENT MAX
Command 6
Prowess 9
Intellect 1
Diplomacy 21
Ambition 5
Aptitude
Fighter D Cavalier D
Mage D Engineer
Mariner D Pilot
Intellect
Diplomacy 10 20
Ambition 11
Aptitude
Fighter D Cavalier D Archer D
Mage D Engineer D Armorer D
Mariner D Pilot D Tactician D
Aptitude
Cavalier D Archer D
Engineer C Armorer D
Pilot D Tactician D
Stats
CURRENT MAX
Command 35 42
Prowess 15 17
Intellect 20 55
Diplomacy 3 38
Ambition 7
Aptitude
Fighter D Cavalier D
Mage C Archer D

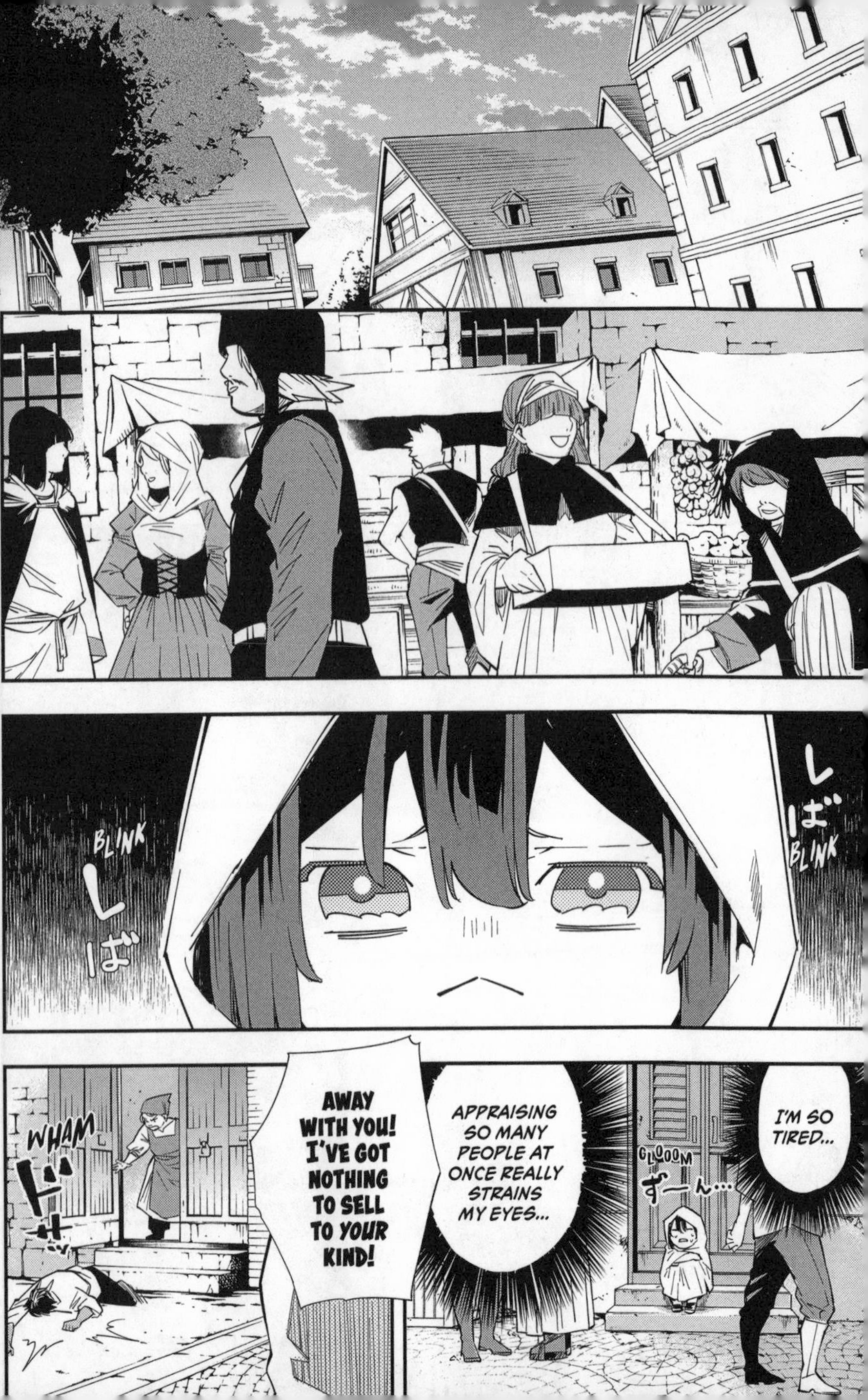
BLINK
BLINK
I'M SO TIRED...
GLOOOM
ずーん...
APPRAISING SO MANY PEOPLE AT ONCE REALLY STRAINS MY EYES...
AWAY WITH YOU! I'VE GOT NOTHING TO SELL TO YOUR KIND!
WHAM

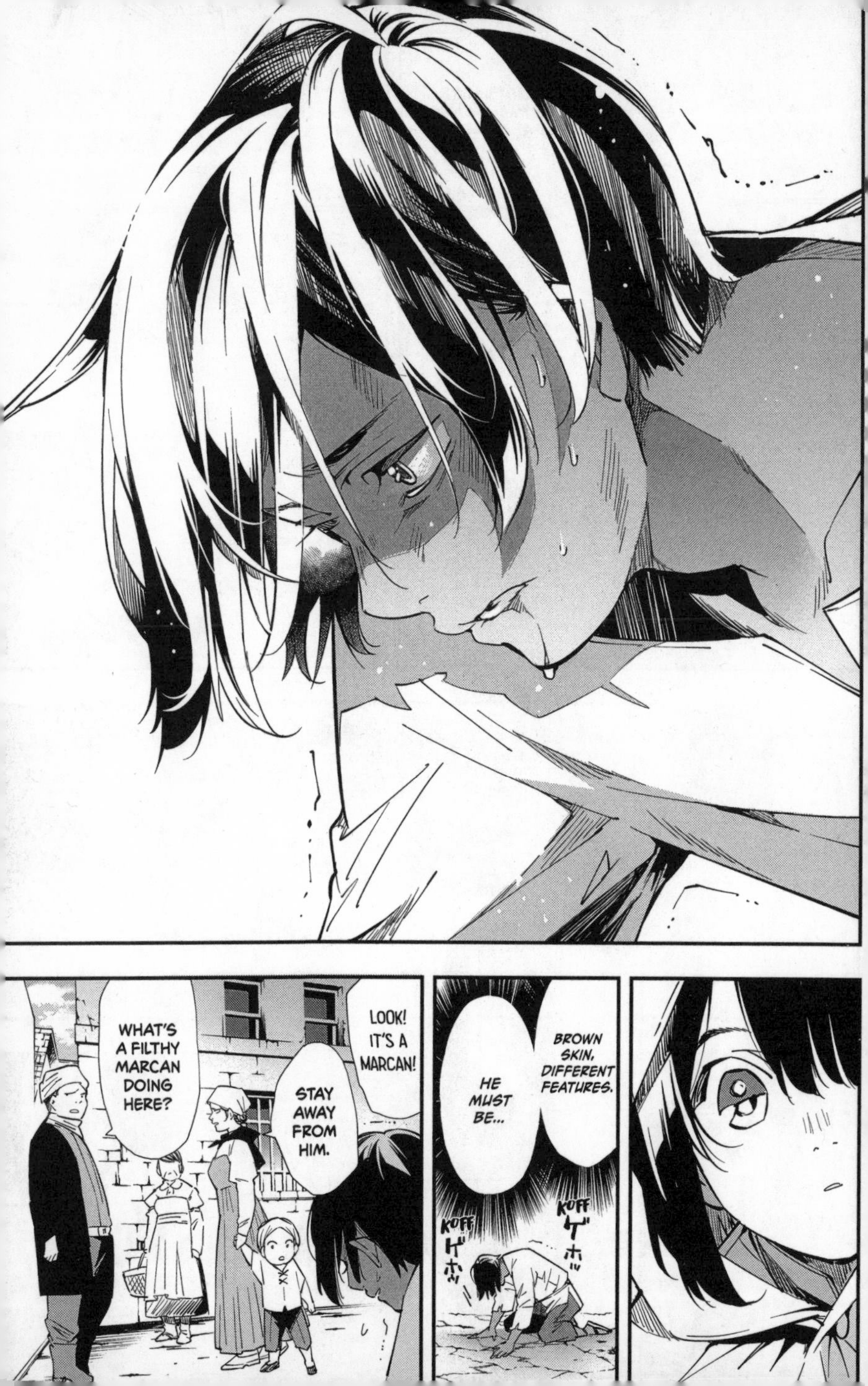
BROWN SKIN, DIFFERENT FEATURES.
HE MUST BE...
KOFF
KOFF
LOOK! IT'S A MARCAN!
STAY AWAY FROM HIM.
WHAT'S A FILTHY MARCAN DOING HERE?

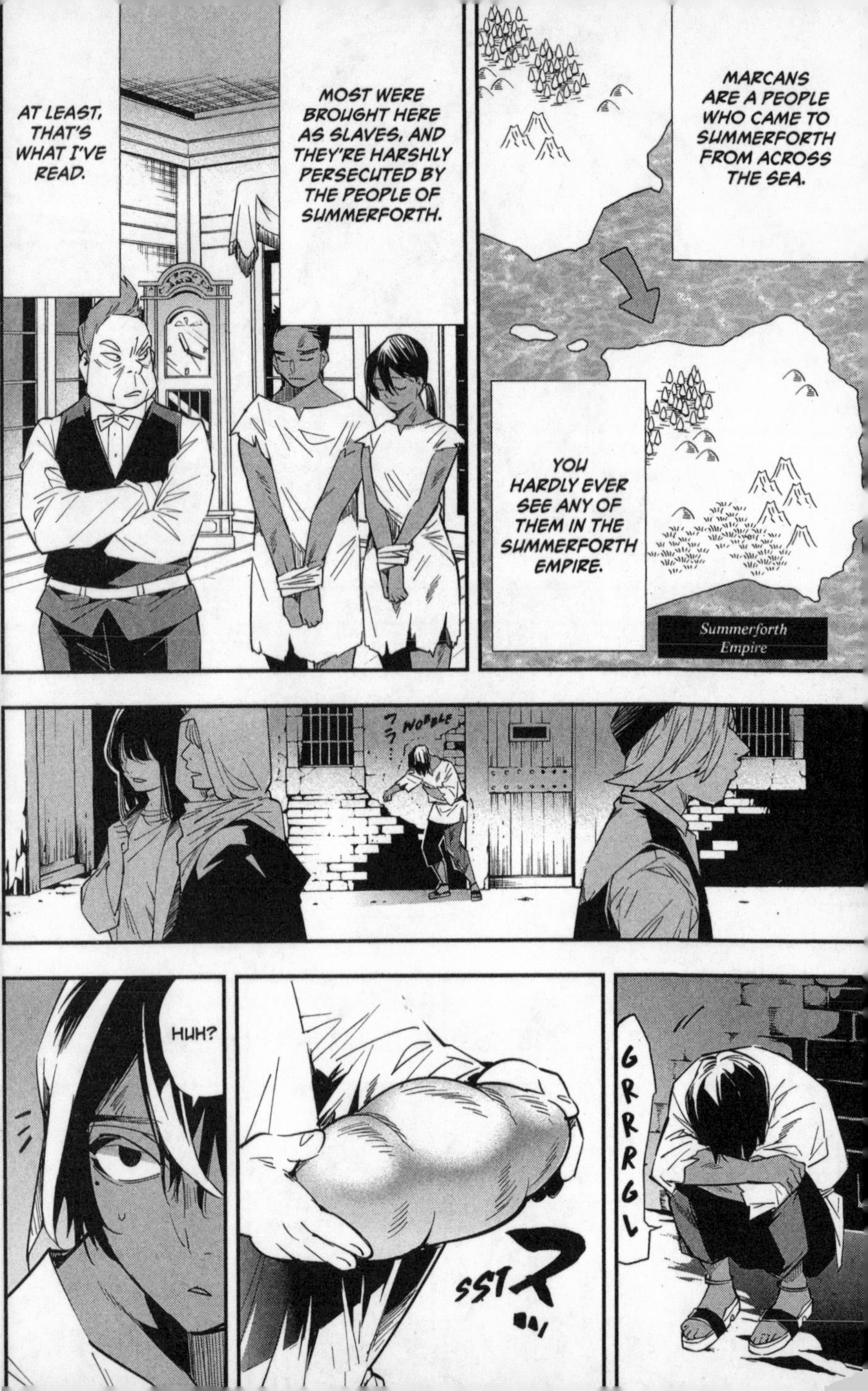
MARCANS ARE A PEOPLE WHO CAME TO SUMMERFORTH FROM ACROSS THE SEA.
YOU HARDLY EVER SEE ANY OF THEM IN THE SUMMERFORTH EMPIRE.
Summerforth Empire
MOST WERE BROUGHT HERE AS SLAVES, AND THEY'RE HARSHLY PERSECUTED BY THE PEOPLE OF SUMMERFORTH.
AT LEAST, THAT'S WHAT I'VE READ.
WOBBLE
GRRRGL
SST
HUH?

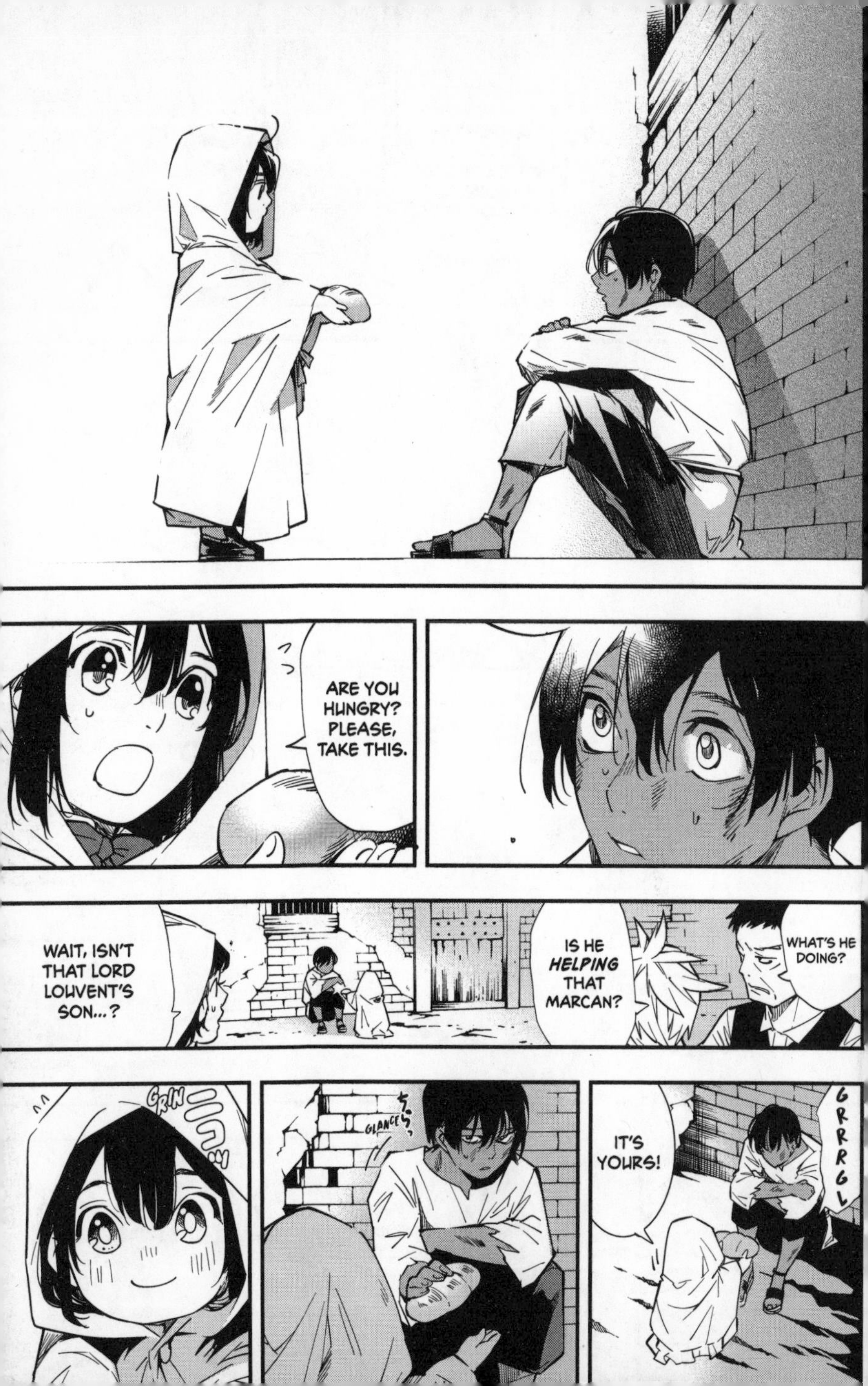
ARE YOU HUNGRY? PLEASE, TAKE THIS.
WHAT'S HE DOING?
IS HE *HELPING* THAT MARCAN?
WAIT, ISN'T THAT LORD LOUVENT'S SON...?
GRRRGL
IT'S YOURS!
GLANCE
GRIN

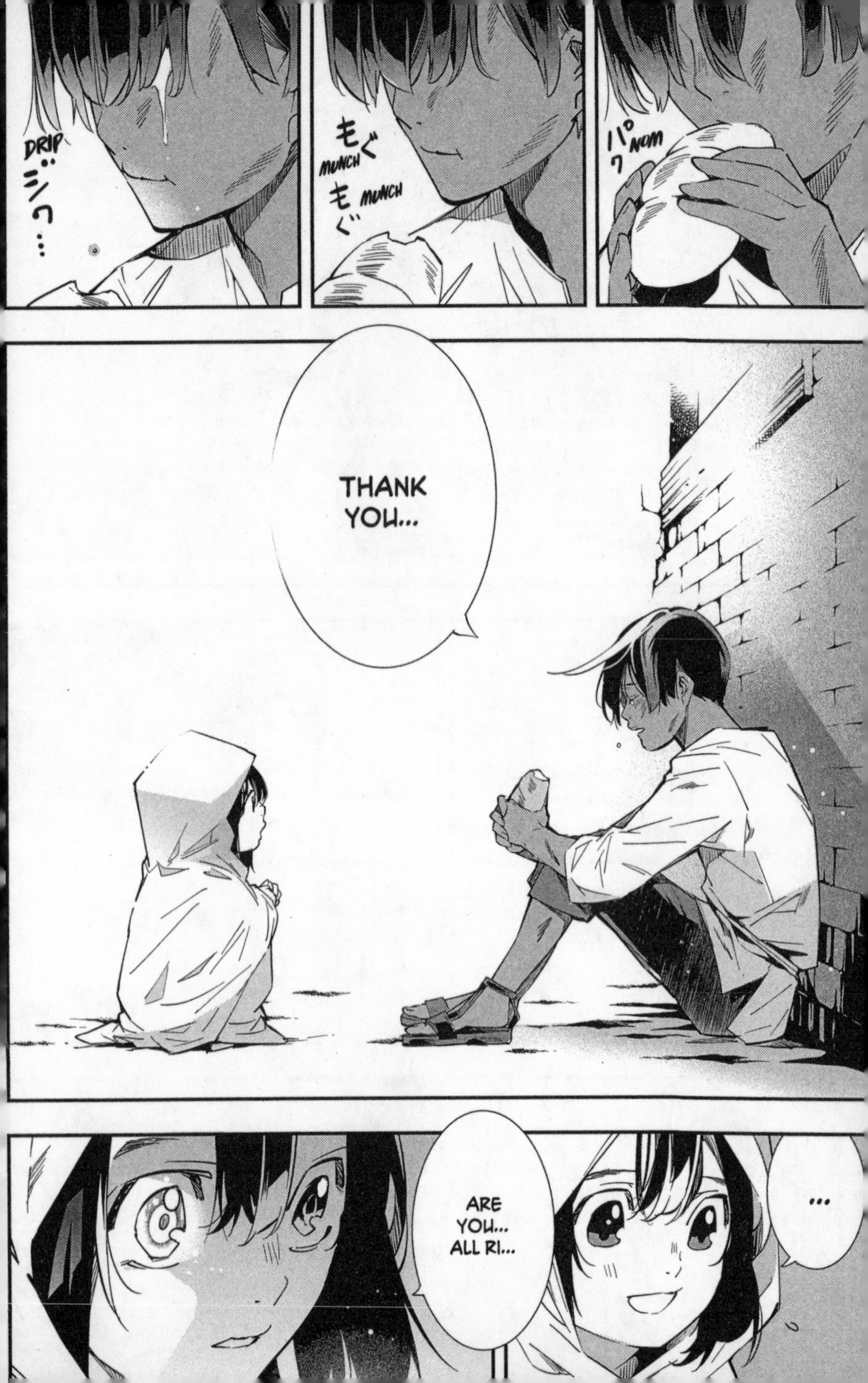
パク NOM
もぐ MUNCH
もぐ MUNCH
DRIP
ジワ…
THANK YOU...
...
ARE YOU... ALL RI...

Rietz Muses - Age 14 ♂

Stats

	CURRENT	MAX
Command	87	99
Prowess	70	90
Intellect	72	99
Diplomacy	78	100

Ambition	21

Aptitude

Fighter	A	Cavalier	S	Archer	A
Mage	C	Engineer	S	Armorer	A
Mariner	D	Pilot	C	Tactician	S

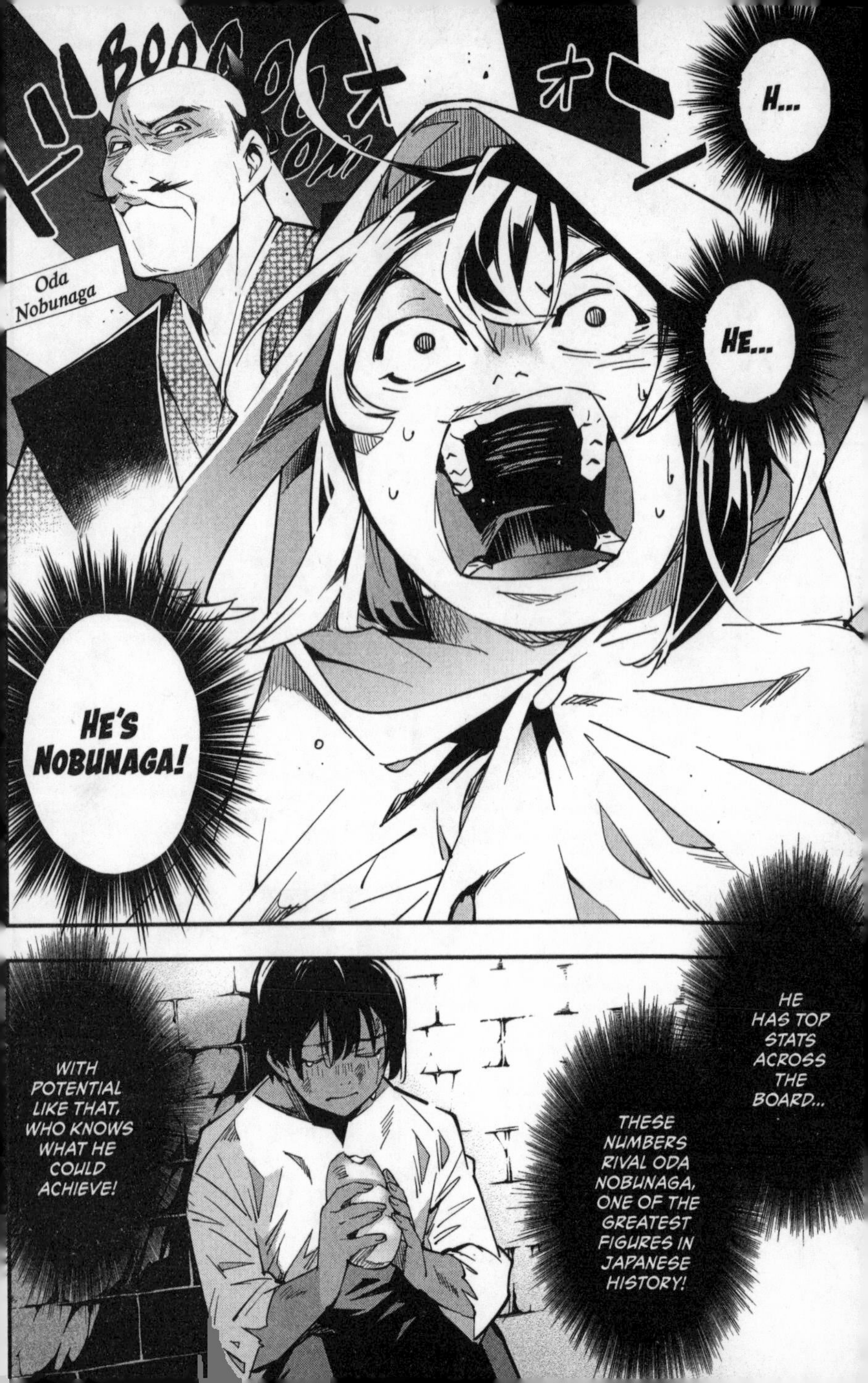
H...
HE...
Oda Nobunaga
HE'S NOBUNAGA!
HE HAS TOP STATS ACROSS THE BOARD...
THESE NUMBERS RIVAL ODA NOBUNAGA, ONE OF THE GREATEST FIGURES IN JAPANESE HISTORY!
WITH POTENTIAL LIKE THAT, WHO KNOWS WHAT HE COULD ACHIEVE!

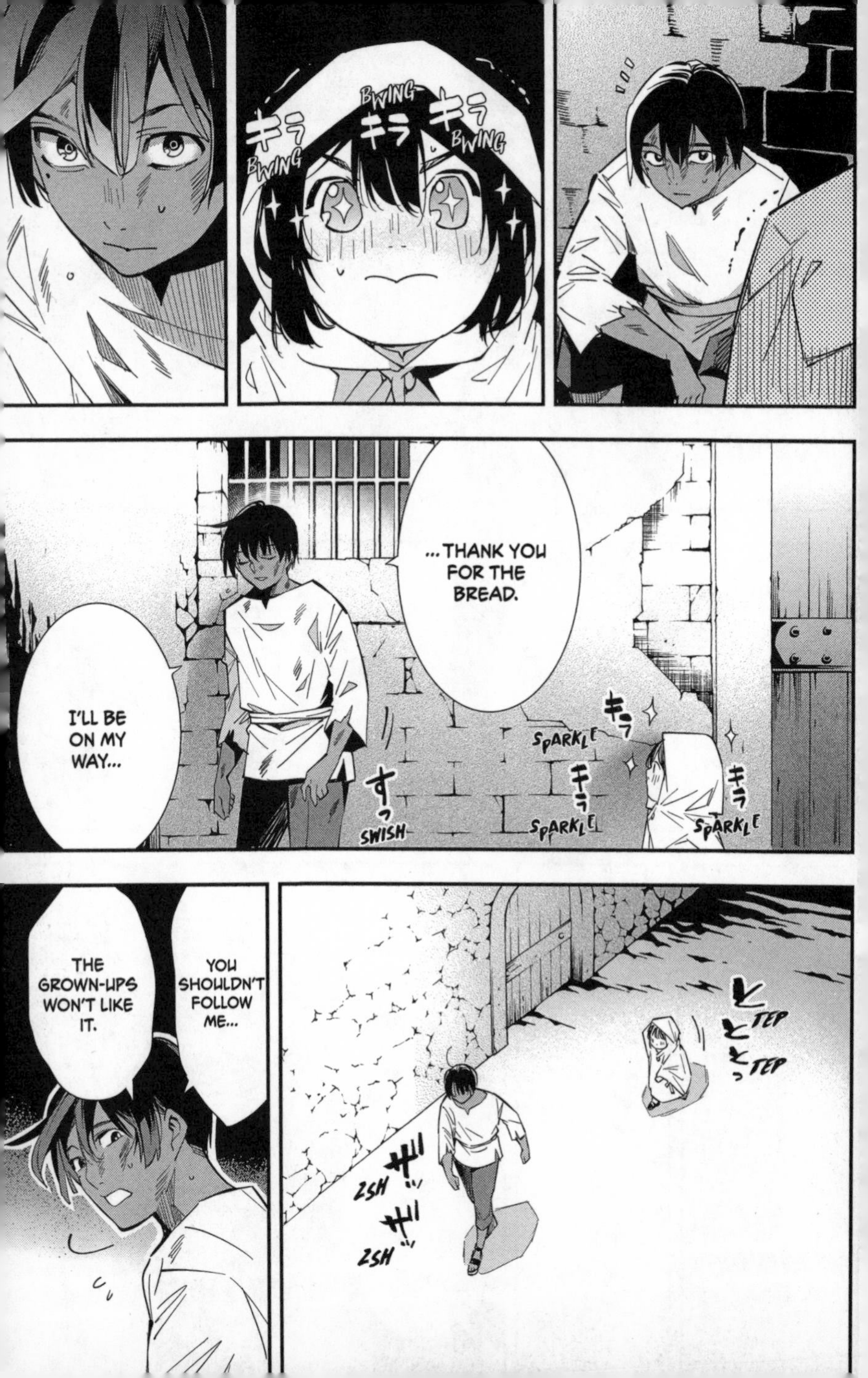
キラ
BWING
キラ
BWING
キラ
BWING
...THANK YOU FOR THE BREAD.
I'LL BE ON MY WAY...
キラ
SPARKLE
キラ
SPARKLE
キラ
SPARKLE
すっ
SWISH
とっ
TEP
とっ
TEP
ザッ
ZSH
ザッ
ZSH
YOU SHOULDN'T FOLLOW ME...
THE GROWN-UPS WON'T LIKE IT.

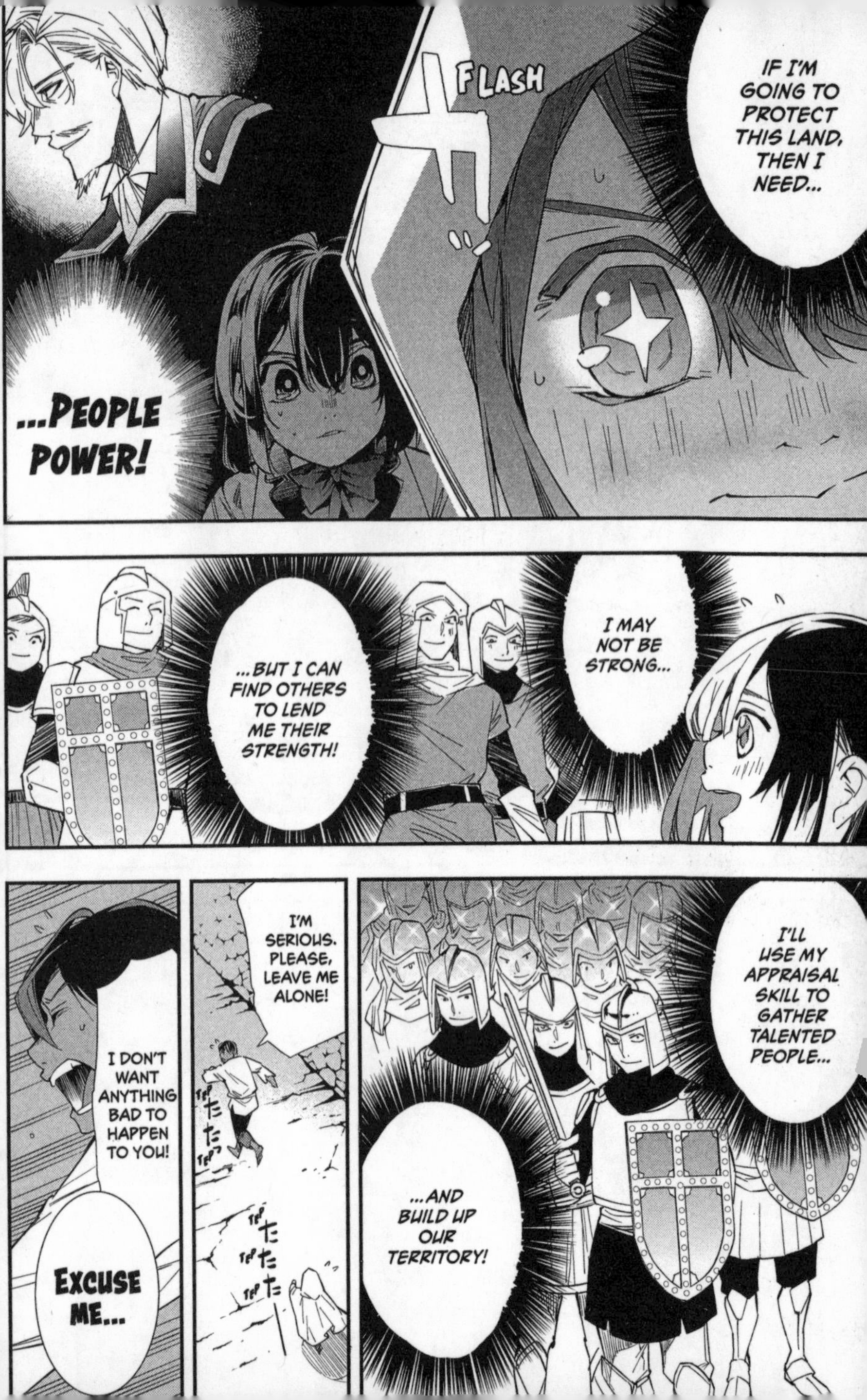
IF I'M GOING TO PROTECT THIS LAND, THEN I NEED...
FLASH
...PEOPLE POWER!
I MAY NOT BE STRONG...
...BUT I CAN FIND OTHERS TO LEND ME THEIR STRENGTH!
I'LL USE MY APPRAISAL SKILL TO GATHER TALENTED PEOPLE...
...AND BUILD UP OUR TERRITORY!
I'M SERIOUS. PLEASE, LEAVE ME ALONE!
I DON'T WANT ANYTHING BAD TO HAPPEN TO YOU!
EXCUSE ME...

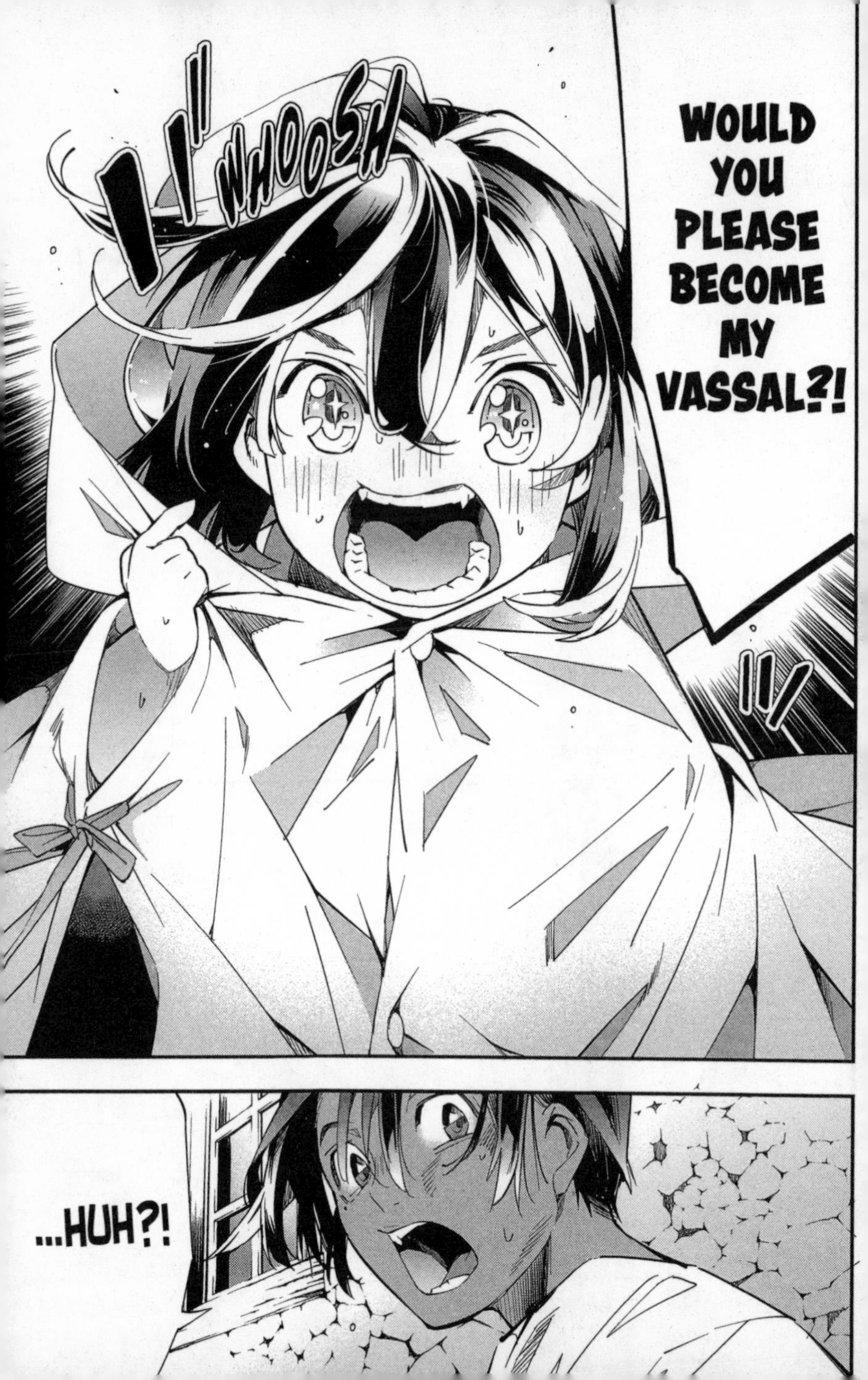
WOULD YOU PLEASE BECOME MY VASSAL?!
WHOOSH
...HUH?!

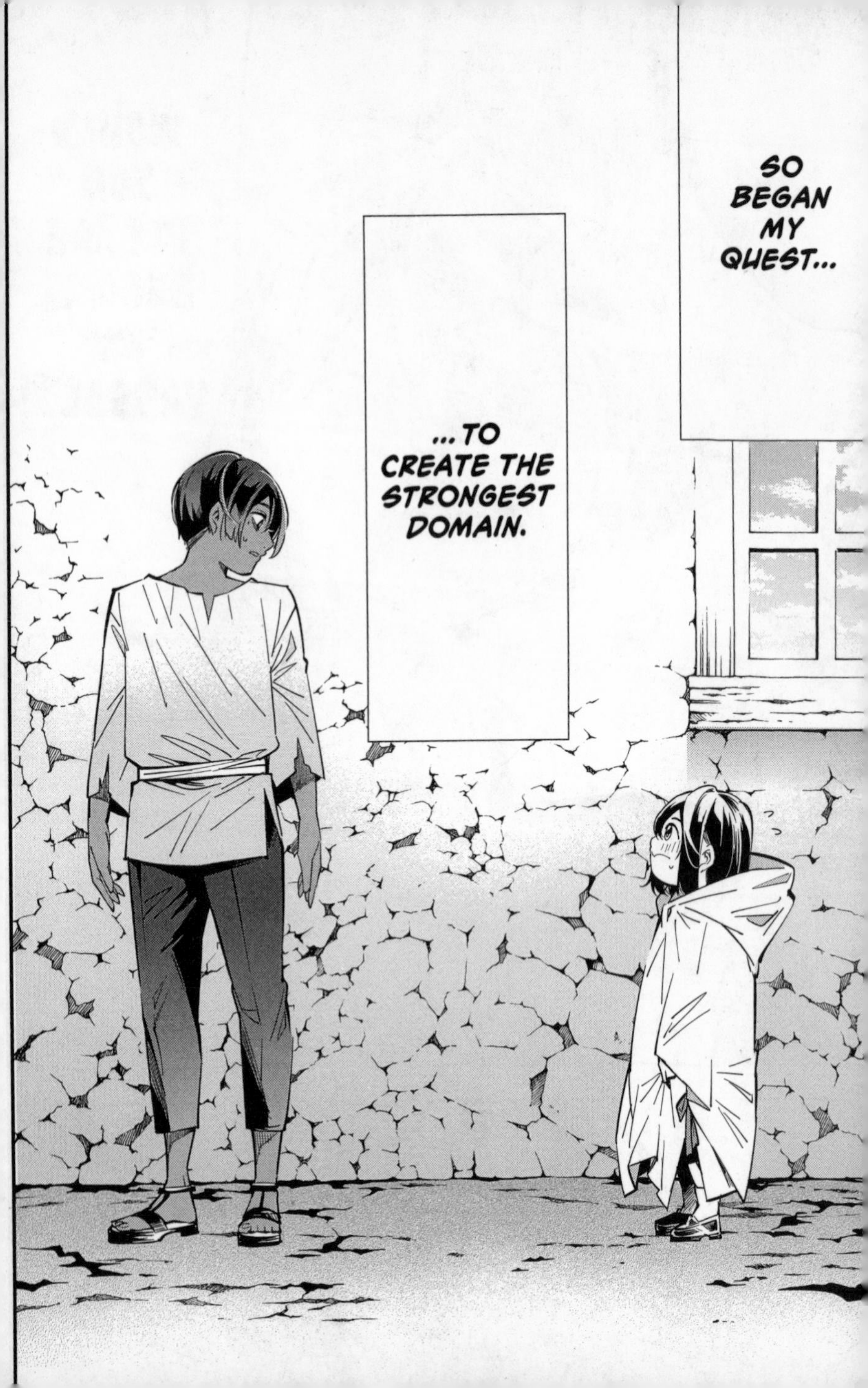
SO BEGAN MY QUEST...
...TO CREATE THE STRONGEST DOMAIN.

Chapter 2: The Test

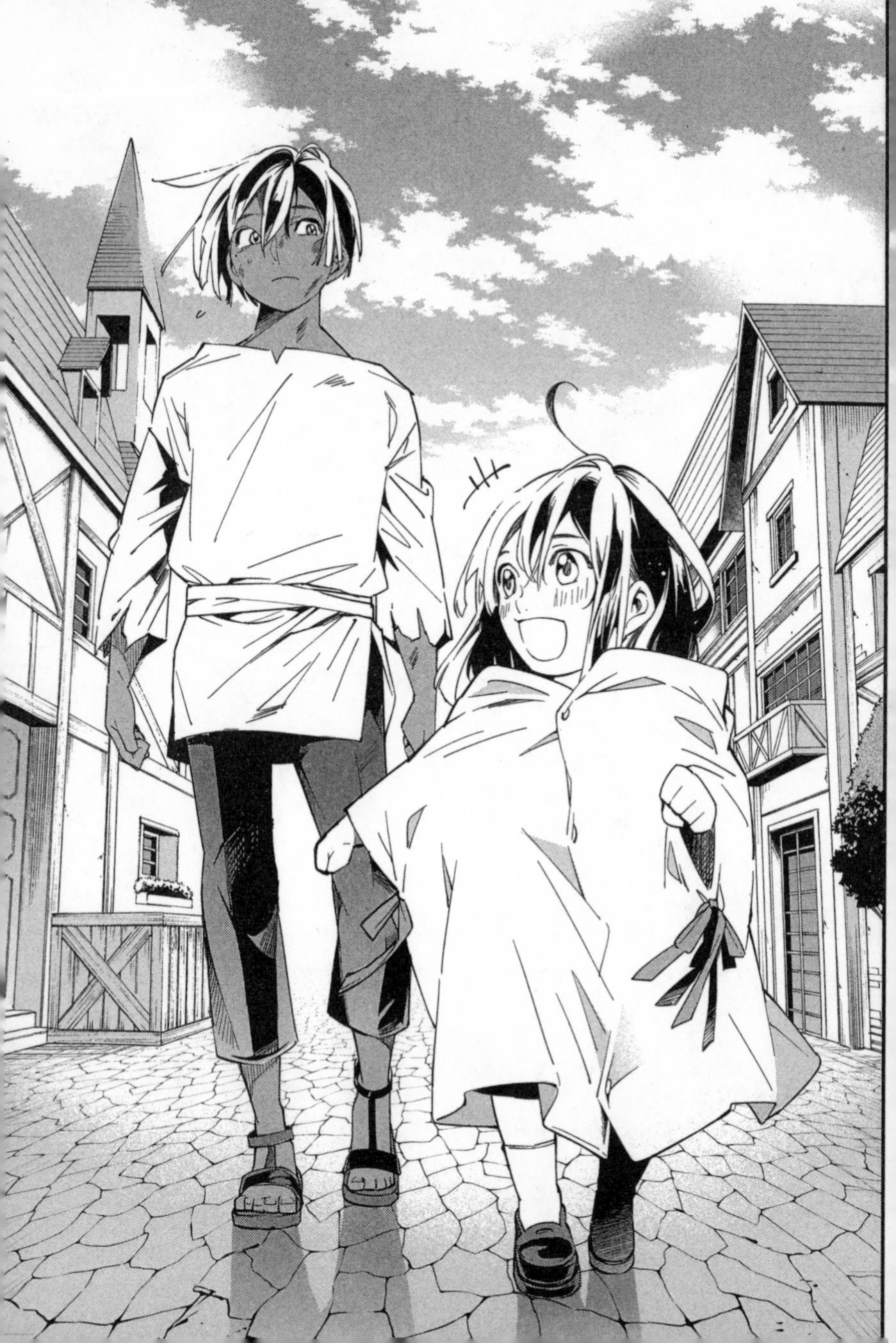

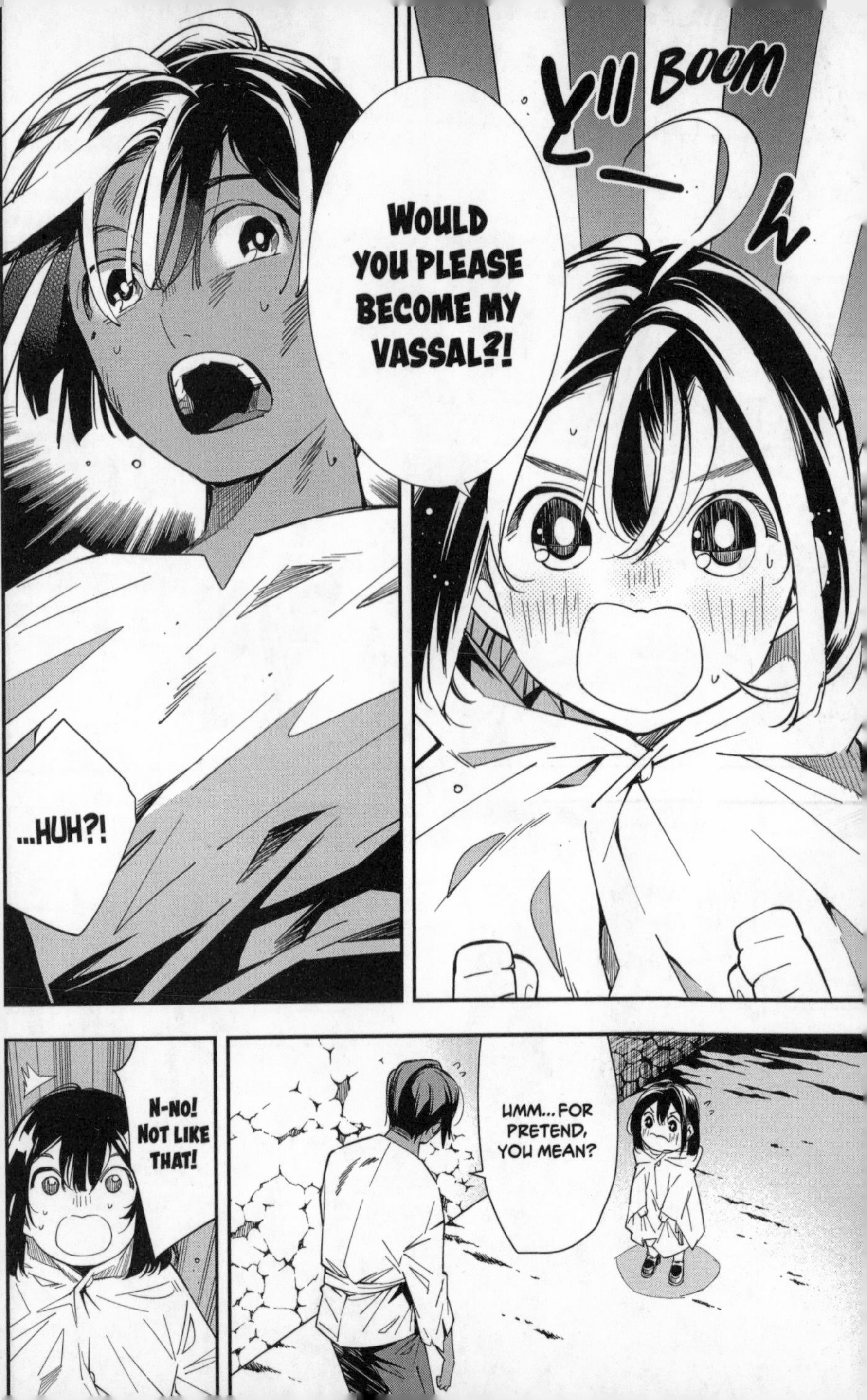
BOOM
WOULD YOU PLEASE BECOME MY VASSAL?!
...HUH?!
UMM... FOR PRETEND, YOU MEAN?
N-NO! NOT LIKE THAT!

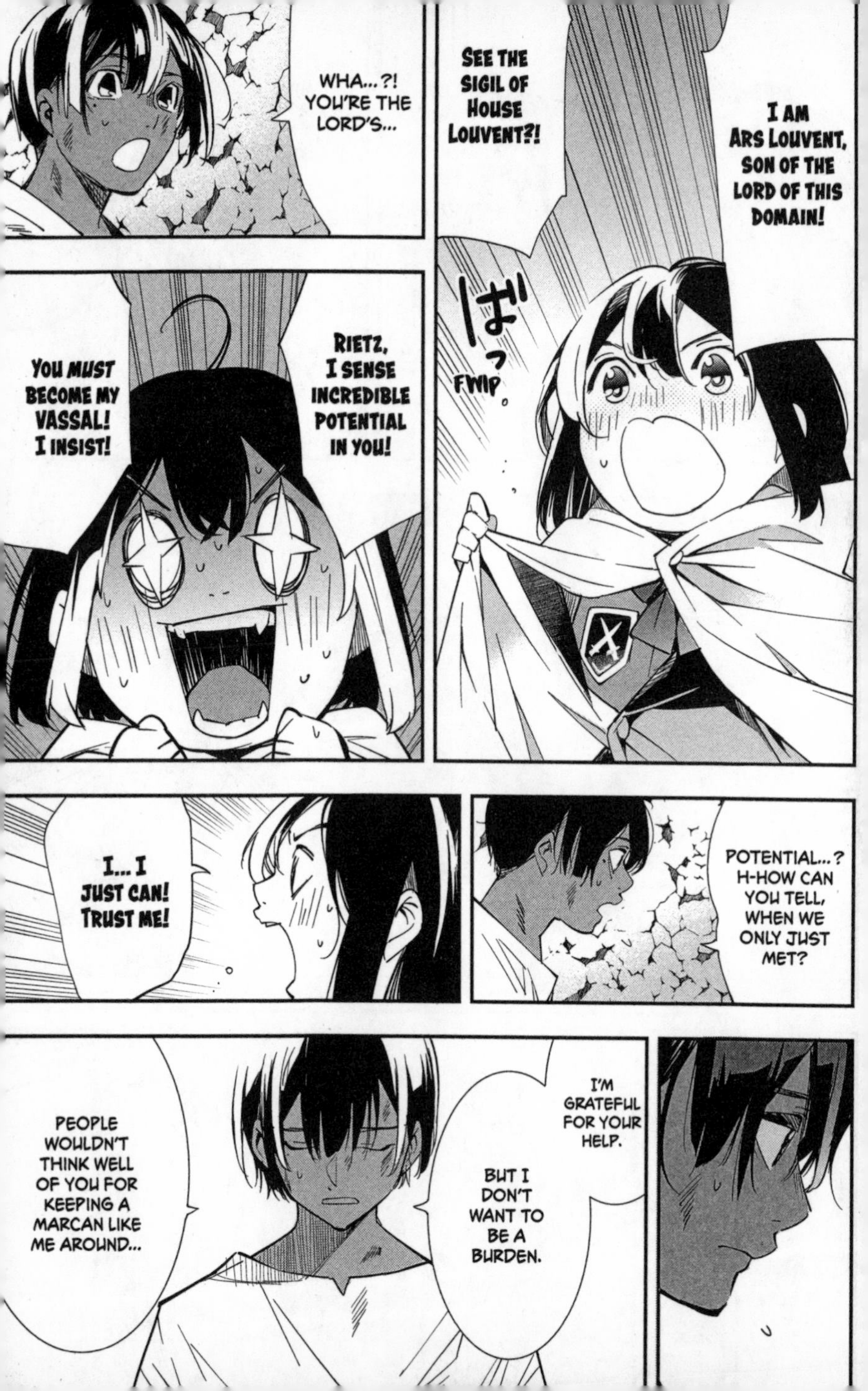
I AM ARS LOUVENT, SON OF THE LORD OF THIS DOMAIN!
SEE THE SIGIL OF HOUSE LOUVENT?!
ぱっ
FWIP
WHA...?! YOU'RE THE LORD'S...
RIETZ, I SENSE INCREDIBLE POTENTIAL IN YOU!
YOU MUST BECOME MY VASSAL! I INSIST!
POTENTIAL...? H-HOW CAN YOU TELL, WHEN WE ONLY JUST MET?
I... I JUST CAN! TRUST ME!
I'M GRATEFUL FOR YOUR HELP.
BUT I DON'T WANT TO BE A BURDEN.
PEOPLE WOULDN'T THINK WELL OF YOU FOR KEEPING A MARCAN LIKE ME AROUND...

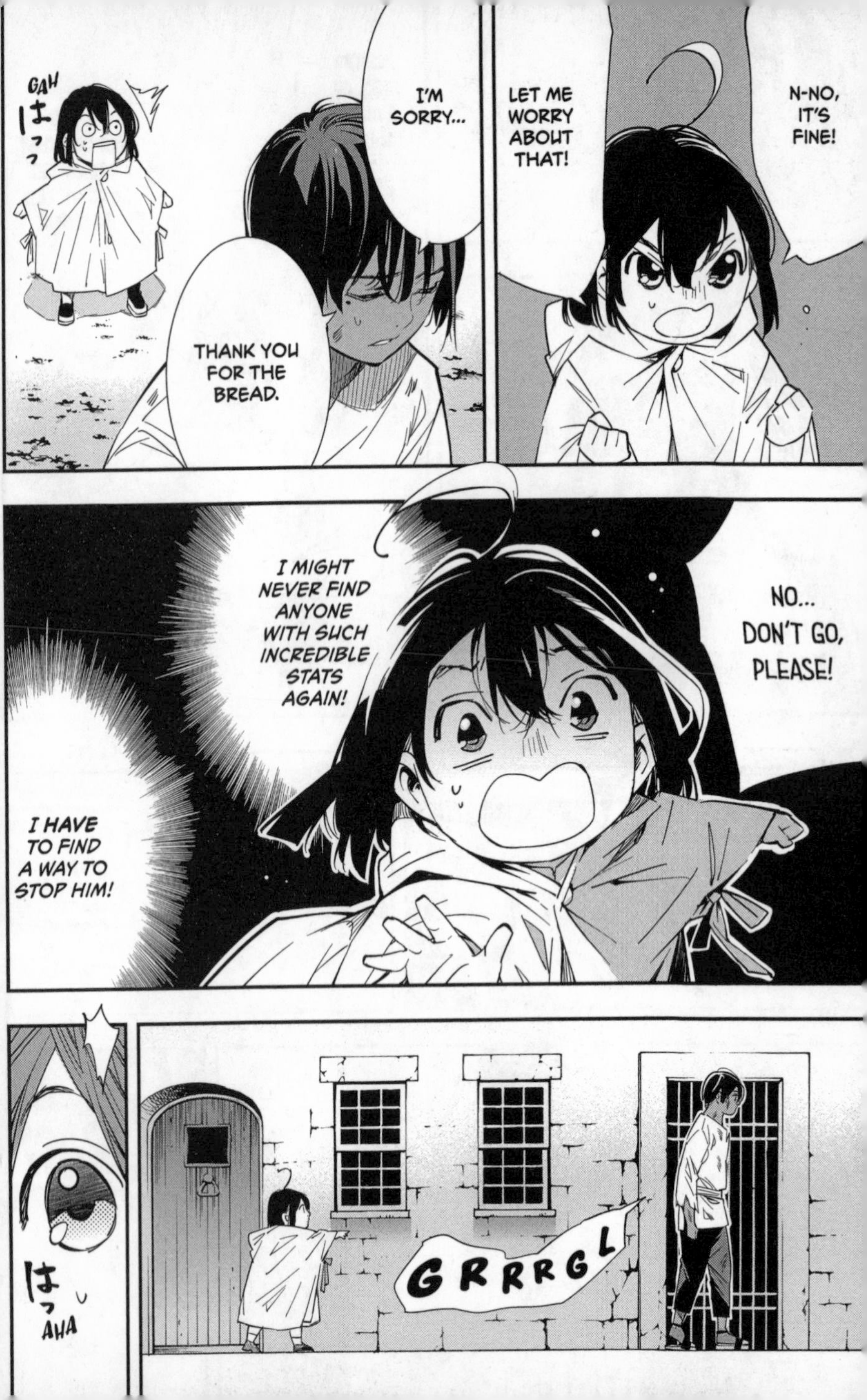
N-NO, IT'S FINE!
LET ME WORRY ABOUT THAT!
I'M SORRY...
THANK YOU FOR THE BREAD.
GAH
はっっ
NO... DON'T GO, PLEASE!
I MIGHT NEVER FIND ANYONE WITH SUCH INCREDIBLE STATS AGAIN!
I HAVE TO FIND A WAY TO STOP HIM!
GRRRGL
はっ
AHA

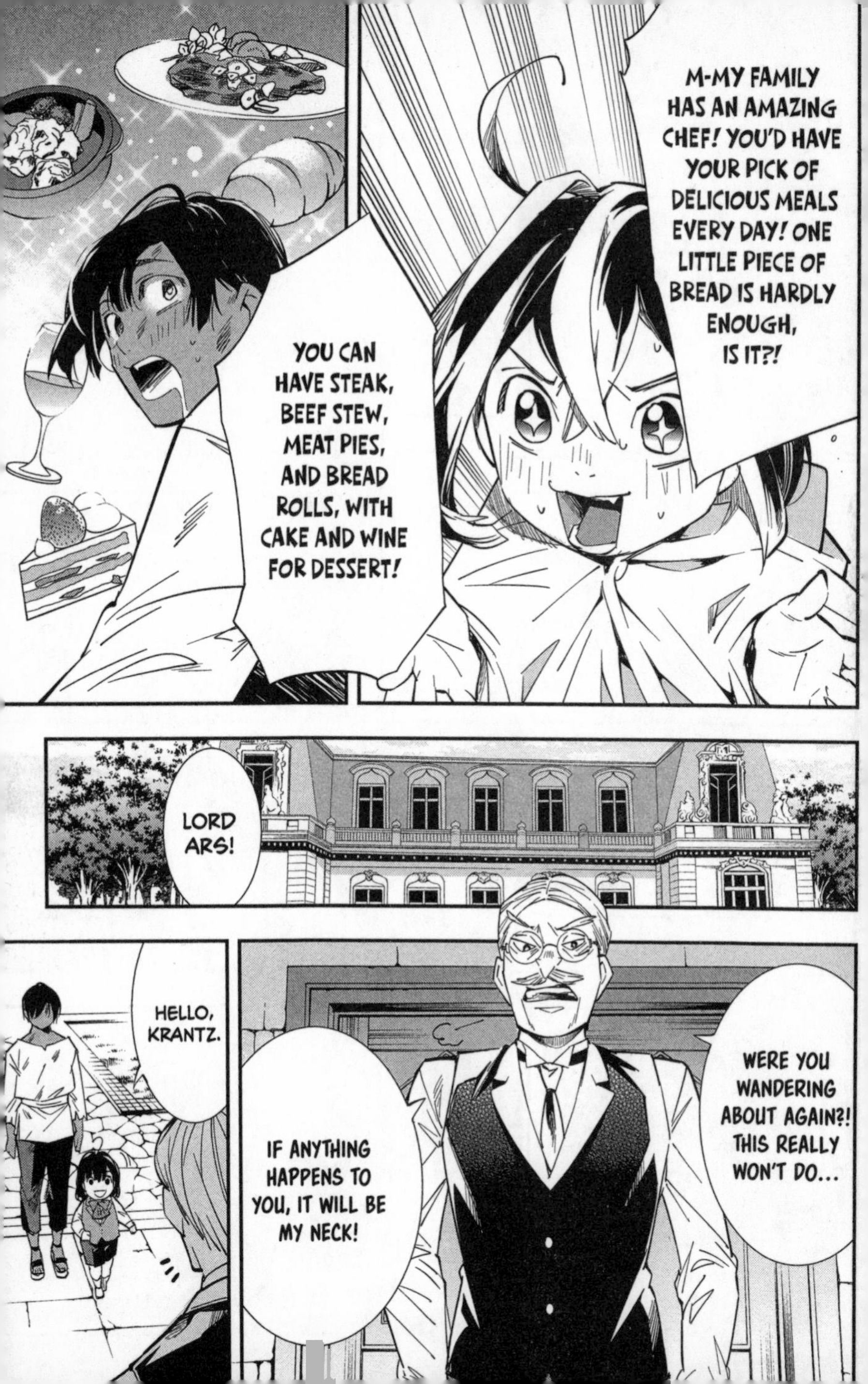
M-MY FAMILY HAS AN AMAZING CHEF! YOU'D HAVE YOUR PICK OF DELICIOUS MEALS EVERY DAY! ONE LITTLE PIECE OF BREAD IS HARDLY ENOUGH, IS IT?!
YOU CAN HAVE STEAK, BEEF STEW, MEAT PIES, AND BREAD ROLLS, WITH CAKE AND WINE FOR DESSERT!
LORD ARS!
WERE YOU WANDERING ABOUT AGAIN?! THIS REALLY WON'T DO...
IF ANYTHING HAPPENS TO YOU, IT WILL BE MY NECK!
HELLO, KRANTZ.

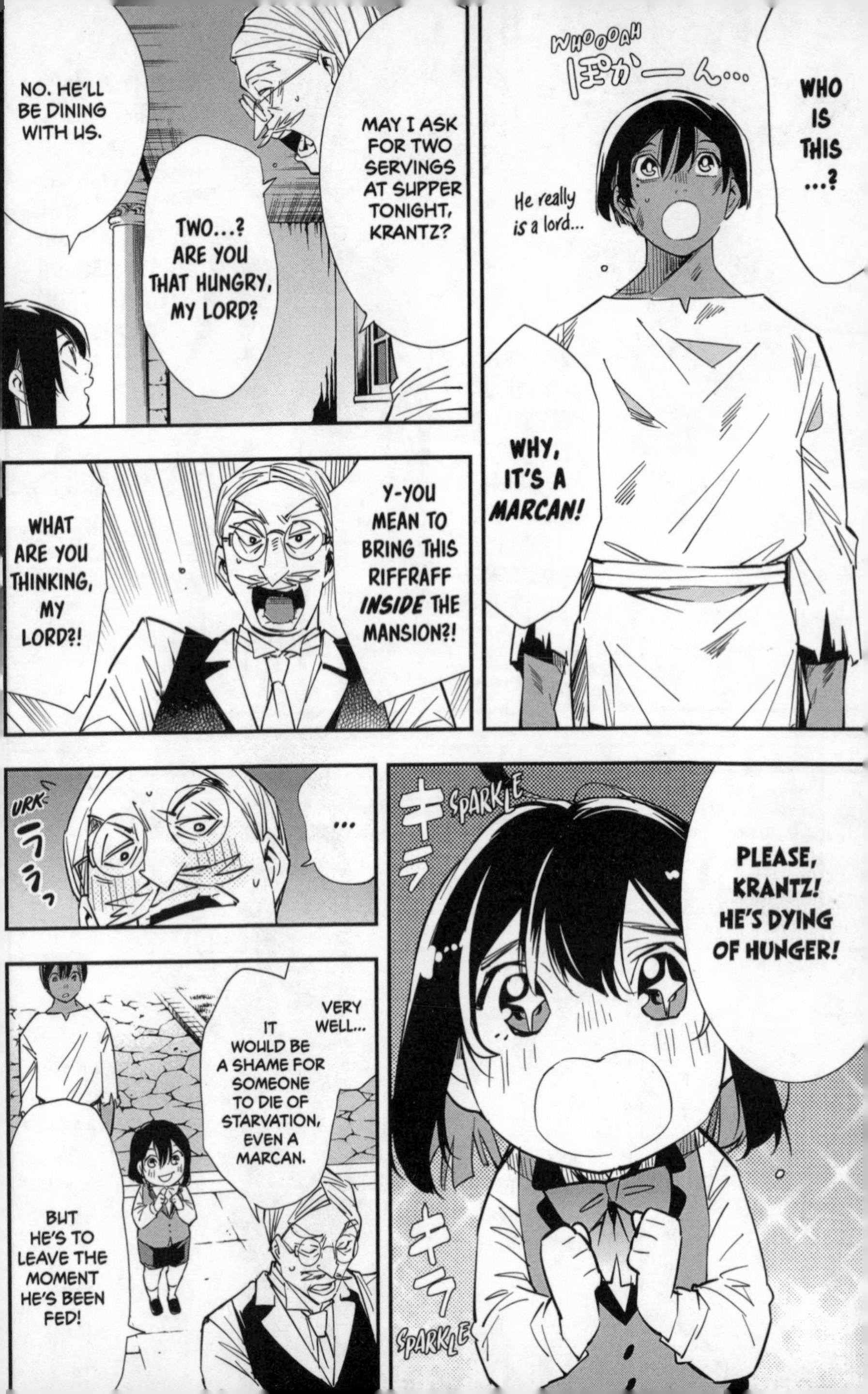
WHOOOAH
ぽかーん…
WHO IS THIS …?
He really is a lord…
WHY, IT'S A MARCAN!
MAY I ASK FOR TWO SERVINGS AT SUPPER TONIGHT, KRANTZ?
TWO…? ARE YOU THAT HUNGRY, MY LORD?
NO. HE'LL BE DINING WITH US.
Y-YOU MEAN TO BRING THIS RIFFRAFF INSIDE THE MANSION?!
WHAT ARE YOU THINKING, MY LORD?!
キラ SPARKLE
PLEASE, KRANTZ! HE'S DYING OF HUNGER!
キラ SPARKLE
URK
ラララ
…
VERY WELL…
IT WOULD BE A SHAME FOR SOMEONE TO DIE OF STARVATION, EVEN A MARCAN.
BUT HE'S TO LEAVE THE MOMENT HE'S BEEN FED!

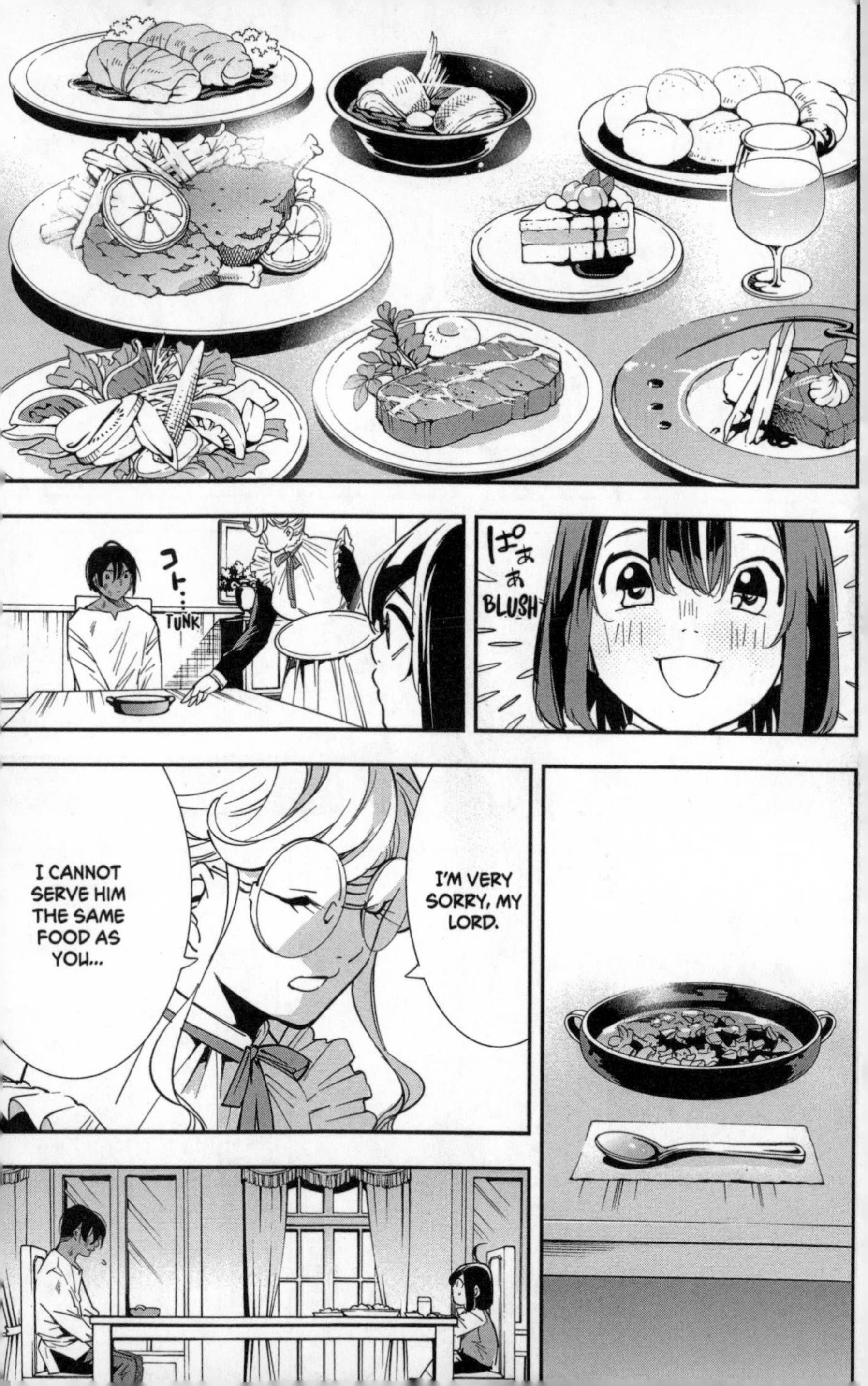
ぱぁあ
BLUSH
コト…
TUNK
I'M VERY SORRY, MY LORD.
I CANNOT SERVE HIM THE SAME FOOD AS YOU...

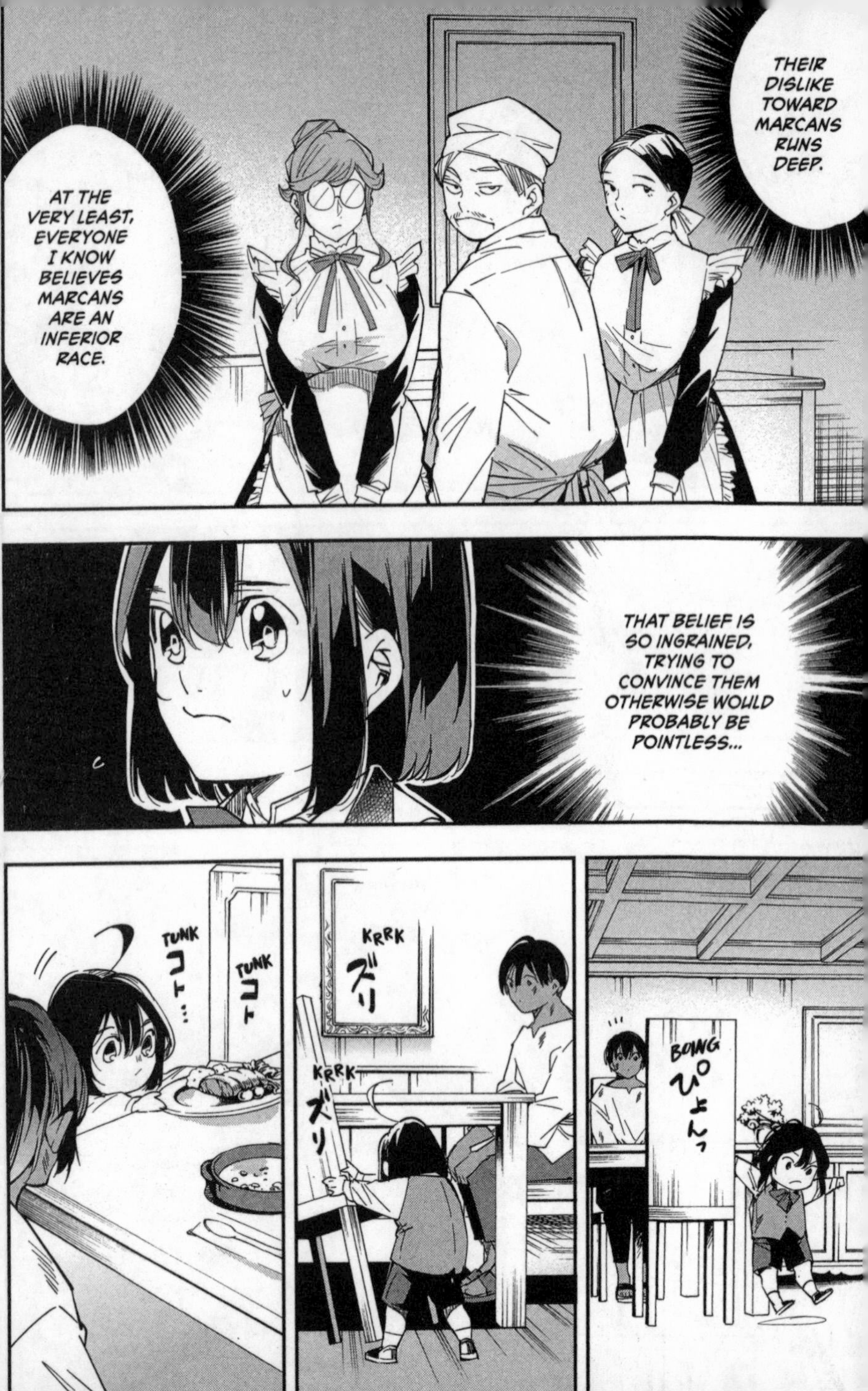
THEIR DISLIKE TOWARD MARCANS RUNS DEEP.
AT THE VERY LEAST, EVERYONE I KNOW BELIEVES MARCANS ARE AN INFERIOR RACE.
THAT BELIEF IS SO INGRAINED, TRYING TO CONVINCE THEM OTHERWISE WOULD PROBABLY BE POINTLESS...
BOING
ぴょんっ
KRRK
ズリ
KRRK
ズリ
TUNK
コト
TUNK
コト…

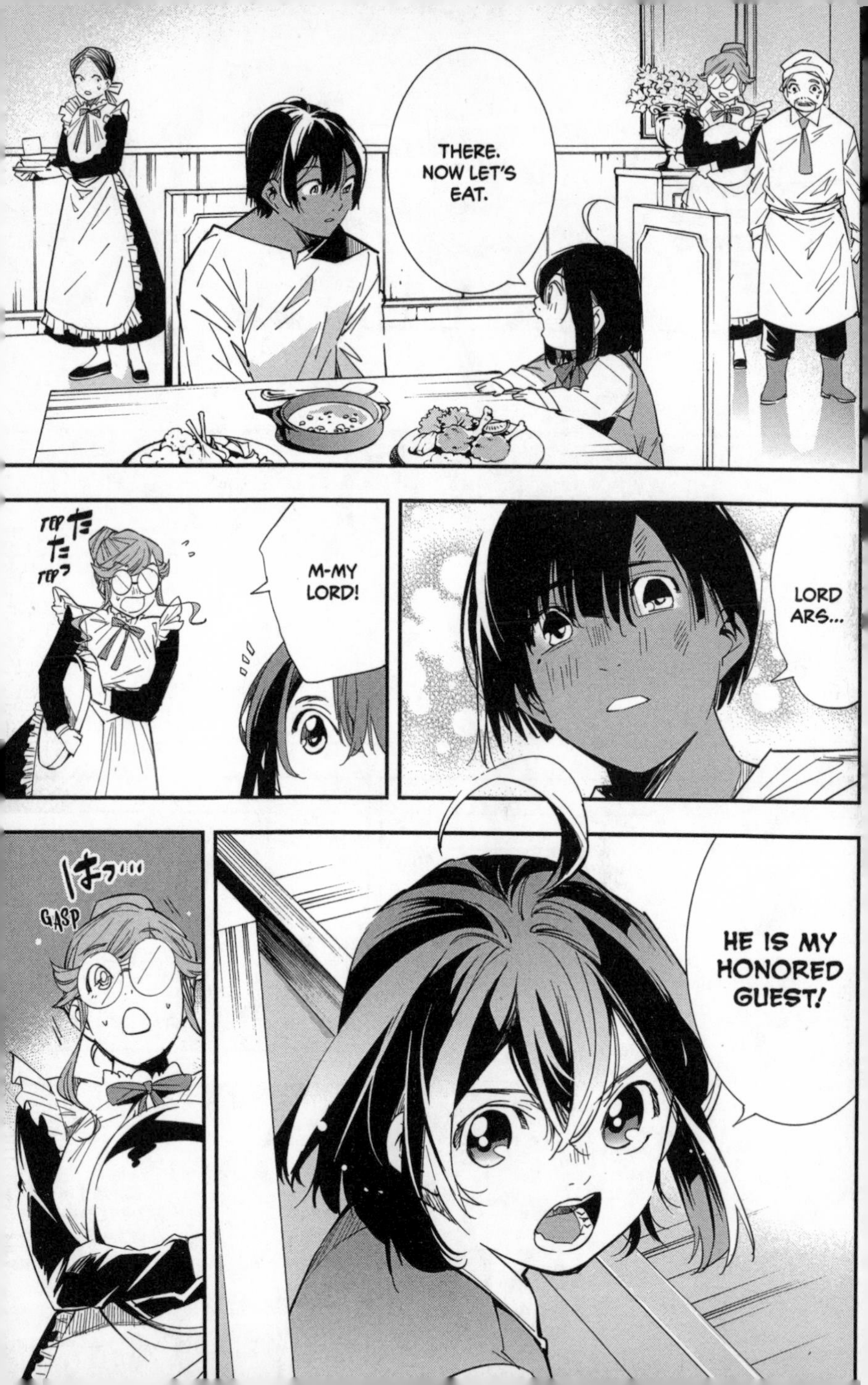
THERE. NOW LET'S EAT.
LORD ARS...
M-MY LORD!
TEP
TEP
HE IS MY HONORED GUEST!
はっ…
GASP

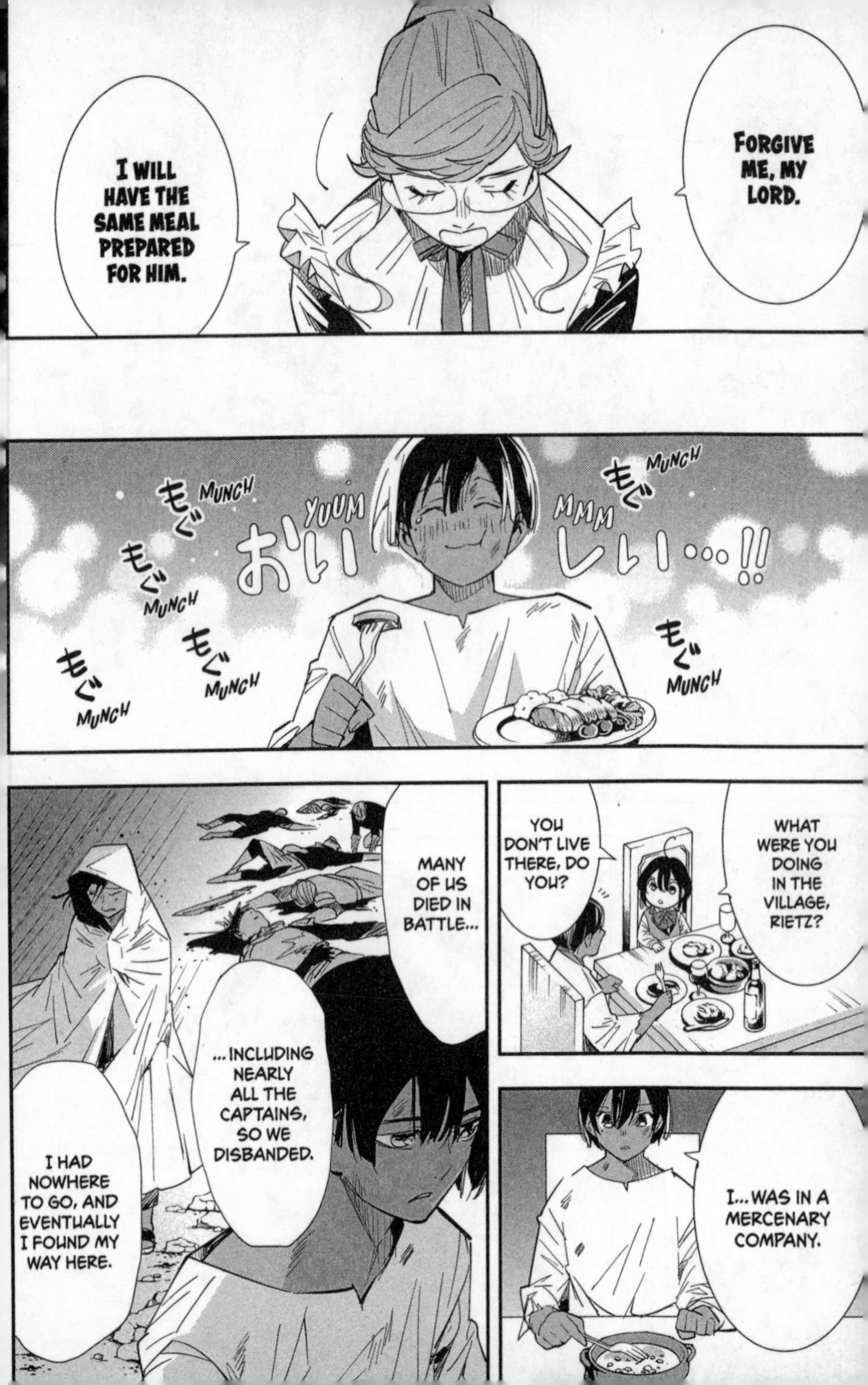
FORGIVE ME, MY LORD.
I WILL HAVE THE SAME MEAL PREPARED FOR HIM.
もぐ MUNCH
おいしい…!!
YUUM MMM
もぐ MUNCH
もぐ MUNCH
もぐ MUNCH
もぐ MUNCH
もぐ MUNCH
WHAT WERE YOU DOING IN THE VILLAGE, RIETZ?
YOU DON'T LIVE THERE, DO YOU?
I...WAS IN A MERCENARY COMPANY.
MANY OF US DIED IN BATTLE...
...INCLUDING NEARLY ALL THE CAPTAINS, SO WE DISBANDED.
I HAD NOWHERE TO GO, AND EVENTUALLY I FOUND MY WAY HERE.

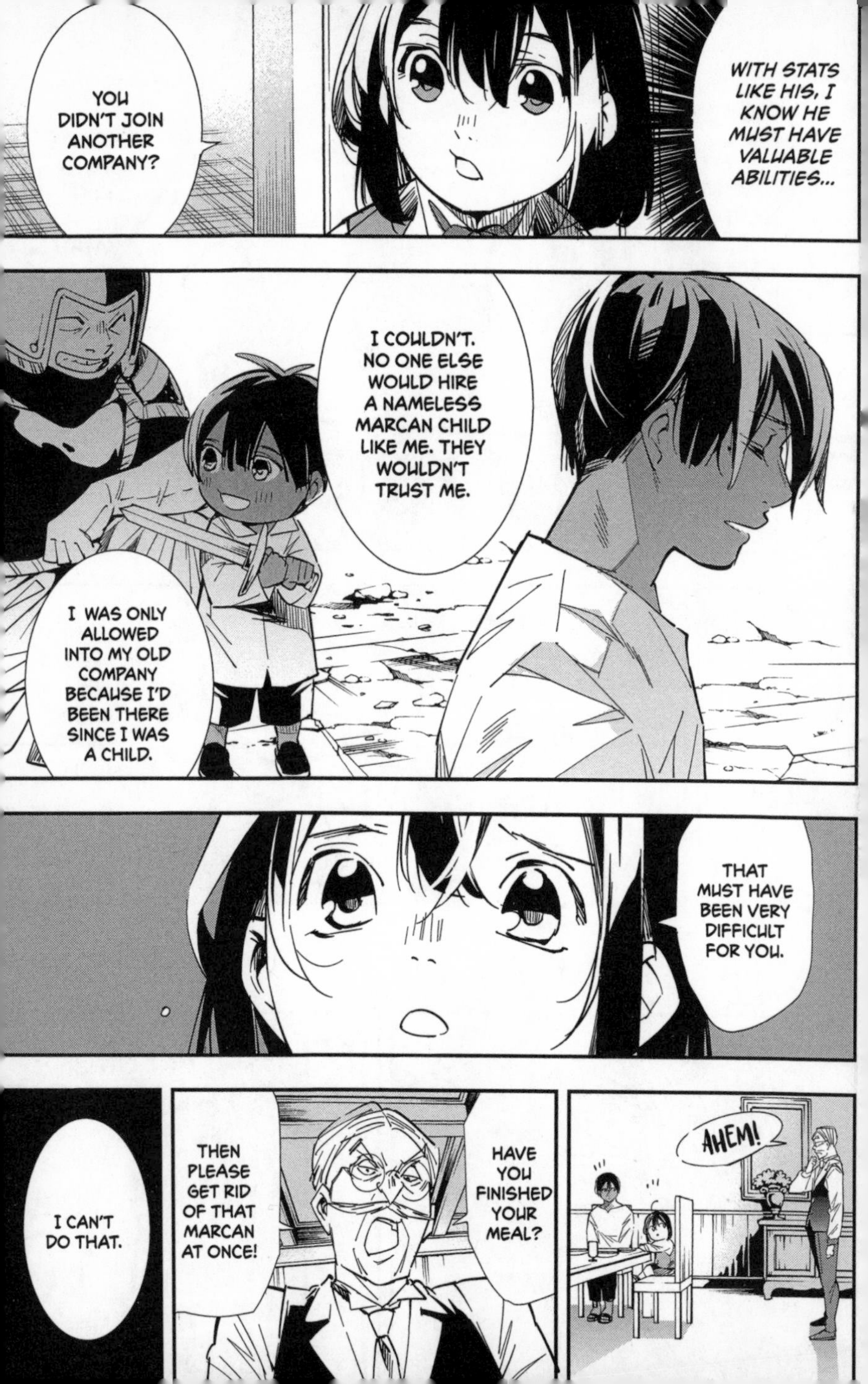
WITH STATS LIKE HIS, I KNOW HE MUST HAVE VALUABLE ABILITIES...
YOU DIDN'T JOIN ANOTHER COMPANY?
I COULDN'T. NO ONE ELSE WOULD HIRE A NAMELESS MARCAN CHILD LIKE ME. THEY WOULDN'T TRUST ME.
I WAS ONLY ALLOWED INTO MY OLD COMPANY BECAUSE I'D BEEN THERE SINCE I WAS A CHILD.
THAT MUST HAVE BEEN VERY DIFFICULT FOR YOU.
AHEM!
HAVE YOU FINISHED YOUR MEAL?
THEN PLEASE GET RID OF THAT MARCAN AT ONCE!
I CAN'T DO THAT.

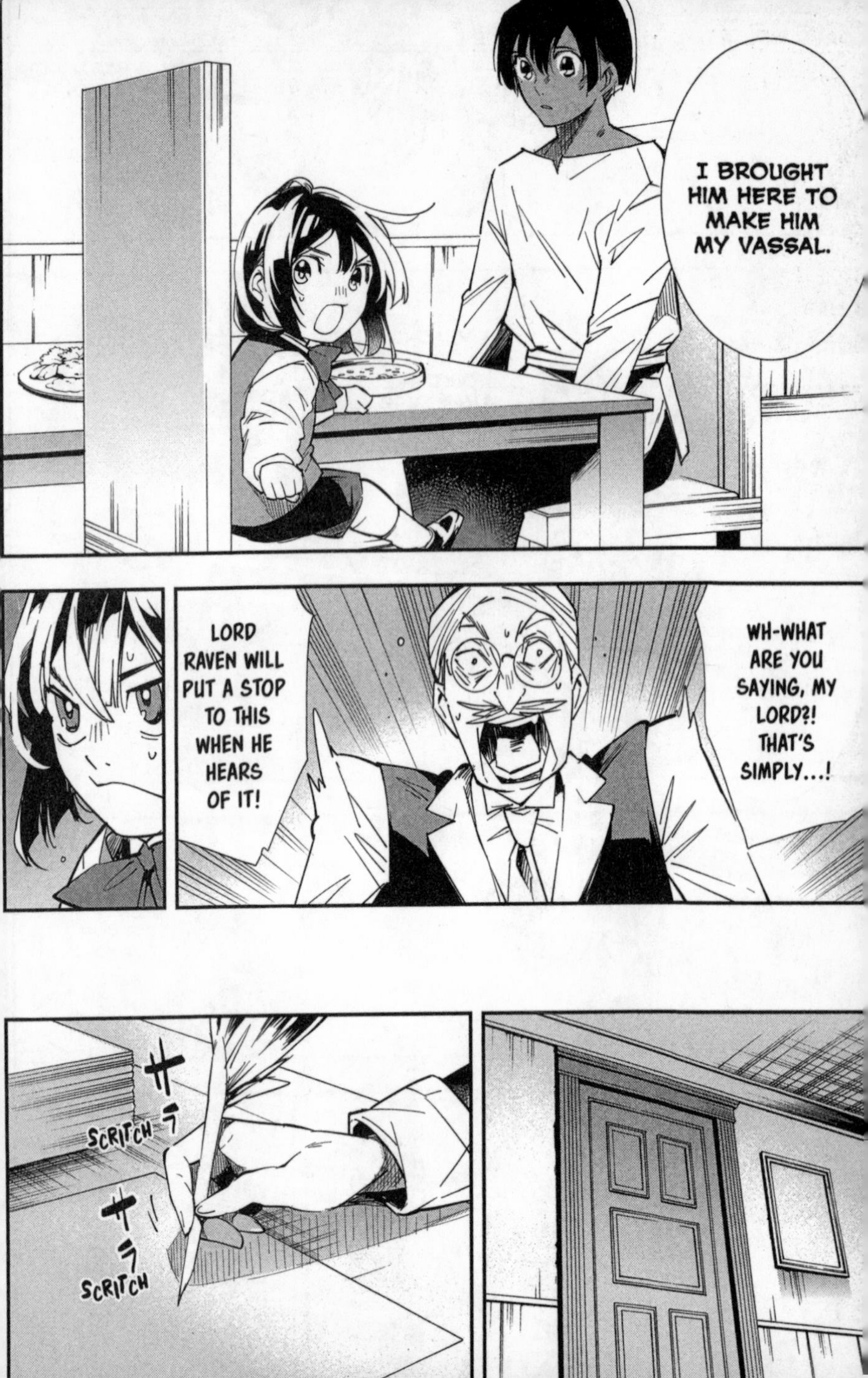
I BROUGHT HIM HERE TO MAKE HIM MY VASSAL.
WH-WHAT ARE YOU SAYING, MY LORD?! THAT'S SIMPLY...!
LORD RAVEN WILL PUT A STOP TO THIS WHEN HE HEARS OF IT!
サラ
SCRITCH
サラ
SCRITCH

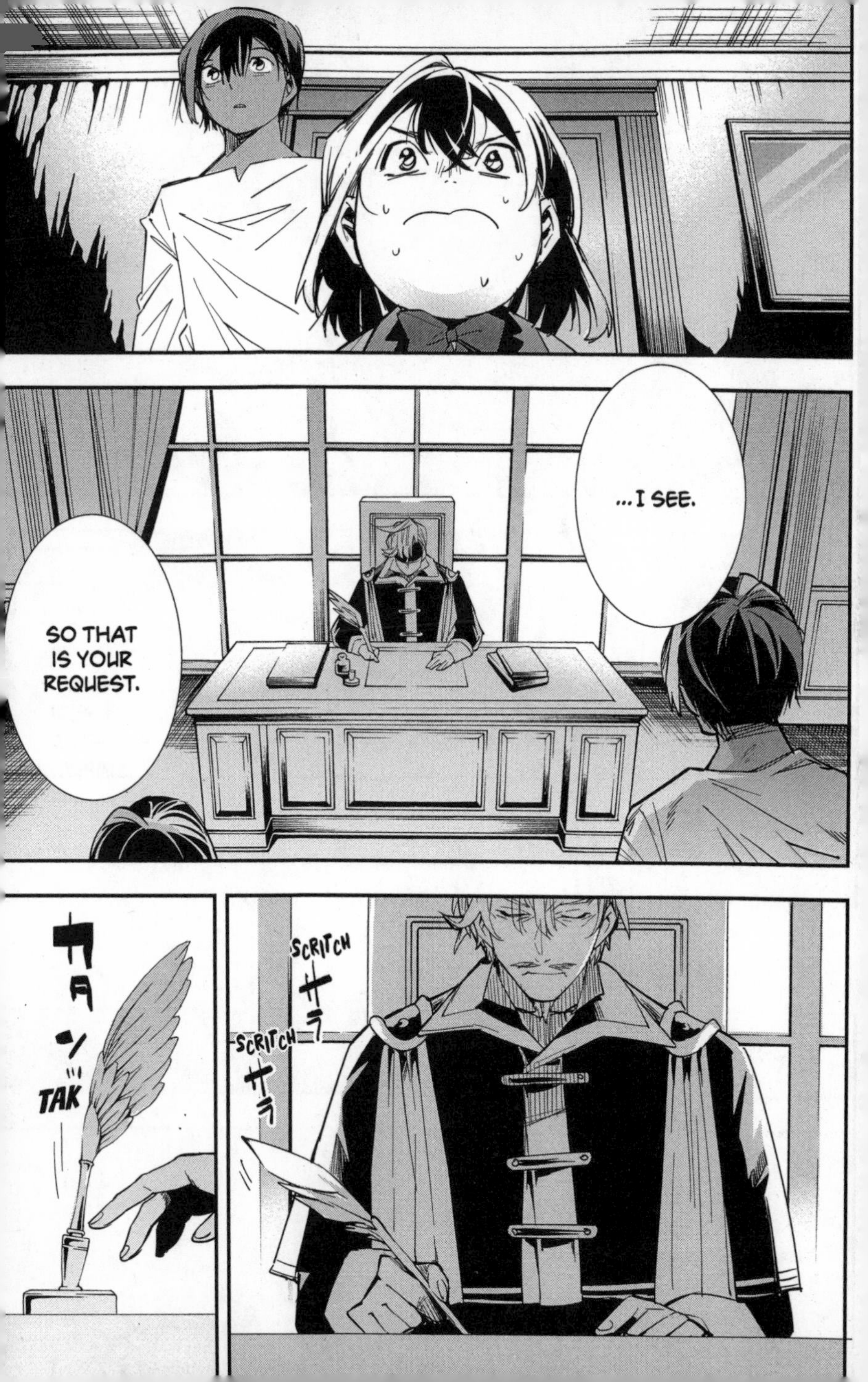
...I SEE.
SO THAT IS YOUR REQUEST.
SCRITCH
サラ
SCRITCH
サラ
カタンッ
TAK

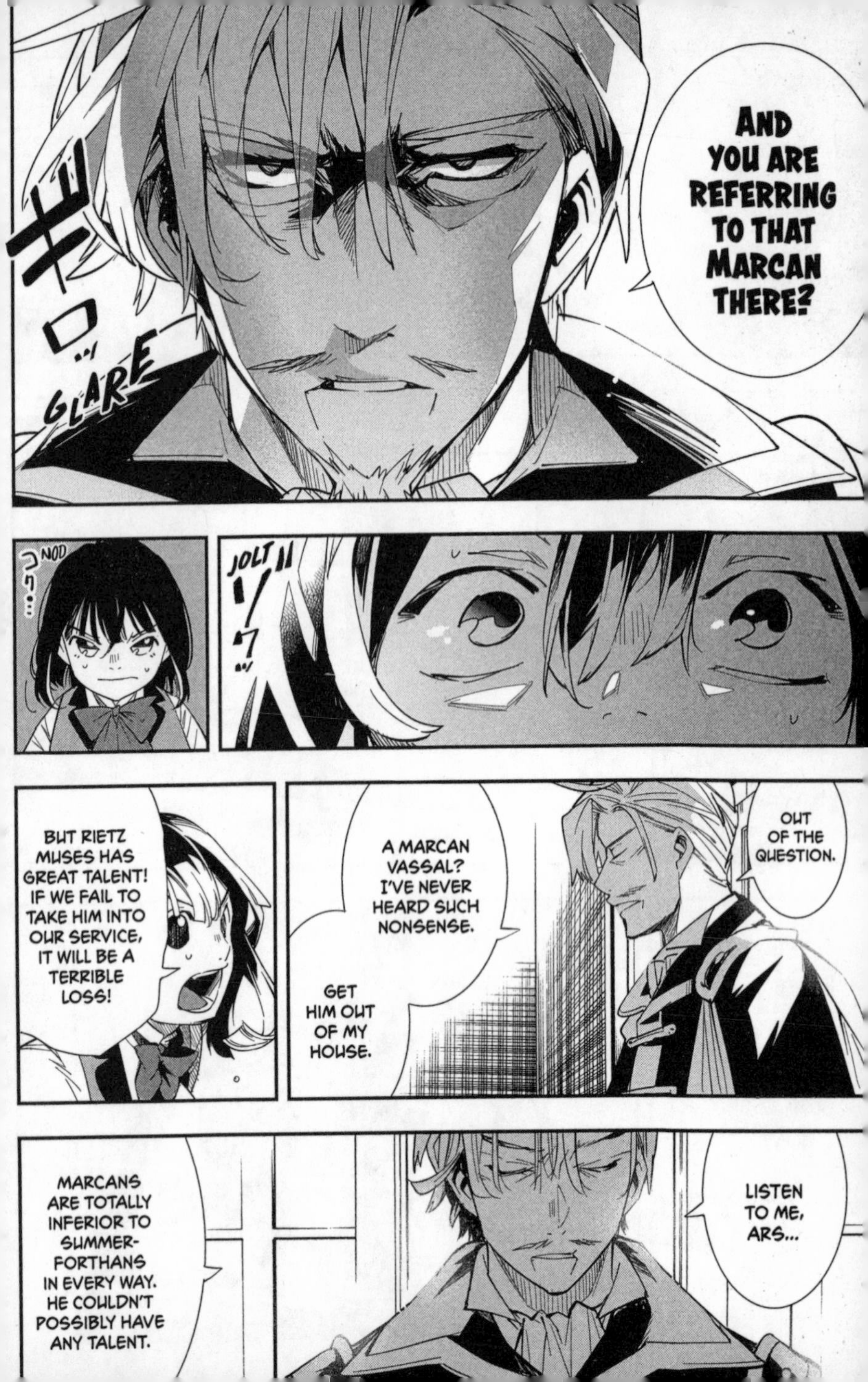
AND YOU ARE REFERRING TO THAT MARCAN THERE?
ギロッ
GLARE
JOLT
NOD
OUT OF THE QUESTION.
A MARCAN VASSAL? I'VE NEVER HEARD SUCH NONSENSE.
GET HIM OUT OF MY HOUSE.
BUT RIETZ MUSES HAS GREAT TALENT! IF WE FAIL TO TAKE HIM INTO OUR SERVICE, IT WILL BE A TERRIBLE LOSS!
LISTEN TO ME, ARS...
MARCANS ARE TOTALLY INFERIOR TO SUMMERFORTHANS IN EVERY WAY. HE COULDN'T POSSIBLY HAVE ANY TALENT.

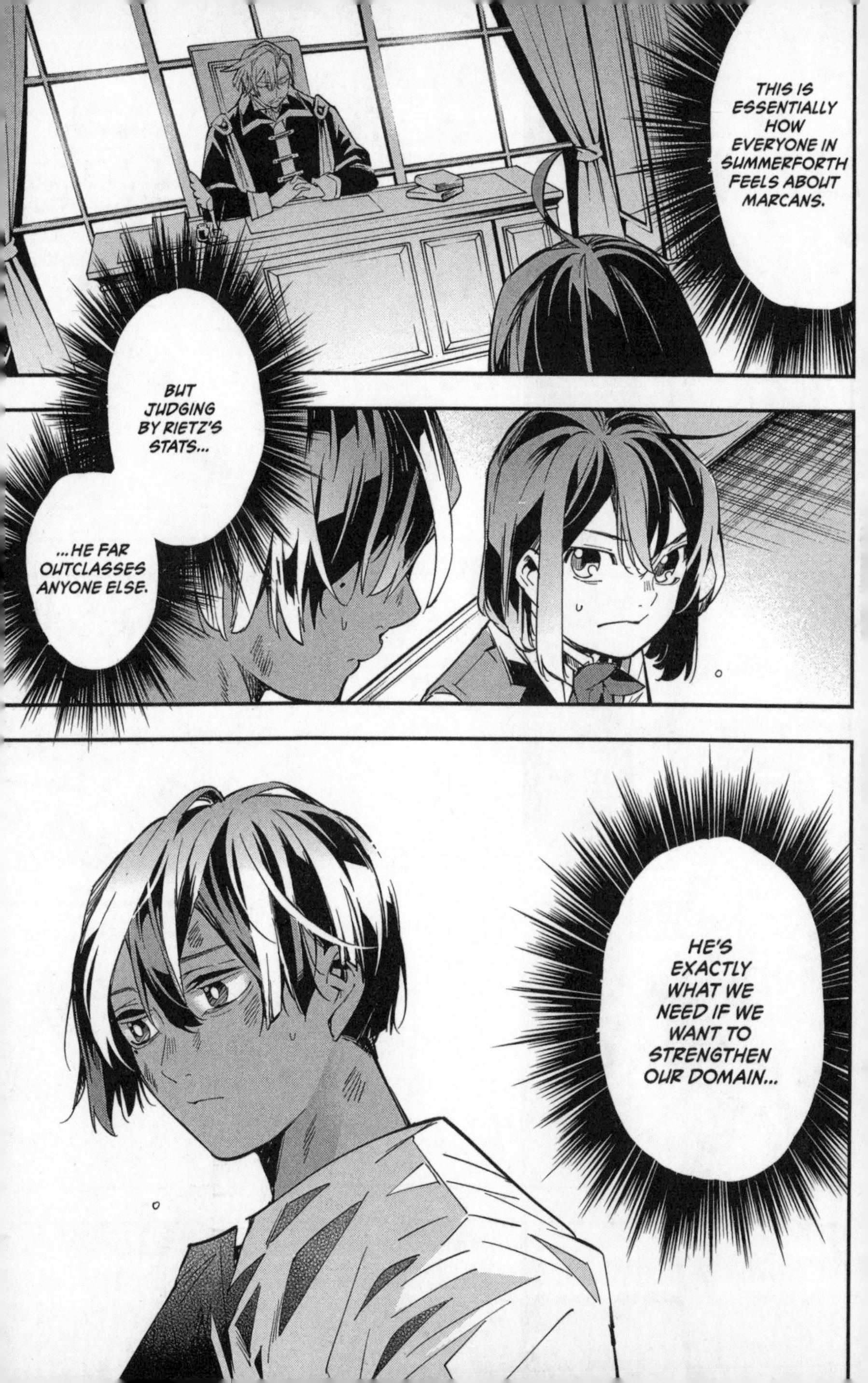
THIS IS ESSENTIALLY HOW EVERYONE IN SUMMERFORTH FEELS ABOUT MARCANS.
BUT JUDGING BY RIETZ'S STATS...
...HE FAR OUTCLASSES ANYONE ELSE.
HE'S EXACTLY WHAT WE NEED IF WE WANT TO STRENGTHEN OUR DOMAIN...

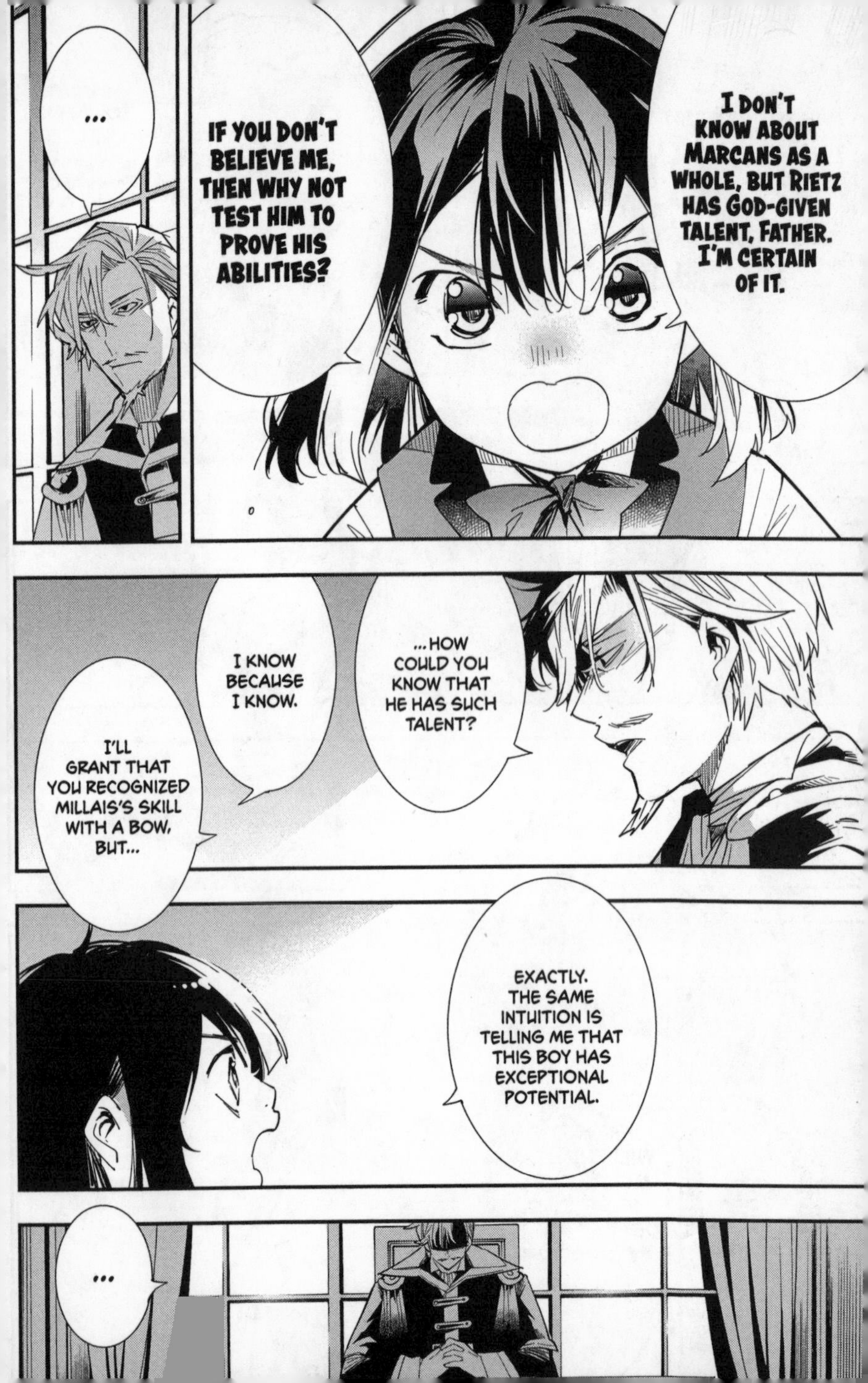
I DON'T KNOW ABOUT MARCANS AS A WHOLE, BUT RIETZ HAS GOD-GIVEN TALENT, FATHER. I'M CERTAIN OF IT.
IF YOU DON'T BELIEVE ME, THEN WHY NOT TEST HIM TO PROVE HIS ABILITIES?
...
...HOW COULD YOU KNOW THAT HE HAS SUCH TALENT?
I KNOW BECAUSE I KNOW.
I'LL GRANT THAT YOU RECOGNIZED MILLAIS'S SKILL WITH A BOW, BUT...
EXACTLY. THE SAME INTUITION IS TELLING ME THAT THIS BOY HAS EXCEPTIONAL POTENTIAL.
...

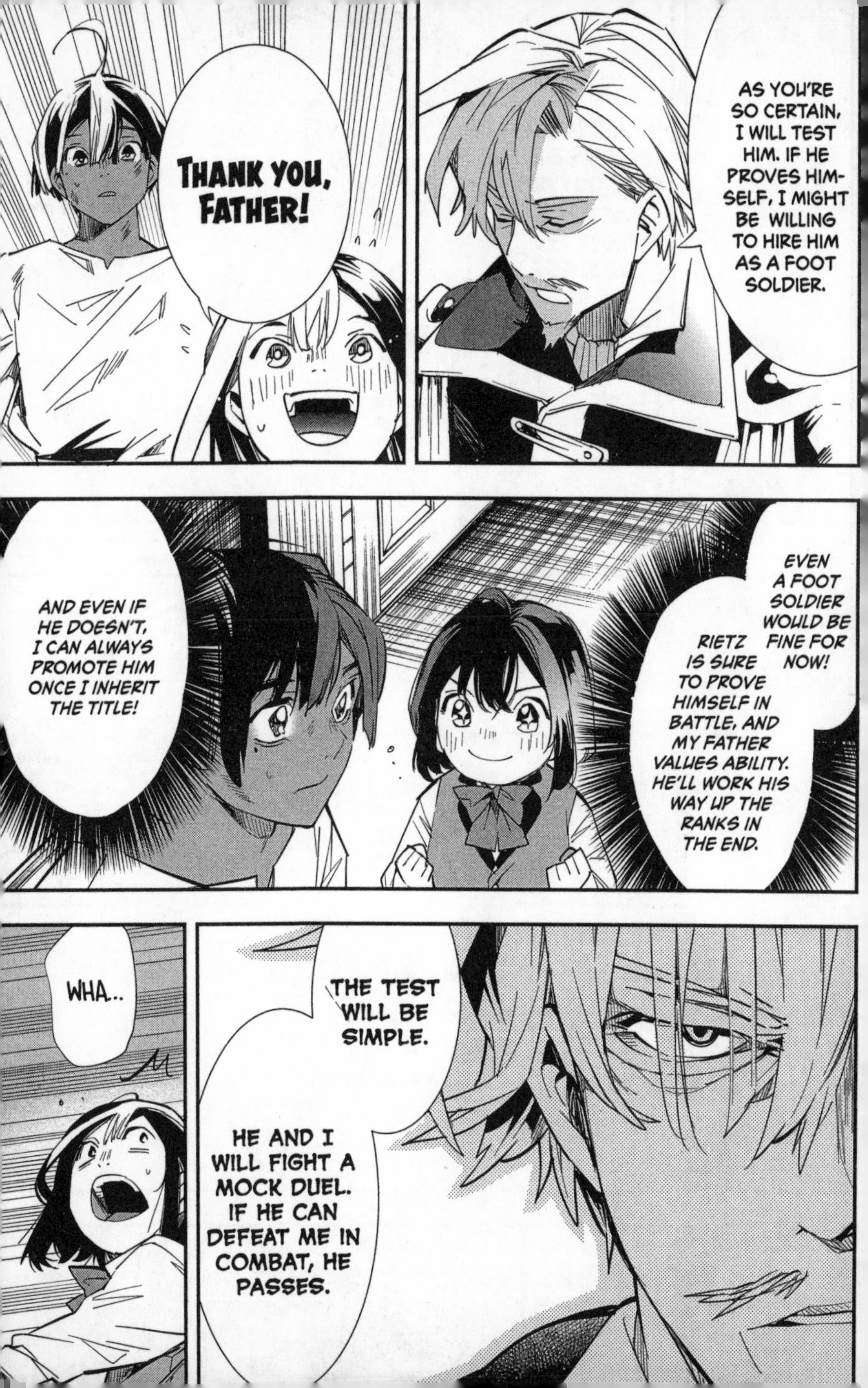
AS YOU'RE SO CERTAIN, I WILL TEST HIM. IF HE PROVES HIMSELF, I MIGHT BE WILLING TO HIRE HIM AS A FOOT SOLDIER.
THANK YOU, FATHER!
EVEN A FOOT SOLDIER WOULD BE FINE FOR NOW!
RIETZ IS SURE TO PROVE HIMSELF IN BATTLE, AND MY FATHER VALUES ABILITY. HE'LL WORK HIS WAY UP THE RANKS IN THE END.
AND EVEN IF HE DOESN'T, I CAN ALWAYS PROMOTE HIM ONCE I INHERIT THE TITLE!
THE TEST WILL BE SIMPLE.
HE AND I WILL FIGHT A MOCK DUEL. IF HE CAN DEFEAT ME IN COMBAT, HE PASSES.
WHA..

HE DOES... BUT...

BUT, FATHER... HE'S ONLY FOURTEEN YEARS OLD.

AND YOU'RE A SUPREMELY GIFTED FIGHTER.

ASKING RIETZ TO DEFEAT *YOU* AS HE IS NOW IS JUST...

HE HAS THE TALENT, NO?

Raven Louvent • Age 30

Stats

	CURRENT	MAX
Command	86	86
Prowess	94	95
Intellect	44	56
Diplomacy	23	31
Ambition	6	7

Aptitude

Fighter A	Cavalier S	Archer B
Mage D	Engineer D	Armorer D
Mariner D	Pilot D	Tactician D

Rietz Muses • Age 14

Stats

	CURRENT	MAX
Command	87	99
Prowess	70	90
Intellect	72	99
Diplomacy	78	100
Ambition	2	1

Aptitude

Fighter A	Cavalier S	Archer A
Mage C	Engineer S	Armorer A
Mariner D	Pilot C	Tactician S

FATHER'S PROWESS IS 94. RIETZ'S IS 70.

RIETZ MIGHT STAND A CHANCE AFTER SOME PROPER TRAINING, BUT RIGHT NOW...

THANK YOU, SIR.

OH, GOOD... IN THAT CASE, HE MIGHT BE ABLE TO WIN!

WHEW

I DON'T INTEND TO TREAT IT AS A REAL DUEL. I WILL FIGHT WITH A HANDICAP.

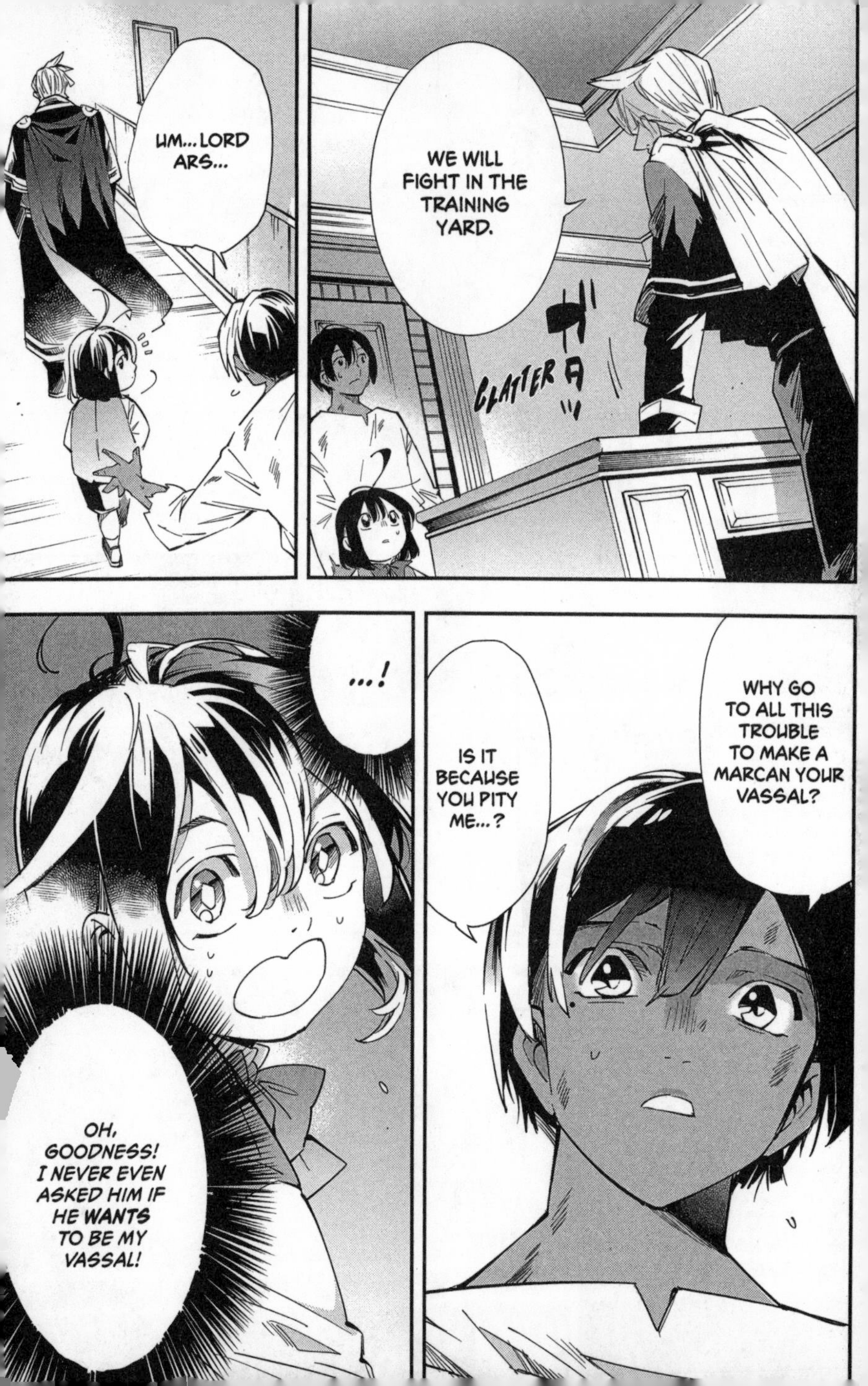
WE WILL FIGHT IN THE TRAINING YARD.
CLATTER
UM... LORD ARS...
WHY GO TO ALL THIS TROUBLE TO MAKE A MARCAN YOUR VASSAL?
IS IT BECAUSE YOU PITY ME...?
...!
OH, GOODNESS! I NEVER EVEN ASKED HIM IF HE WANTS TO BE MY VASSAL!

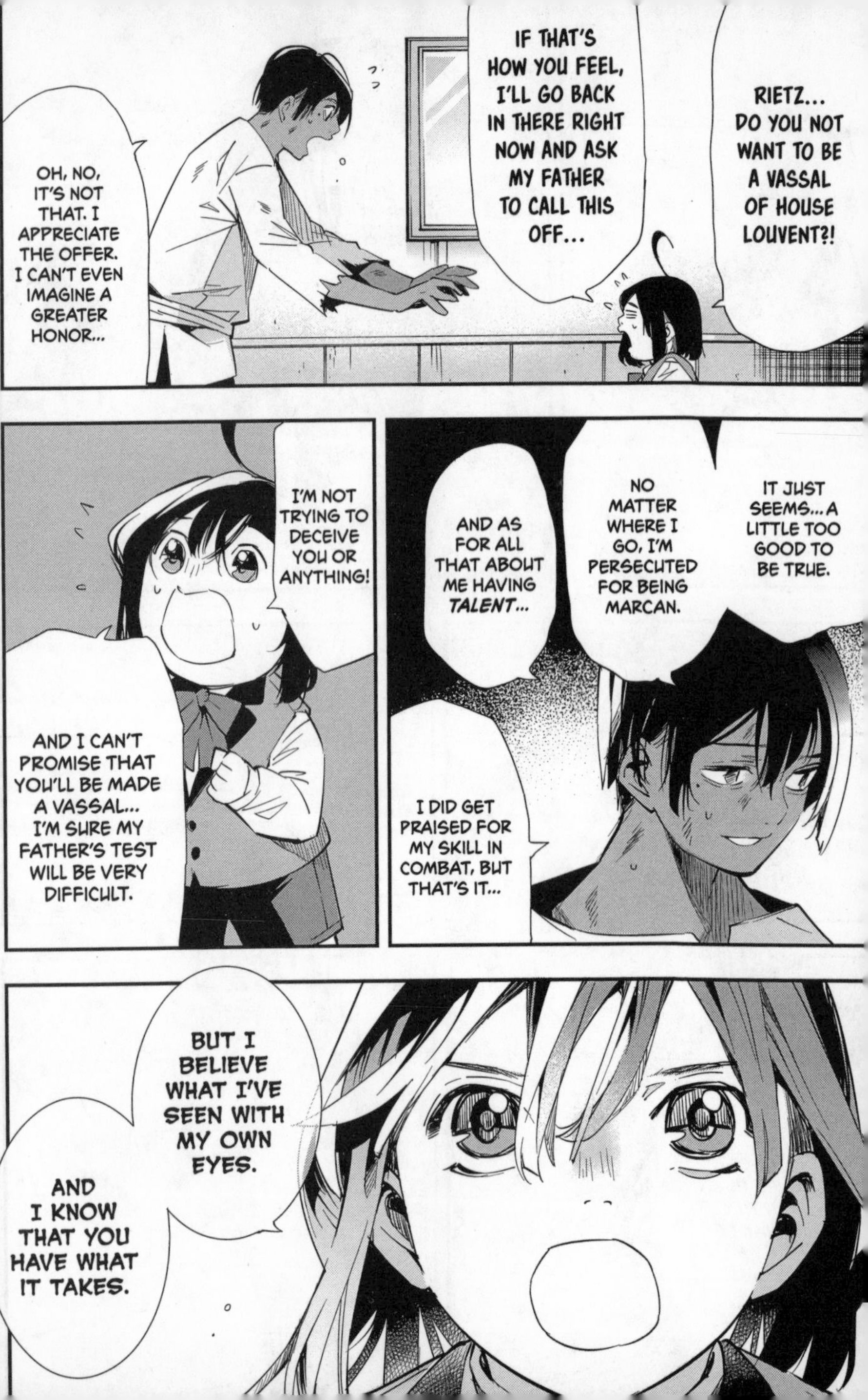
RIETZ... DO YOU NOT WANT TO BE A VASSAL OF HOUSE LOUVENT?!
IF THAT'S HOW YOU FEEL, I'LL GO BACK IN THERE RIGHT NOW AND ASK MY FATHER TO CALL THIS OFF...
OH, NO, IT'S NOT THAT. I APPRECIATE THE OFFER. I CAN'T EVEN IMAGINE A GREATER HONOR...
IT JUST SEEMS... A LITTLE TOO GOOD TO BE TRUE.
NO MATTER WHERE I GO, I'M PERSECUTED FOR BEING MARCAN.
AND AS FOR ALL THAT ABOUT ME HAVING *TALENT*...
I DID GET PRAISED FOR MY SKILL IN COMBAT, BUT THAT'S IT...
I'M NOT TRYING TO DECEIVE YOU OR ANYTHING!
AND I CAN'T PROMISE THAT YOU'LL BE MADE A VASSAL... I'M SURE MY FATHER'S TEST WILL BE VERY DIFFICULT.
BUT I BELIEVE WHAT I'VE SEEN WITH MY OWN EYES.
AND I KNOW THAT YOU HAVE WHAT IT TAKES.

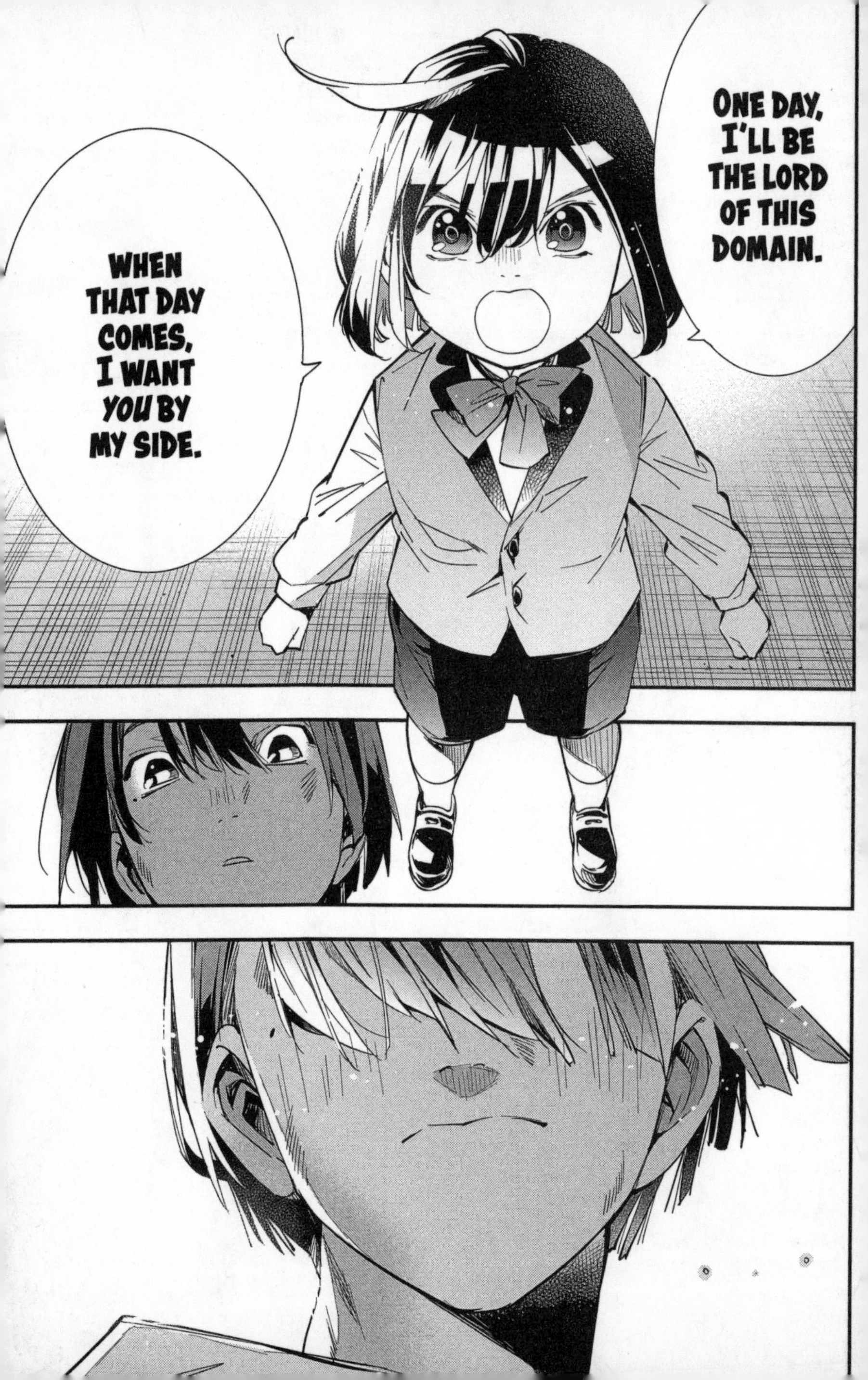
ONE DAY, I'LL BE THE LORD OF THIS DOMAIN.
WHEN THAT DAY COMES, I WANT *YOU* BY MY SIDE.

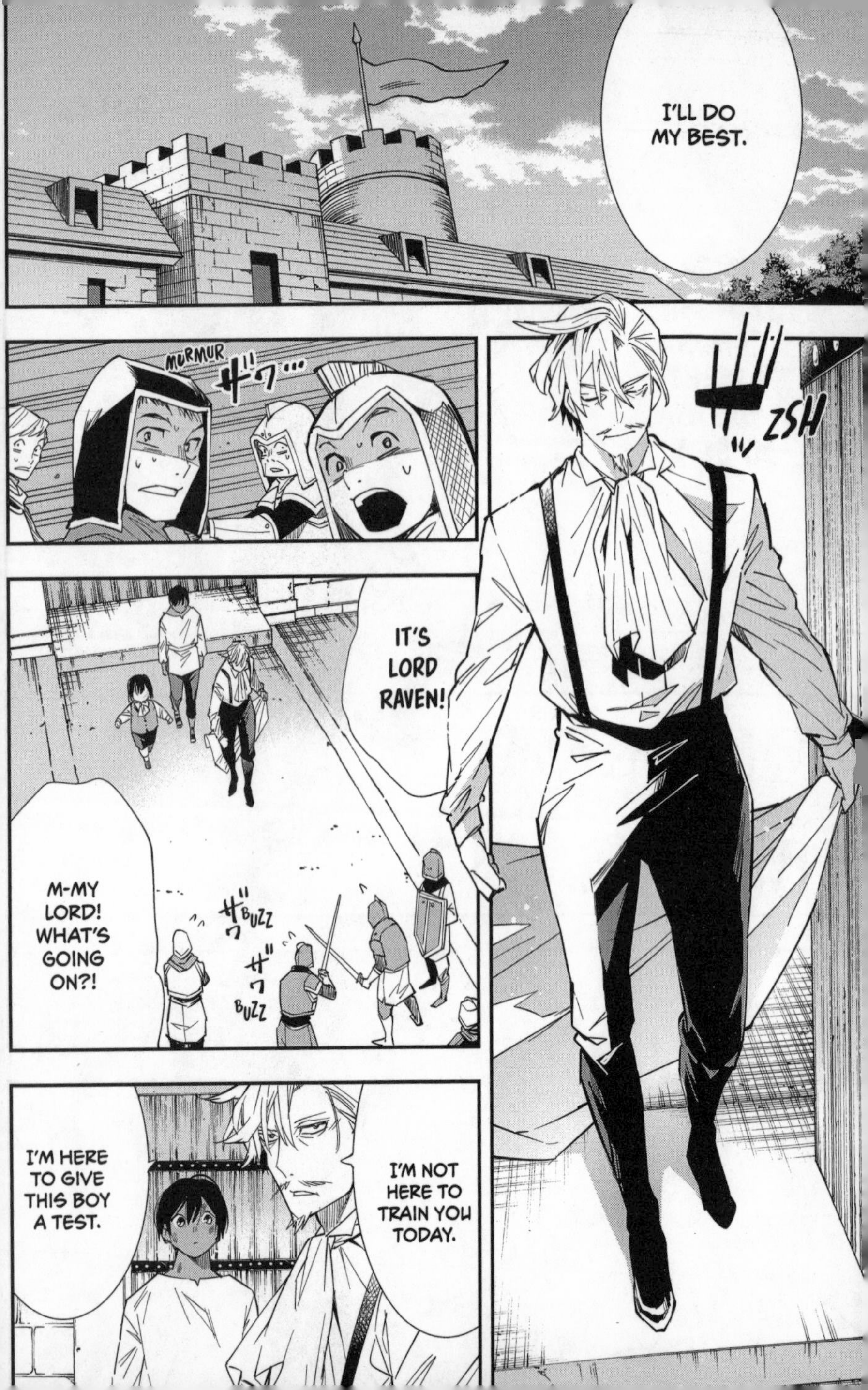
I'LL DO MY BEST.
ザッ
ZSH
MURMUR
ザワ…
IT'S LORD RAVEN!
M-MY LORD! WHAT'S GOING ON?!
ザワ
BUZZ
ザワ
BUZZ
I'M NOT HERE TO TRAIN YOU TODAY.
I'M HERE TO GIVE THIS BOY A TEST.

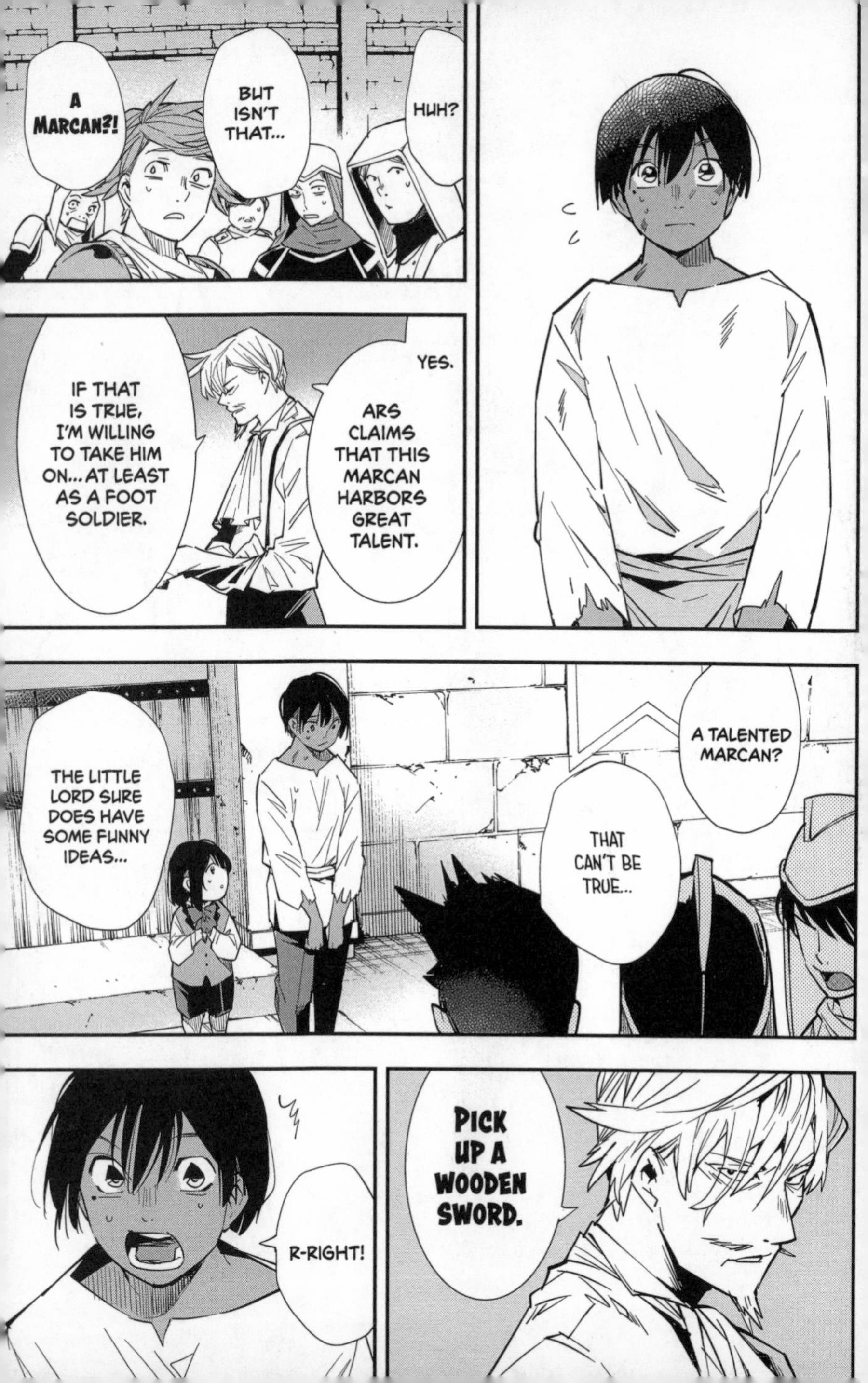
HUH?
BUT ISN'T THAT...
A MARCAN?!
YES.
ARS CLAIMS THAT THIS MARCAN HARBORS GREAT TALENT.
IF THAT IS TRUE, I'M WILLING TO TAKE HIM ON... AT LEAST AS A FOOT SOLDIER.
A TALENTED MARCAN?
THAT CAN'T BE TRUE...
THE LITTLE LORD SURE DOES HAVE SOME FUNNY IDEAS...
PICK UP A WOODEN SWORD.
R-RIGHT!

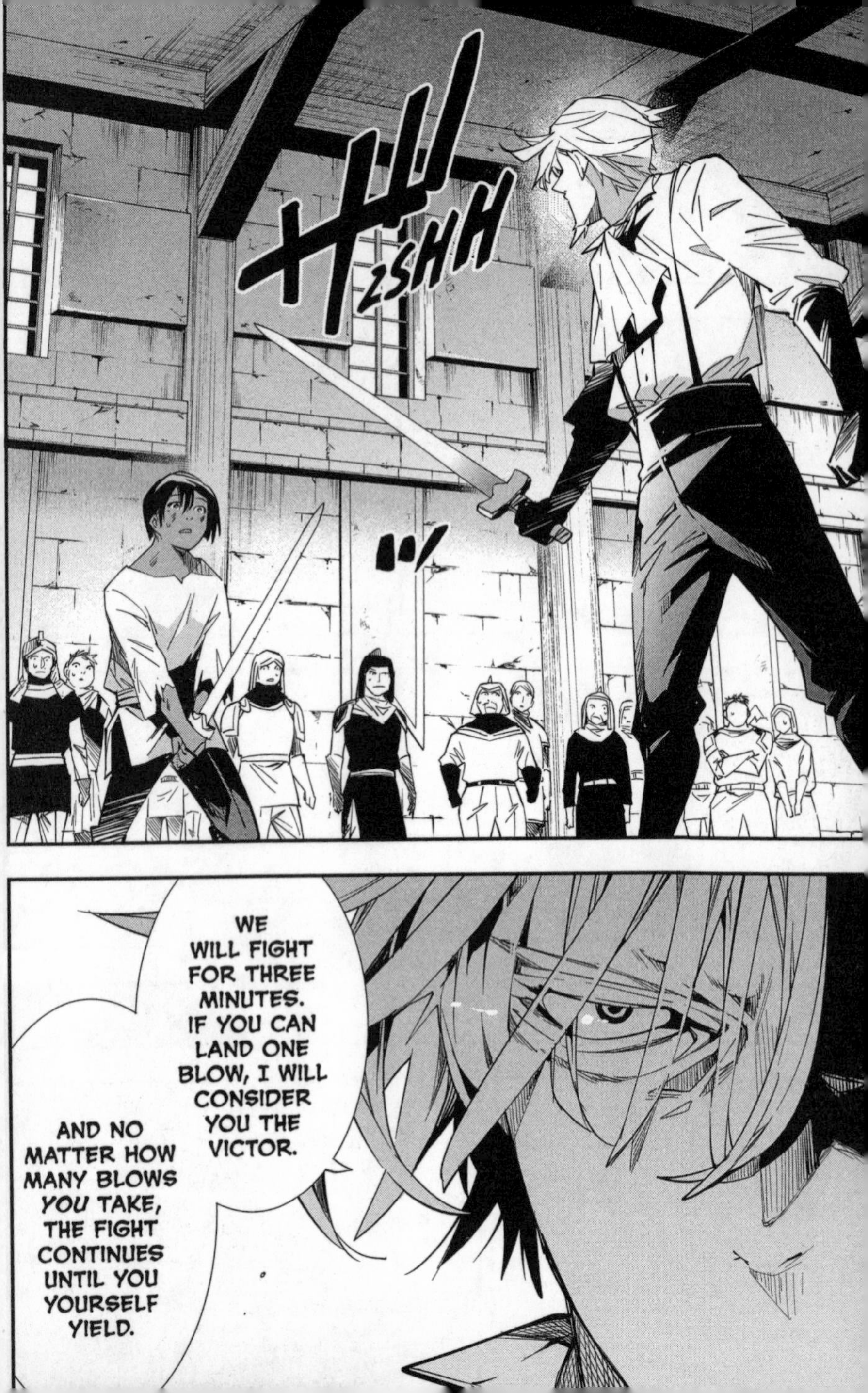
ZSHH
WE WILL FIGHT FOR THREE MINUTES. IF YOU CAN LAND ONE BLOW, I WILL CONSIDER YOU THE VICTOR.
AND NO MATTER HOW MANY BLOWS *YOU* TAKE, THE FIGHT CONTINUES UNTIL YOU YOURSELF YIELD.

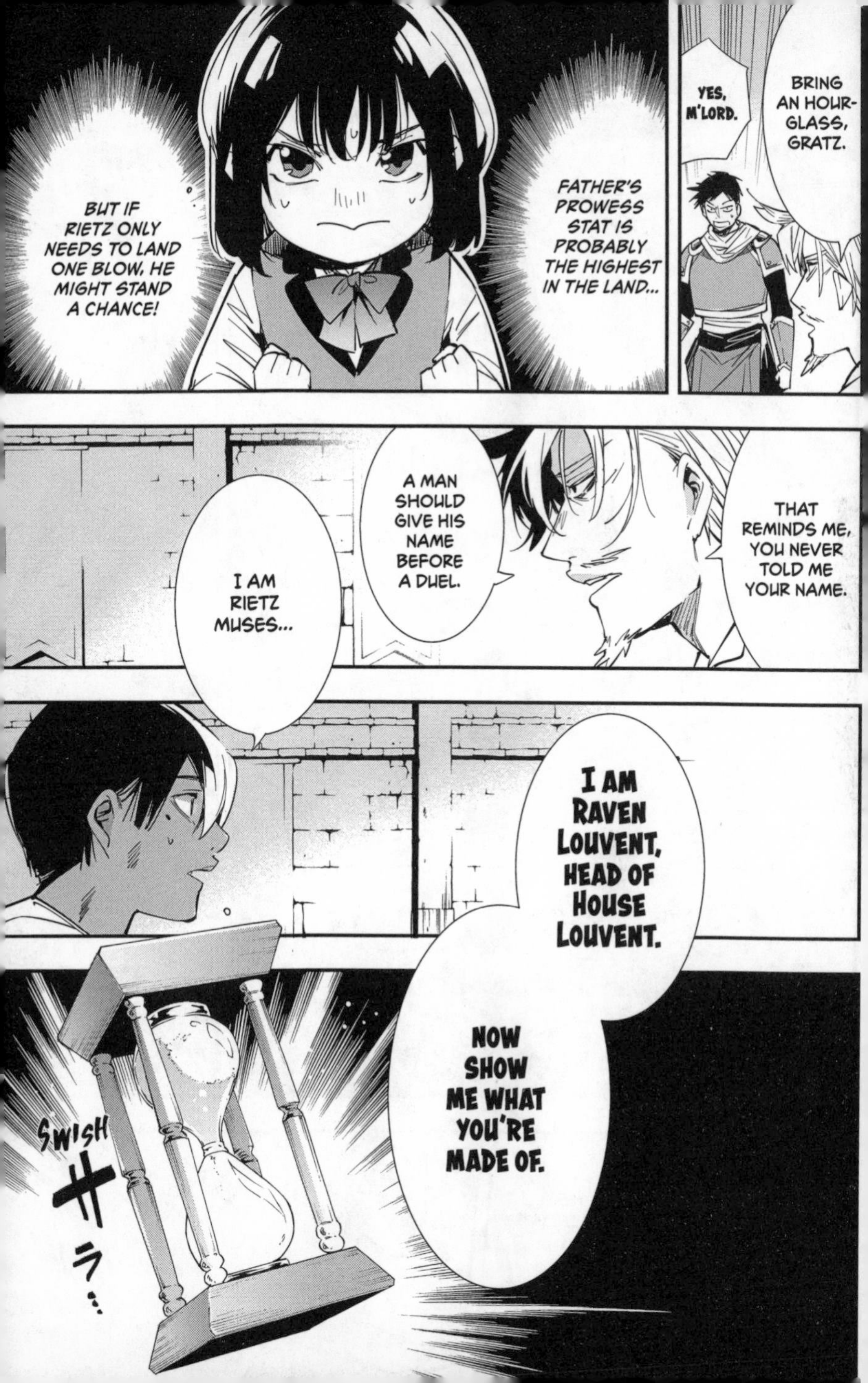
BRING AN HOUR-GLASS, GRATZ.
YES, M'LORD.
FATHER'S PROWESS STAT IS PROBABLY THE HIGHEST IN THE LAND...
BUT IF RIETZ ONLY NEEDS TO LAND ONE BLOW, HE MIGHT STAND A CHANCE!
THAT REMINDS ME, YOU NEVER TOLD ME YOUR NAME.
A MAN SHOULD GIVE HIS NAME BEFORE A DUEL.
I AM RIETZ MUSES...
I AM RAVEN LOUVENT, HEAD OF HOUSE LOUVENT.
NOW SHOW ME WHAT YOU'RE MADE OF.
SWISH
サラ…

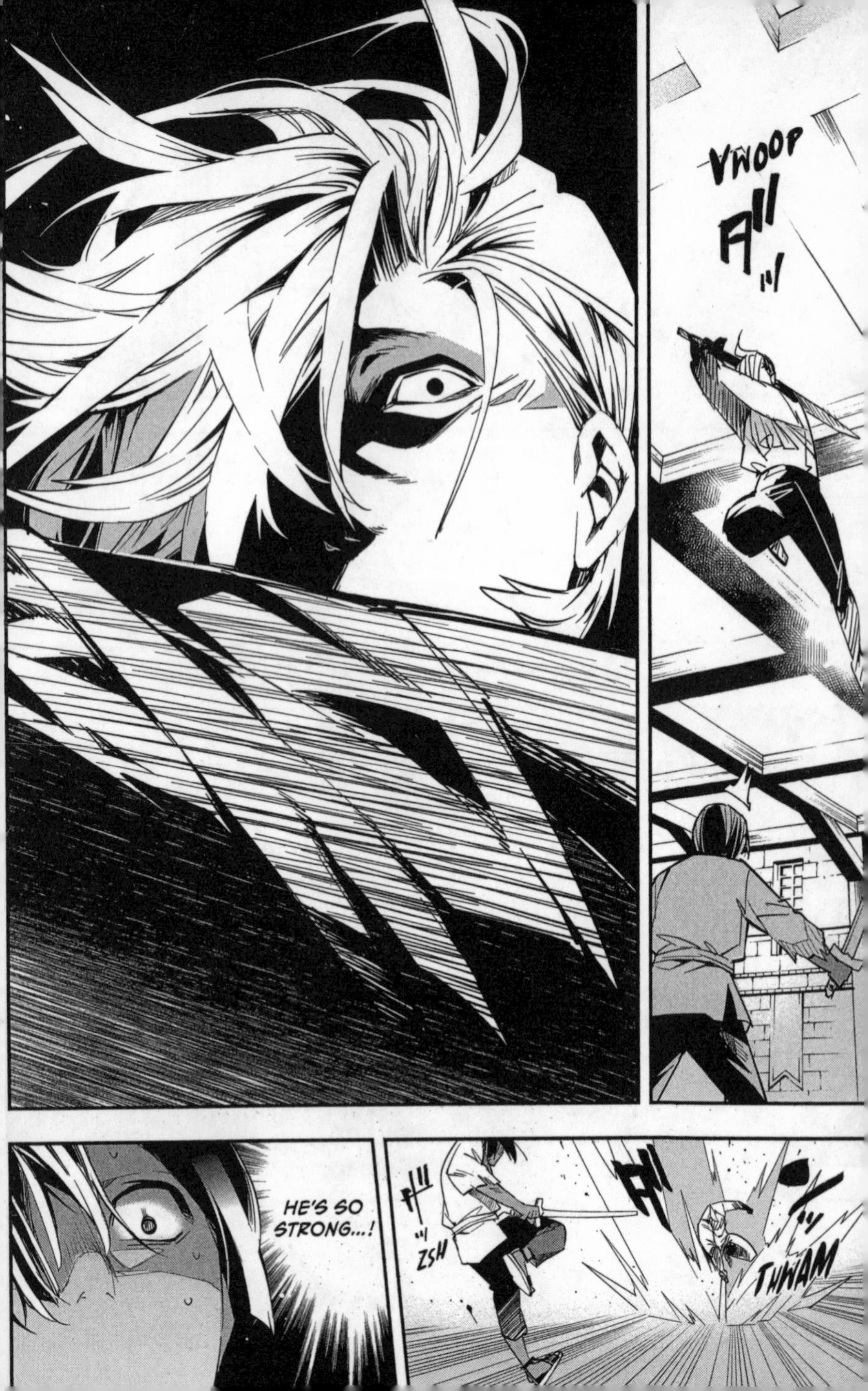
VWOOP
ZSH
THWAM
HE'S SO STRONG...!

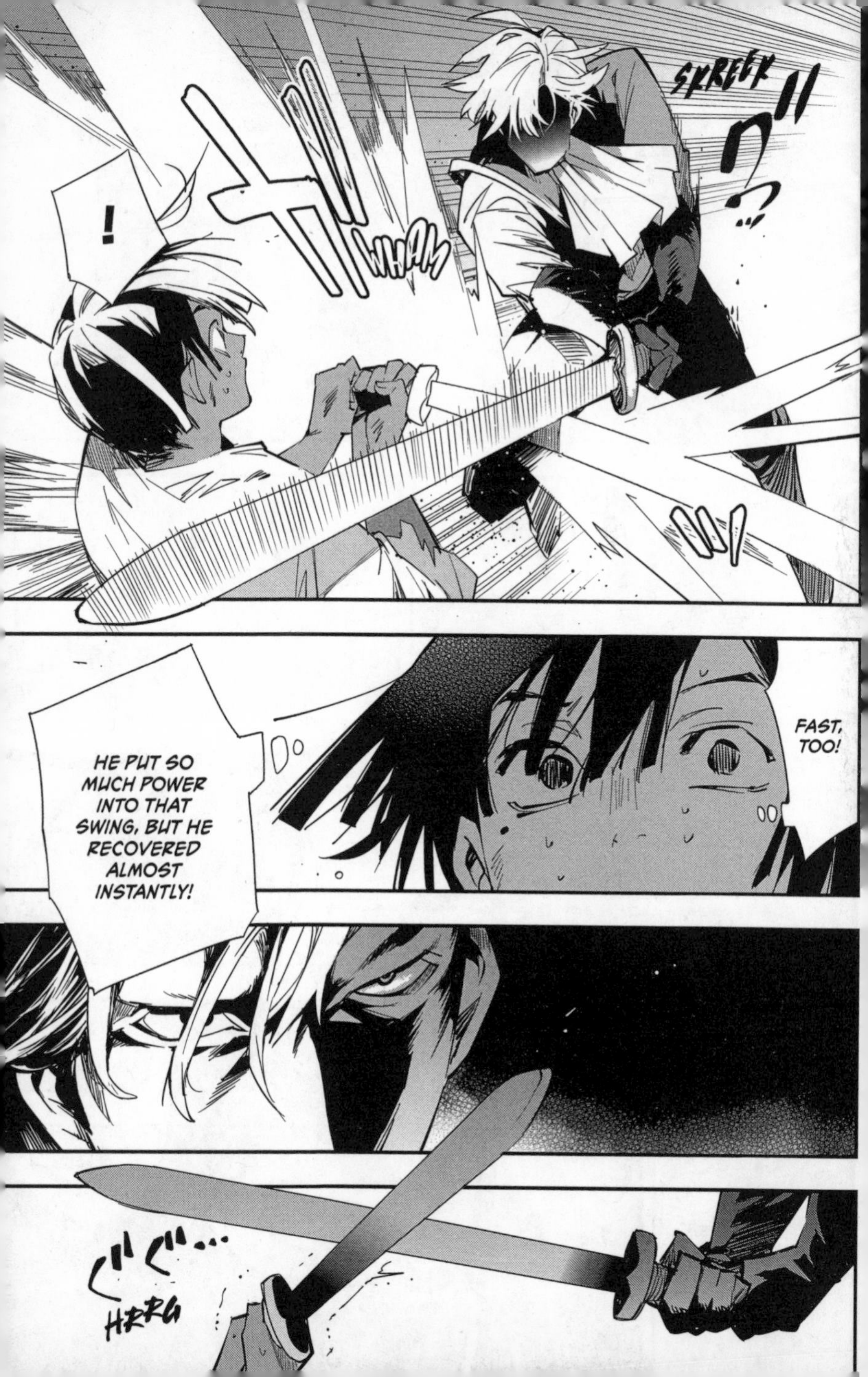
SKREEK
WHAM
!
FAST, TOO!
HE PUT SO MUCH POWER INTO THAT SWING, BUT HE RECOVERED ALMOST INSTANTLY!
HRRG

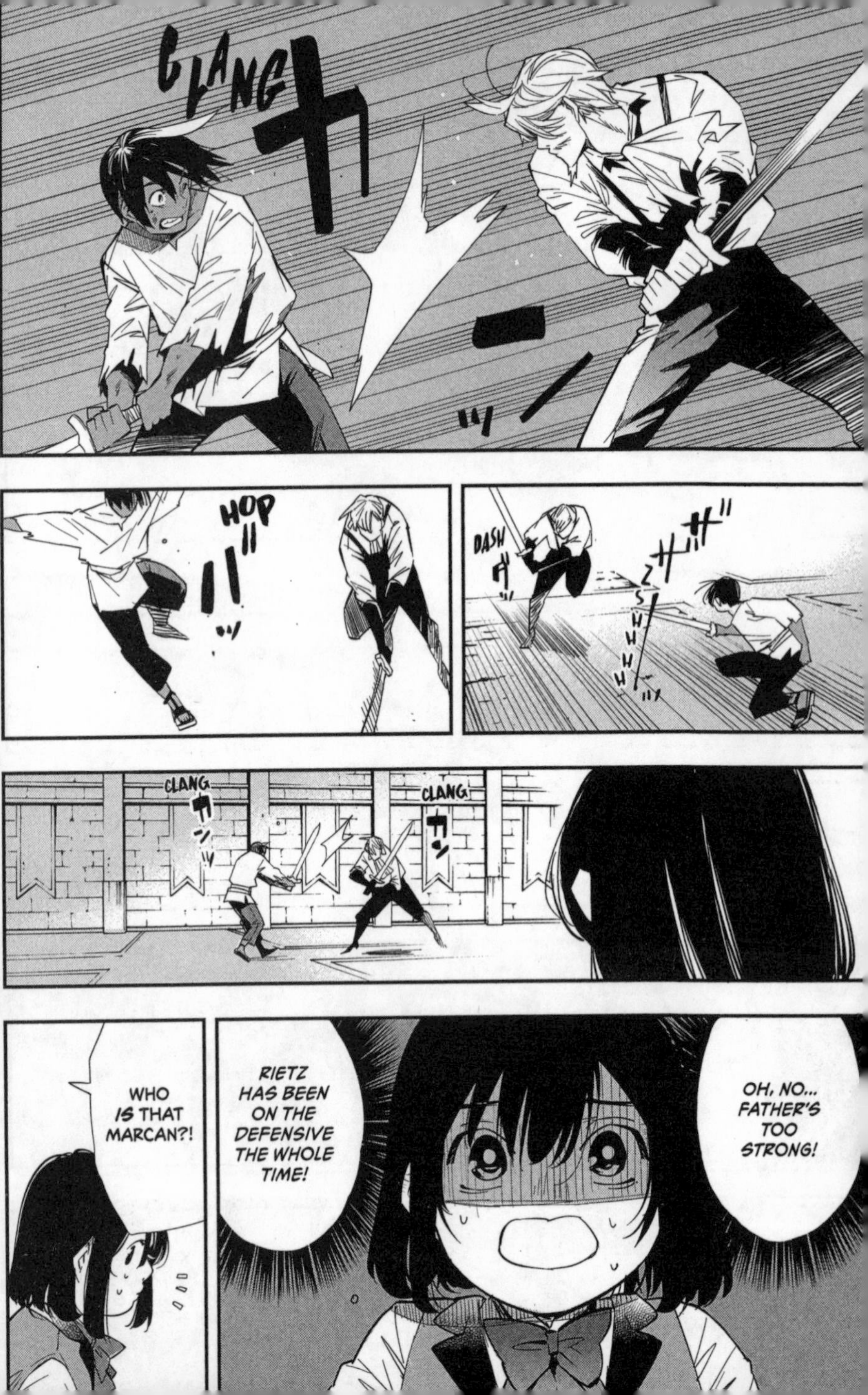
CLANG
DASH
ZSHHHH
HOP
CLANG
CLANG
OH, NO... FATHER'S TOO STRONG!
RIETZ HAS BEEN ON THE DEFENSIVE THE WHOLE TIME!
WHO IS THAT MARCAN?!

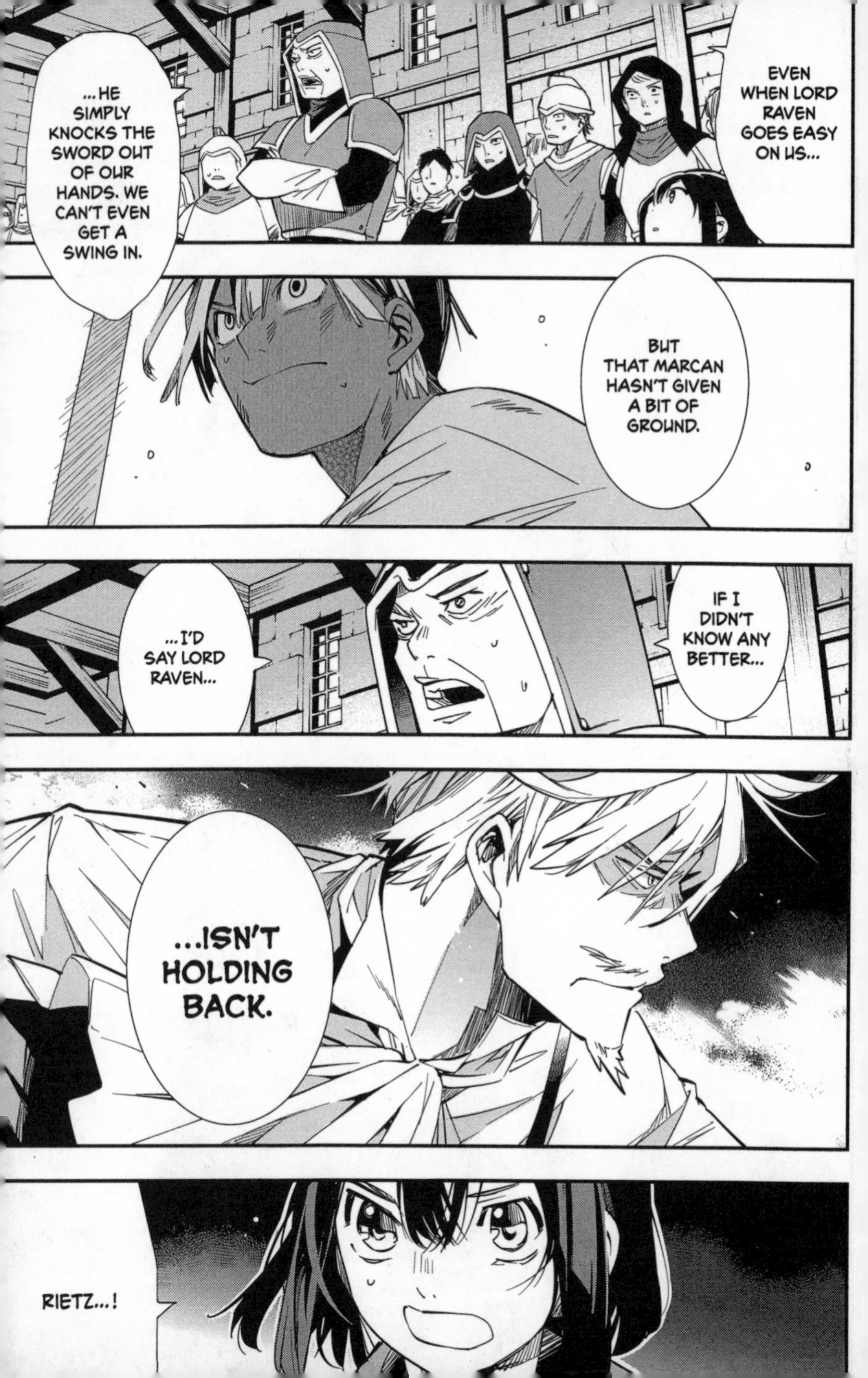
EVEN WHEN LORD RAVEN GOES EASY ON US...
...HE SIMPLY KNOCKS THE SWORD OUT OF OUR HANDS. WE CAN'T EVEN GET A SWING IN.
BUT THAT MARCAN HASN'T GIVEN A BIT OF GROUND.
IF I DIDN'T KNOW ANY BETTER...
...I'D SAY LORD RAVEN...
...ISN'T HOLDING BACK.
RIETZ...!

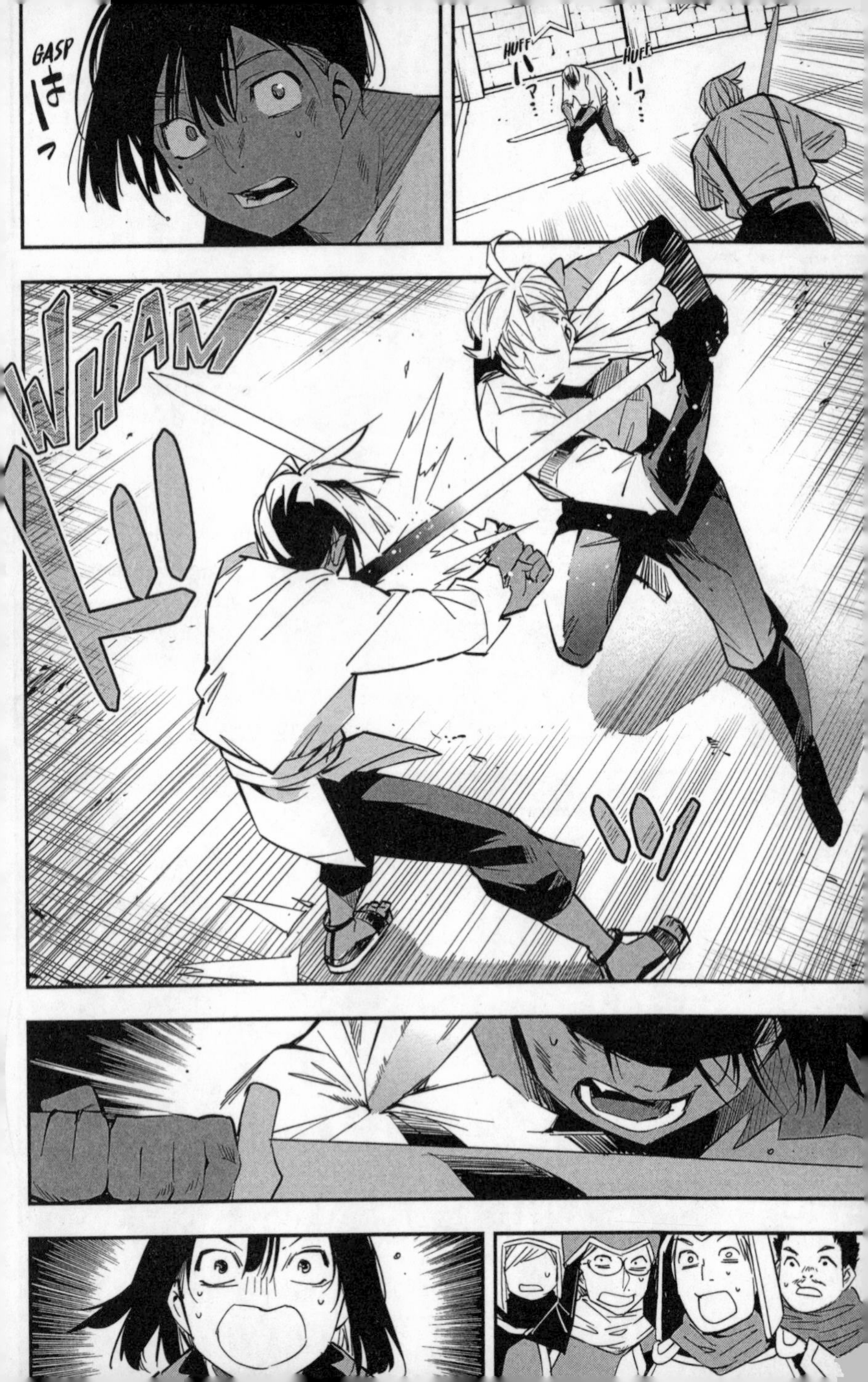
HUFF
ハァ…
HUFF
ハァ…
GASP
はっ
WHAM
ドッ

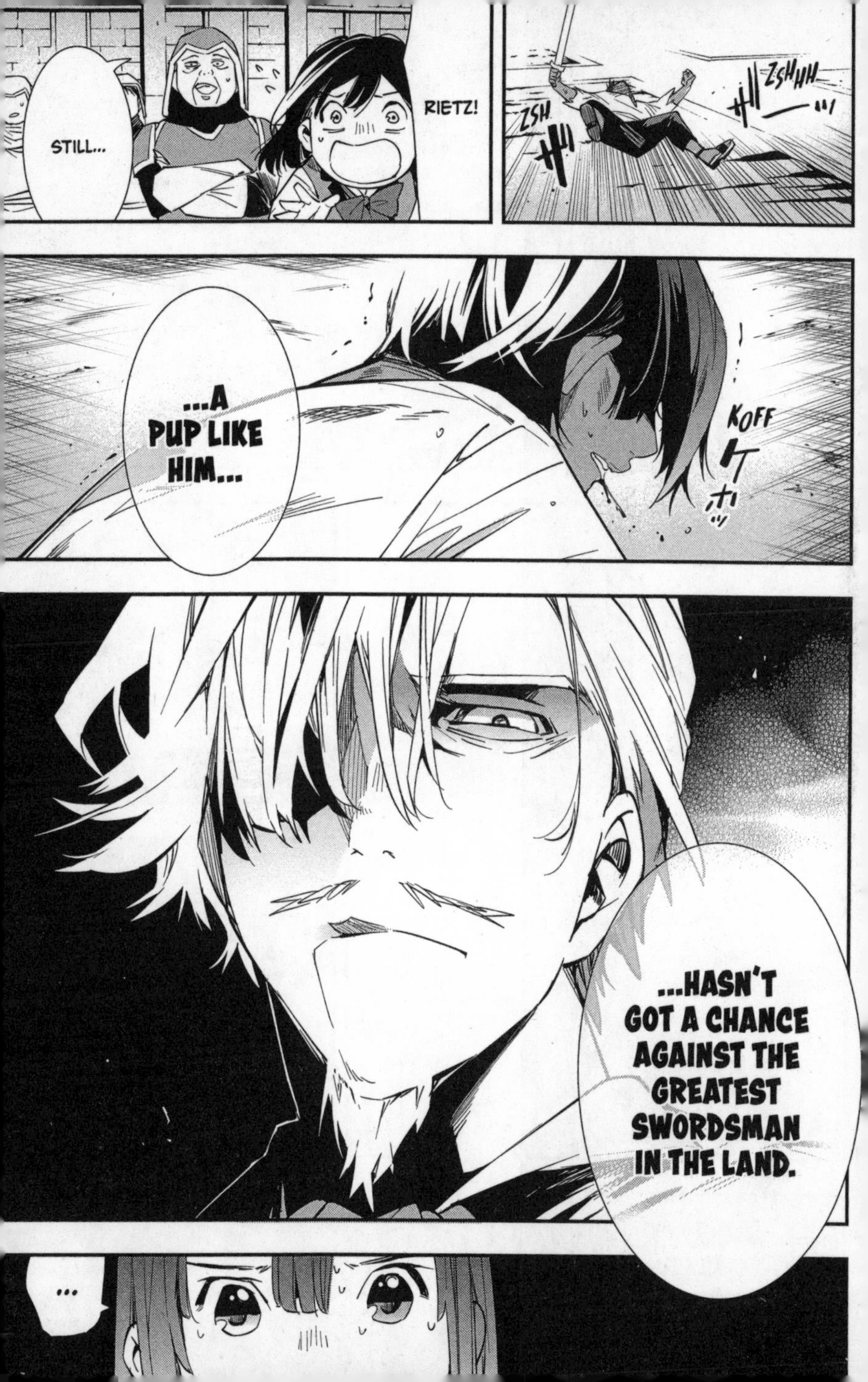
ZSHHH
ZSH
RIETZ!
STILL...
...A PUP LIKE HIM...
KOFF
ケホッ
...HASN'T GOT A CHANCE AGAINST THE GREATEST SWORDSMAN IN THE LAND.
...

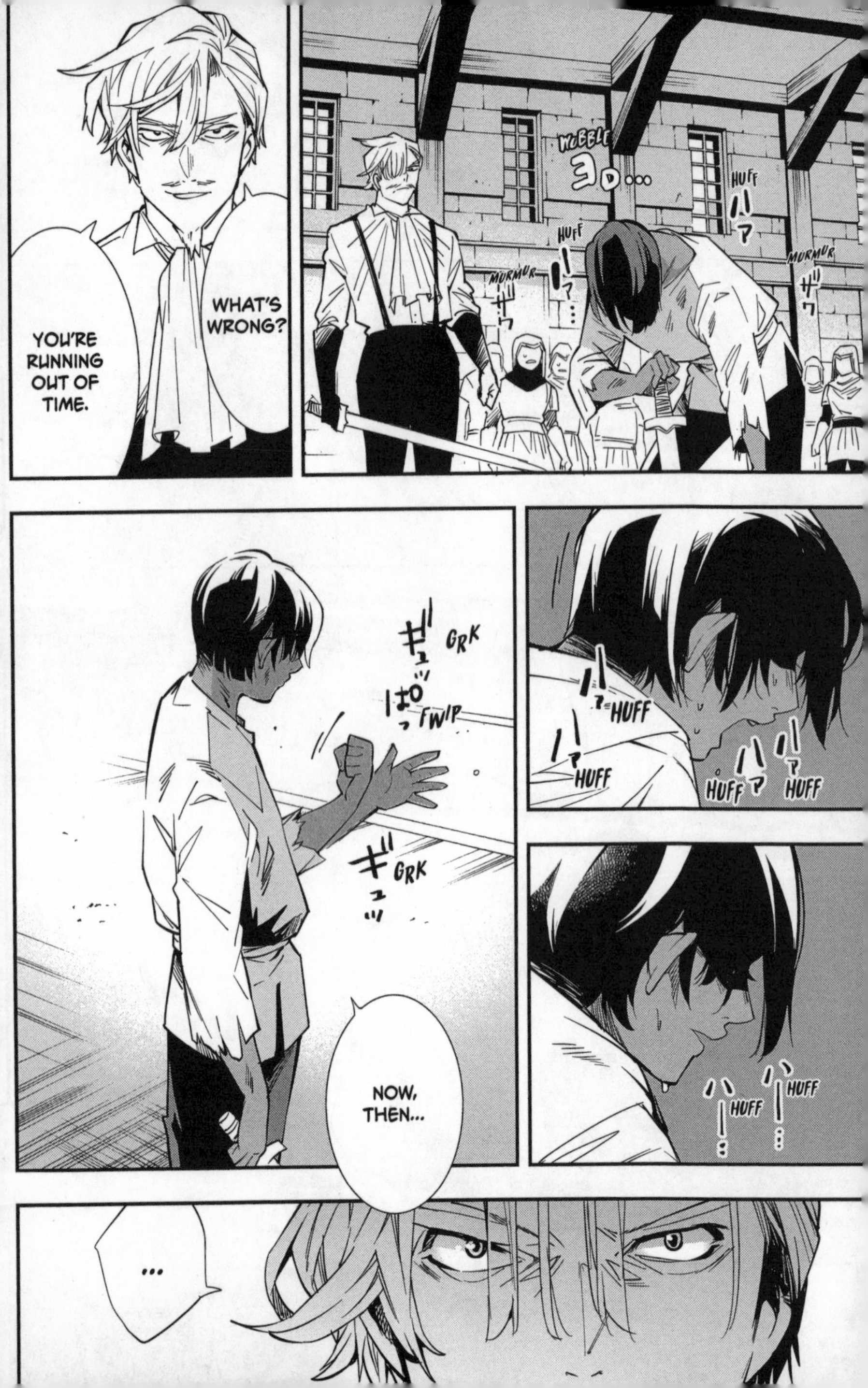
WOBBLE
HUFF
HUFF
MURMUR
MURMUR
WHAT'S WRONG?
YOU'RE RUNNING OUT OF TIME.
HUFF
HUFF
HUFF
HUFF
HUFF
HUFF
GRK
FWIP
GRK
NOW, THEN...
...

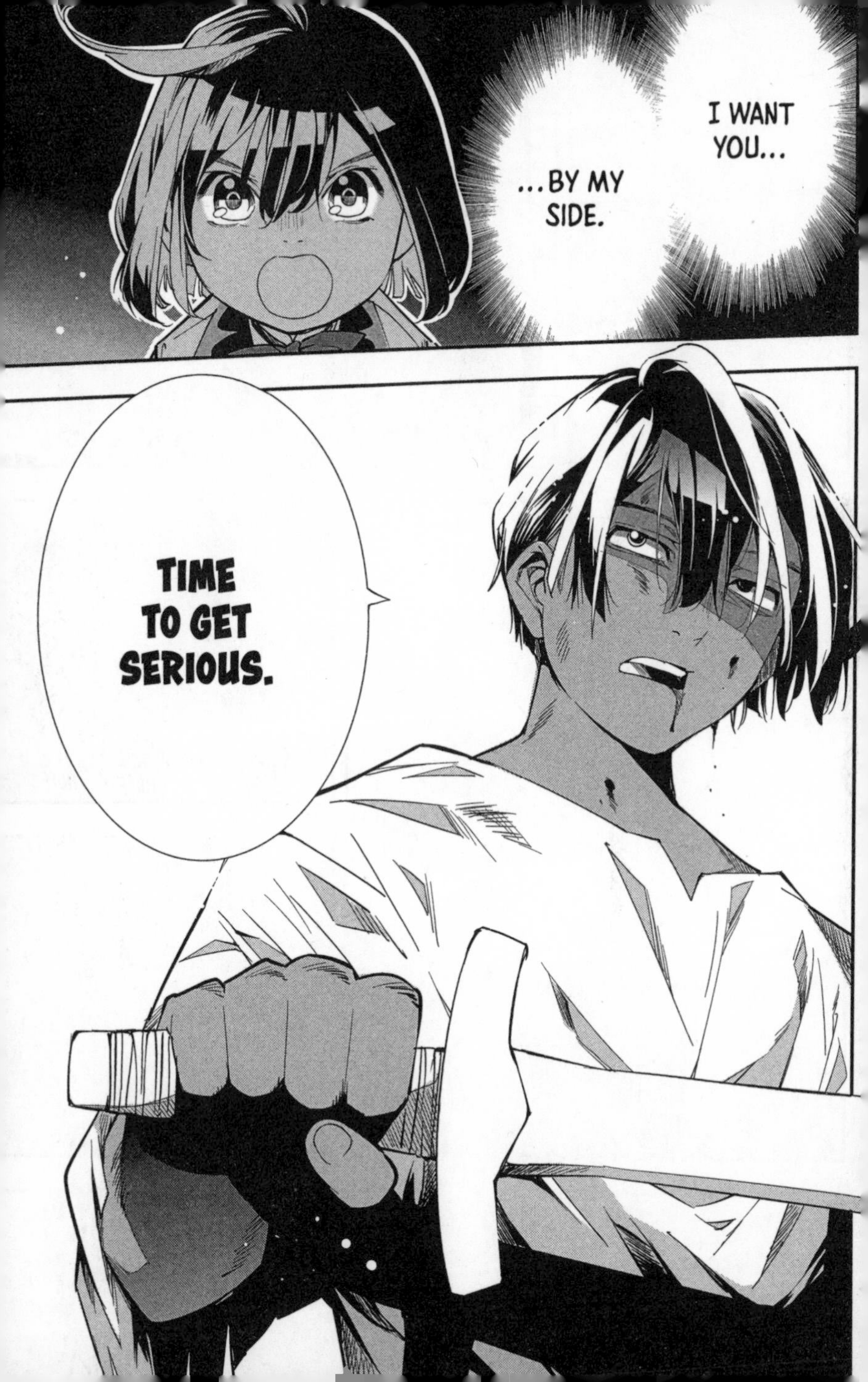
I WANT YOU...
...BY MY SIDE.
TIME TO GET SERIOUS.

As a Reincarnated ARISTOCRAT, I'll Use My Appraisal Skill to Rise in the World

Chapter 3: Victory or Defeat

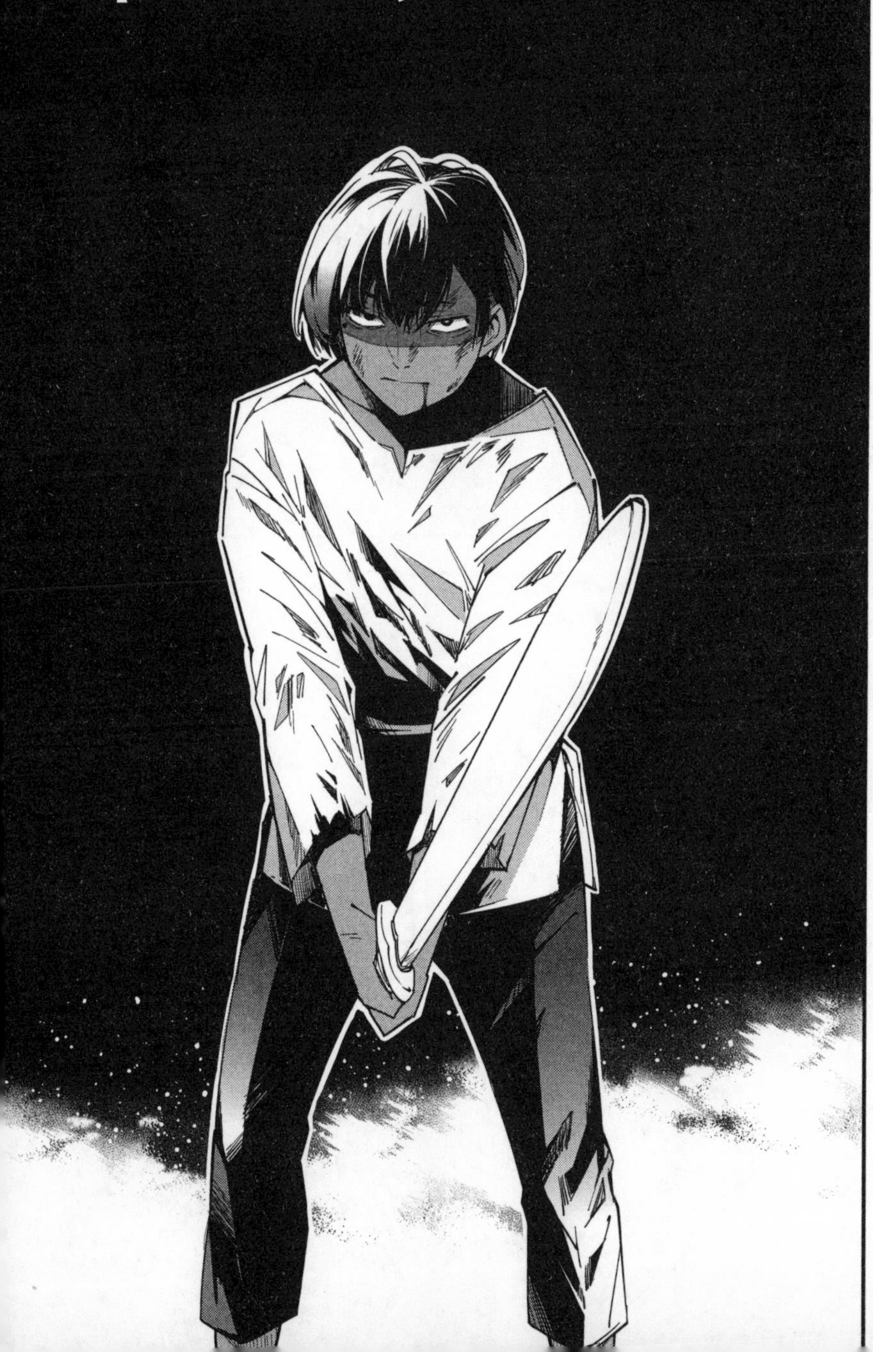

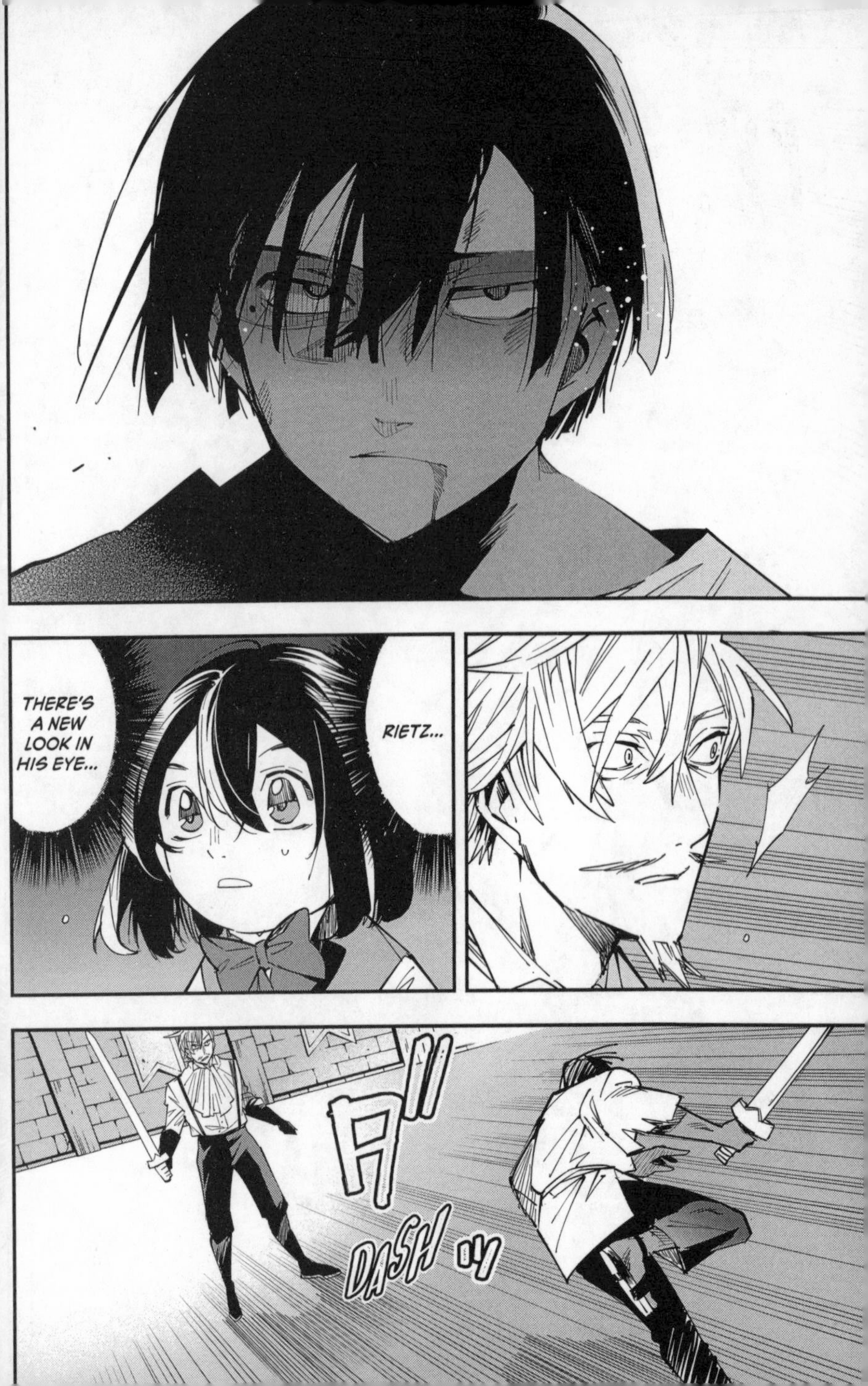
RIETZ...
THERE'S A NEW LOOK IN HIS EYE...
DASH

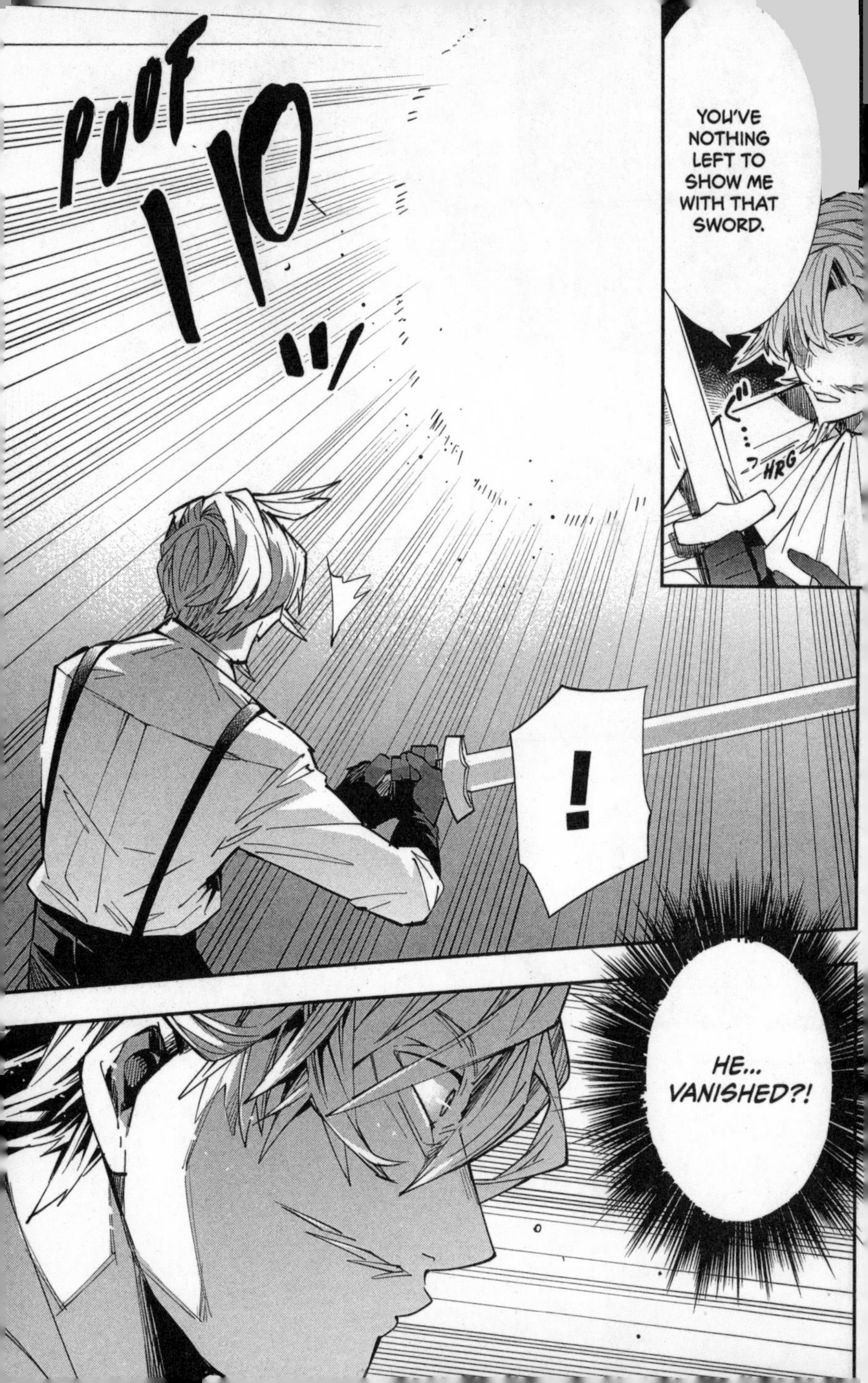
YOU'VE NOTHING LEFT TO SHOW ME WITH THAT SWORD.
HRG
POOF
!
HE... VANISHED?!

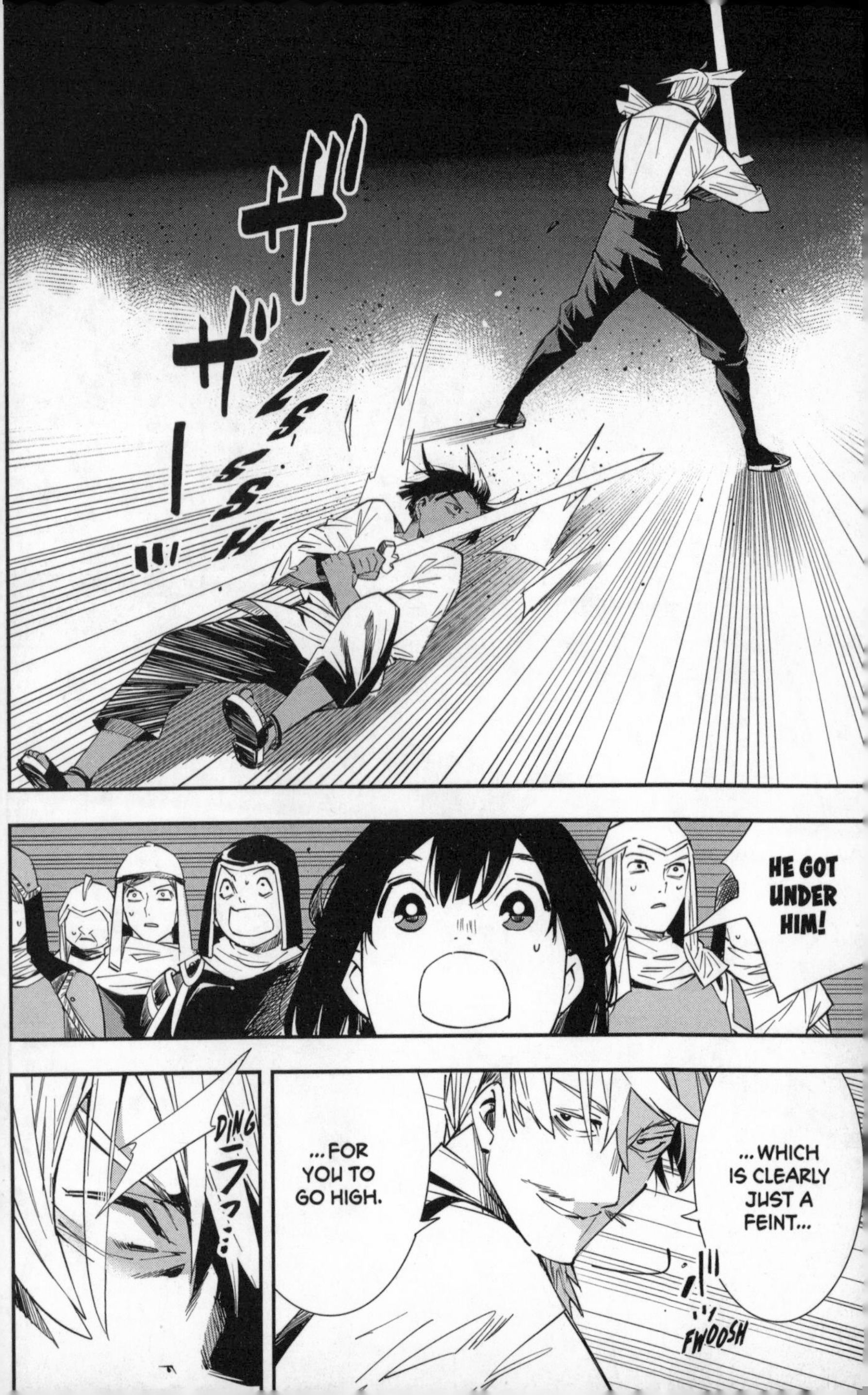
ザザー!!
ZSSSH
HE GOT UNDER HIM!
...WHICH IS CLEARLY JUST A FEINT...
...FOR YOU TO GO HIGH.
FWOOSH
DING
フッ...

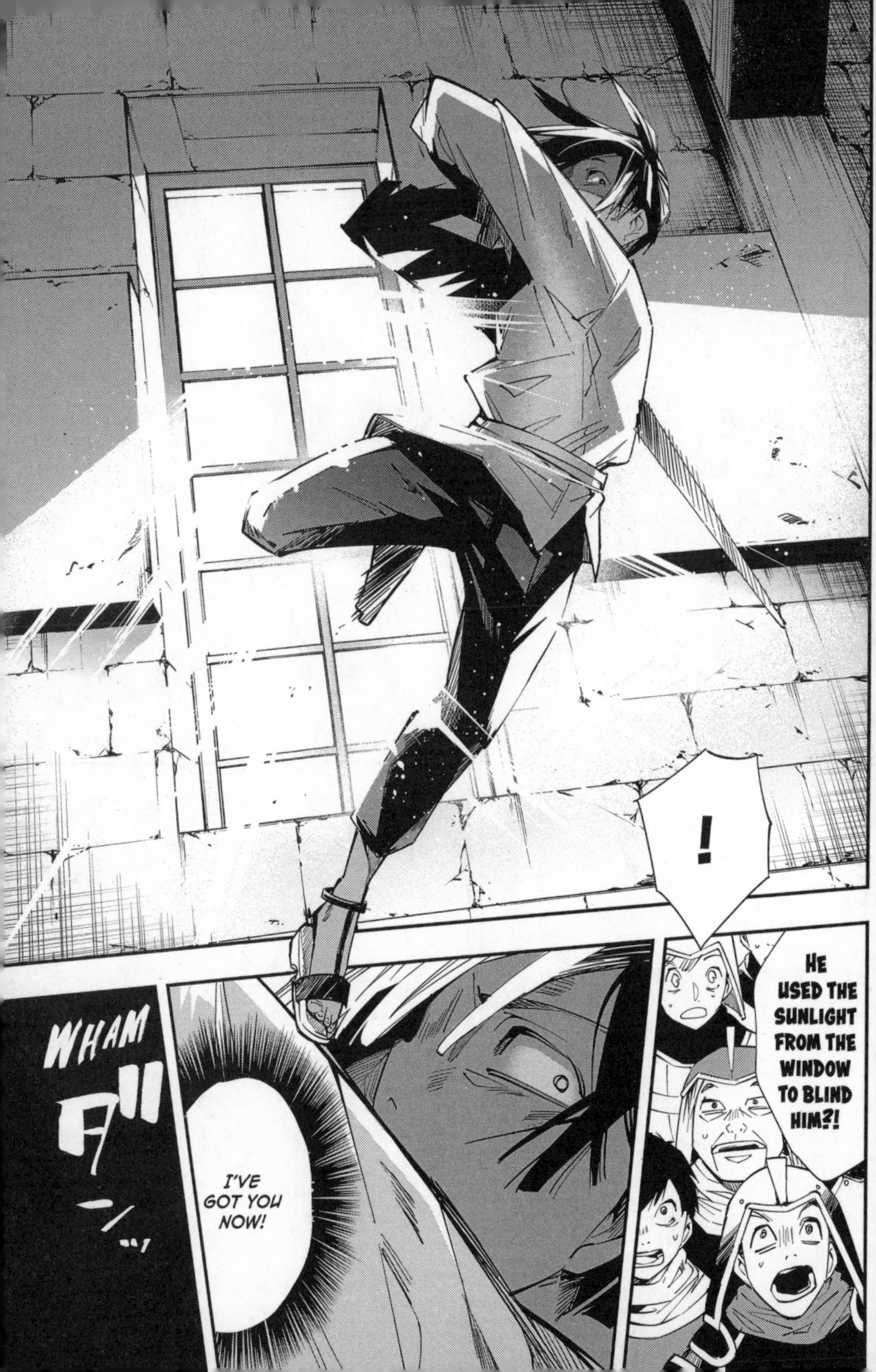
!
HE USED THE SUNLIGHT FROM THE WINDOW TO BLIND HIM?!
I'VE GOT YOU NOW!
WHAM

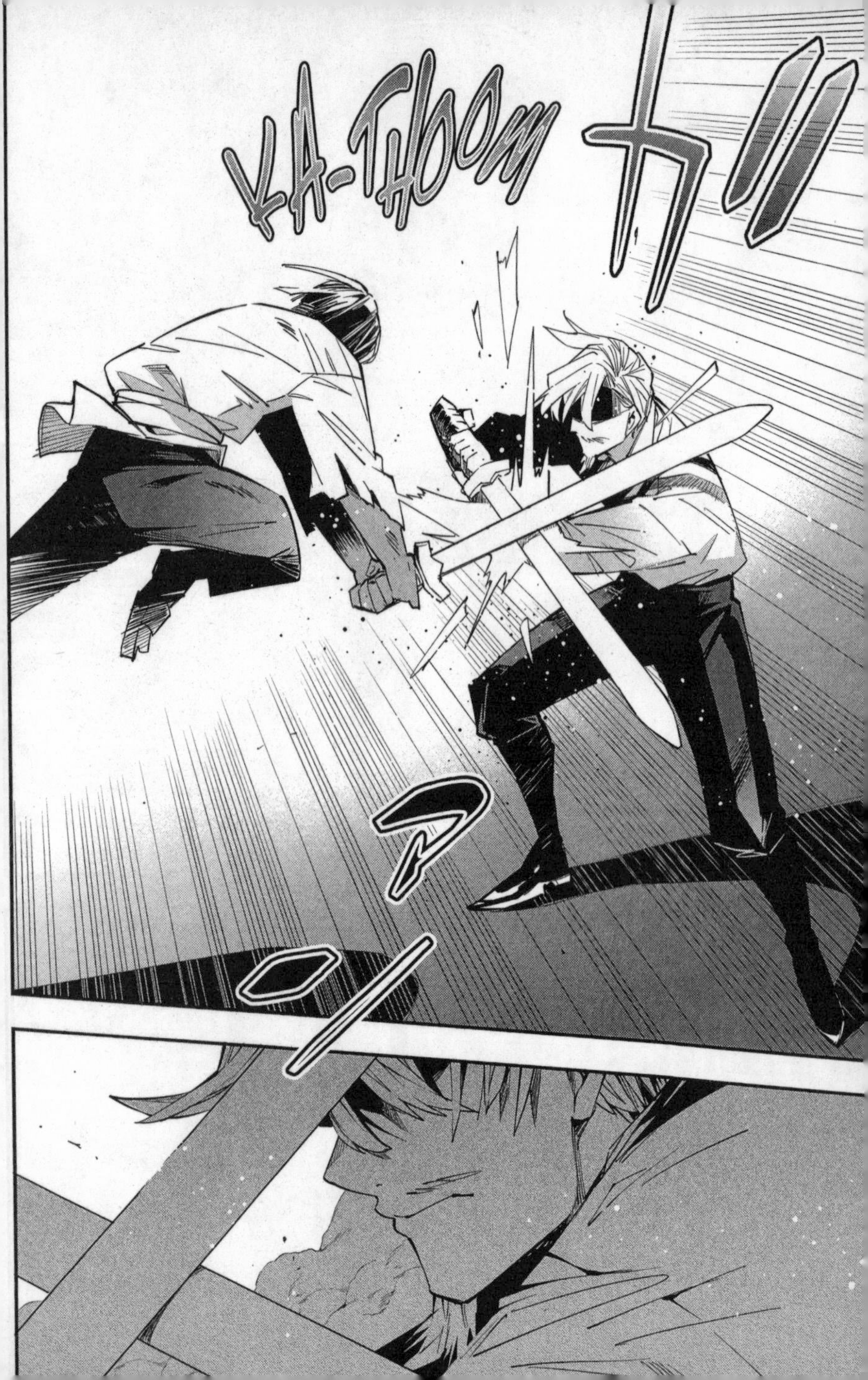
KA-THOOM

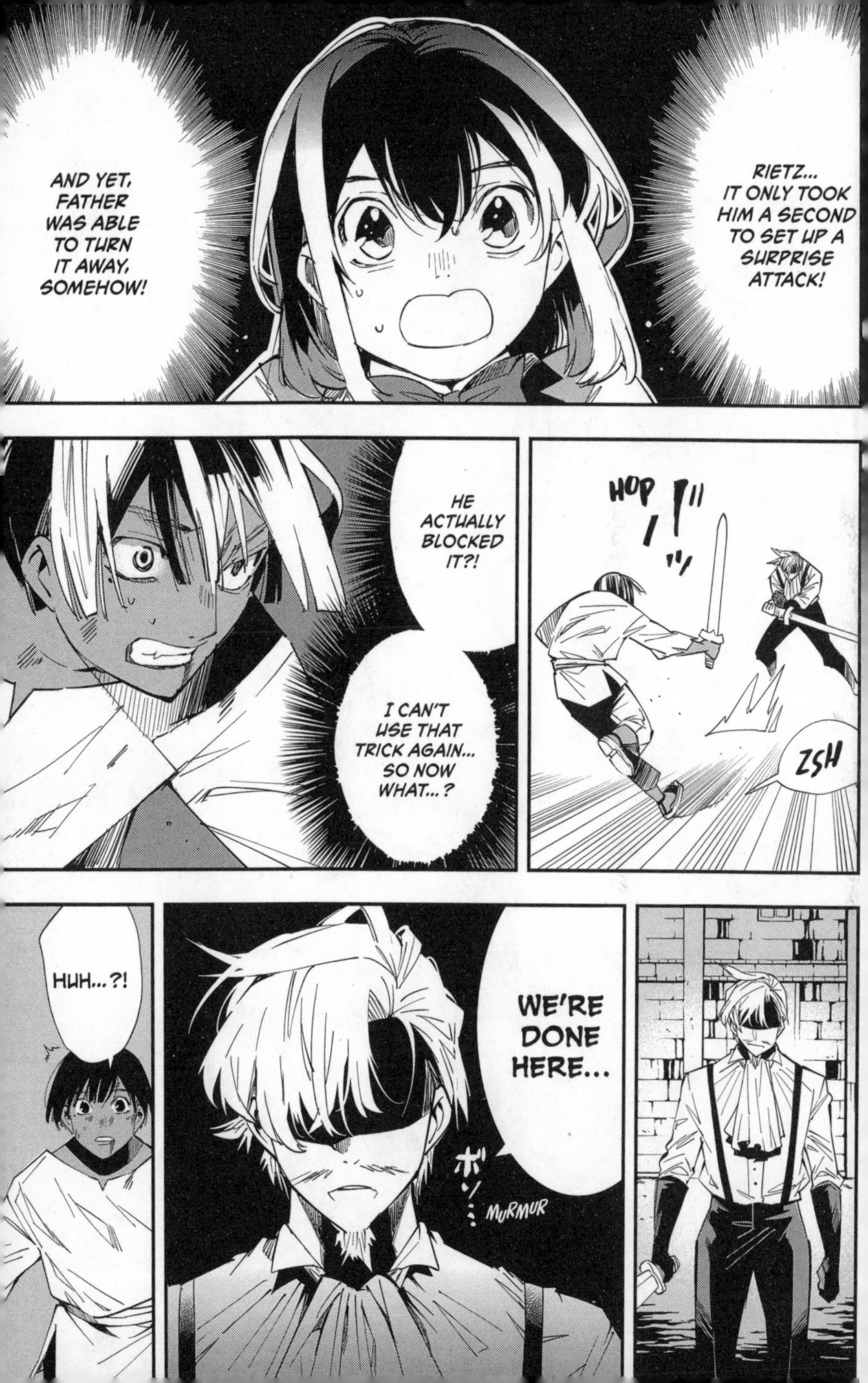
RIETZ... IT ONLY TOOK HIM A SECOND TO SET UP A SURPRISE ATTACK!
AND YET, FATHER WAS ABLE TO TURN IT AWAY, SOMEHOW!
HOP
ZSH
HE ACTUALLY BLOCKED IT?!
I CAN'T USE THAT TRICK AGAIN... SO NOW WHAT...?
WE'RE DONE HERE...
MURMUR
HUH...?!

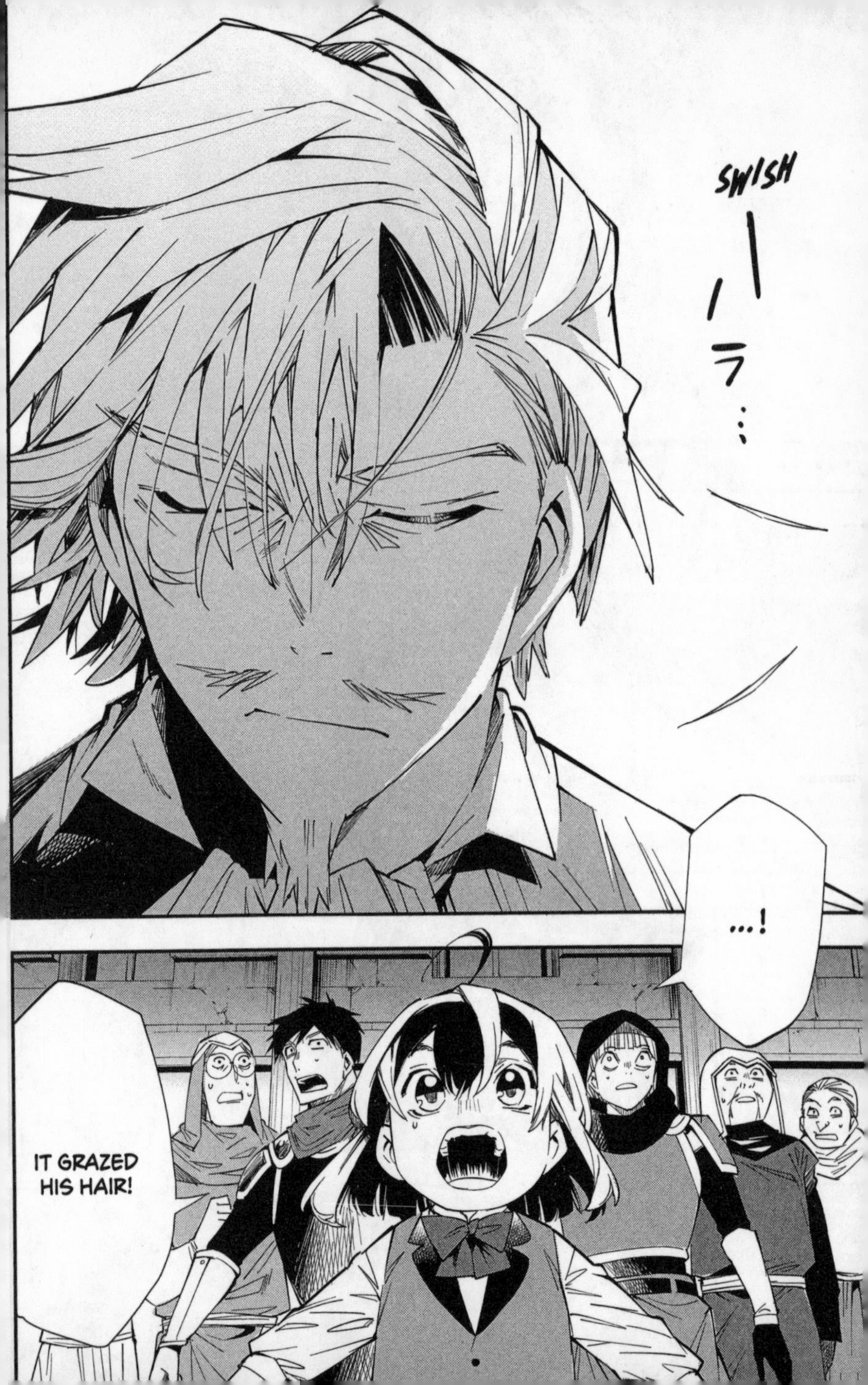
SWISH
サラ…
...!
IT GRAZED HIS HAIR!

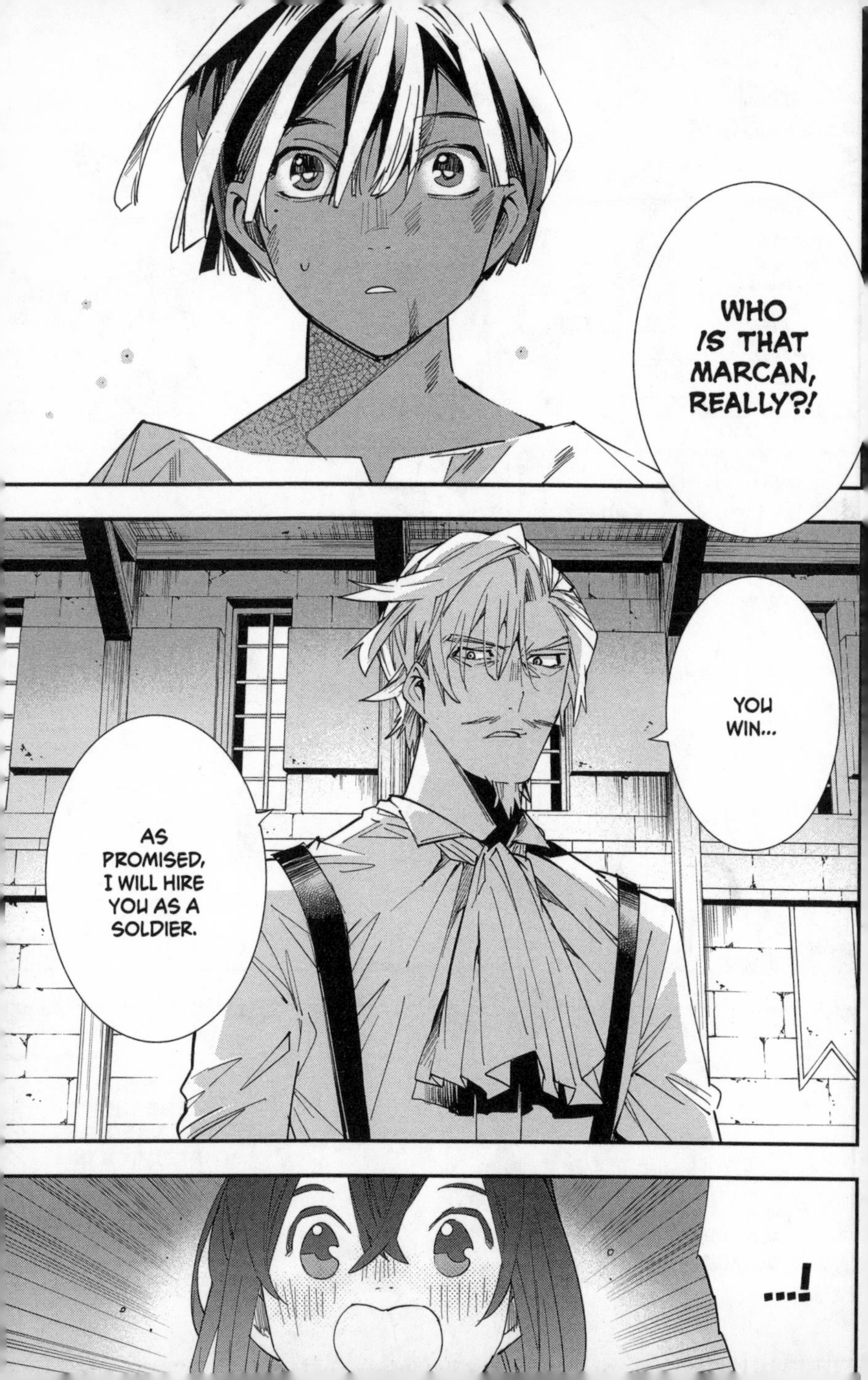
WHO IS THAT MARCAN, REALLY?!
YOU WIN...
AS PROMISED, I WILL HIRE YOU AS A SOLDIER.
...!

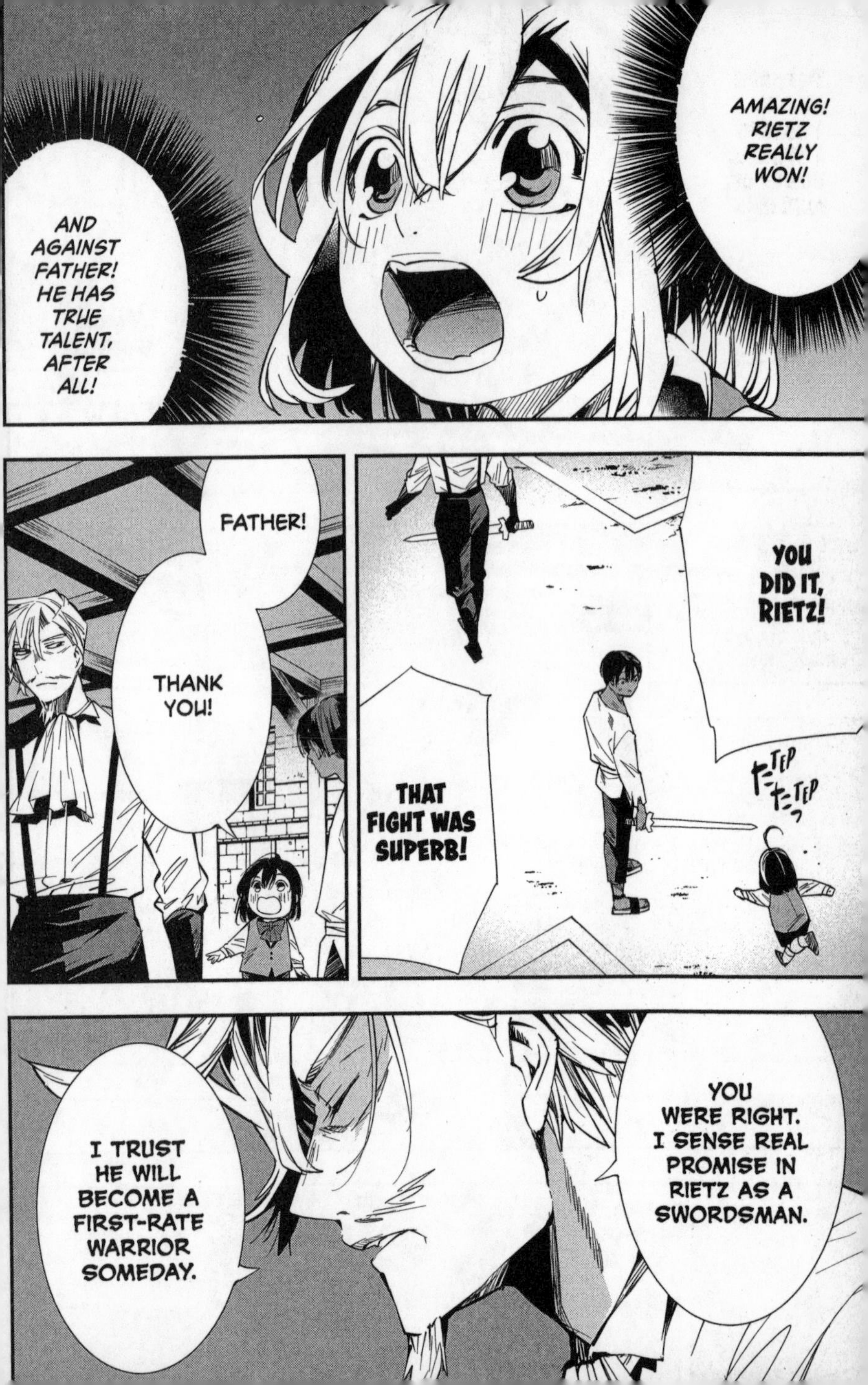
AMAZING! RIETZ REALLY WON!
AND AGAINST FATHER! HE HAS TRUE TALENT, AFTER ALL!
YOU DID IT, RIETZ!
TEP TEP
THAT FIGHT WAS SUPERB!
FATHER!
THANK YOU!
YOU WERE RIGHT. I SENSE REAL PROMISE IN RIETZ AS A SWORDSMAN.
I TRUST HE WILL BECOME A FIRST-RATE WARRIOR SOMEDAY.

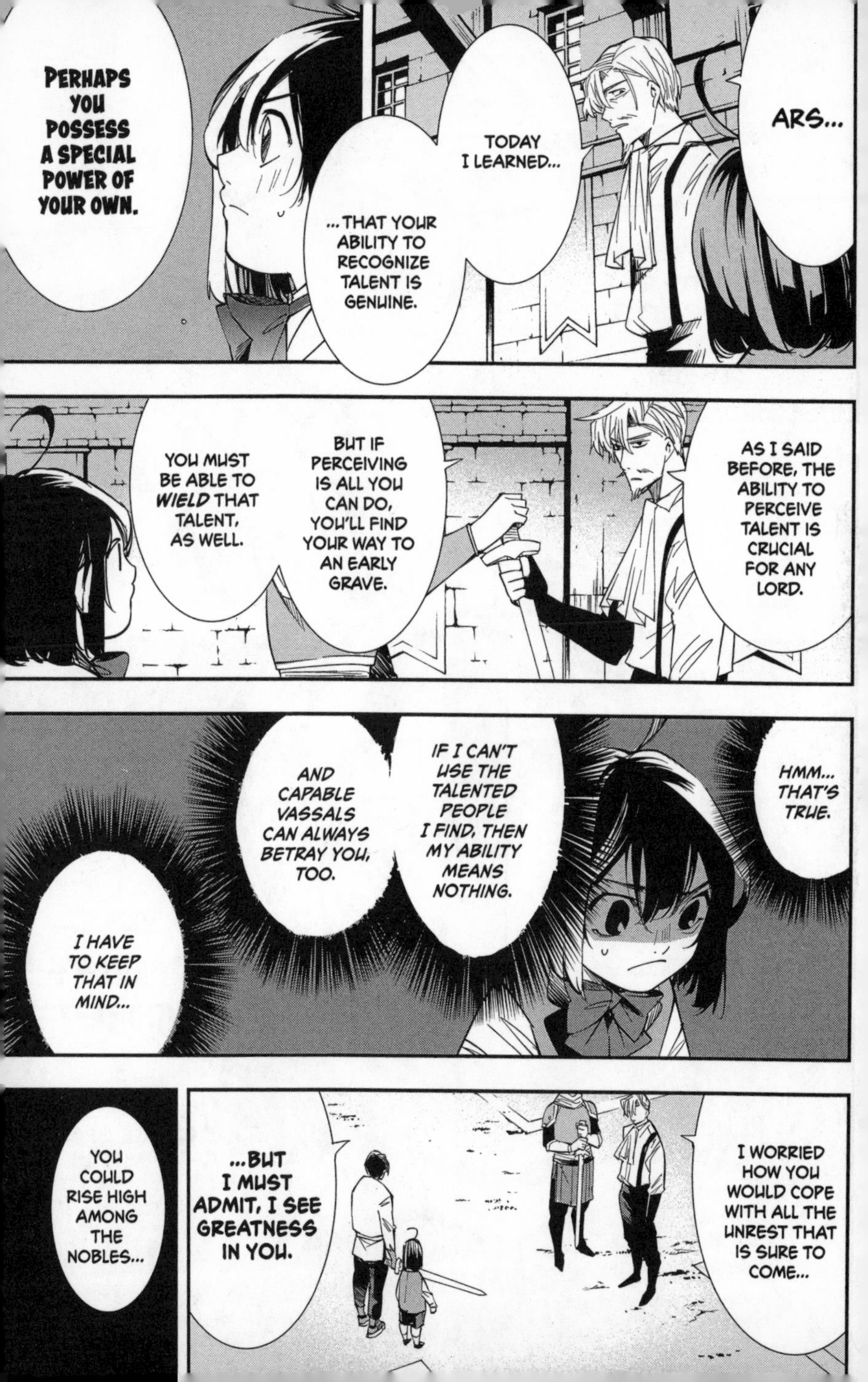
ARS...
TODAY I LEARNED...
...THAT YOUR ABILITY TO RECOGNIZE TALENT IS GENUINE.
PERHAPS YOU POSSESS A SPECIAL POWER OF YOUR OWN.
AS I SAID BEFORE, THE ABILITY TO PERCEIVE TALENT IS CRUCIAL FOR ANY LORD.
BUT IF PERCEIVING IS ALL YOU CAN DO, YOU'LL FIND YOUR WAY TO AN EARLY GRAVE.
YOU MUST BE ABLE TO *WIELD* THAT TALENT, AS WELL.
HMM... THAT'S TRUE.
IF I CAN'T USE THE TALENTED PEOPLE I FIND, THEN MY ABILITY MEANS NOTHING.
AND CAPABLE VASSALS CAN ALWAYS BETRAY YOU, TOO.
I HAVE TO KEEP THAT IN MIND...
I WORRIED HOW YOU WOULD COPE WITH ALL THE UNREST THAT IS SURE TO COME...
...BUT I MUST ADMIT, I SEE GREATNESS IN YOU.
YOU COULD RISE HIGH AMONG THE NOBLES...

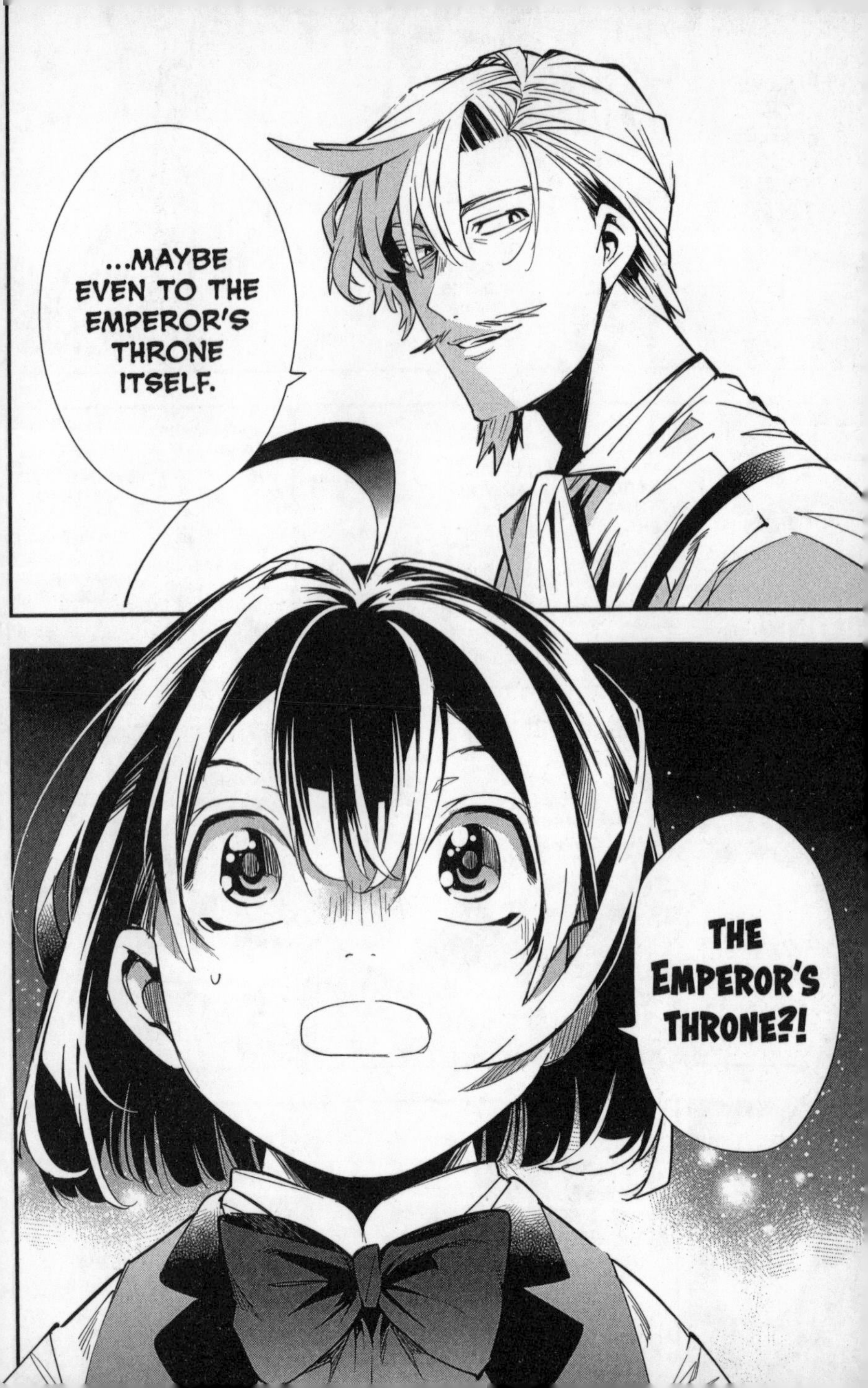
...MAYBE EVEN TO THE EMPEROR'S THRONE ITSELF.
THE EMPEROR'S THRONE?!

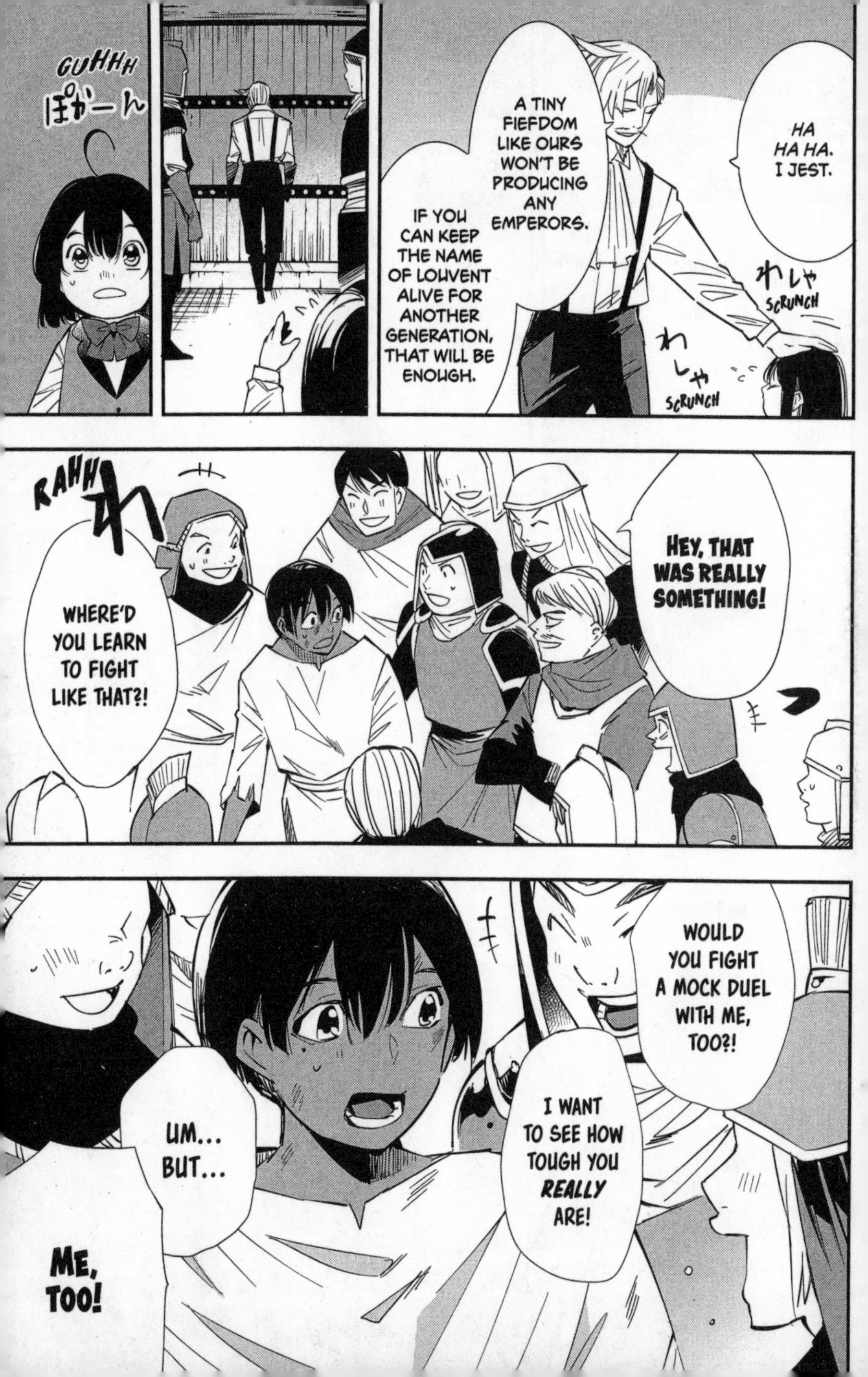
HA HA HA. I JEST.
A TINY FIEFDOM LIKE OURS WON'T BE PRODUCING ANY EMPERORS.
IF YOU CAN KEEP THE NAME OF LOUVENT ALIVE FOR ANOTHER GENERATION, THAT WILL BE ENOUGH.
わしゃ SCRUNCH
わしゃ SCRUNCH
GUHHH ぽかーん
HEY, THAT WAS REALLY SOMETHING!
WHERE'D YOU LEARN TO FIGHT LIKE THAT?!
RAHHH わ
WOULD YOU FIGHT A MOCK DUEL WITH ME, TOO?!
I WANT TO SEE HOW TOUGH YOU REALLY ARE!
UM... BUT...
ME, TOO!

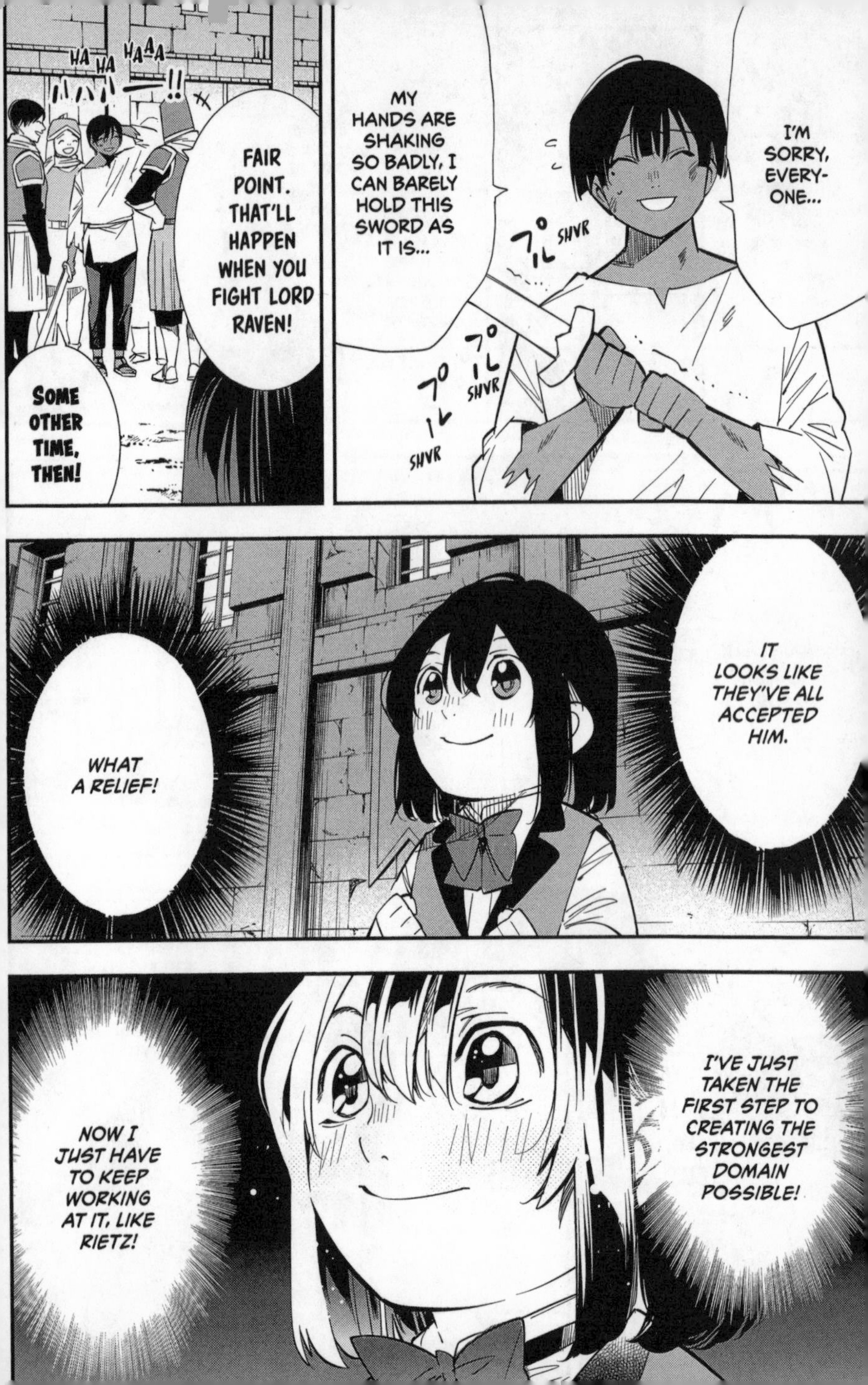
I'M SORRY, EVERY-ONE...
MY HANDS ARE SHAKING SO BADLY, I CAN BARELY HOLD THIS SWORD AS IT IS...
プル SHVR
プル SHVR
プル SHVR
HA HA HAAA
ハハハー!!
FAIR POINT. THAT'LL HAPPEN WHEN YOU FIGHT LORD RAVEN!
SOME OTHER TIME, THEN!
IT LOOKS LIKE THEY'VE ALL ACCEPTED HIM.
WHAT A RELIEF!
I'VE JUST TAKEN THE FIRST STEP TO CREATING THE STRONGEST DOMAIN POSSIBLE!
NOW I JUST HAVE TO KEEP WORKING AT IT, LIKE RIETZ!

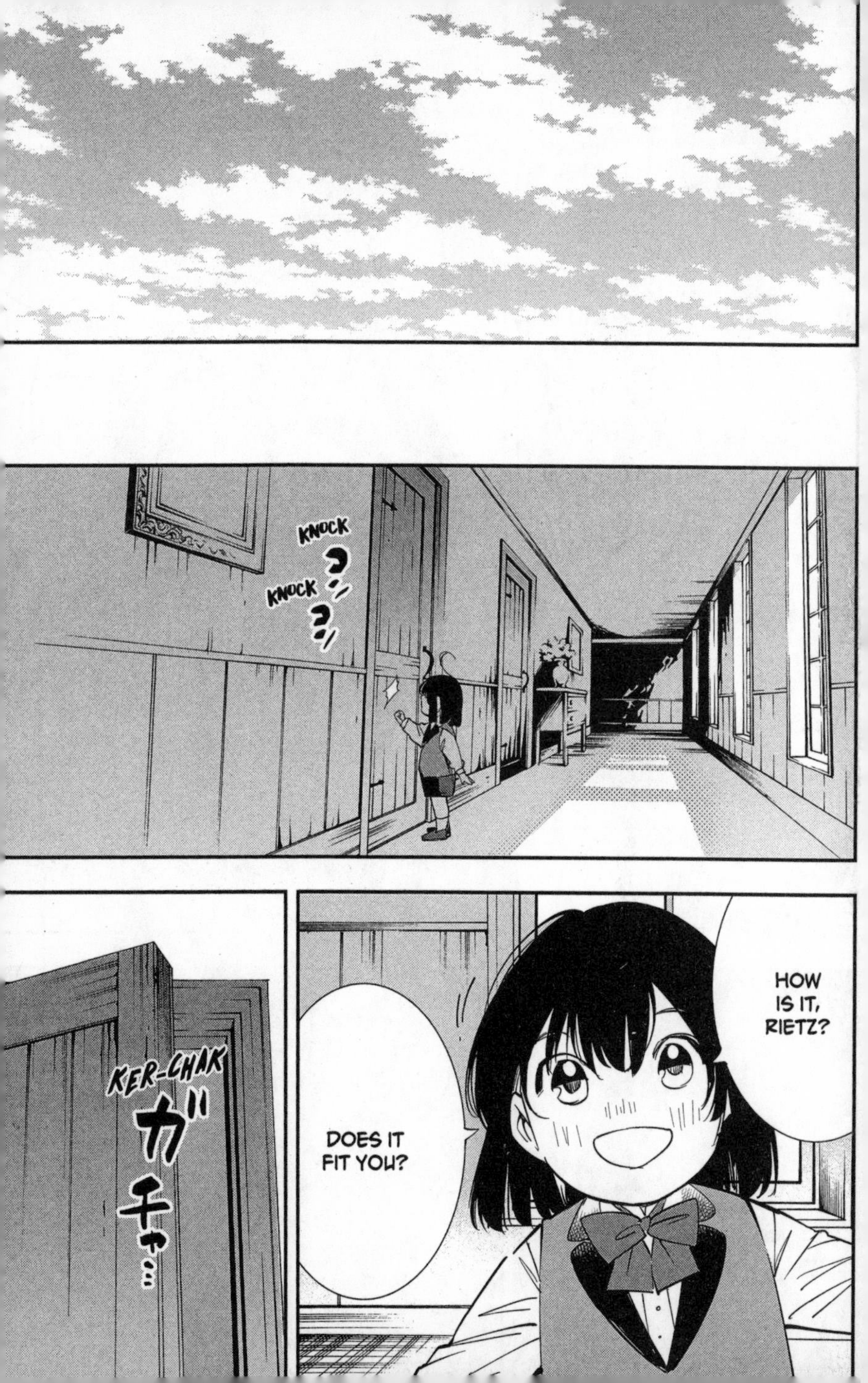
KNOCK
コン
KNOCK
コン
HOW IS IT, RIETZ?
DOES IT FIT YOU?
KER-CHAK
ガチャ…

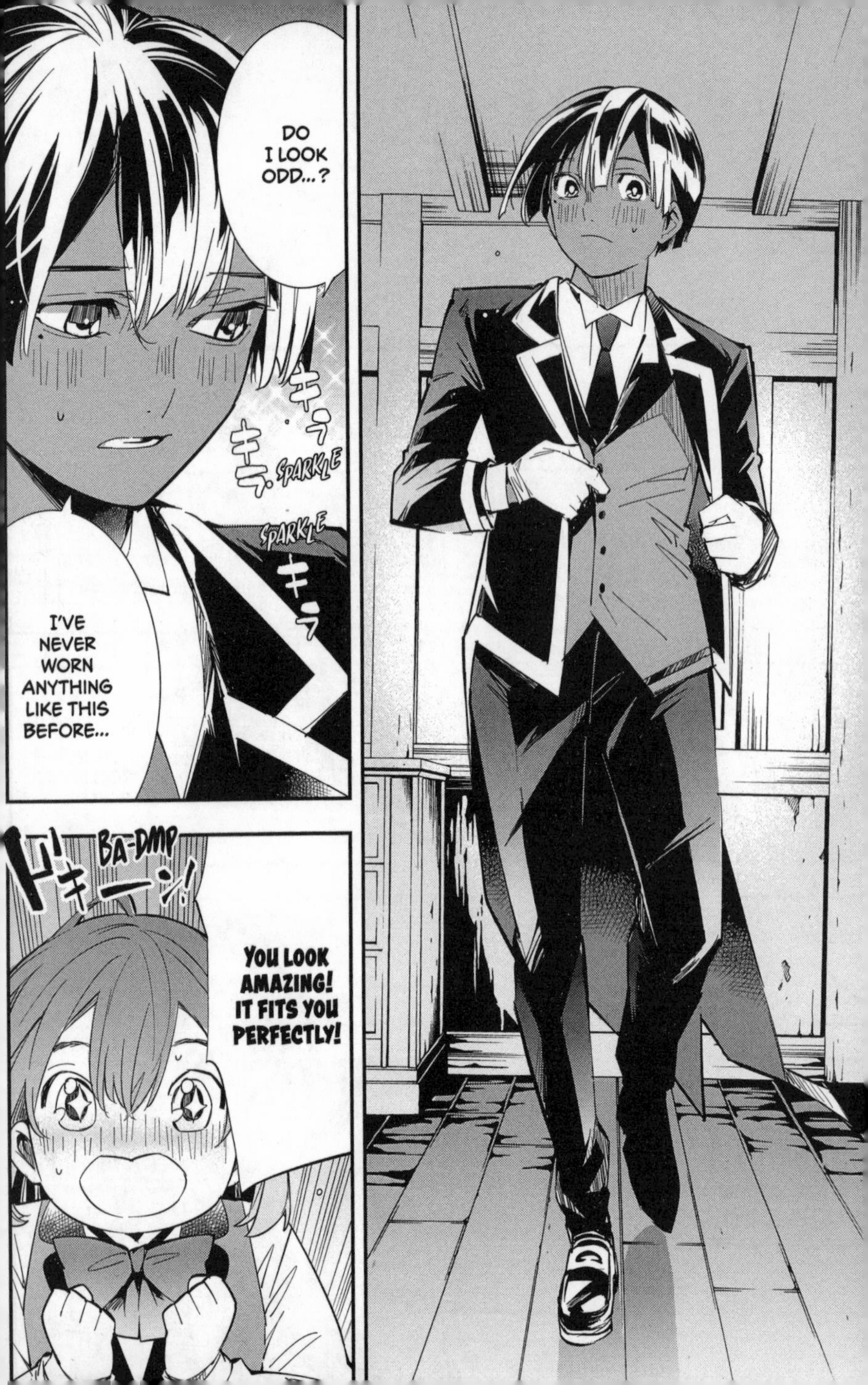
DO I LOOK ODD...?
キラ
キラ
SPARKLE
SPARKLE
キラ
I'VE NEVER WORN ANYTHING LIKE THIS BEFORE...
ドキーン!
BA-DMP
YOU LOOK AMAZING! IT FITS YOU PERFECTLY!

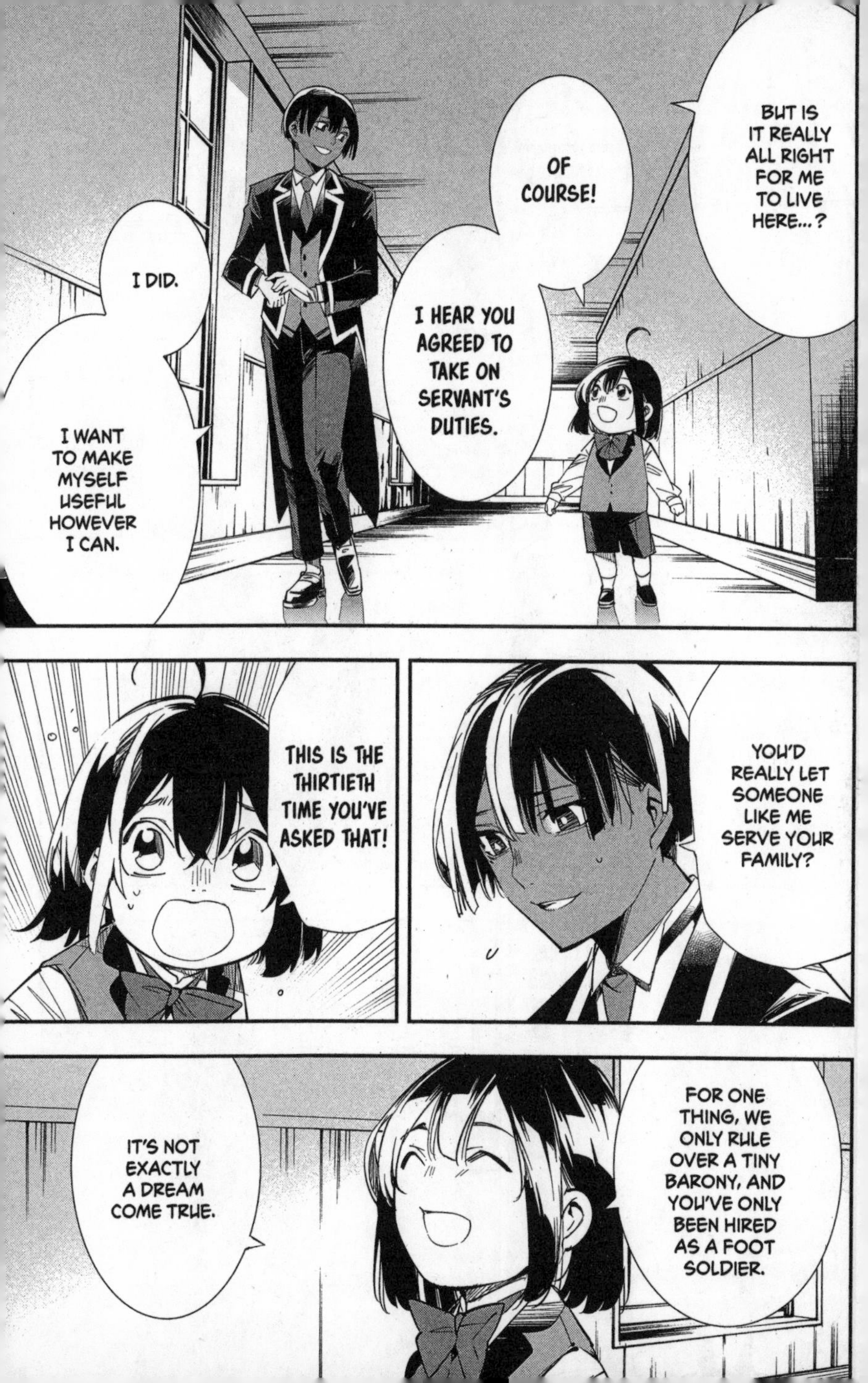
BUT IS IT REALLY ALL RIGHT FOR ME TO LIVE HERE...?
OF COURSE!
I HEAR YOU AGREED TO TAKE ON SERVANT'S DUTIES.
I DID.
I WANT TO MAKE MYSELF USEFUL HOWEVER I CAN.
YOU'D REALLY LET SOMEONE LIKE ME SERVE YOUR FAMILY?
THIS IS THE THIRTIETH TIME YOU'VE ASKED THAT!
FOR ONE THING, WE ONLY RULE OVER A TINY BARONY, AND YOU'VE ONLY BEEN HIRED AS A FOOT SOLDIER.
IT'S NOT EXACTLY A DREAM COME TRUE.

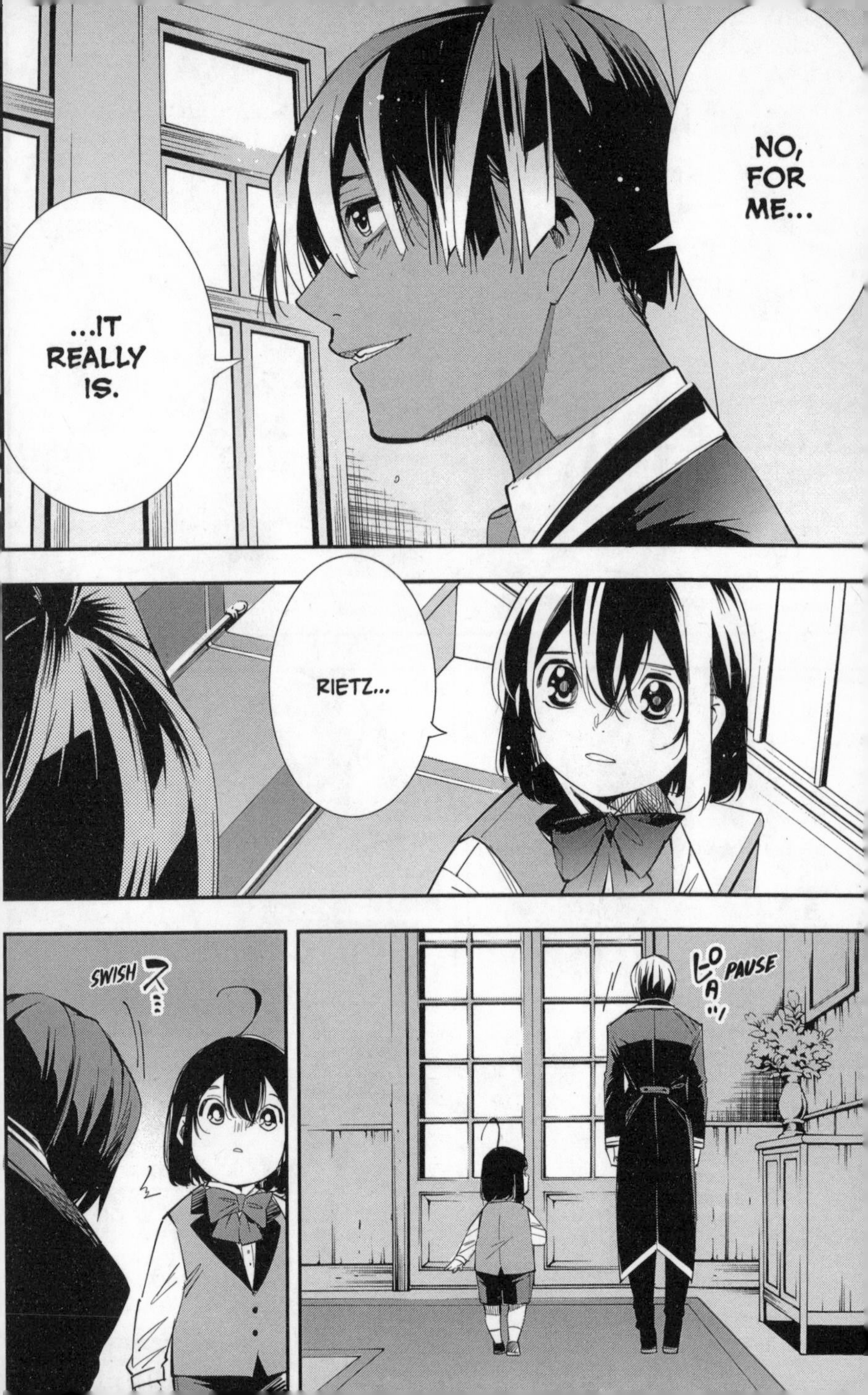
NO, FOR ME...
...IT REALLY IS.
RIETZ...
ピタッ PAUSE
SWISH ス…

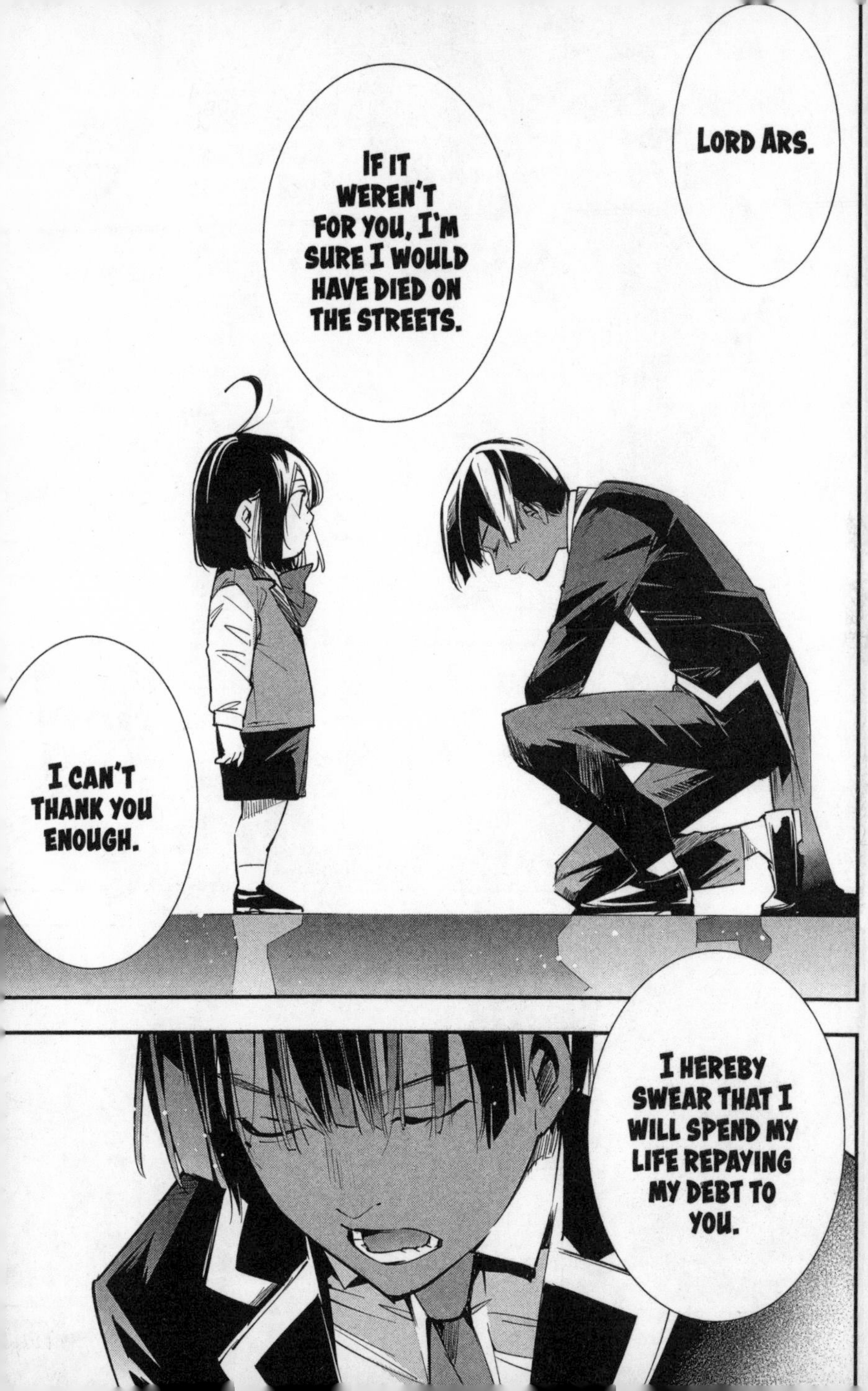
LORD ARS.
IF IT WEREN'T FOR YOU, I'M SURE I WOULD HAVE DIED ON THE STREETS.
I CAN'T THANK YOU ENOUGH.
I HEREBY SWEAR THAT I WILL SPEND MY LIFE REPAYING MY DEBT TO YOU.

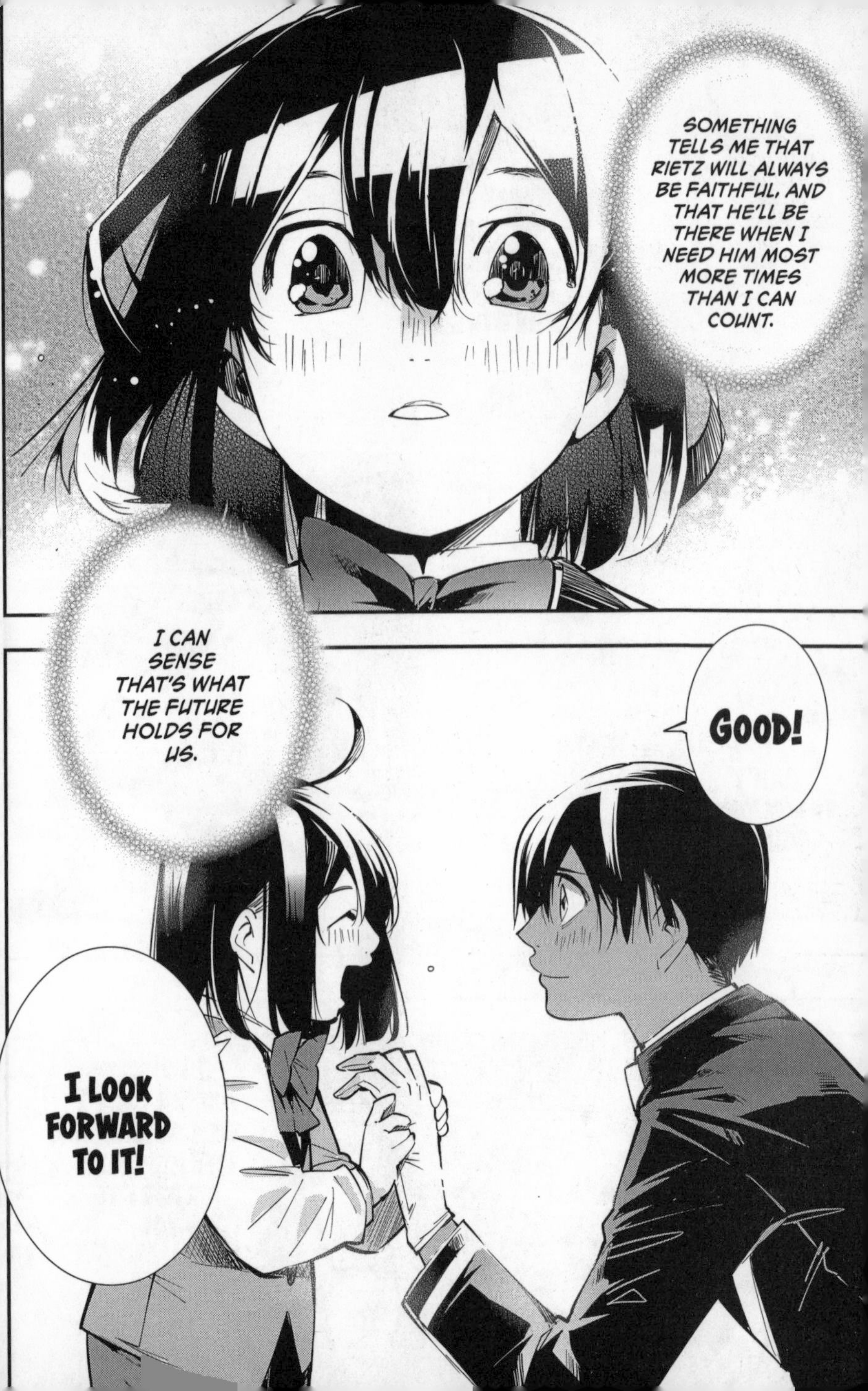
SOMETHING TELLS ME THAT RIETZ WILL ALWAYS BE FAITHFUL, AND THAT HE'LL BE THERE WHEN I NEED HIM MOST MORE TIMES THAN I CAN COUNT.
I CAN SENSE THAT'S WHAT THE FUTURE HOLDS FOR US.
GOOD!
I LOOK FORWARD TO IT!

I USED TO BE A SALARYMAN IN MODERN JAPAN, BUT I DIED AND WAS REBORN IN THIS STRANGE WORLD.

MY NAME IS ARS LOUVENT. I'M THREE YEARS OLD, AND I'M THE SON OF A BARON.

I CAN SEE THEIR STATS AND APTITUDES AS NUMBERS.

I LEARNED THAT I HAVE THE POWER TO APPRAISE PEOPLE'S ABILITIES.

USING THIS SKILL OF MINE, I SUCCEEDED IN SCOUTING RIETZ AND BRINGING HIS OUTSTANDING ABILITIES TO OUR SIDE.

Rietz Muses · Age 14

Stats	CURRENT	MAX
Command	87	99
Prowess	70	90
Intellect	72	99
Diplomacy	78	100
Ambition	21	

Aptitude		
Fighter A	Cavalier S	Archer A
Mage C	Engineer S	Armorer A
Mariner D	Pilot C	Tactician S

...I'LL HAVE TO USE MY APPRAISAL SKILL TO FIND THE MOST TALENTED PEOPLE AND BUILD THE STRONGEST DOMAIN POSSIBLE!

IN ORDER TO SURVIVE THE COMING TURMOIL...

PUMP

Chapter 4: On the Brink

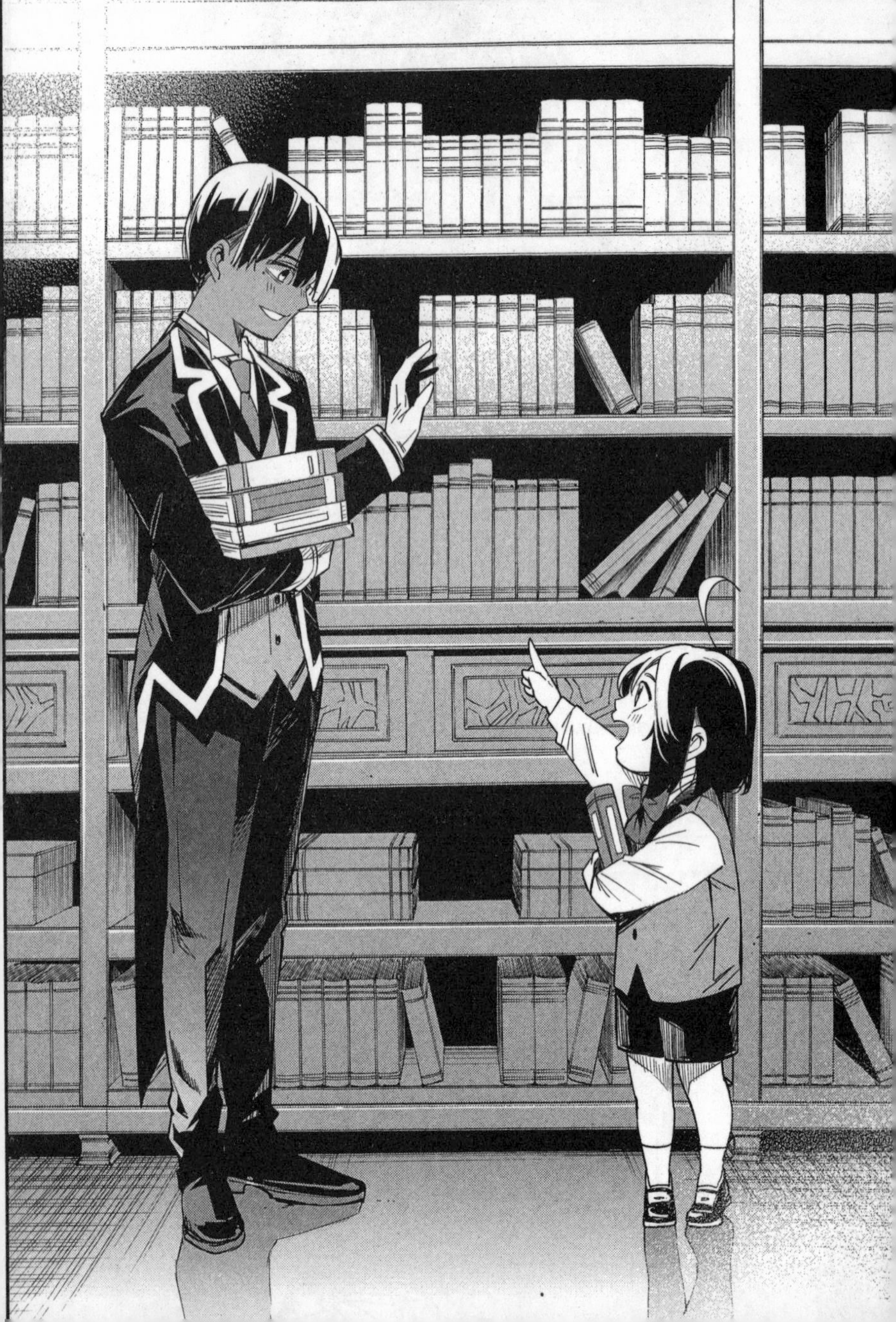

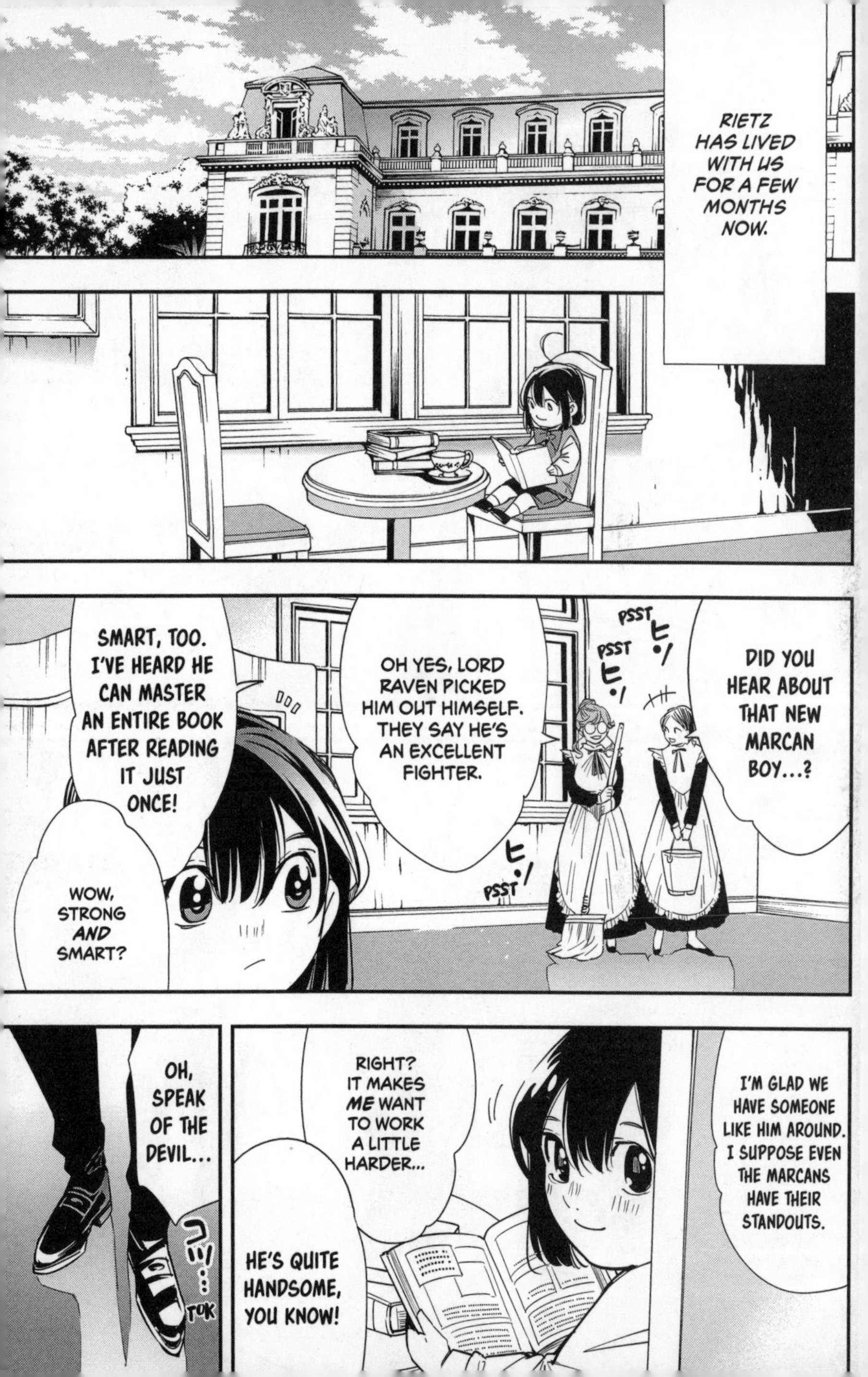
RIETZ HAS LIVED WITH US FOR A FEW MONTHS NOW.
PSST
PSST
DID YOU HEAR ABOUT THAT NEW MARCAN BOY...?
OH YES, LORD RAVEN PICKED HIM OUT HIMSELF. THEY SAY HE'S AN EXCELLENT FIGHTER.
PSST
SMART, TOO. I'VE HEARD HE CAN MASTER AN ENTIRE BOOK AFTER READING IT JUST ONCE!
WOW, STRONG *AND* SMART?
I'M GLAD WE HAVE SOMEONE LIKE HIM AROUND. I SUPPOSE EVEN THE MARCANS HAVE THEIR STANDOUTS.
RIGHT? IT MAKES *ME* WANT TO WORK A LITTLE HARDER...
HE'S QUITE HANDSOME, YOU KNOW!
OH, SPEAK OF THE DEVIL...
TOK

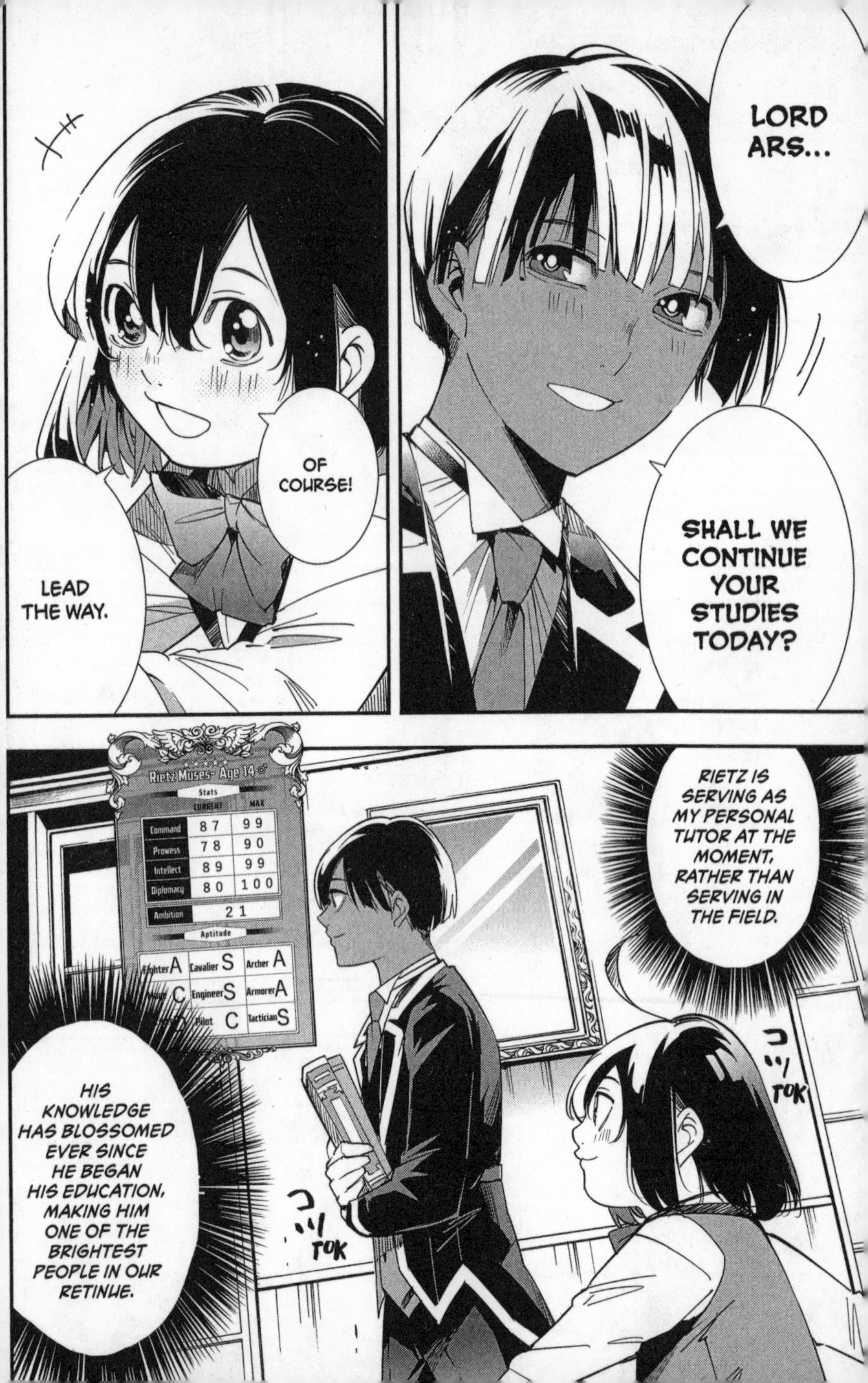
LORD ARS...
SHALL WE CONTINUE YOUR STUDIES TODAY?
OF COURSE!
LEAD THE WAY.
RIETZ IS SERVING AS MY PERSONAL TUTOR AT THE MOMENT, RATHER THAN SERVING IN THE FIELD.
Rietz Muses- Age 14 ♂
Stats
CURRENT MAX
Command 87 99
Prowess 78 90
Intellect 89 99
Diplomacy 80 100
Ambition 21
Aptitude
Cavalier S Archer A
Engineer S Armorer A
Pilot C Tactician S
コツ TOK
HIS KNOWLEDGE HAS BLOSSOMED EVER SINCE HE BEGAN HIS EDUCATION, MAKING HIM ONE OF THE BRIGHTEST PEOPLE IN OUR RETINUE.
コツ TOK

LET'S DISCUSS THE CURRENT STATE OF THE SUMMERFORTH EMPIRE.
AS YOU'LL REMEMBER FROM OUR LAST LESSON, THE CONTINENT OF SUMMERFORTH WAS ORIGINALLY COMPOSED OF SEVEN KINGDOMS, WHICH UNIFIED UNDER THE SUMMERFORTH EMPIRE.
Kingdom of Rofeille
Kingdom of Canshiep
Kingdom of Ansel
Kingdom of Paradille
Kingdom of Sheutz
Kingdom of Missian
Kingdom of Seitz
Summerforth Empire
RIGHT.
THE KINGDOM OF ANSEL, WHICH SAT UPON A STRAIT BETWEEN SUMMERFORTH AND ANOTHER CONTINENT...
Ansel
Other Conti-nent
...WAS ABLE TO TRADE WITH LANDS BEYOND SUMMER-FORTH...
...THEREBY GROWING POWERFUL ENOUGH TO CONQUER THE OTHER KINGDOMS.
AFTER INVADING THE OTHER KINGDOMS, KING ANATHIS BYDORAS OF ANSEL NAMED HIMSELF EMPEROR OF SUMMER-FORTH.
THAT WAS 203 YEARS AGO.
King Bydoras
HURRAH

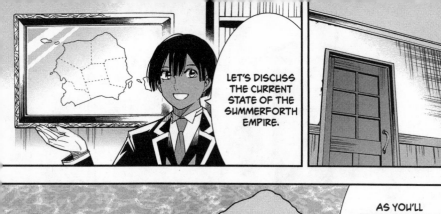

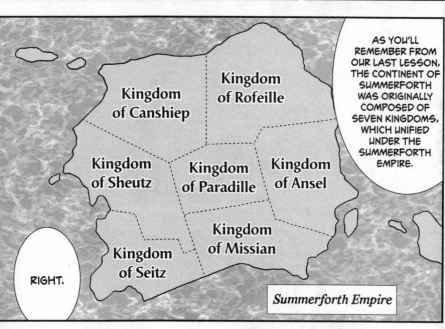

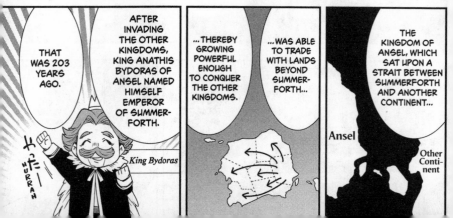

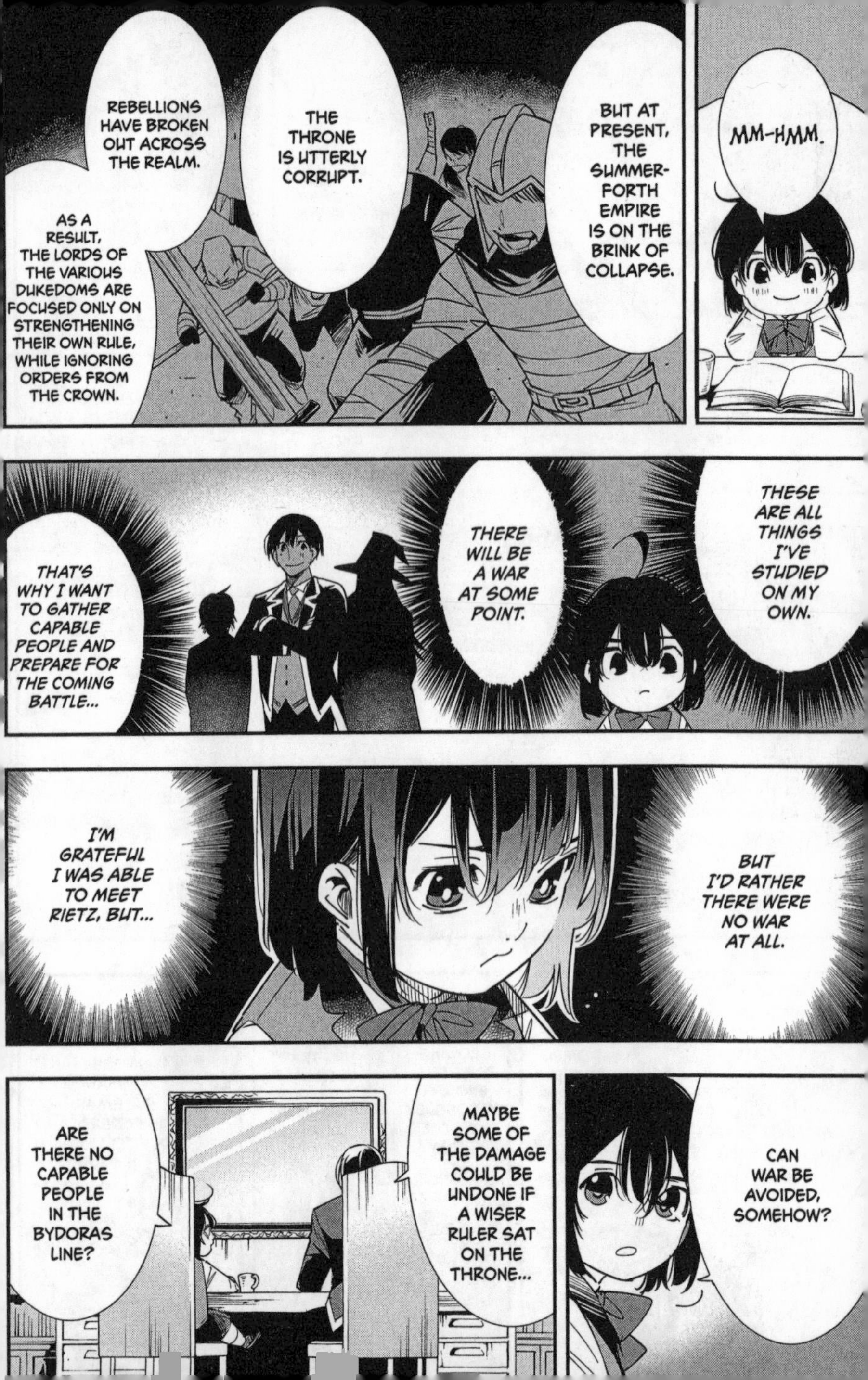
MM-HMM.
BUT AT PRESENT, THE SUMMER-FORTH EMPIRE IS ON THE BRINK OF COLLAPSE.
THE THRONE IS UTTERLY CORRUPT.
REBELLIONS HAVE BROKEN OUT ACROSS THE REALM.
AS A RESULT, THE LORDS OF THE VARIOUS DUKEDOMS ARE FOCUSED ONLY ON STRENGTHENING THEIR OWN RULE, WHILE IGNORING ORDERS FROM THE CROWN.
THESE ARE ALL THINGS I'VE STUDIED ON MY OWN.
THERE WILL BE A WAR AT SOME POINT.
THAT'S WHY I WANT TO GATHER CAPABLE PEOPLE AND PREPARE FOR THE COMING BATTLE...
BUT I'D RATHER THERE WERE NO WAR AT ALL.
I'M GRATEFUL I WAS ABLE TO MEET RIETZ, BUT...
CAN WAR BE AVOIDED, SOMEHOW?
MAYBE SOME OF THE DAMAGE COULD BE UNDONE IF A WISER RULER SAT ON THE THRONE...
ARE THERE NO CAPABLE PEOPLE IN THE BYDORAS LINE?

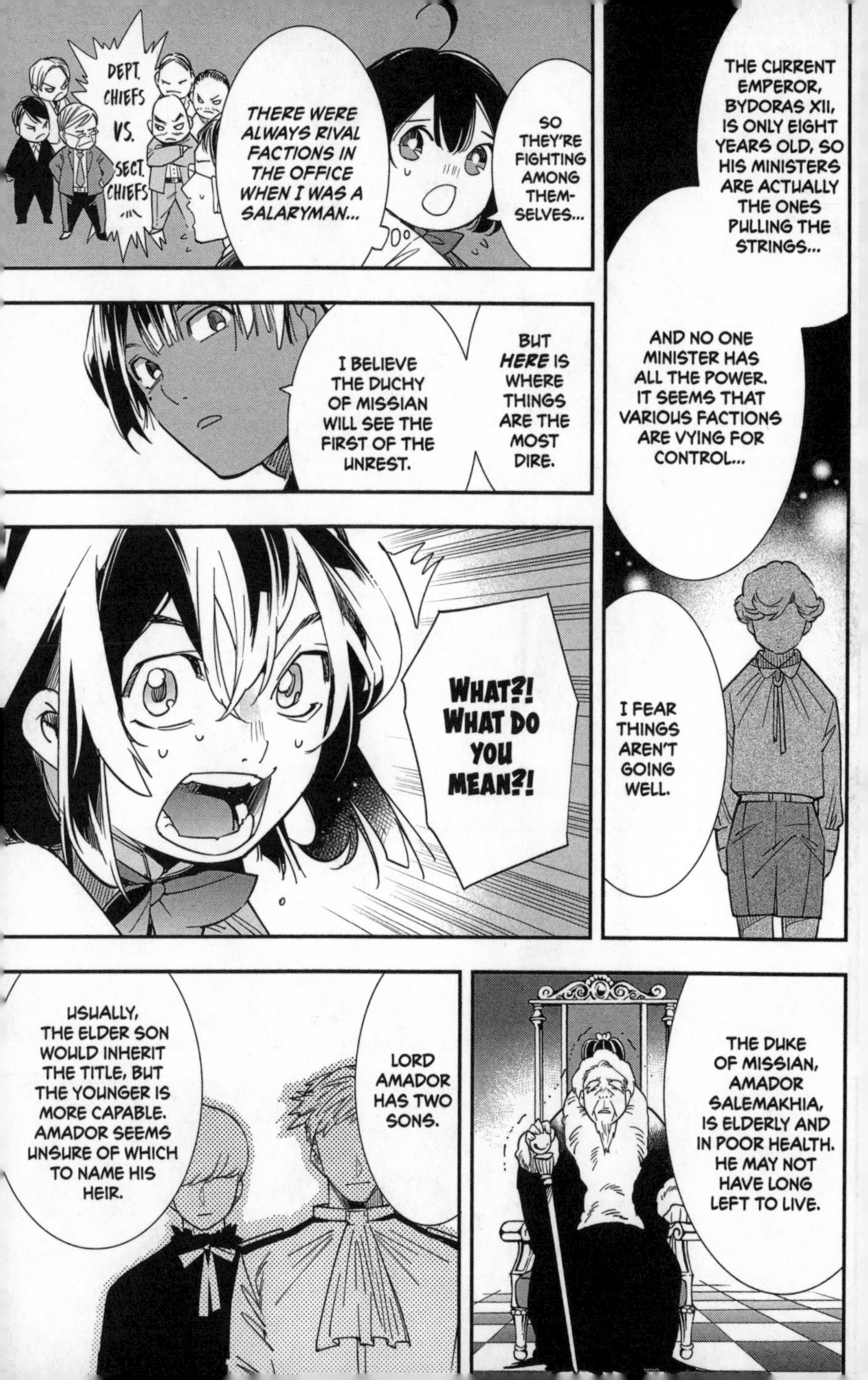
THE CURRENT EMPEROR, BYDORAS XII, IS ONLY EIGHT YEARS OLD, SO HIS MINISTERS ARE ACTUALLY THE ONES PULLING THE STRINGS...
AND NO ONE MINISTER HAS ALL THE POWER. IT SEEMS THAT VARIOUS FACTIONS ARE VYING FOR CONTROL...
I FEAR THINGS AREN'T GOING WELL.
SO THEY'RE FIGHTING AMONG THEM-SELVES...
THERE WERE ALWAYS RIVAL FACTIONS IN THE OFFICE WHEN I WAS A SALARYMAN...
DEPT. CHIEFS
VS.
SECT. CHIEFS
BUT HERE IS WHERE THINGS ARE THE MOST DIRE.
I BELIEVE THE DUCHY OF MISSIAN WILL SEE THE FIRST OF THE UNREST.
WHAT?! WHAT DO YOU MEAN?!
THE DUKE OF MISSIAN, AMADOR SALEMAKHIA, IS ELDERLY AND IN POOR HEALTH. HE MAY NOT HAVE LONG LEFT TO LIVE.
LORD AMADOR HAS TWO SONS.
USUALLY, THE ELDER SON WOULD INHERIT THE TITLE, BUT THE YOUNGER IS MORE CAPABLE. AMADOR SEEMS UNSURE OF WHICH TO NAME HIS HEIR.

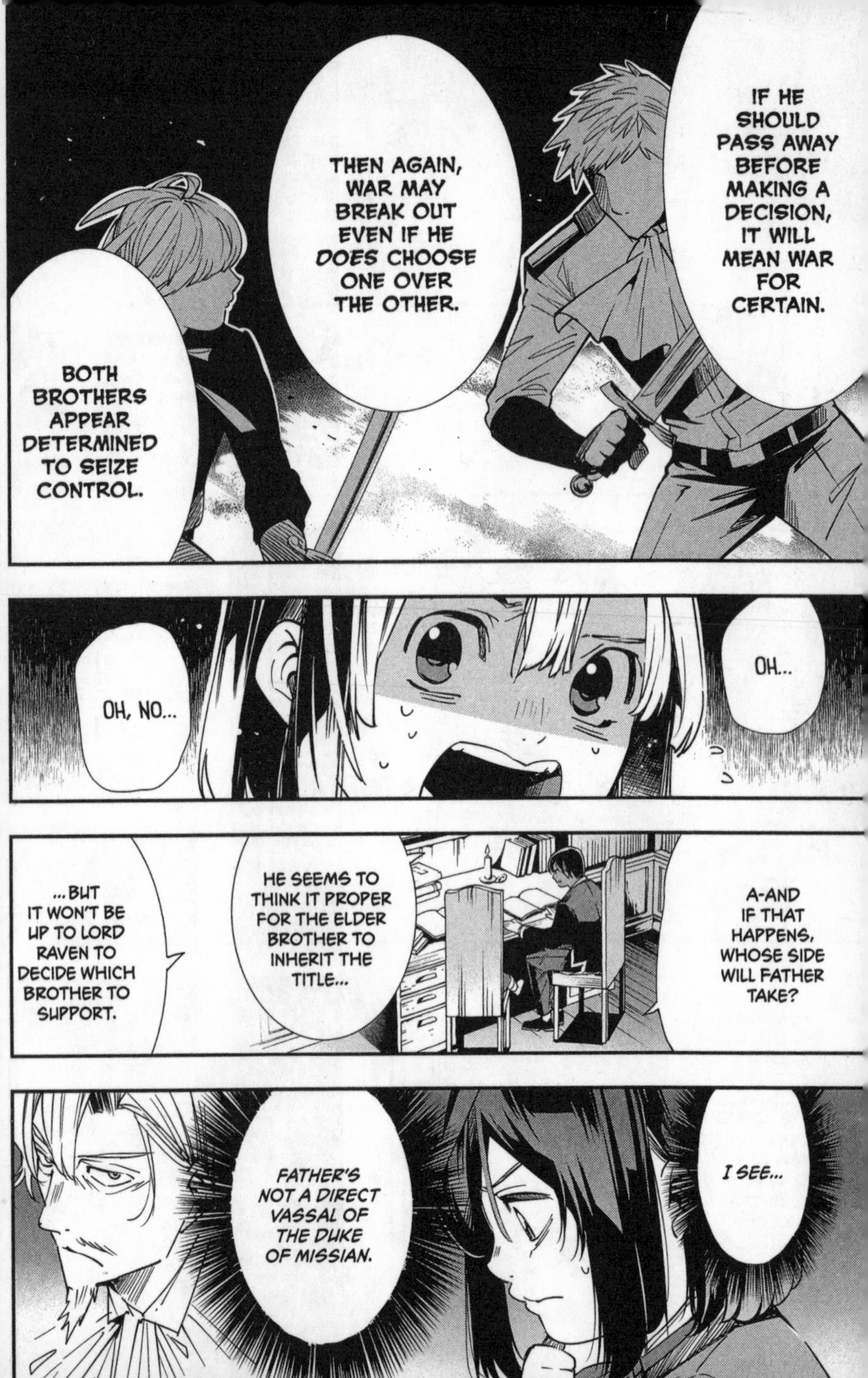
IF HE SHOULD PASS AWAY BEFORE MAKING A DECISION, IT WILL MEAN WAR FOR CERTAIN.
THEN AGAIN, WAR MAY BREAK OUT EVEN IF HE *DOES* CHOOSE ONE OVER THE OTHER.
BOTH BROTHERS APPEAR DETERMINED TO SEIZE CONTROL.
OH...
OH, NO...
A-AND IF THAT HAPPENS, WHOSE SIDE WILL FATHER TAKE?
HE SEEMS TO THINK IT PROPER FOR THE ELDER BROTHER TO INHERIT THE TITLE...
...BUT IT WON'T BE UP TO LORD RAVEN TO DECIDE WHICH BROTHER TO SUPPORT.
I SEE...
FATHER'S NOT A DIRECT VASSAL OF THE DUKE OF MISSIAN.

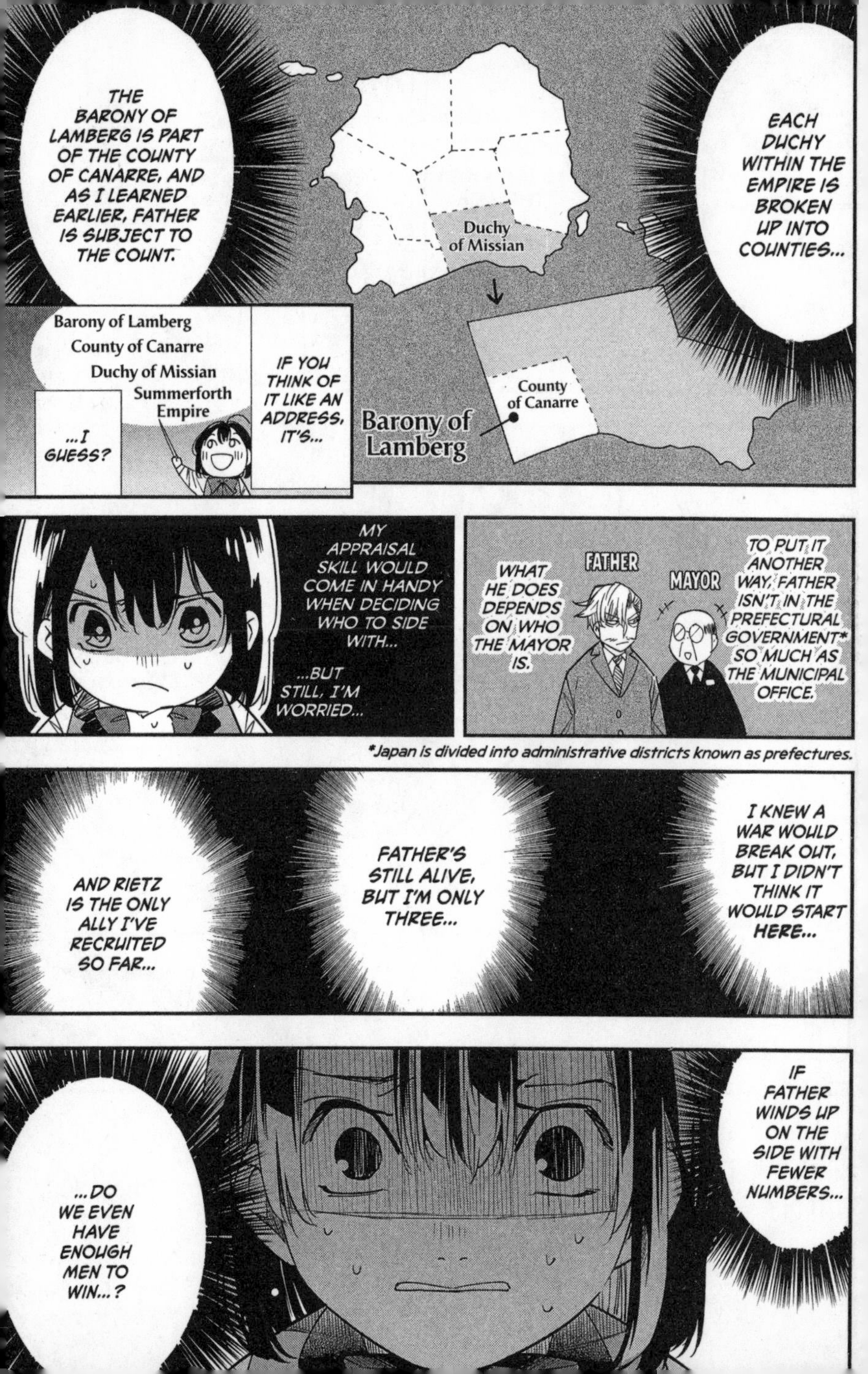
EACH DUCHY WITHIN THE EMPIRE IS BROKEN UP INTO COUNTIES...
Duchy of Missian
County of Canarre
Barony of Lamberg
THE BARONY OF LAMBERG IS PART OF THE COUNTY OF CANARRE, AND AS I LEARNED EARLIER, FATHER IS SUBJECT TO THE COUNT.
IF YOU THINK OF IT LIKE AN ADDRESS, IT'S...
Barony of Lamberg
County of Canarre
Duchy of Missian
Summerforth Empire
...I GUESS?
TO PUT IT ANOTHER WAY, FATHER ISN'T IN THE PREFECTURAL GOVERNMENT* SO MUCH AS THE MUNICIPAL OFFICE.
MAYOR
FATHER
WHAT HE DOES DEPENDS ON WHO THE MAYOR IS.
MY APPRAISAL SKILL WOULD COME IN HANDY WHEN DECIDING WHO TO SIDE WITH...
...BUT STILL, I'M WORRIED...
I KNEW A WAR WOULD BREAK OUT, BUT I DIDN'T THINK IT WOULD START HERE...
FATHER'S STILL ALIVE, BUT I'M ONLY THREE...
AND RIETZ IS THE ONLY ALLY I'VE RECRUITED SO FAR...
IF FATHER WINDS UP ON THE SIDE WITH FEWER NUMBERS...
...DO WE EVEN HAVE ENOUGH MEN TO WIN...?

*Japan is divided into administrative districts known as prefectures.

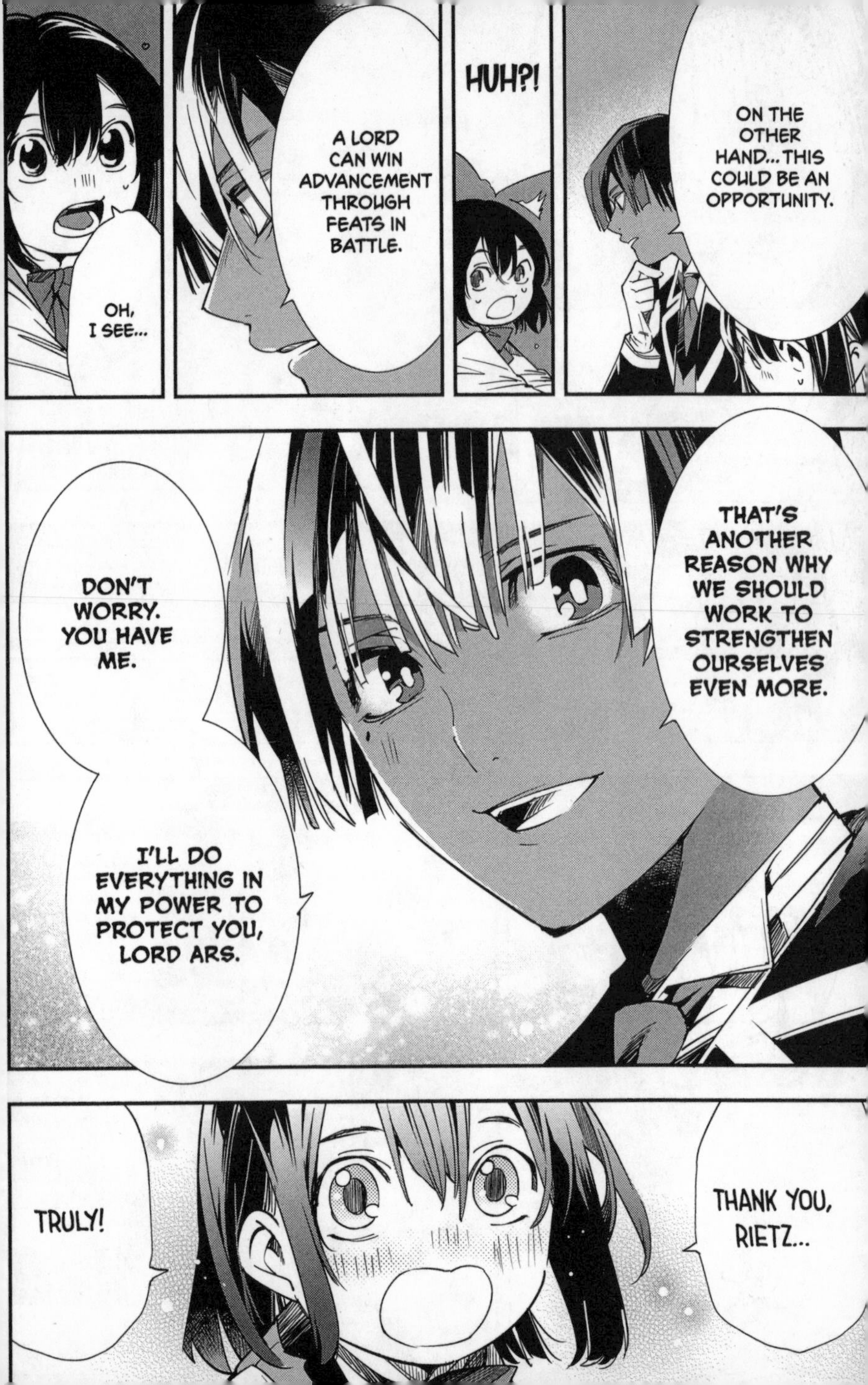
ON THE OTHER HAND... THIS COULD BE AN OPPORTUNITY.
HUH?!
A LORD CAN WIN ADVANCEMENT THROUGH FEATS IN BATTLE.
OH, I SEE...
THAT'S ANOTHER REASON WHY WE SHOULD WORK TO STRENGTHEN OURSELVES EVEN MORE.
DON'T WORRY. YOU HAVE ME.
I'LL DO EVERYTHING IN MY POWER TO PROTECT YOU, LORD ARS.
THANK YOU, RIETZ...
TRULY!

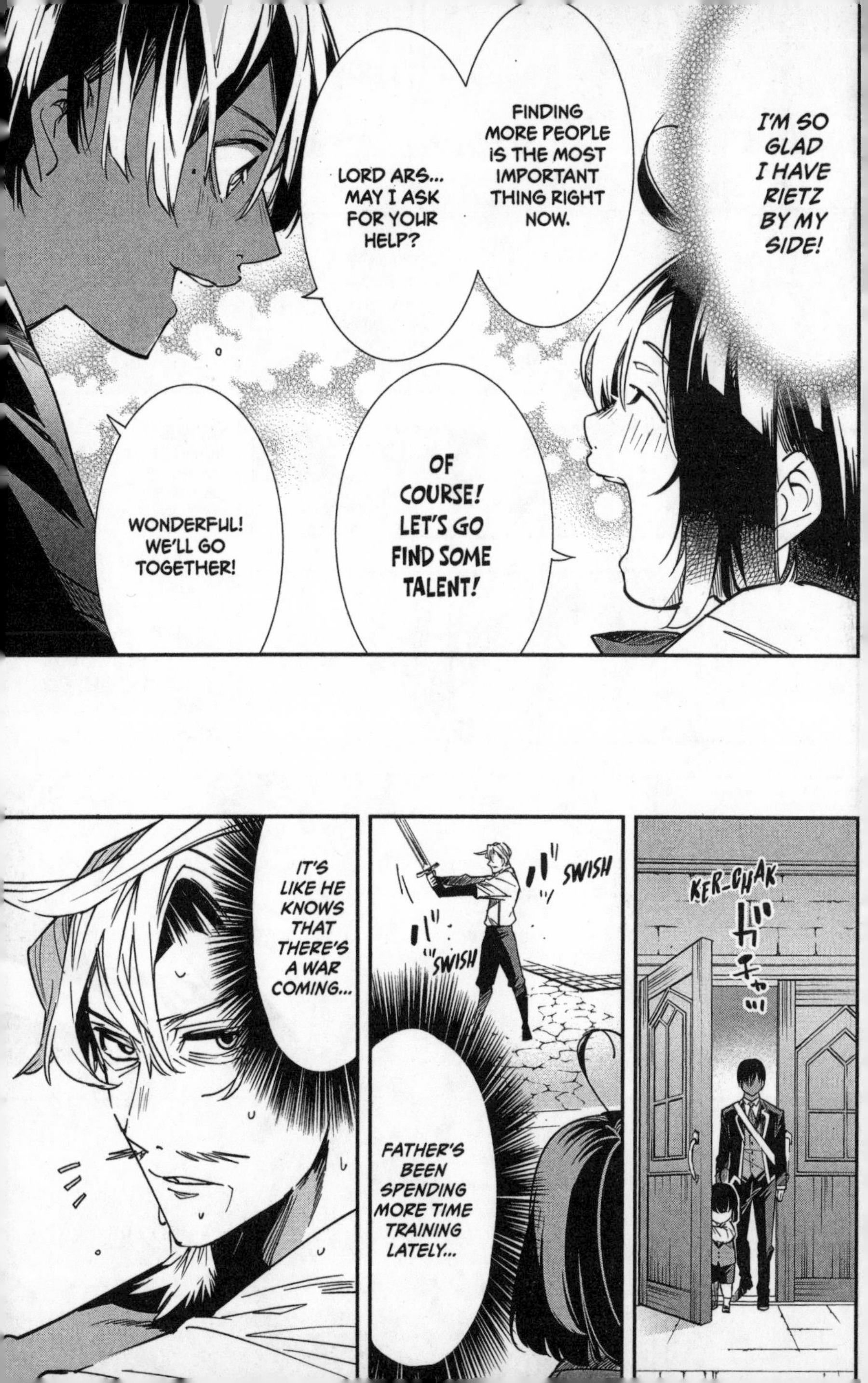
I'M SO GLAD I HAVE RIETZ BY MY SIDE!
FINDING MORE PEOPLE IS THE MOST IMPORTANT THING RIGHT NOW.
LORD ARS... MAY I ASK FOR YOUR HELP?
OF COURSE! LET'S GO FIND SOME TALENT!
WONDERFUL! WE'LL GO TOGETHER!
KER-CHAK
ガチャ
SWISH
SWISH
FATHER'S BEEN SPENDING MORE TIME TRAINING LATELY...
IT'S LIKE HE KNOWS THAT THERE'S A WAR COMING...

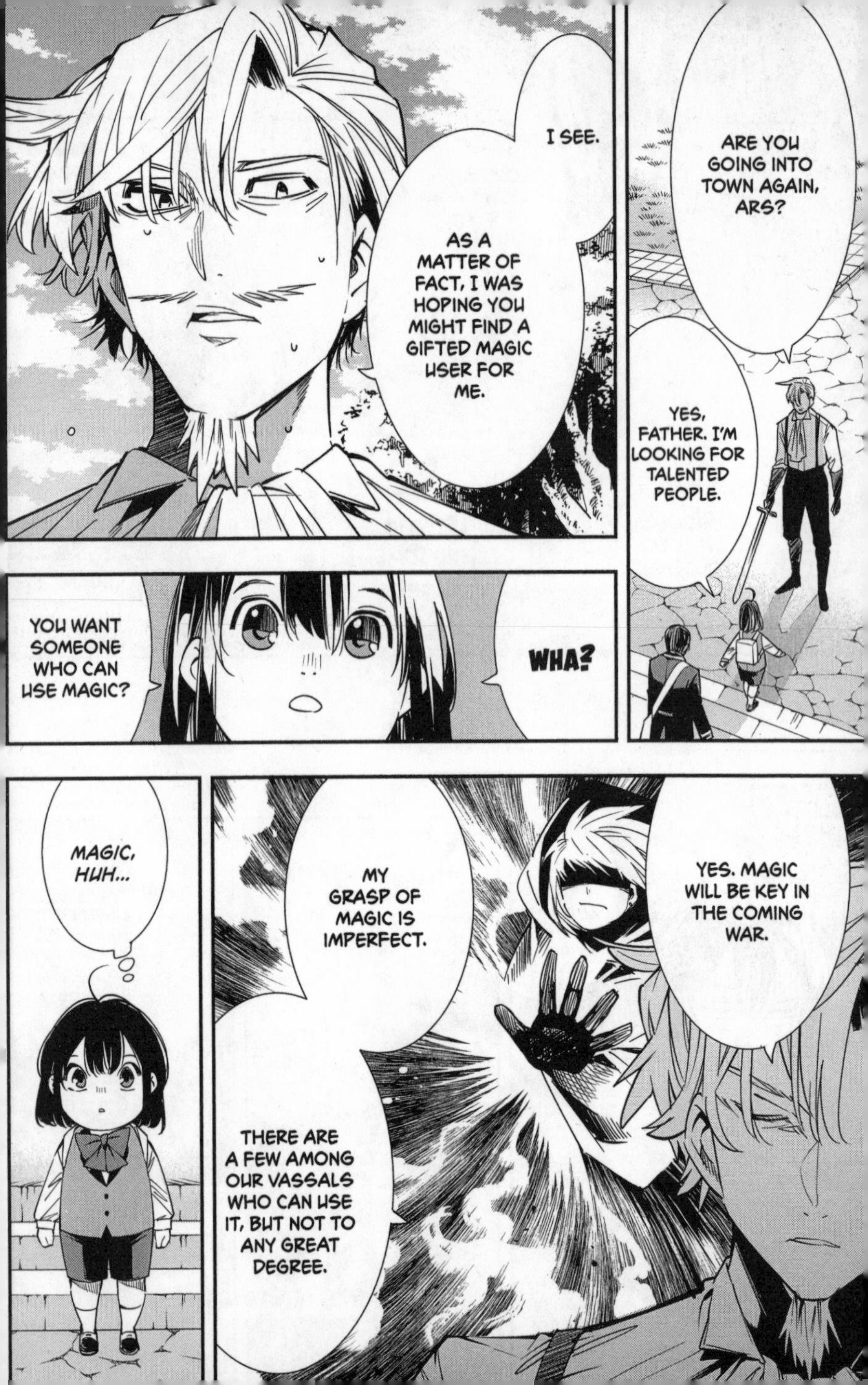
ARE YOU GOING INTO TOWN AGAIN, ARS?
YES, FATHER. I'M LOOKING FOR TALENTED PEOPLE.
I SEE.
AS A MATTER OF FACT, I WAS HOPING YOU MIGHT FIND A GIFTED MAGIC USER FOR ME.
WHA?
YOU WANT SOMEONE WHO CAN USE MAGIC?
YES. MAGIC WILL BE KEY IN THE COMING WAR.
MY GRASP OF MAGIC IS IMPERFECT.
THERE ARE A FEW AMONG OUR VASSALS WHO CAN USE IT, BUT NOT TO ANY GREAT DEGREE.
MAGIC, HUH...

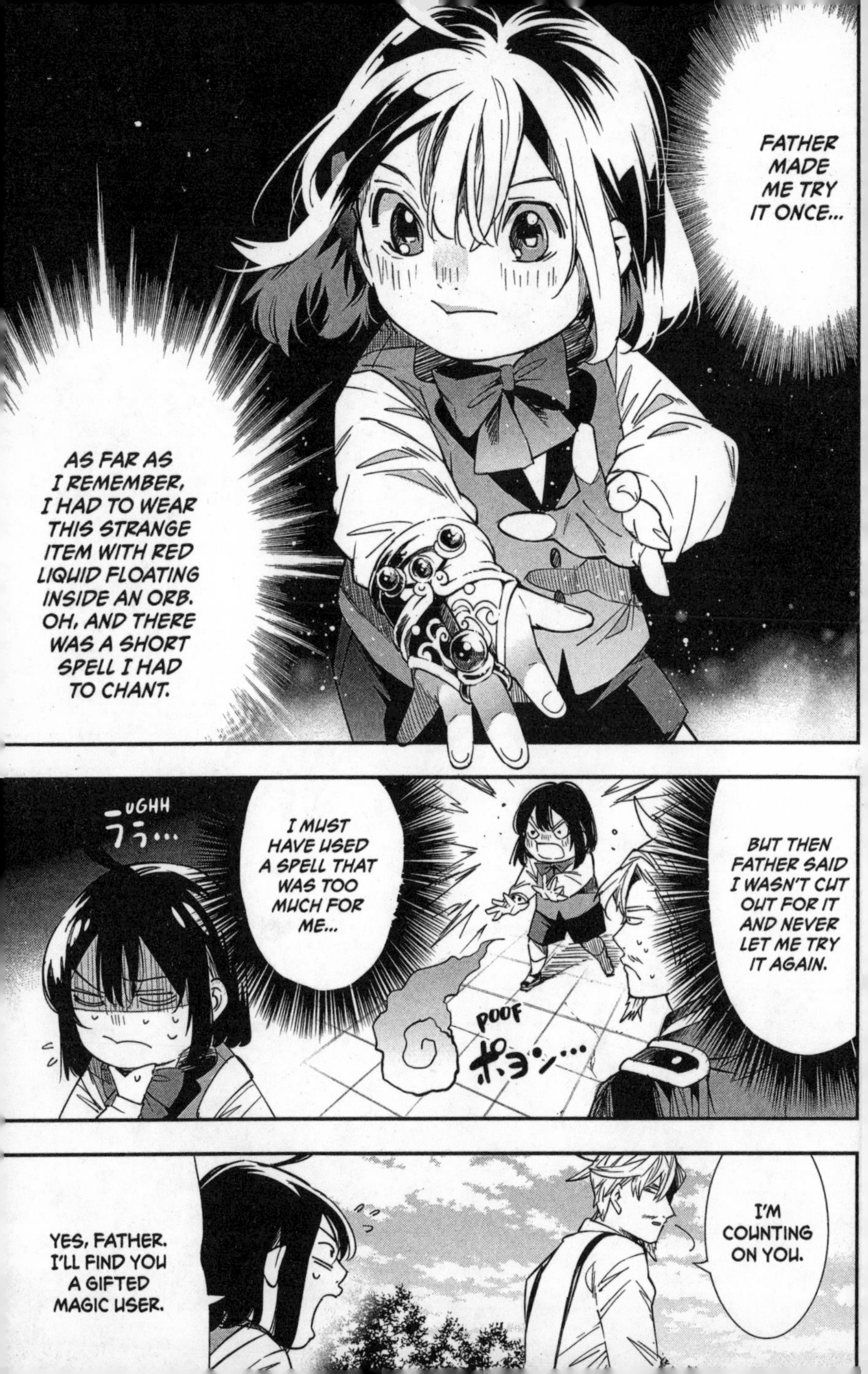
FATHER MADE ME TRY IT ONCE...
AS FAR AS I REMEMBER, I HAD TO WEAR THIS STRANGE ITEM WITH RED LIQUID FLOATING INSIDE AN ORB. OH, AND THERE WAS A SHORT SPELL I HAD TO CHANT.
BUT THEN FATHER SAID I WASN'T CUT OUT FOR IT AND NEVER LET ME TRY IT AGAIN.
I MUST HAVE USED A SPELL THAT WAS TOO MUCH FOR ME...
POOF
ポヨン…
UGHH
フラ…
I'M COUNTING ON YOU.
YES, FATHER. I'LL FIND YOU A GIFTED MAGIC USER.

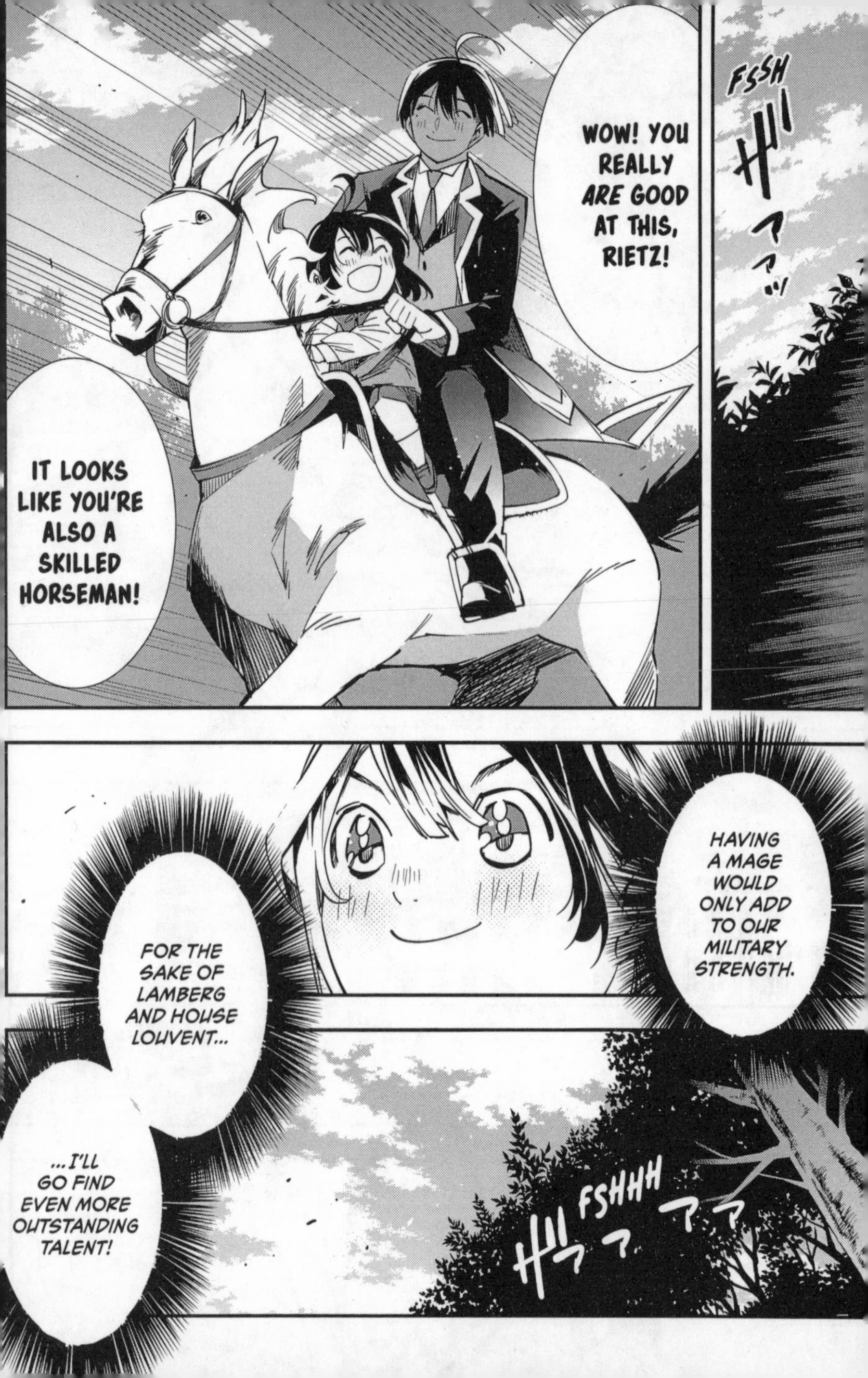
FSSH
WOW! YOU REALLY ARE GOOD AT THIS, RIETZ!
IT LOOKS LIKE YOU'RE ALSO A SKILLED HORSEMAN!
HAVING A MAGE WOULD ONLY ADD TO OUR MILITARY STRENGTH.
FOR THE SAKE OF LAMBERG AND HOUSE LOUVENT...
...I'LL GO FIND EVEN MORE OUTSTANDING TALENT!
FSHHH

Chapter 5: Inequality and Change

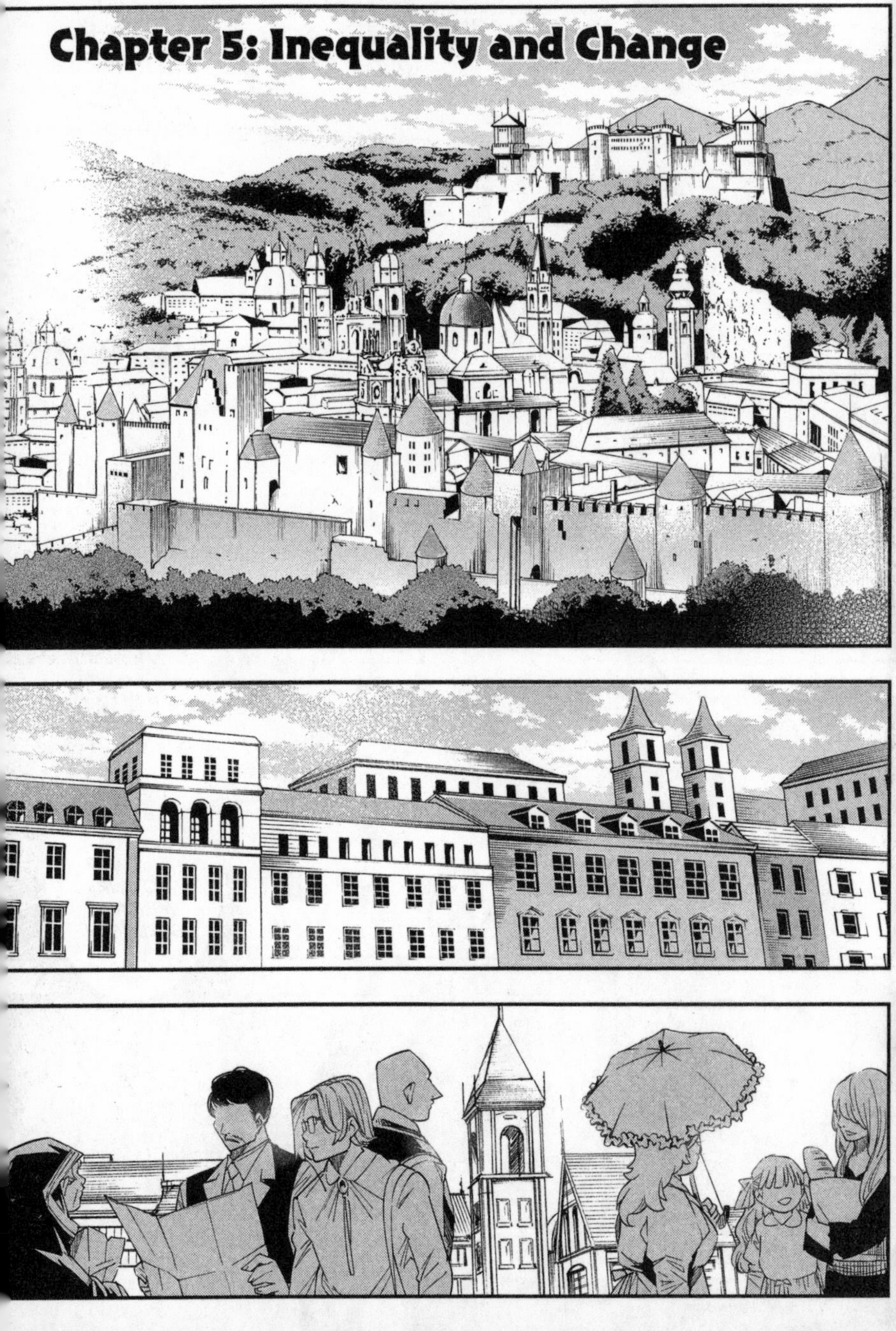

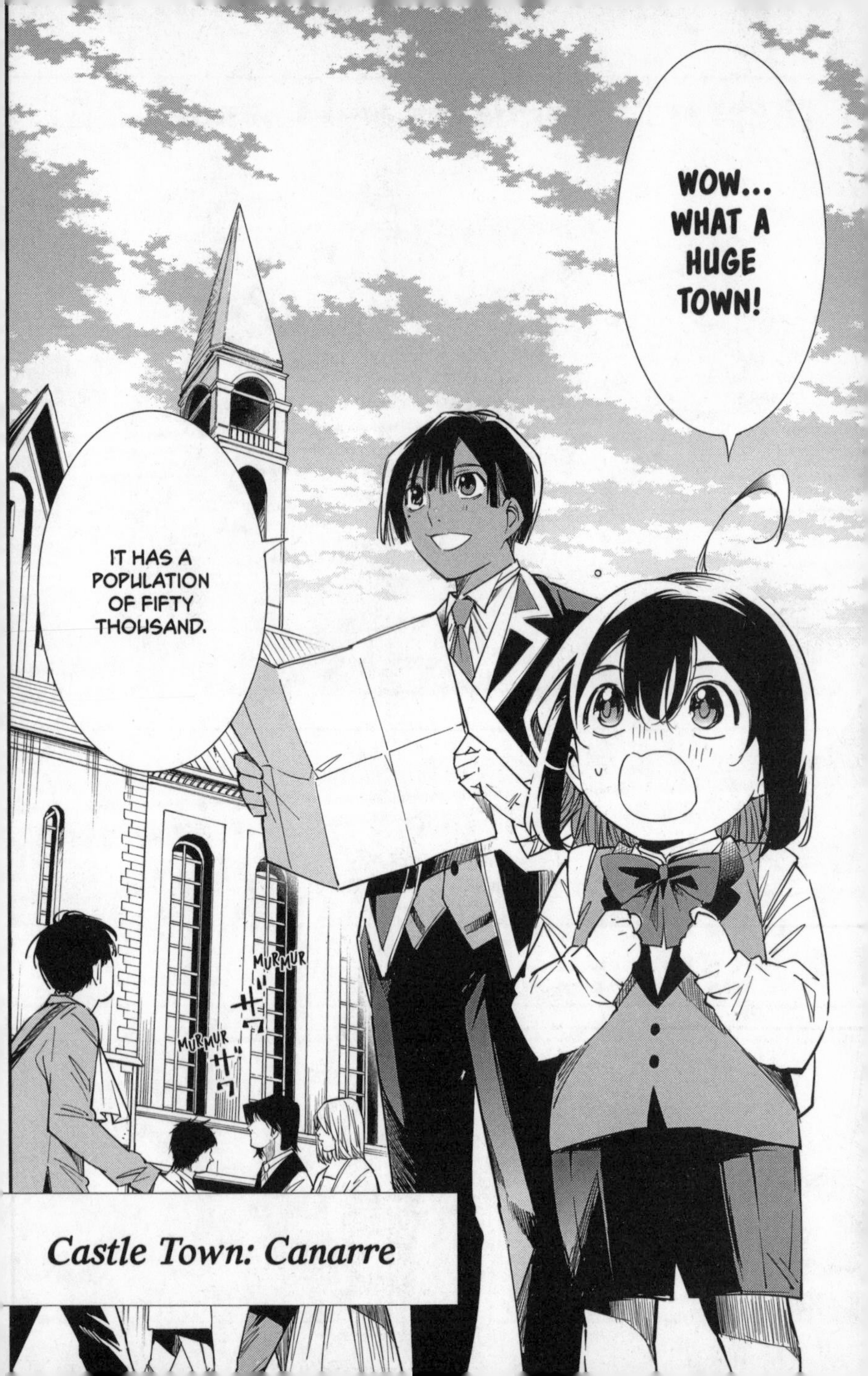
WOW... WHAT A HUGE TOWN!
IT HAS A POPULATION OF FIFTY THOUSAND.
MURMUR
MURMUR
Castle Town: Canarre

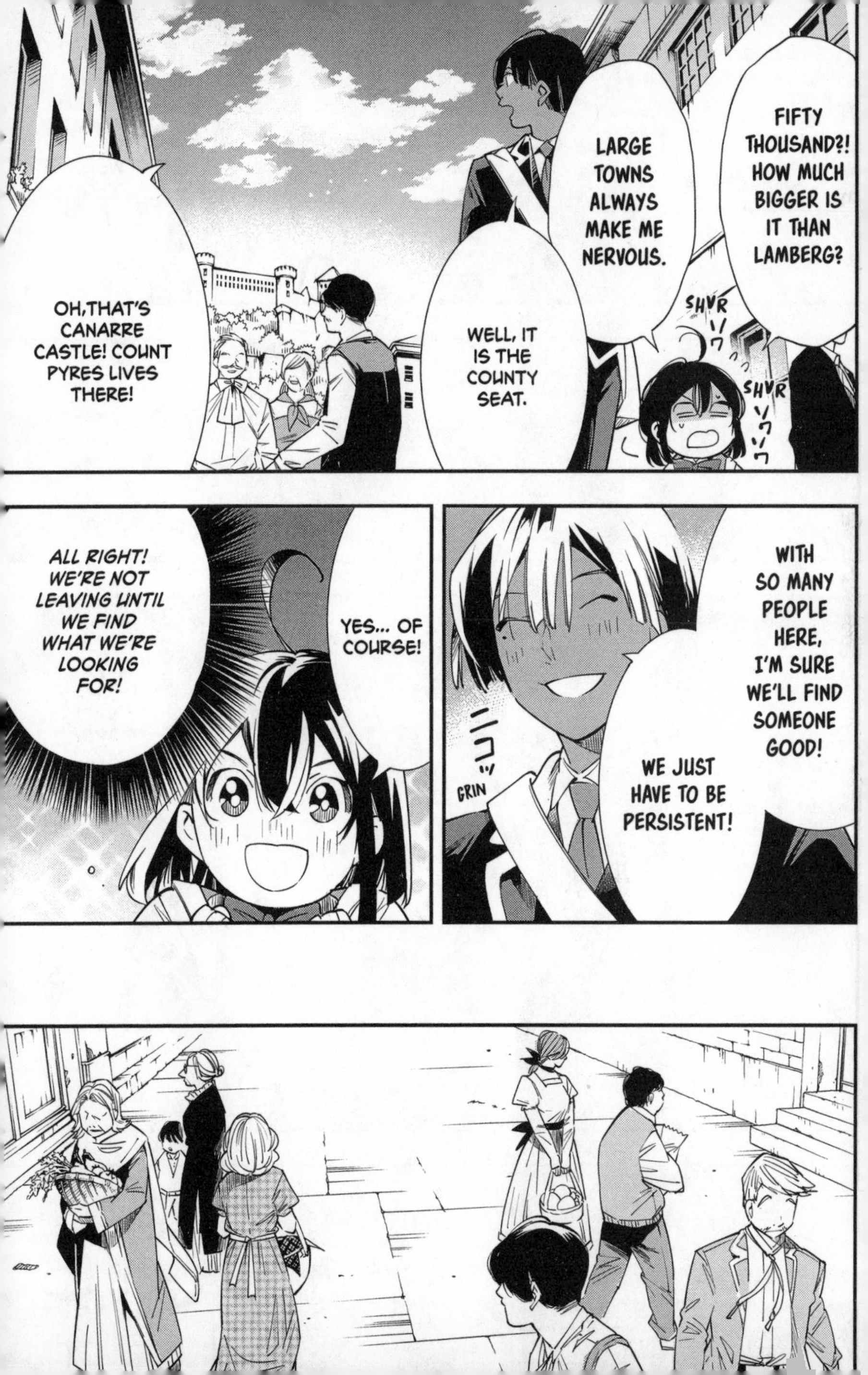
FIFTY THOUSAND?! HOW MUCH BIGGER IS IT THAN LAMBERG?
LARGE TOWNS ALWAYS MAKE ME NERVOUS.
SHVR
SHVR
WELL, IT IS THE COUNTY SEAT.
OH,THAT'S CANARRE CASTLE! COUNT PYRES LIVES THERE!
WITH SO MANY PEOPLE HERE, I'M SURE WE'LL FIND SOMEONE GOOD!
WE JUST HAVE TO BE PERSISTENT!
GRIN
YES... OF COURSE!
ALL RIGHT! WE'RE NOT LEAVING UNTIL WE FIND WHAT WE'RE LOOKING FOR!

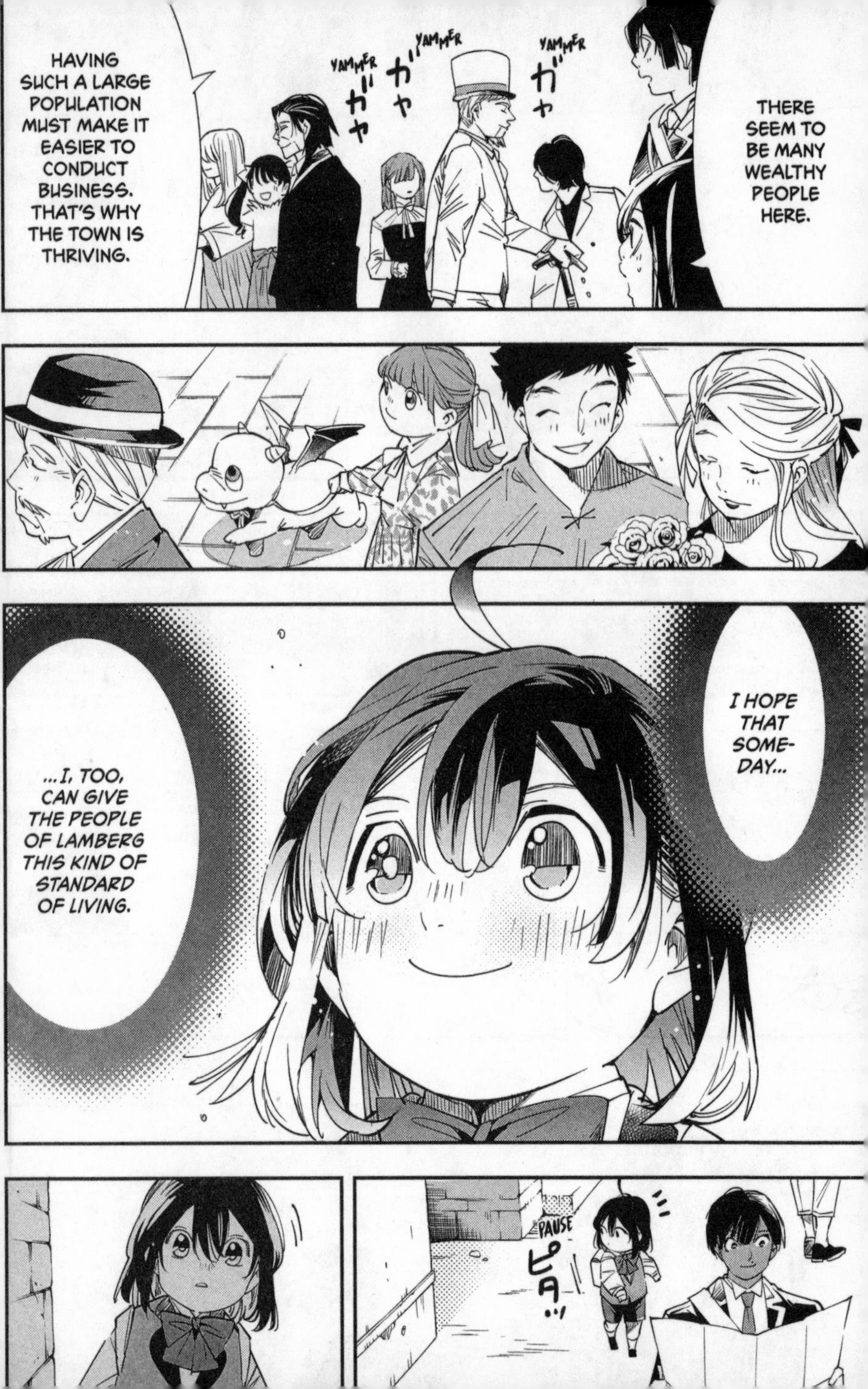
THERE SEEM TO BE MANY WEALTHY PEOPLE HERE.
YAMMER ガヤ
YAMMER ガヤ
YAMMER ガヤ
HAVING SUCH A LARGE POPULATION MUST MAKE IT EASIER TO CONDUCT BUSINESS. THAT'S WHY THE TOWN IS THRIVING.
I HOPE THAT SOME-DAY...
...I, TOO, CAN GIVE THE PEOPLE OF LAMBERG THIS KIND OF STANDARD OF LIVING.
PAUSE ピタッ

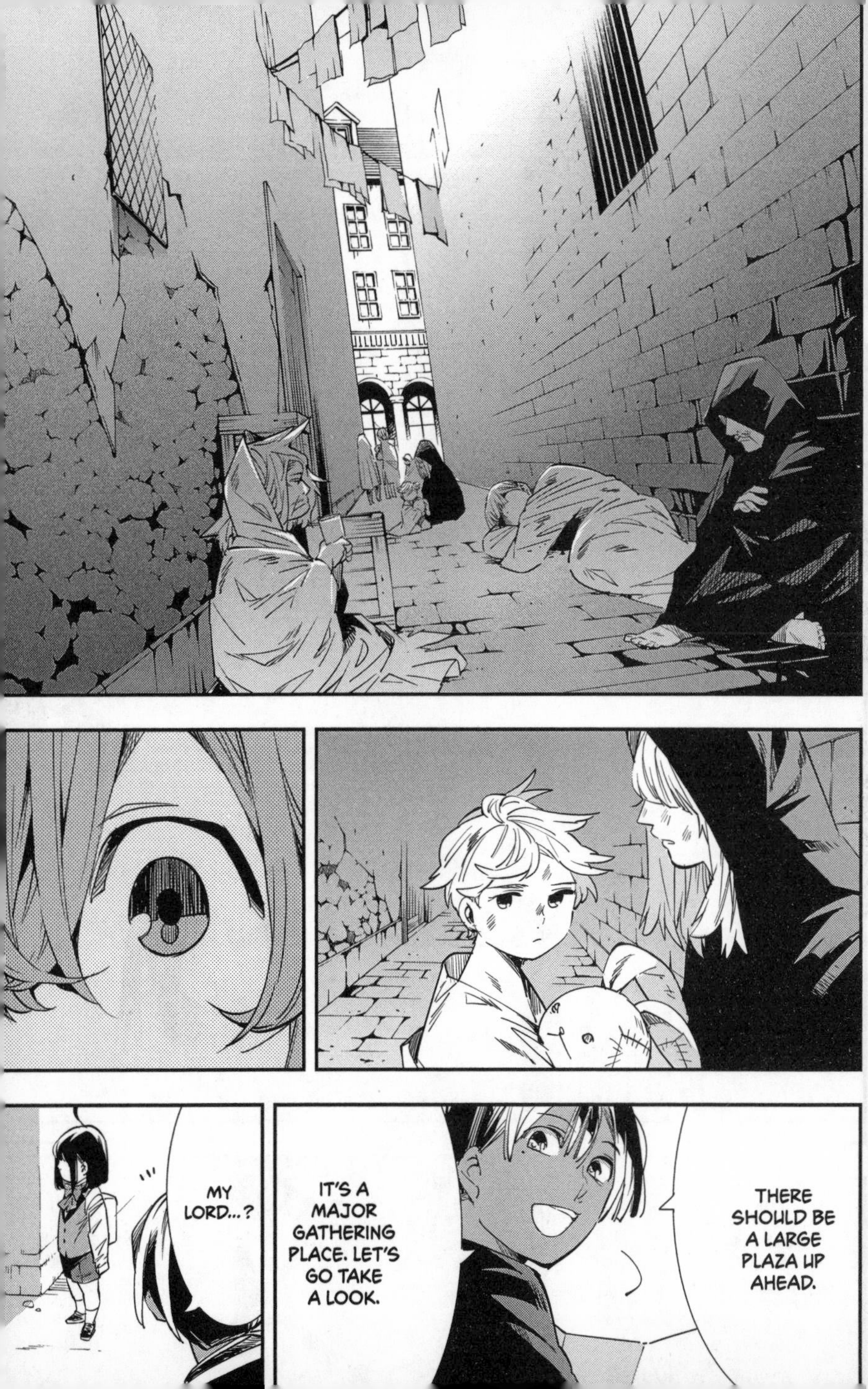
THERE SHOULD BE A LARGE PLAZA UP AHEAD.
IT'S A MAJOR GATHERING PLACE. LET'S GO TAKE A LOOK.
MY LORD...?

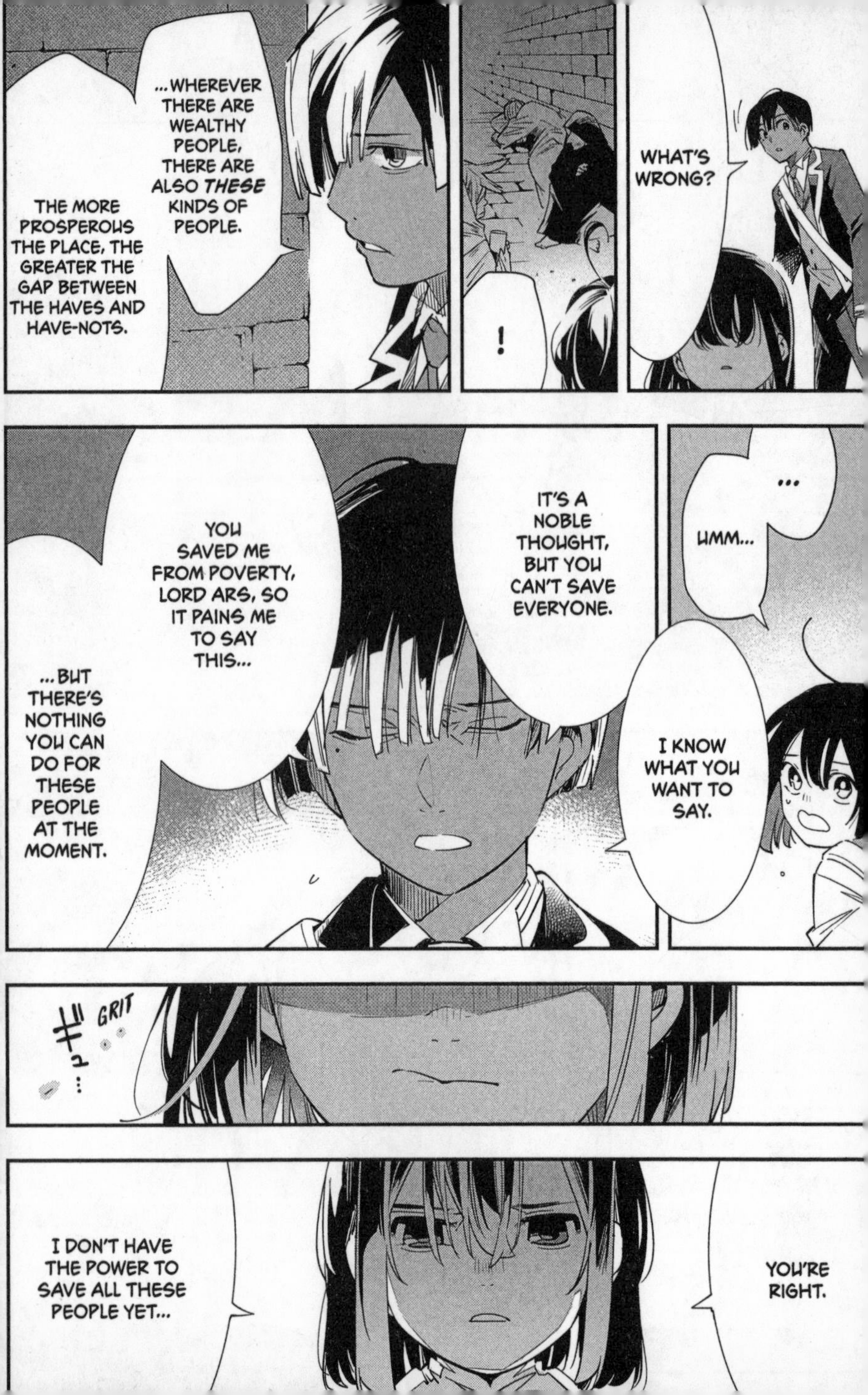
WHAT'S WRONG?
!
...WHEREVER THERE ARE WEALTHY PEOPLE, THERE ARE ALSO *THESE* KINDS OF PEOPLE.
THE MORE PROSPEROUS THE PLACE, THE GREATER THE GAP BETWEEN THE HAVES AND HAVE-NOTS.
...
UMM...
IT'S A NOBLE THOUGHT, BUT YOU CAN'T SAVE EVERYONE.
YOU SAVED ME FROM POVERTY, LORD ARS, SO IT PAINS ME TO SAY THIS...
...BUT THERE'S NOTHING YOU CAN DO FOR THESE PEOPLE AT THE MOMENT.
I KNOW WHAT YOU WANT TO SAY.
GRIT
YOU'RE RIGHT.
I DON'T HAVE THE POWER TO SAVE ALL THESE PEOPLE YET...

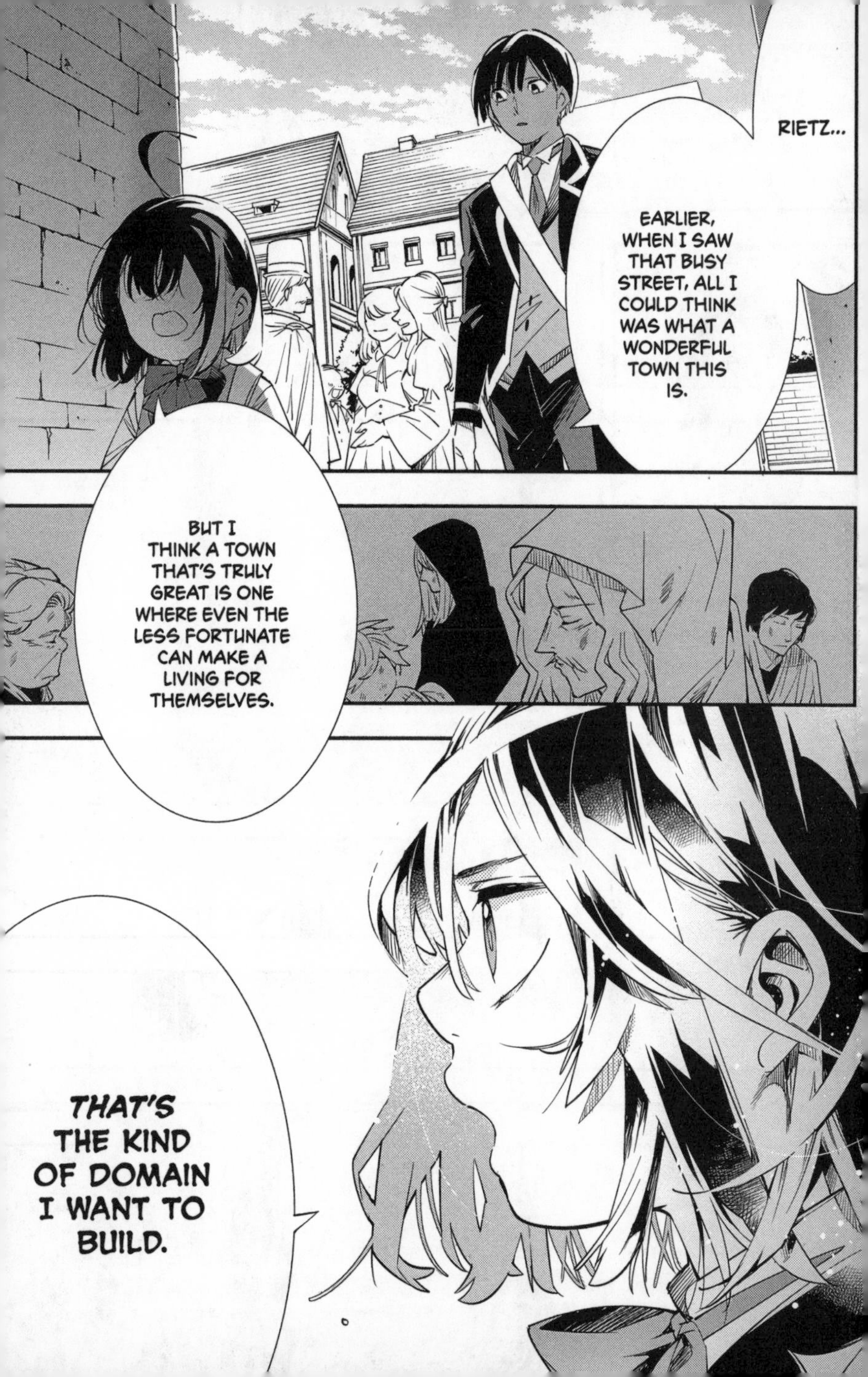
RIETZ...
EARLIER, WHEN I SAW THAT BUSY STREET, ALL I COULD THINK WAS WHAT A WONDERFUL TOWN THIS IS.
BUT I THINK A TOWN THAT'S TRULY GREAT IS ONE WHERE EVEN THE LESS FORTUNATE CAN MAKE A LIVING FOR THEMSELVES.
THAT'S THE KIND OF DOMAIN I WANT TO BUILD.

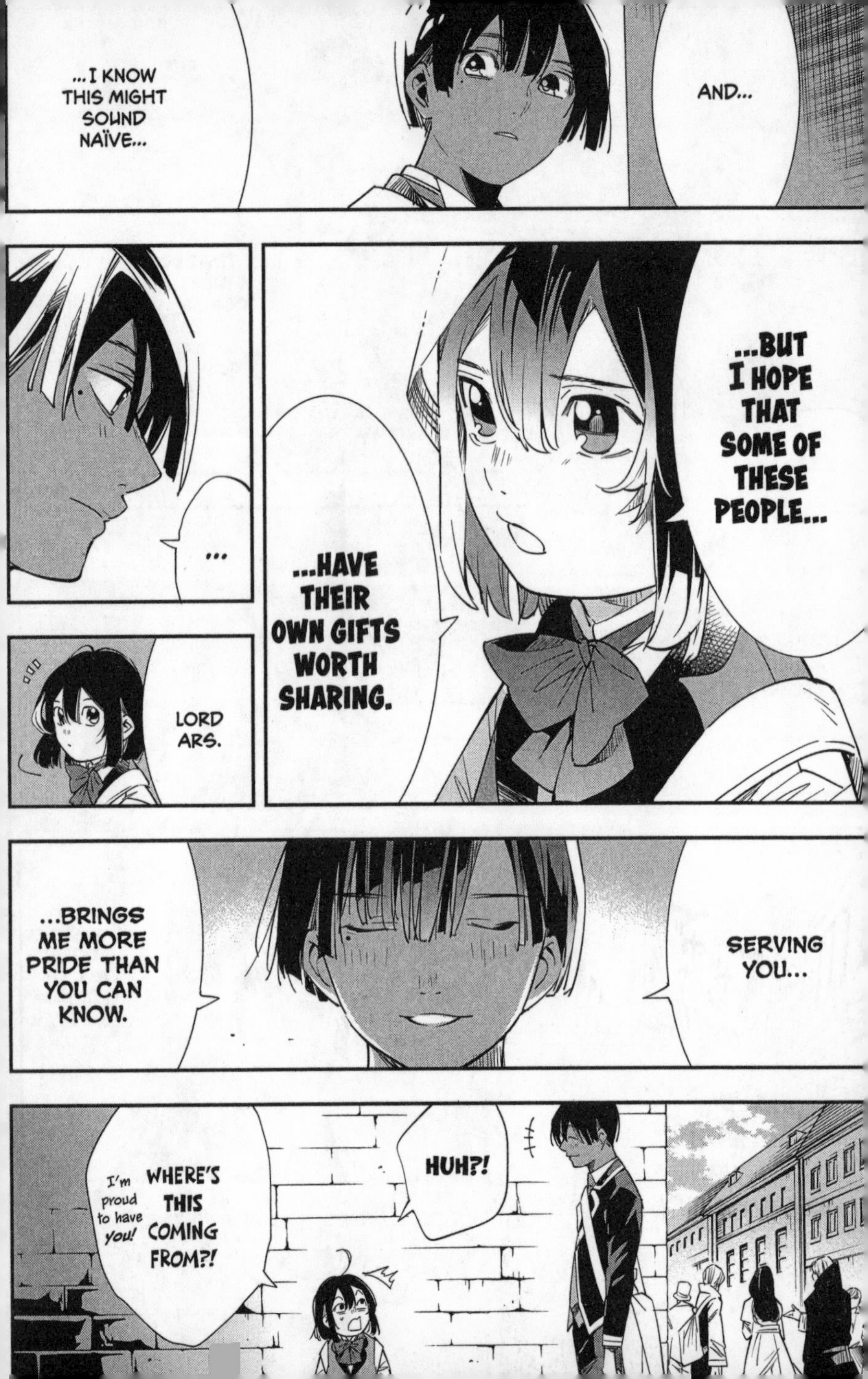
AND...
...I KNOW THIS MIGHT SOUND NAÏVE...
...BUT I HOPE THAT SOME OF THESE PEOPLE...
...HAVE THEIR OWN GIFTS WORTH SHARING.
...
LORD ARS.
SERVING YOU...
...BRINGS ME MORE PRIDE THAN YOU CAN KNOW.
HUH?!
WHERE'S THIS COMING FROM?!
I'm proud to have you!

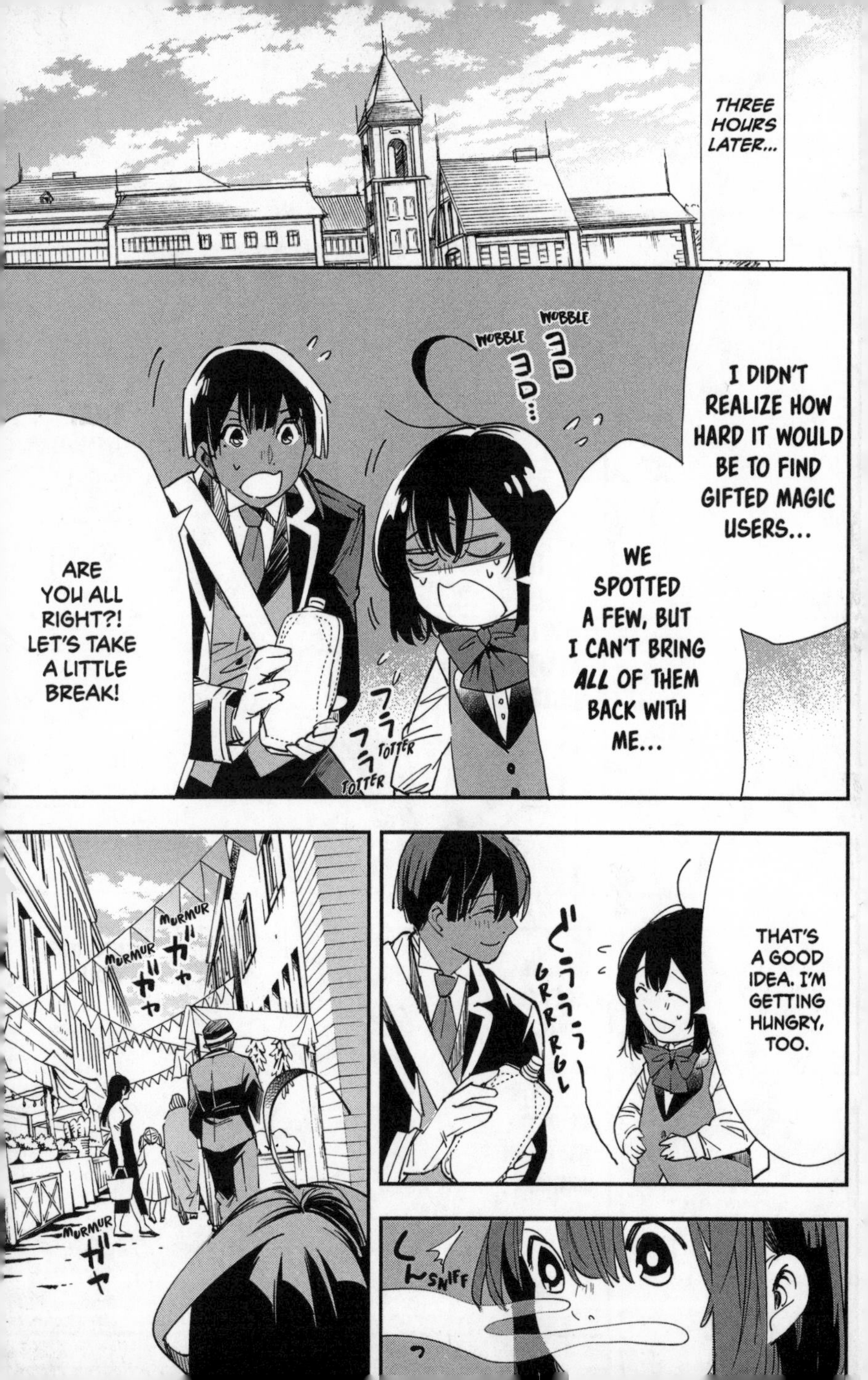
THREE HOURS LATER...
I DIDN'T REALIZE HOW HARD IT WOULD BE TO FIND GIFTED MAGIC USERS...
WOBBLE WOBBLE
ヨロ ヨロ...
WE SPOTTED A FEW, BUT I CAN'T BRING ALL OF THEM BACK WITH ME...
フラ フラ
TOTTER TOTTER
ARE YOU ALL RIGHT?! LET'S TAKE A LITTLE BREAK!
THAT'S A GOOD IDEA. I'M GETTING HUNGRY, TOO.
GRRRRGL
くん SNIFF
MURMUR MURMUR
ガヤ ガヤ
MURMUR
ガヤ

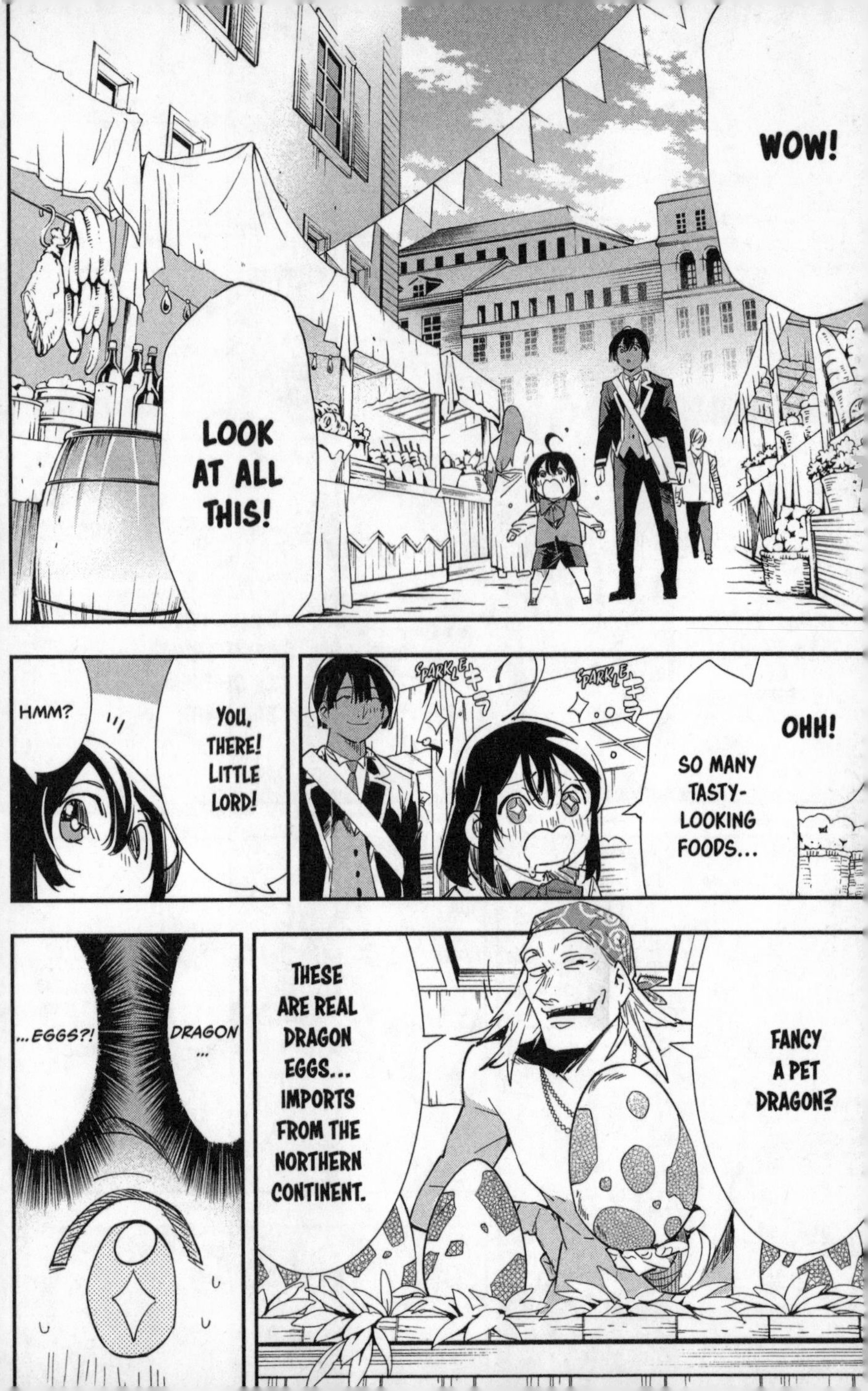
WOW!
LOOK AT ALL THIS!
OHH!
SO MANY TASTY-LOOKING FOODS...
SPARKLE
SPARKLE
YOU, THERE! LITTLE LORD!
HMM?
FANCY A PET DRAGON?
THESE ARE REAL DRAGON EGGS... IMPORTS FROM THE NORTHERN CONTINENT.
DRAGON...
...EGGS?!

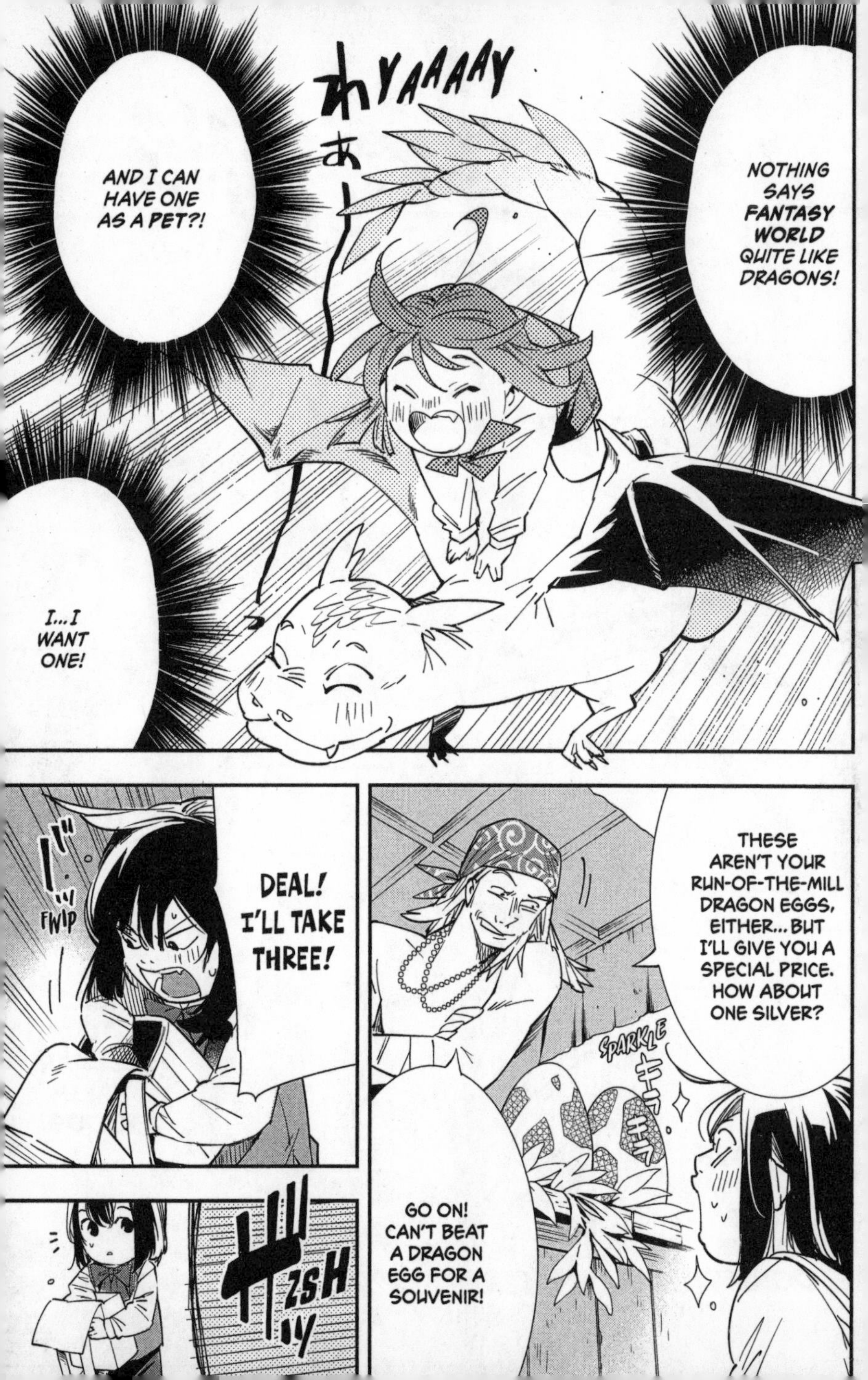
NOTHING SAYS FANTASY WORLD QUITE LIKE DRAGONS!
YAAAAY
AND I CAN HAVE ONE AS A PET?!
I...I WANT ONE!
THESE AREN'T YOUR RUN-OF-THE-MILL DRAGON EGGS, EITHER... BUT I'LL GIVE YOU A SPECIAL PRICE. HOW ABOUT ONE SILVER?
SPARKLE
GO ON! CAN'T BEAT A DRAGON EGG FOR A SOUVENIR!
DEAL! I'LL TAKE THREE!
FWIP
ZSH

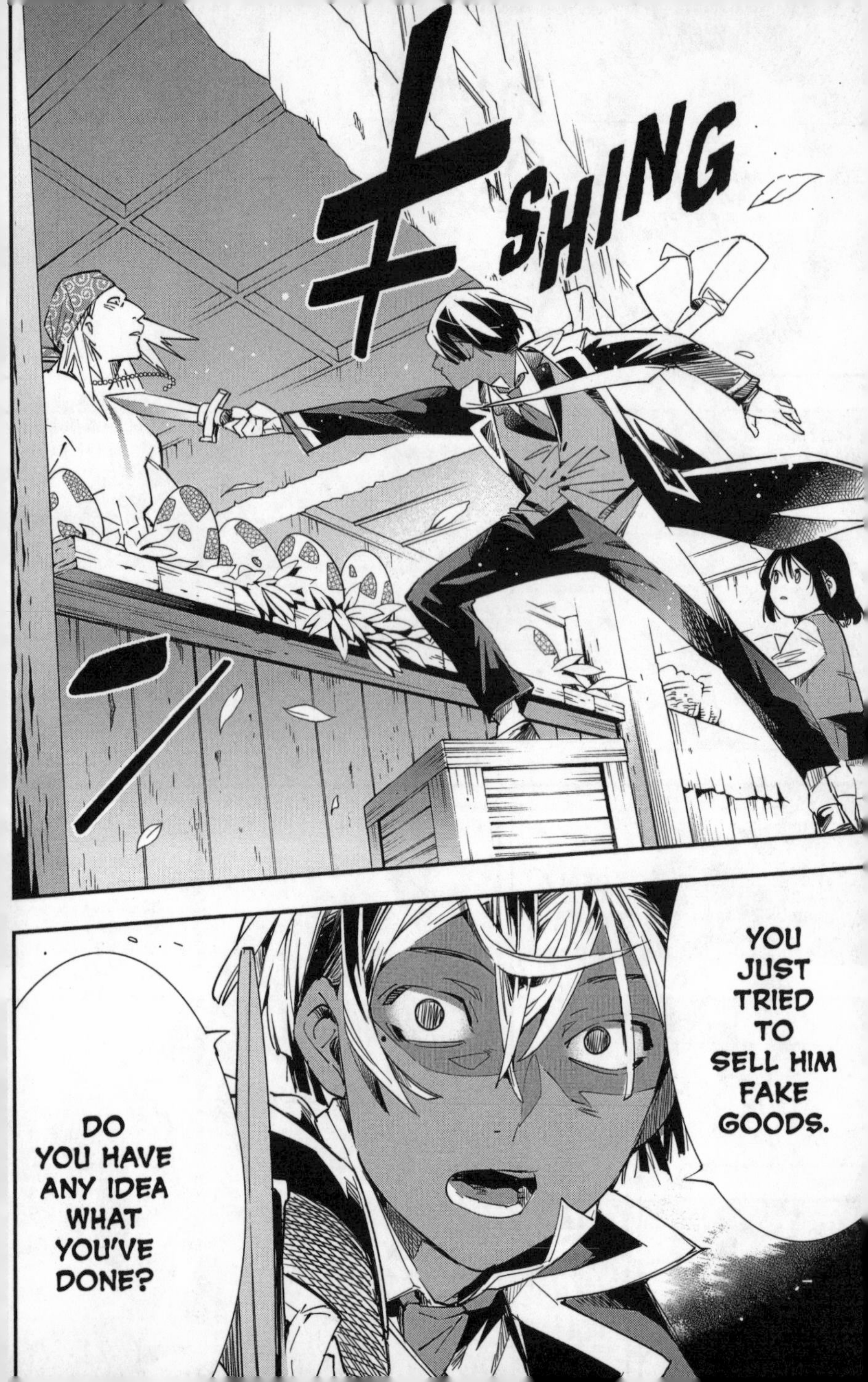
SHING
YOU JUST TRIED TO SELL HIM FAKE GOODS.
DO YOU HAVE ANY IDEA WHAT YOU'VE DONE?

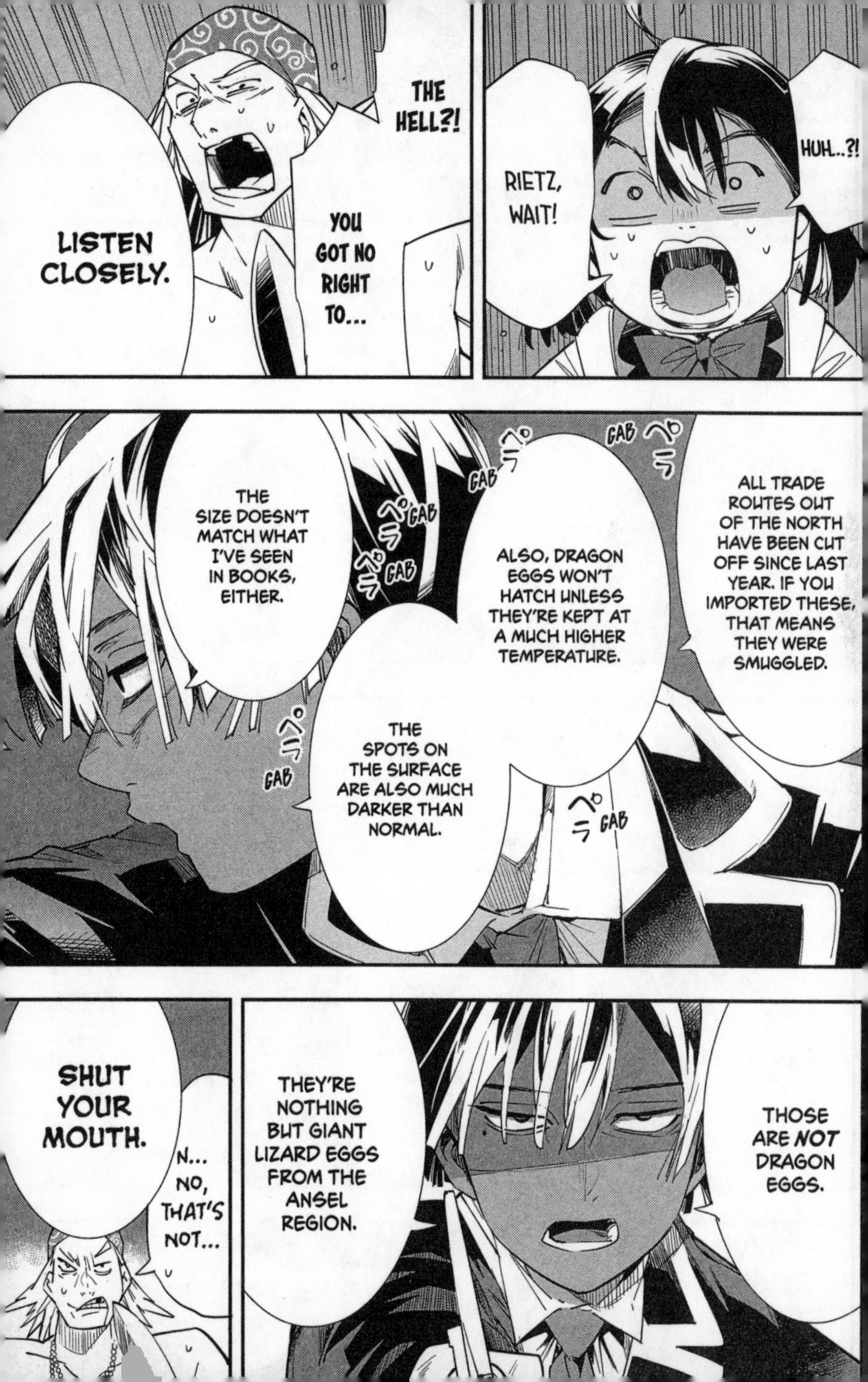

HUH..?!
RIETZ, WAIT!
THE HELL?!
YOU GOT NO RIGHT TO...
LISTEN CLOSELY.
GAB
ALL TRADE ROUTES OUT OF THE NORTH HAVE BEEN CUT OFF SINCE LAST YEAR. IF YOU IMPORTED THESE, THAT MEANS THEY WERE SMUGGLED.
GAB
ALSO, DRAGON EGGS WON'T HATCH UNLESS THEY'RE KEPT AT A MUCH HIGHER TEMPERATURE.
GAB
GAB
GAB
THE SIZE DOESN'T MATCH WHAT I'VE SEEN IN BOOKS, EITHER.
GAB
THE SPOTS ON THE SURFACE ARE ALSO MUCH DARKER THAN NORMAL.
GAB
THOSE ARE *NOT* DRAGON EGGS.
THEY'RE NOTHING BUT GIANT LIZARD EGGS FROM THE ANSEL REGION.
N... NO, THAT'S NOT...
SHUT YOUR MOUTH.

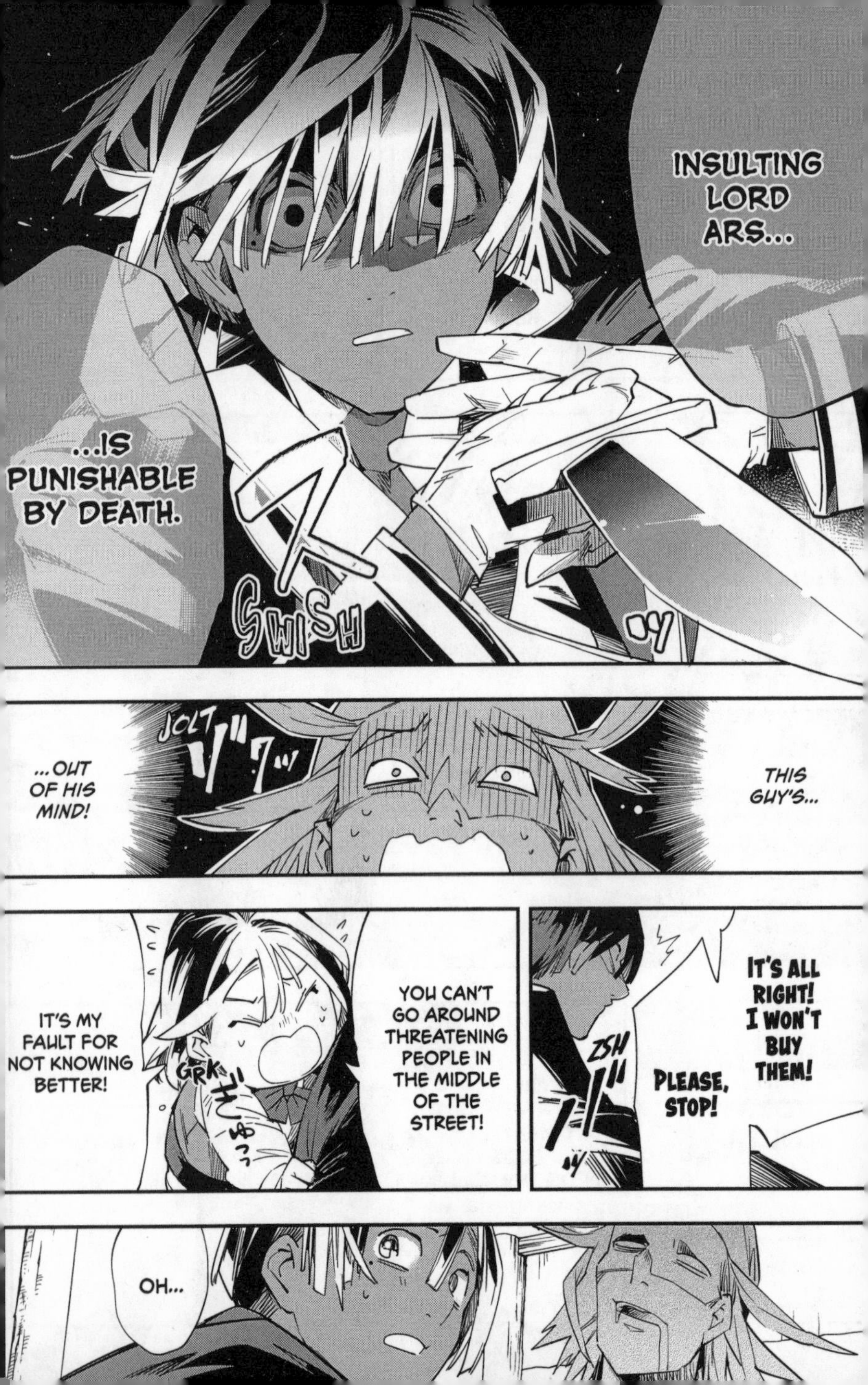
INSULTING LORD ARS...
...IS PUNISHABLE BY DEATH.
SWISH
JOLT
THIS GUY'S...
...OUT OF HIS MIND!
IT'S ALL RIGHT! I WON'T BUY THEM!
PLEASE, STOP!
ZSH
YOU CAN'T GO AROUND THREATENING PEOPLE IN THE MIDDLE OF THE STREET!
IT'S MY FAULT FOR NOT KNOWING BETTER!
GRK
OH...

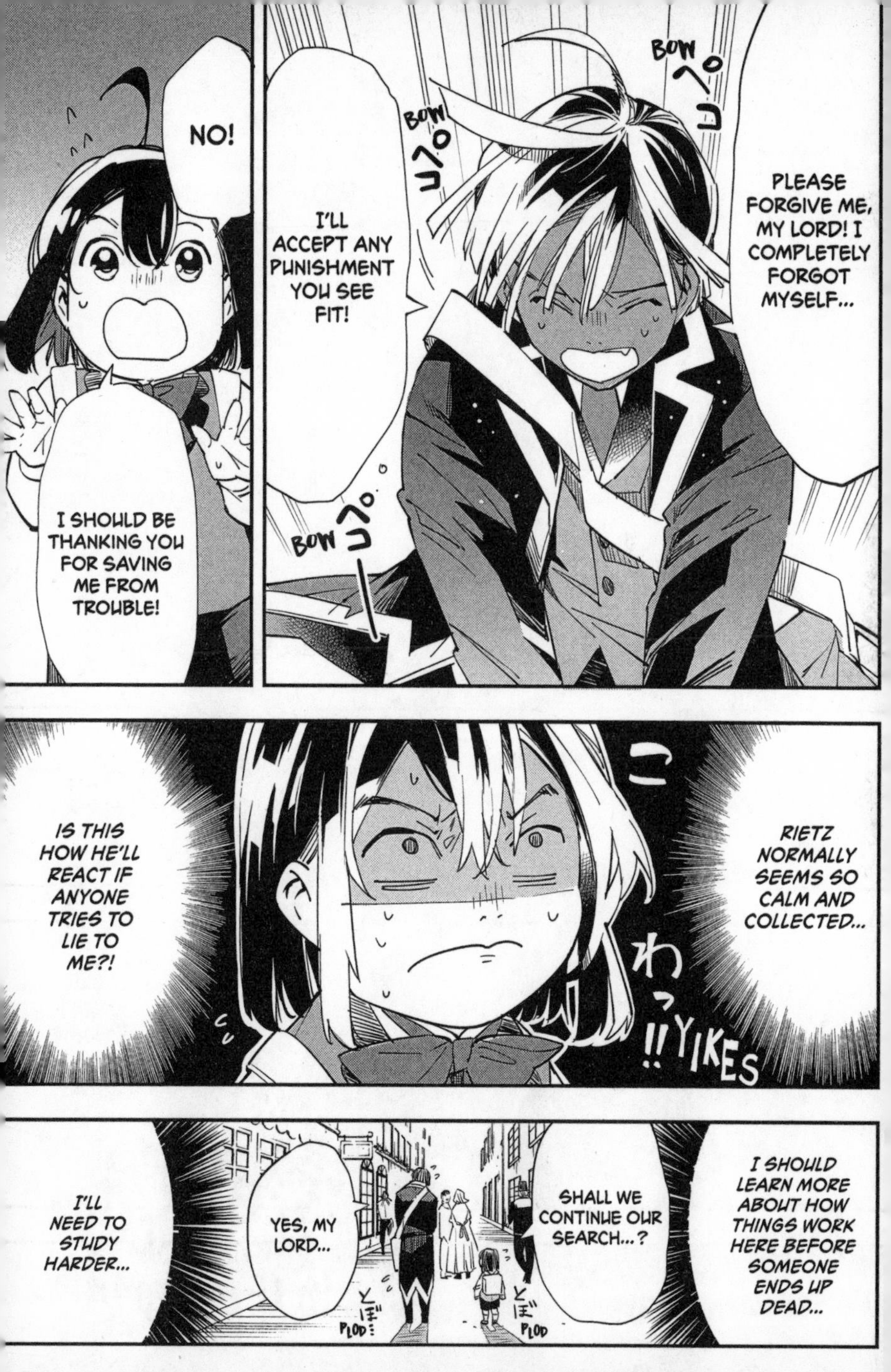
BOW へコ
PLEASE FORGIVE ME, MY LORD! I COMPLETELY FORGOT MYSELF...
BOW ペコ
I'LL ACCEPT ANY PUNISHMENT YOU SEE FIT!
BOW ペコ
NO!
I SHOULD BE THANKING YOU FOR SAVING ME FROM TROUBLE!
RIETZ NORMALLY SEEMS SO CALM AND COLLECTED...
こわっ!! YIKES
IS THIS HOW HE'LL REACT IF ANYONE TRIES TO LIE TO ME?!
I SHOULD LEARN MORE ABOUT HOW THINGS WORK HERE BEFORE SOMEONE ENDS UP DEAD...
SHALL WE CONTINUE OUR SEARCH...?
とぼ PLOD
YES, MY LORD...
とぼ PLOD
I'LL NEED TO STUDY HARDER...

As a Reincarnated
ARISTOCRAT,
I'll Use My Appraisal Skill to
Rise in the World

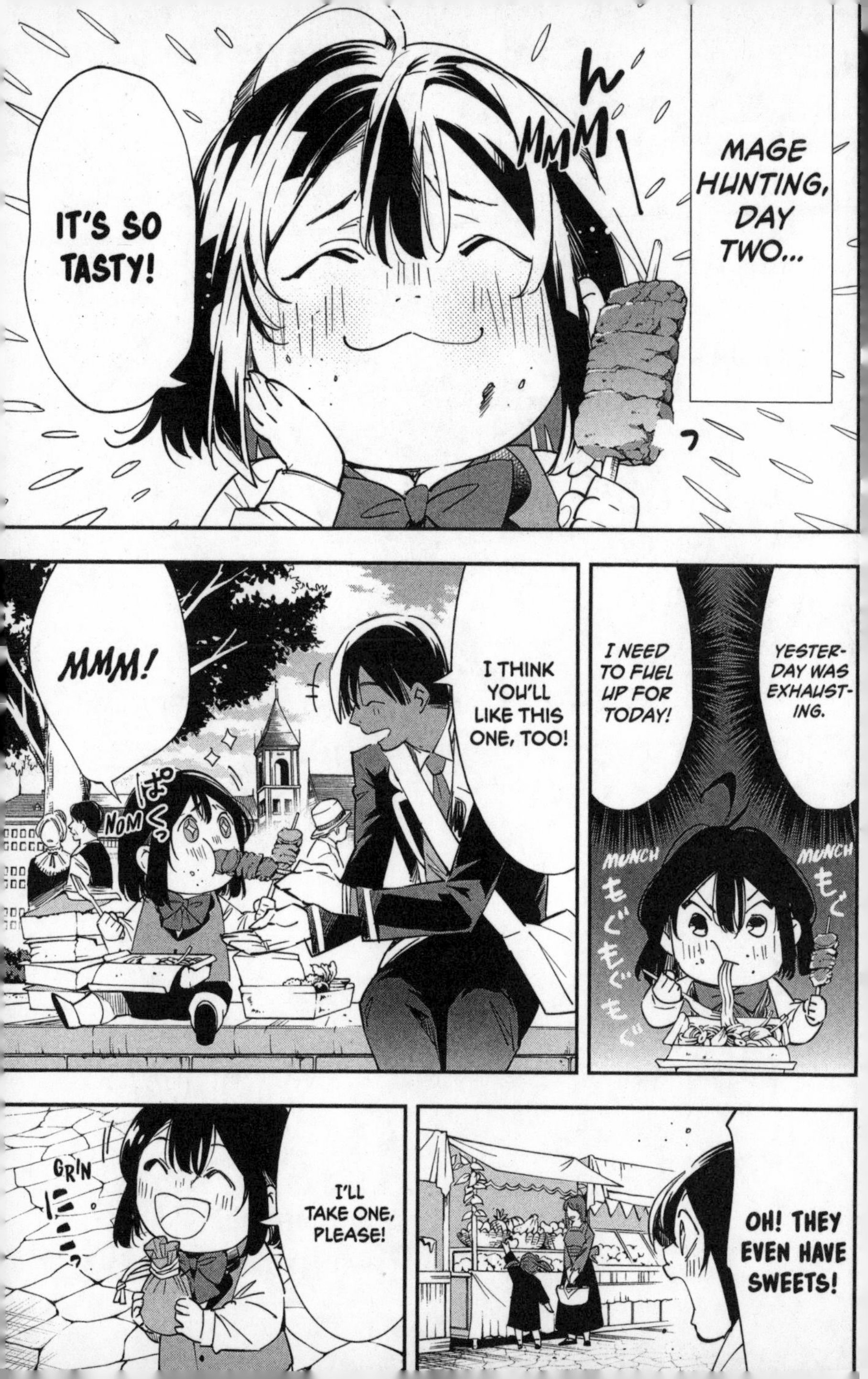
MAGE HUNTING, DAY TWO...
MMMM
IT'S SO TASTY!
YESTER-DAY WAS EXHAUST-ING.
I NEED TO FUEL UP FOR TODAY!
MUNCH もぐ
MUNCH もぐもぐもぐ
I THINK YOU'LL LIKE THIS ONE, TOO!
MMM!
NOM ぱく
OH! THEY EVEN HAVE SWEETS!
I'LL TAKE ONE, PLEASE!
GRIN

Chapter 6: Charlotte Lace

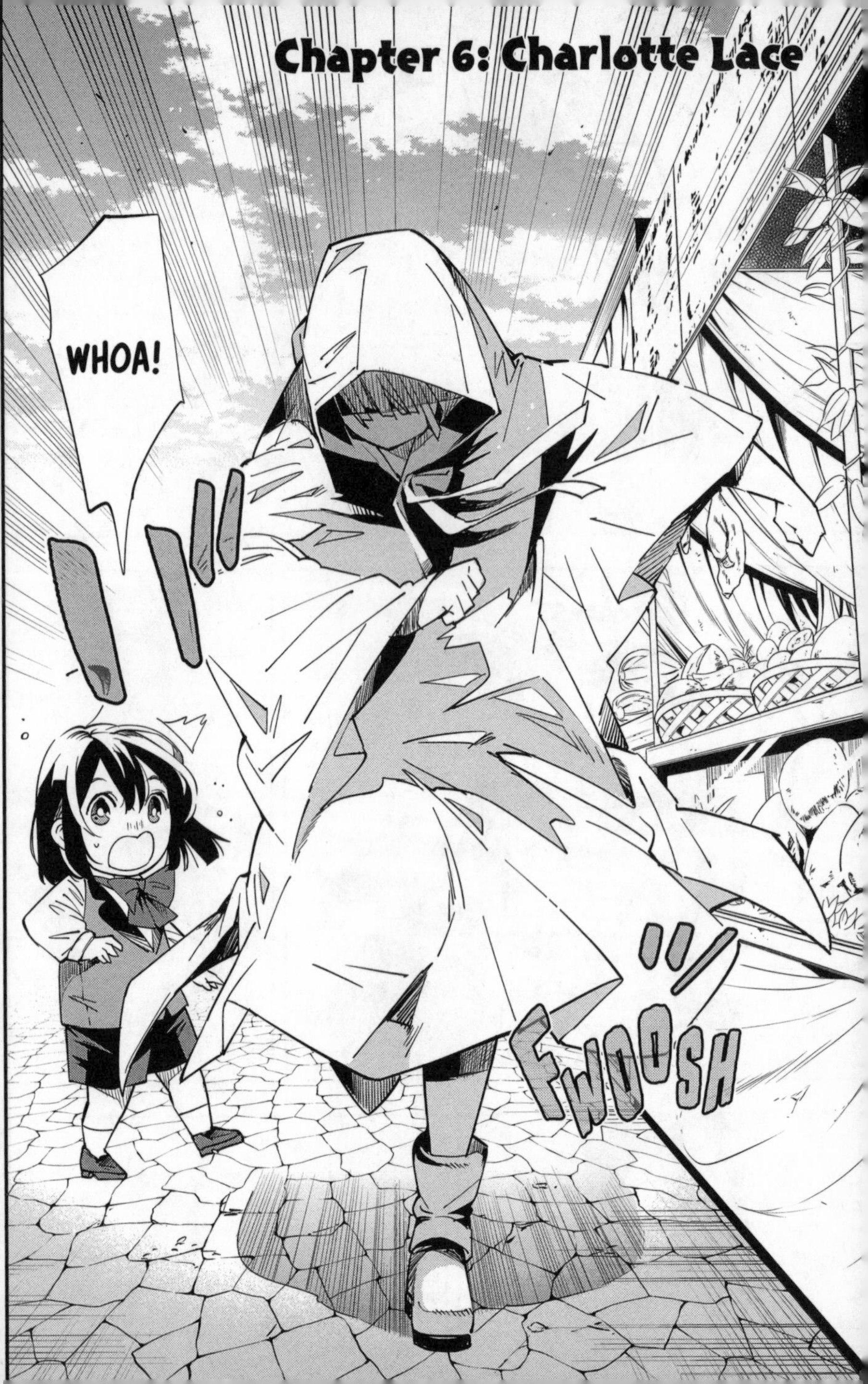
WHOA!
FWOOSH

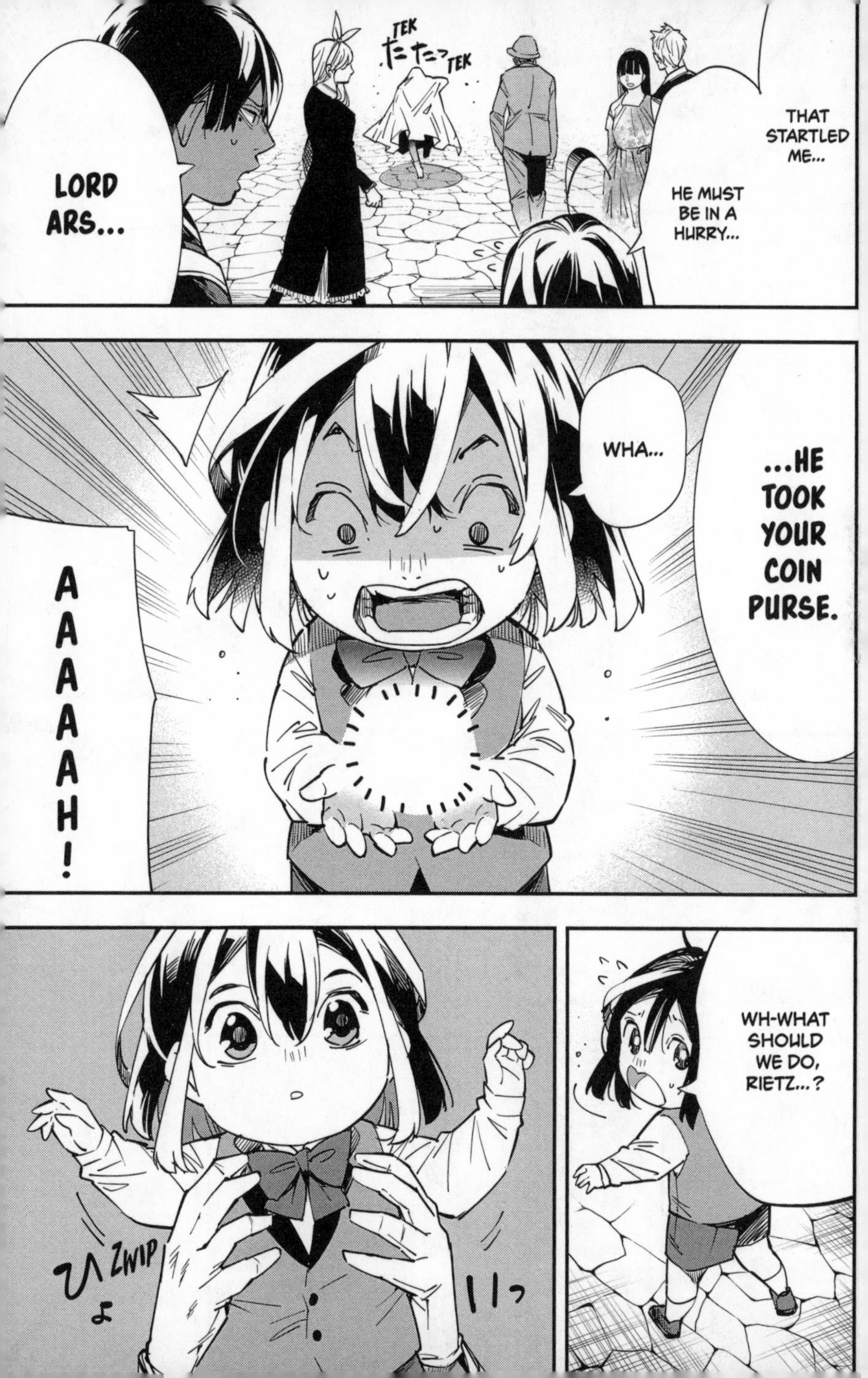
TEK
たたっ
TEK
THAT STARTLED ME...
HE MUST BE IN A HURRY...
LORD ARS...
...HE TOOK YOUR COIN PURSE.
WHA...
AAAAAAH!
WH-WHAT SHOULD WE DO, RIETZ...?
ZWIP
ひょ

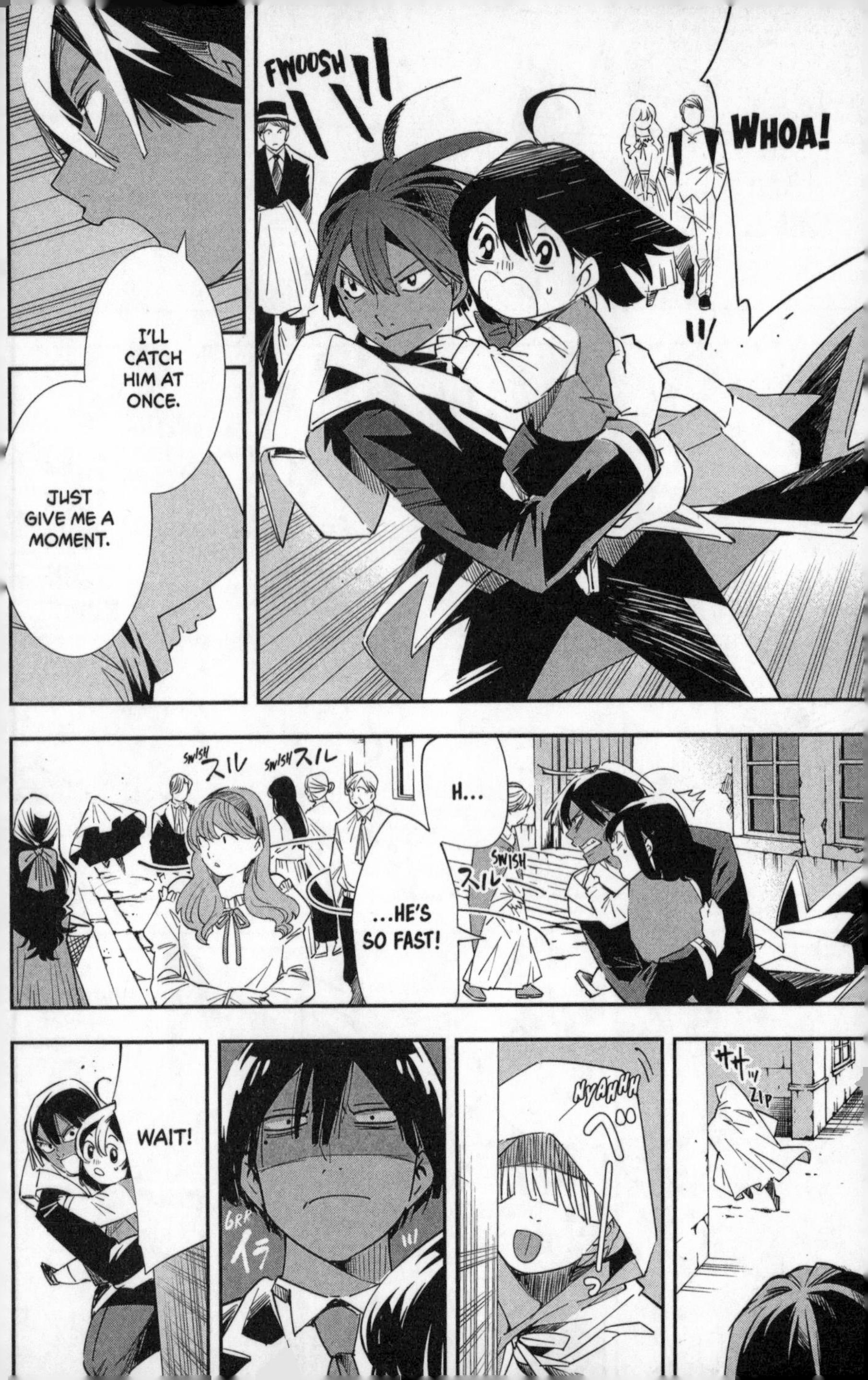
WHOA!
FWOOSH
I'LL CATCH HIM AT ONCE.
JUST GIVE ME A MOMENT.
H...
...HE'S SO FAST!
SWISH スルー
SWISH スル
SWISH スル
ZIP ササッ
NYAHHH べー
GRR イラ
WAIT!

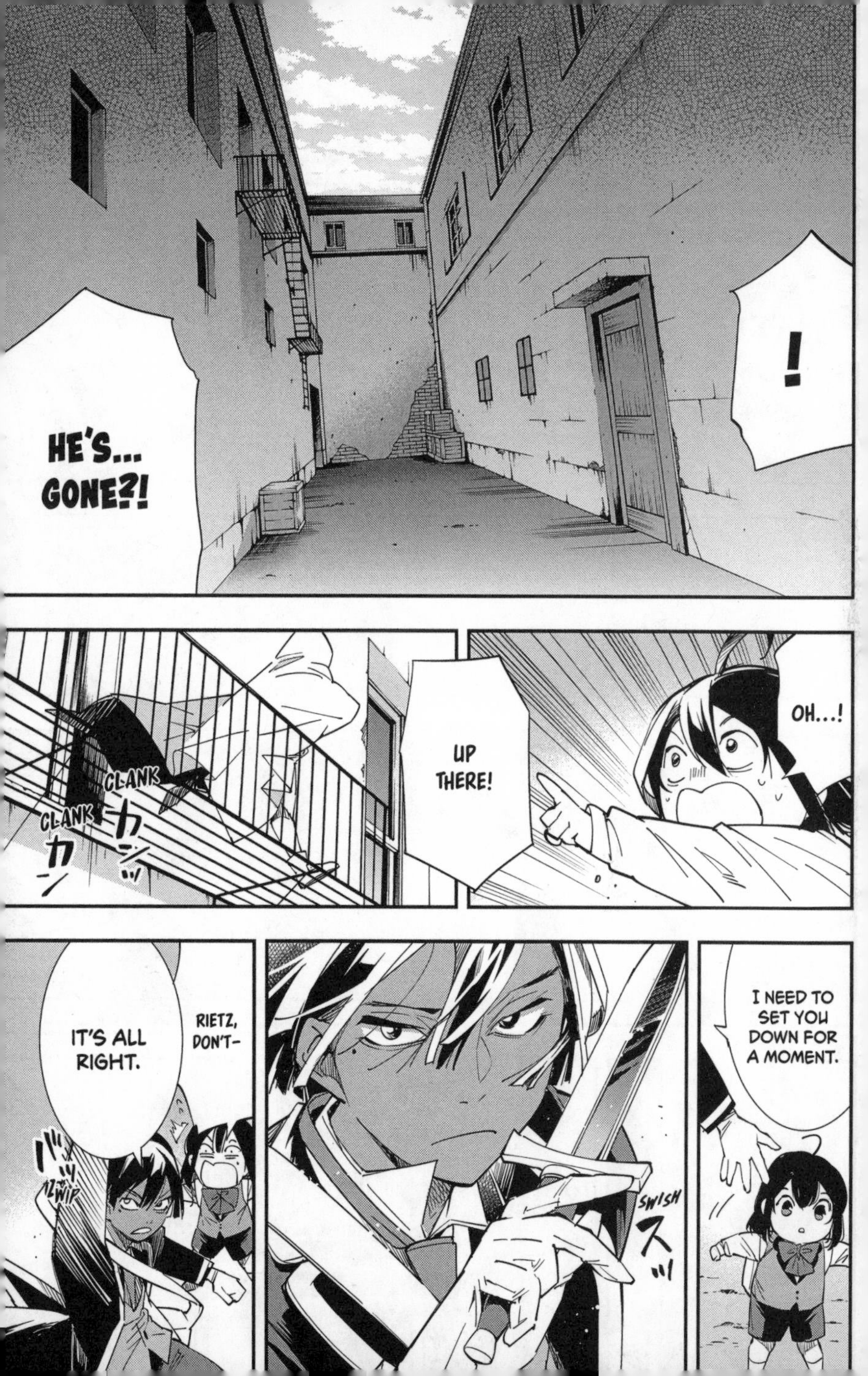
!
HE'S... GONE?!
OH...!
UP THERE!
CLANK
CLANK
I NEED TO SET YOU DOWN FOR A MOMENT.
SWISH
RIETZ, DON'T-
IT'S ALL RIGHT.
WIP

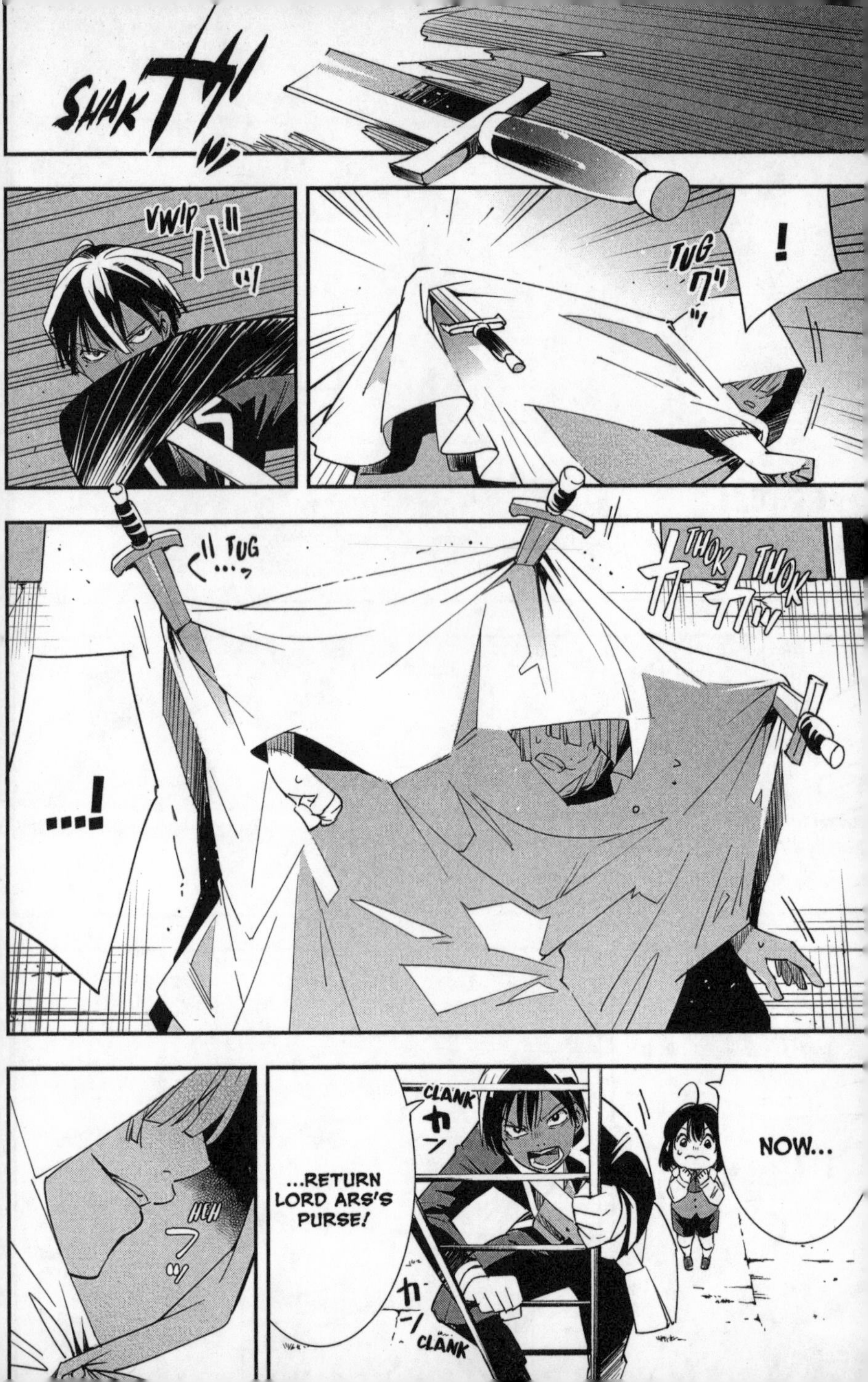
SHAK
!
TUG
VWIP
THOK
THOK
TUG
...!
NOW...
...RETURN LORD ARS'S PURSE!
CLANK
CLANK
HEH

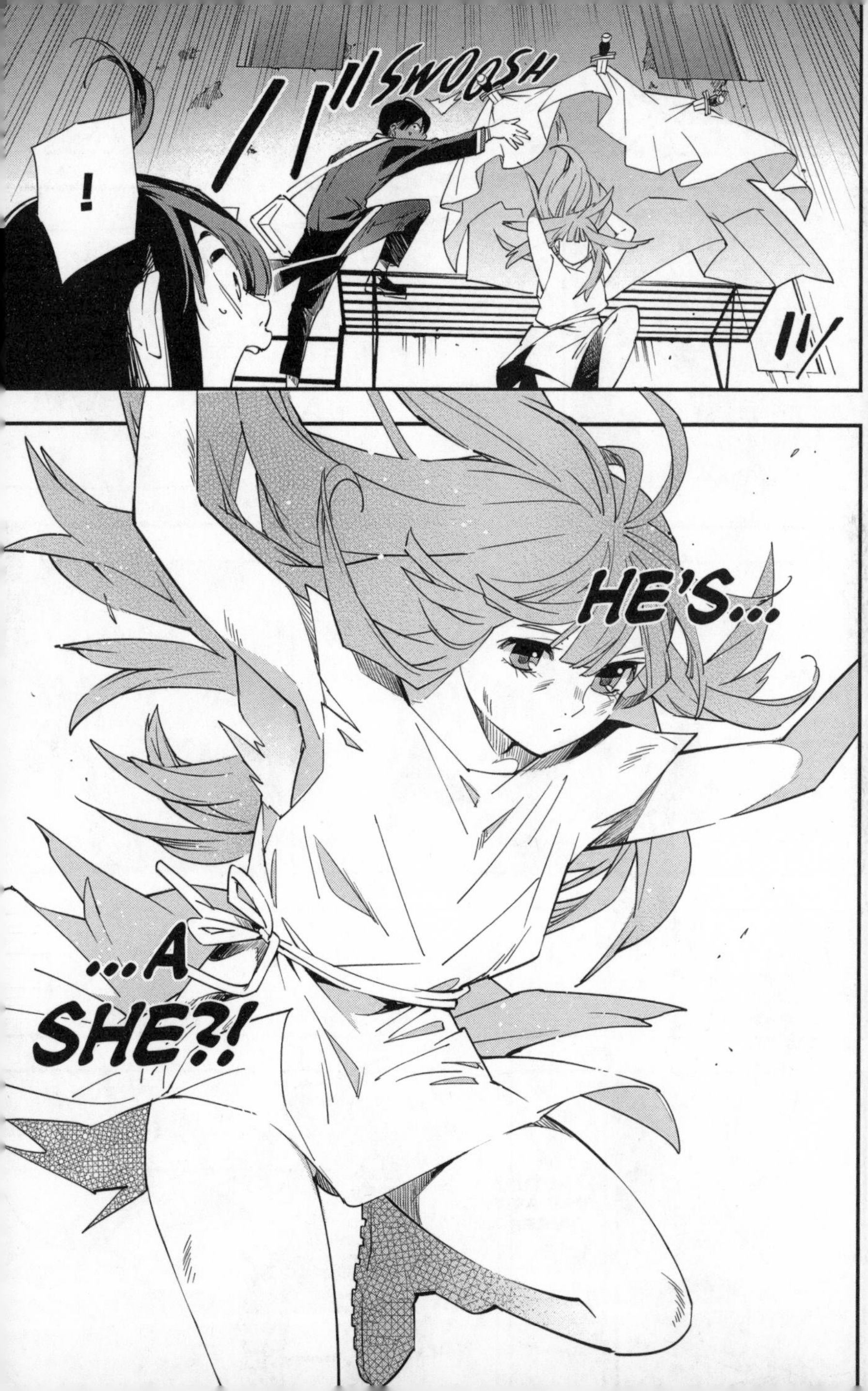
SWOOSH
!
HE'S...
...A SHE?!

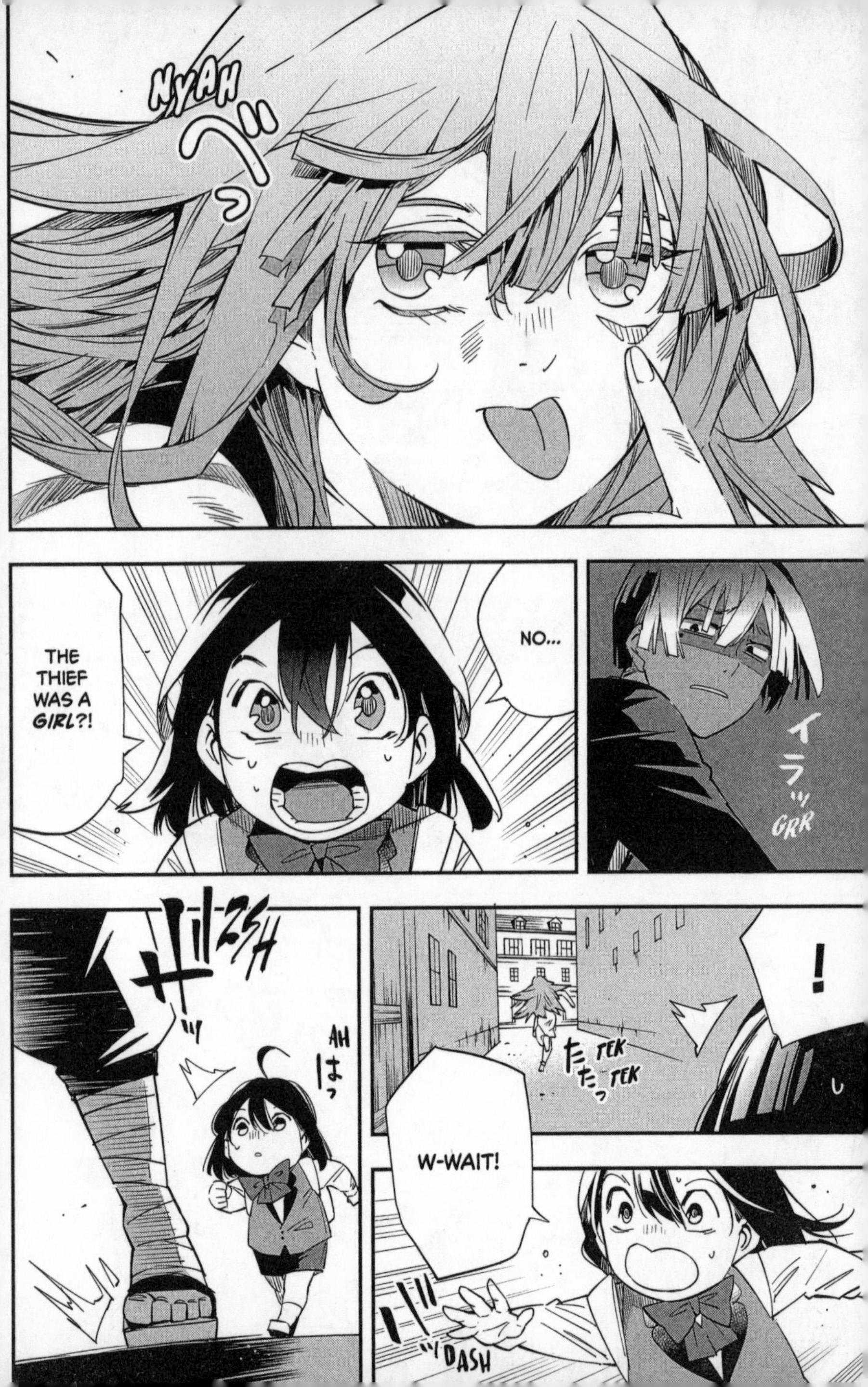
NYAH
イラッ
GRR
NO...
THE THIEF WAS A GIRL?!
!
たたっ
TEK TEK
W-WAIT!
DASH
DASH
はっ
AH

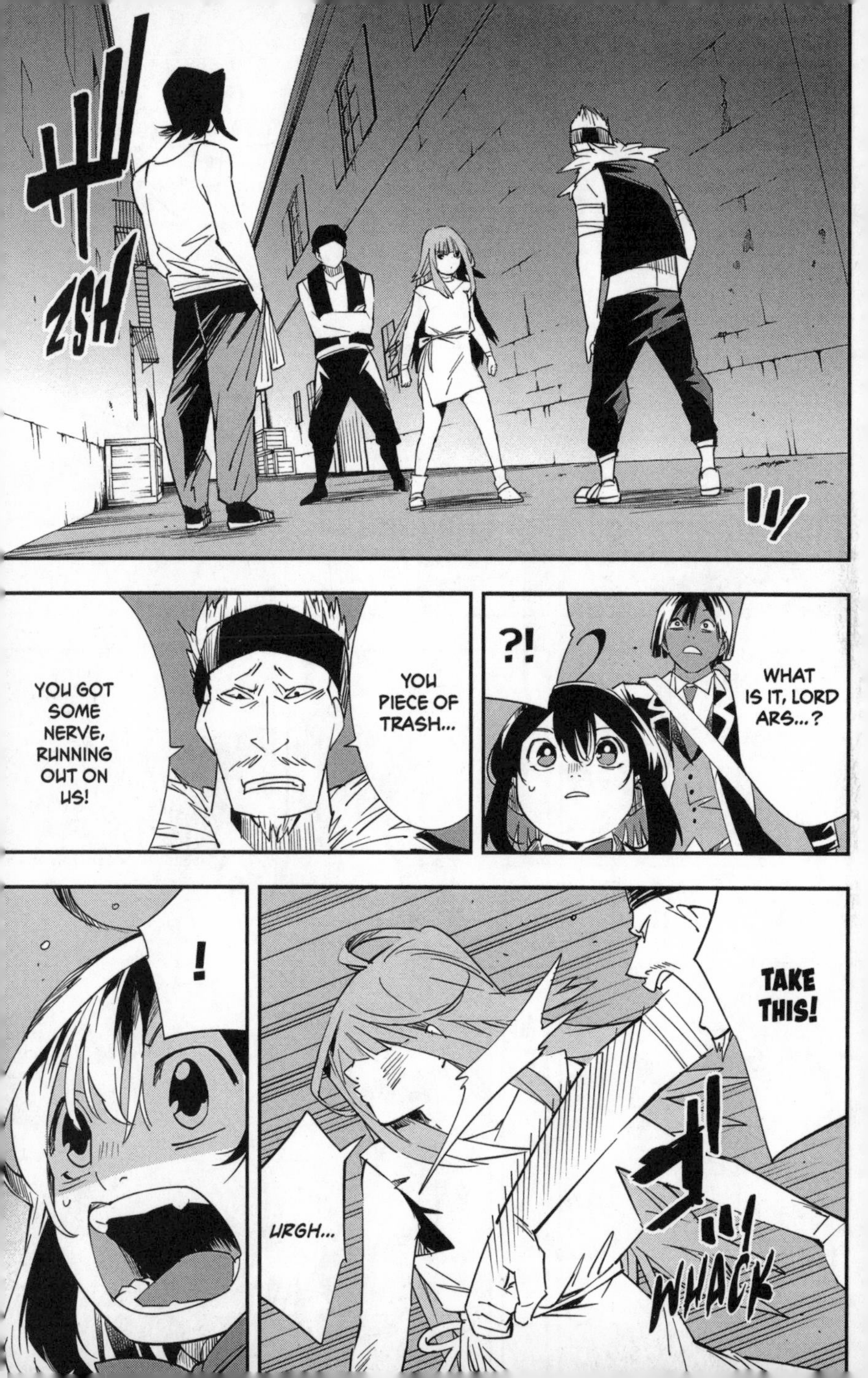
ZSH
?!
WHAT IS IT, LORD ARS...?
YOU PIECE OF TRASH...
YOU GOT SOME NERVE, RUNNING OUT ON US!
TAKE THIS!
WHACK
URGH...
!

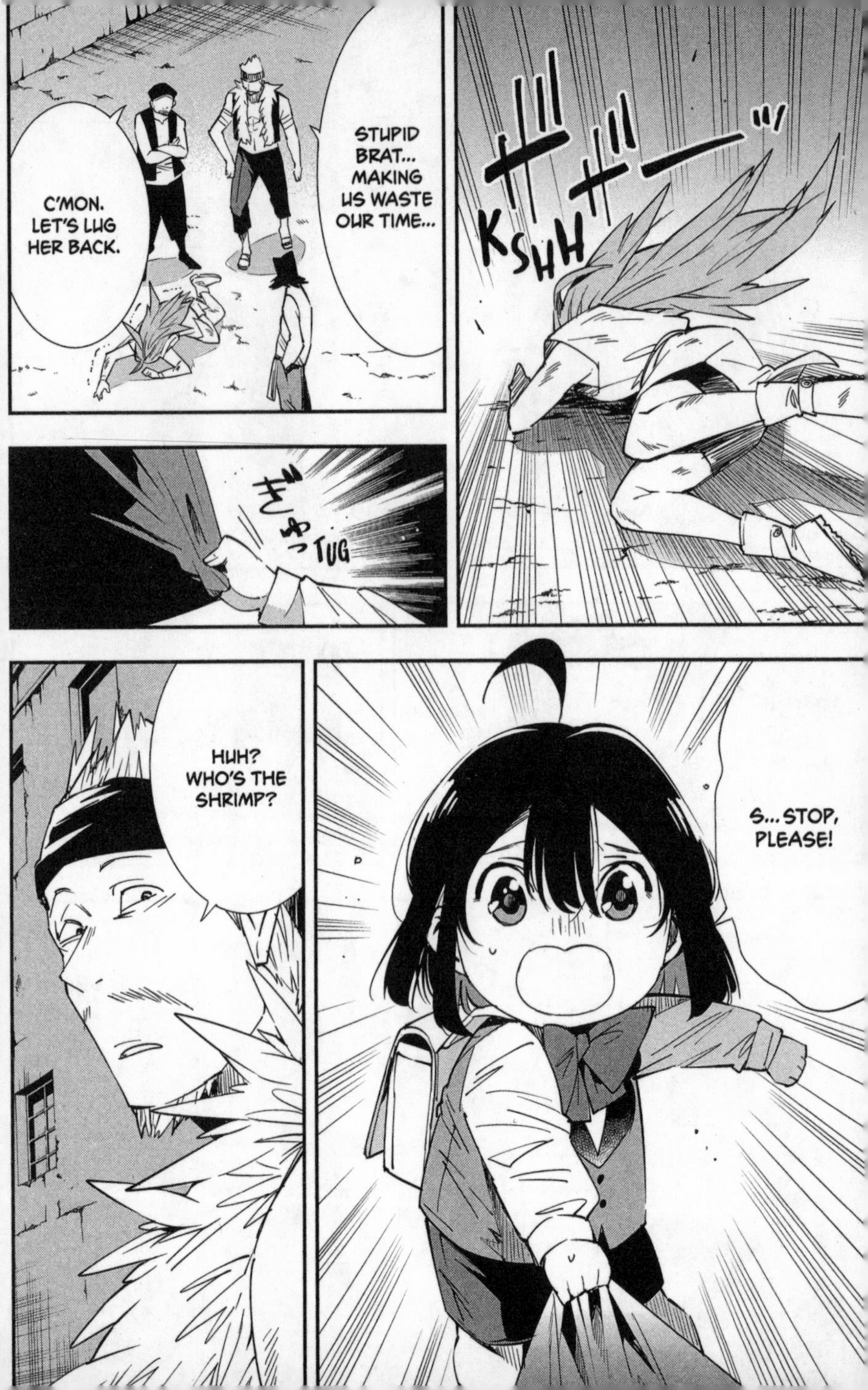
KSHH
STUPID BRAT... MAKING US WASTE OUR TIME...
C'MON. LET'S LUG HER BACK.
TUG
S... STOP, PLEASE!
HUH? WHO'S THE SHRIMP?

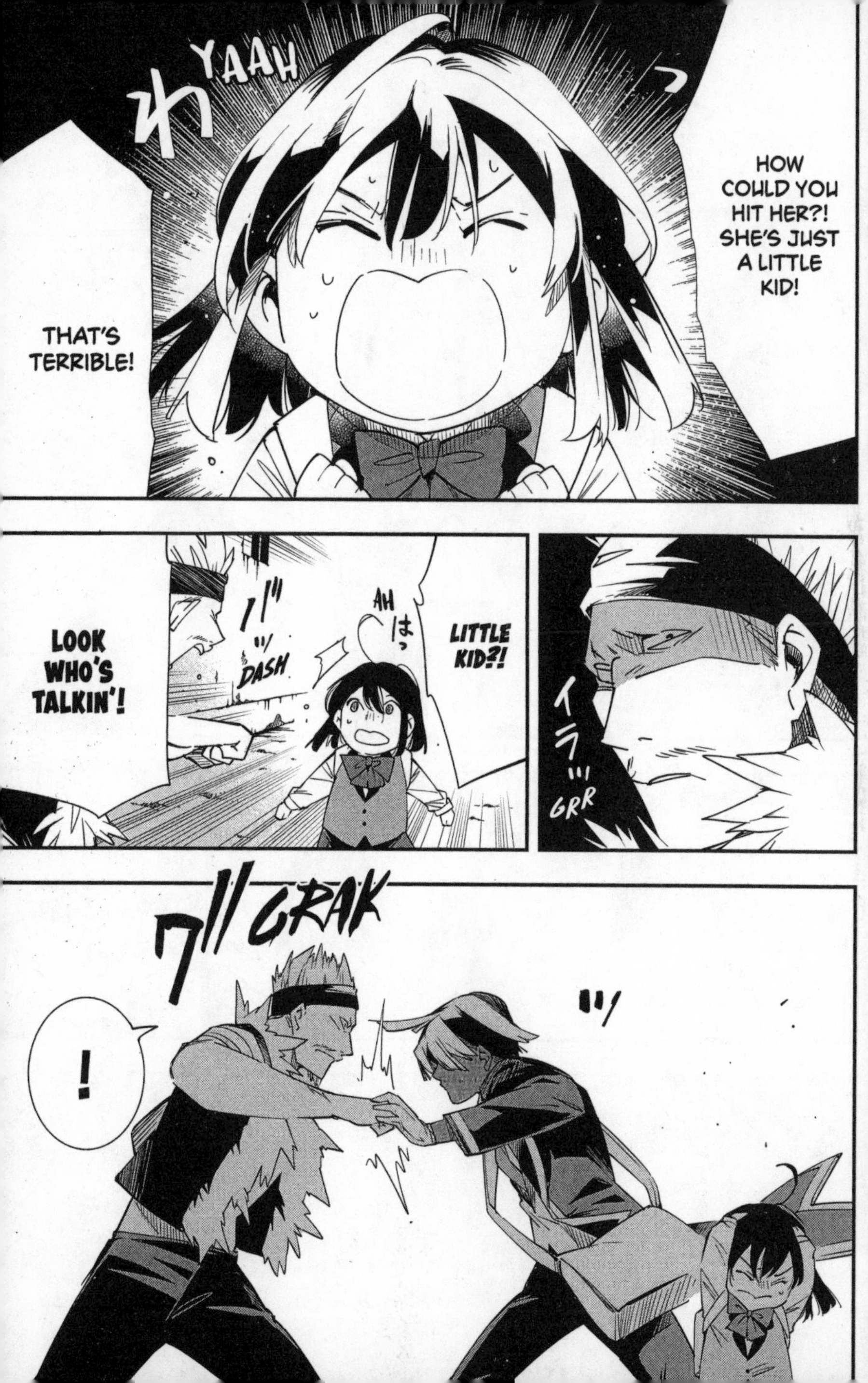
YAAH
HOW COULD YOU HIT HER?! SHE'S JUST A LITTLE KID!
THAT'S TERRIBLE!
GRR
LITTLE KID?!
AH
DASH
LOOK WHO'S TALKIN'!
GRAK
!

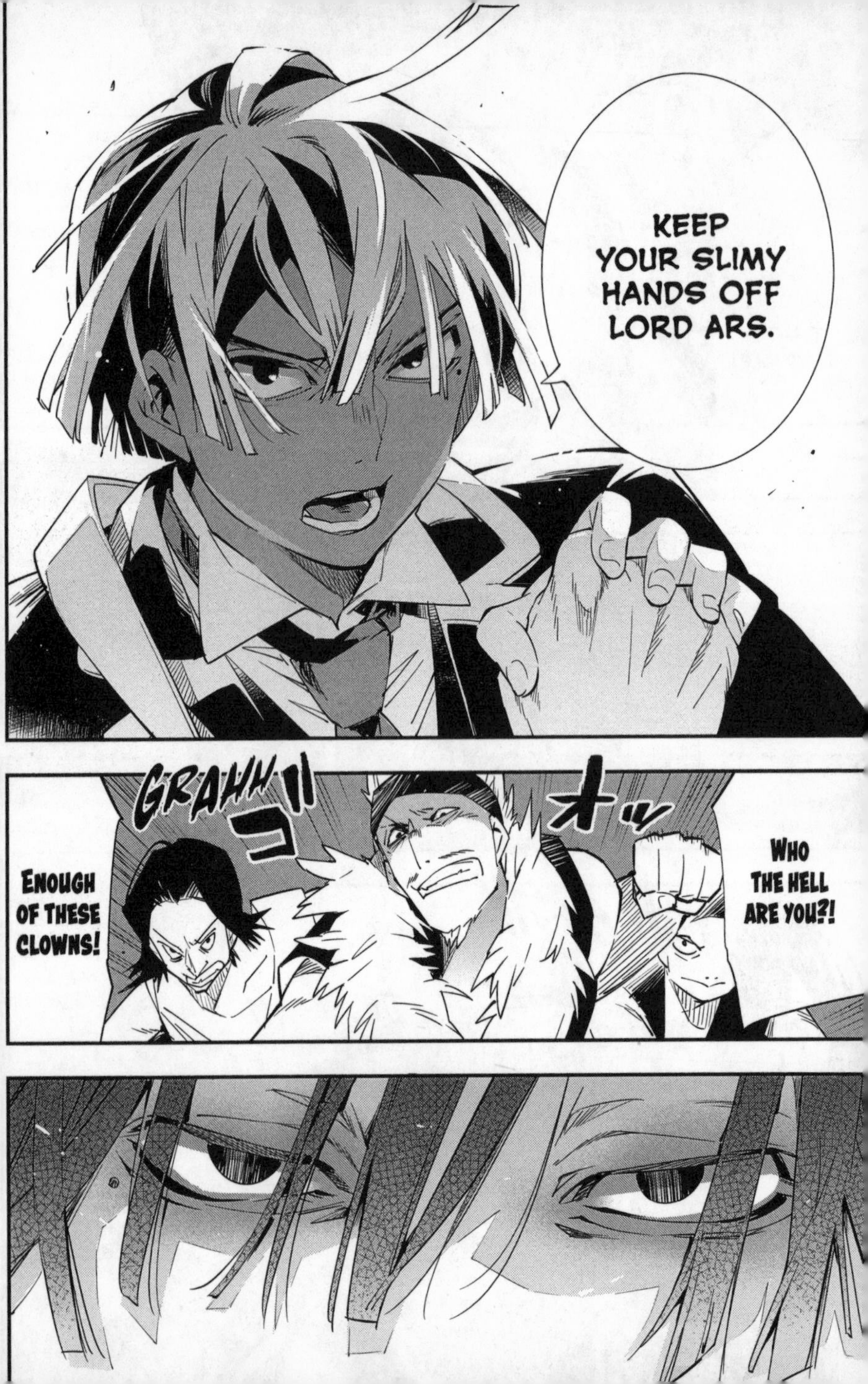
KEEP YOUR SLIMY HANDS OFF LORD ARS.
オッ
GRAHH
WHO THE HELL ARE YOU?!
ENOUGH OF THESE CLOWNS!

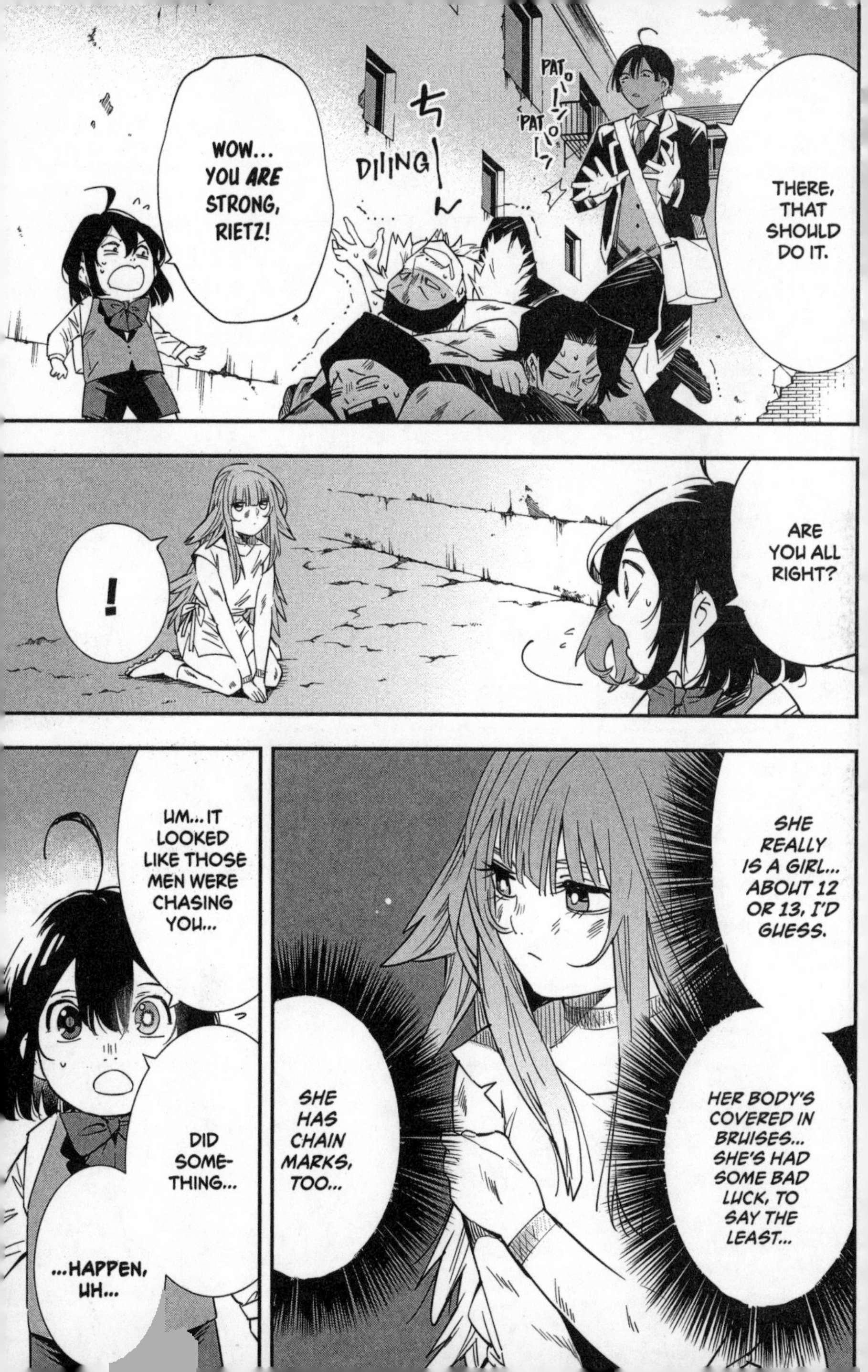
THERE, THAT SHOULD DO IT.
PAT PAT
DIIING
WOW... YOU ARE STRONG, RIETZ!
ARE YOU ALL RIGHT?
!
SHE REALLY IS A GIRL... ABOUT 12 OR 13, I'D GUESS.
HER BODY'S COVERED IN BRUISES... SHE'S HAD SOME BAD LUCK, TO SAY THE LEAST...
SHE HAS CHAIN MARKS, TOO...
UM... IT LOOKED LIKE THOSE MEN WERE CHASING YOU...
DID SOME-THING...
...HAPPEN, UH...

★★★★★
Charlotte Lace - Age 11 ♀

Stats

	CURRENT	MAX
Command	6 5	9 2
Prowess	9 3	1 1 6
Intellect	3 4	4 5
Diplomacy	3 1	4 0

Ambition	1

Aptitude

Fighter	D	Cavalier	D	Archer	D
Mage	S	Engineer	D	Armorer	D
Mariner	D	Pilot	D	Tactician	D

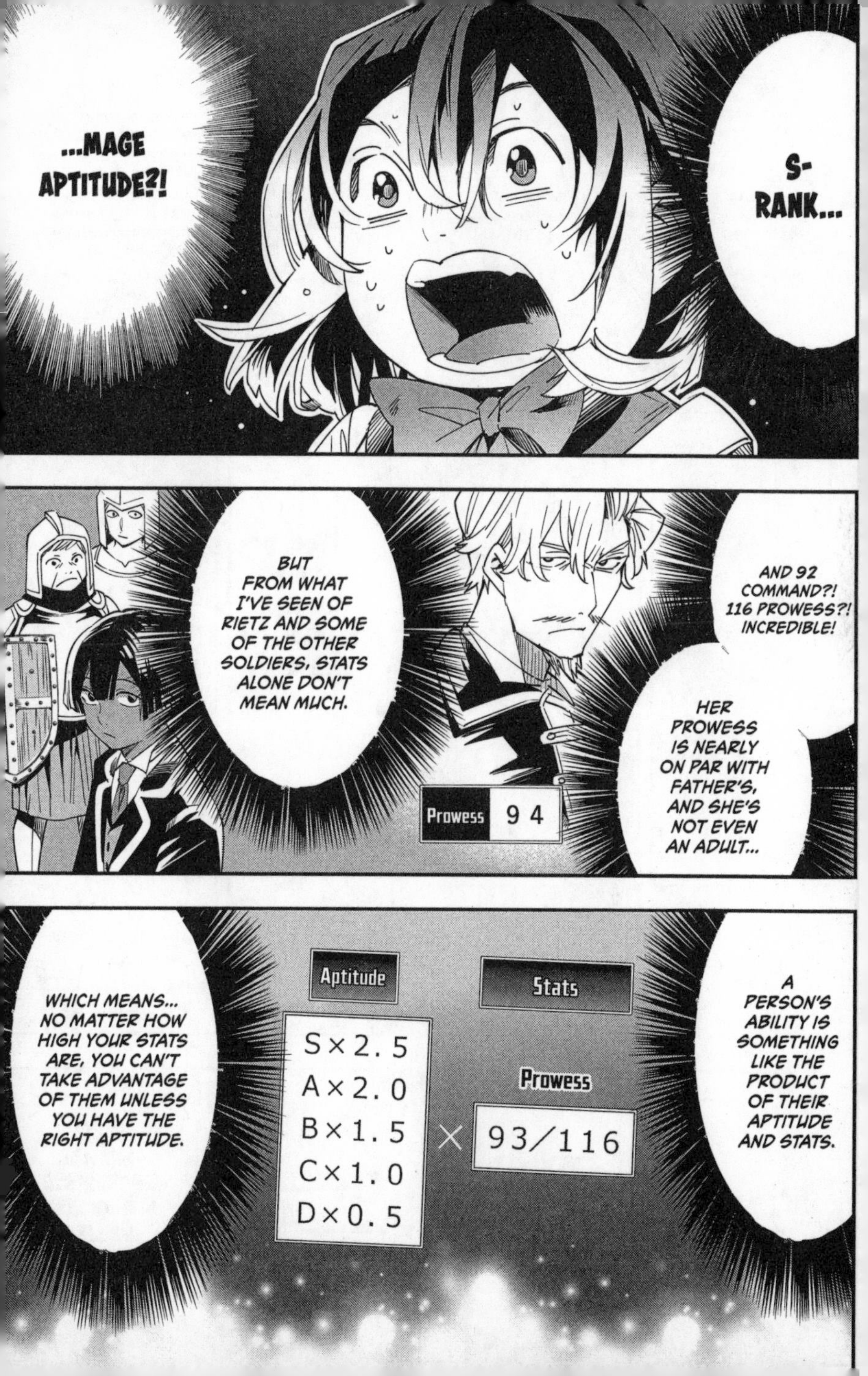
S-RANK...
...MAGE APTITUDE?!
AND 92 COMMAND?! 116 PROWESS?! INCREDIBLE!
HER PROWESS IS NEARLY ON PAR WITH FATHER'S, AND SHE'S NOT EVEN AN ADULT...
Prowess 94
BUT FROM WHAT I'VE SEEN OF RIETZ AND SOME OF THE OTHER SOLDIERS, STATS ALONE DON'T MEAN MUCH.
A PERSON'S ABILITY IS SOMETHING LIKE THE PRODUCT OF THEIR APTITUDE AND STATS.
Stats
Prowess
93/116
×
Aptitude
S×2.5
A×2.0
B×1.5
C×1.0
D×0.5
WHICH MEANS... NO MATTER HOW HIGH YOUR STATS ARE, YOU CAN'T TAKE ADVANTAGE OF THEM UNLESS YOU HAVE THE RIGHT APTITUDE.

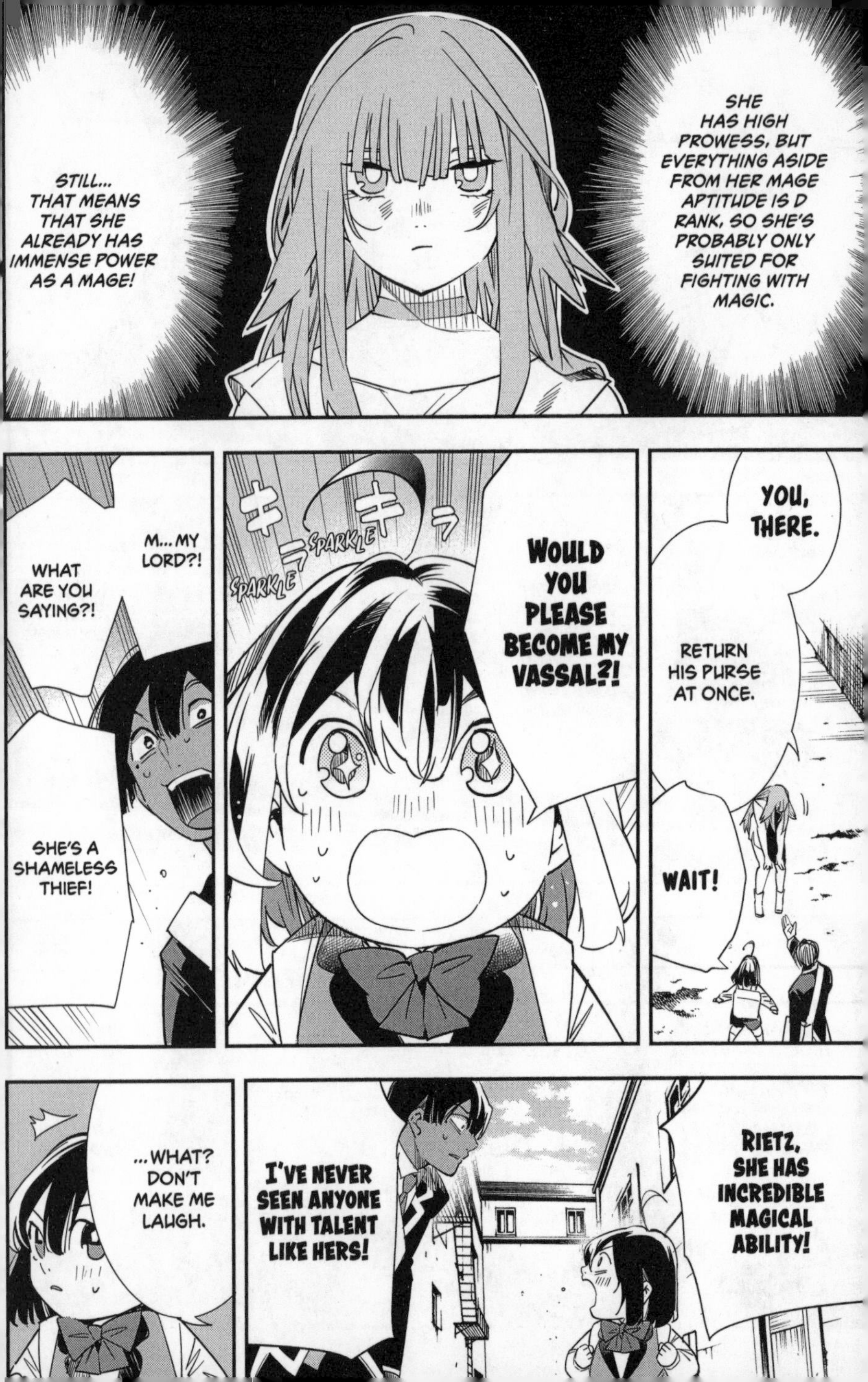
SHE HAS HIGH PROWESS, BUT EVERYTHING ASIDE FROM HER MAGE APTITUDE IS D RANK, SO SHE'S PROBABLY ONLY SUITED FOR FIGHTING WITH MAGIC.
STILL... THAT MEANS THAT SHE ALREADY HAS IMMENSE POWER AS A MAGE!
YOU, THERE.
RETURN HIS PURSE AT ONCE.
WAIT!
キラキラ
SPARKLE SPARKLE
WOULD YOU PLEASE BECOME MY VASSAL?!
M... MY LORD?!
WHAT ARE YOU SAYING?!
SHE'S A SHAMELESS THIEF!
RIETZ, SHE HAS INCREDIBLE MAGICAL ABILITY!
I'VE NEVER SEEN ANYONE WITH TALENT LIKE HERS!
...WHAT? DON'T MAKE ME LAUGH.

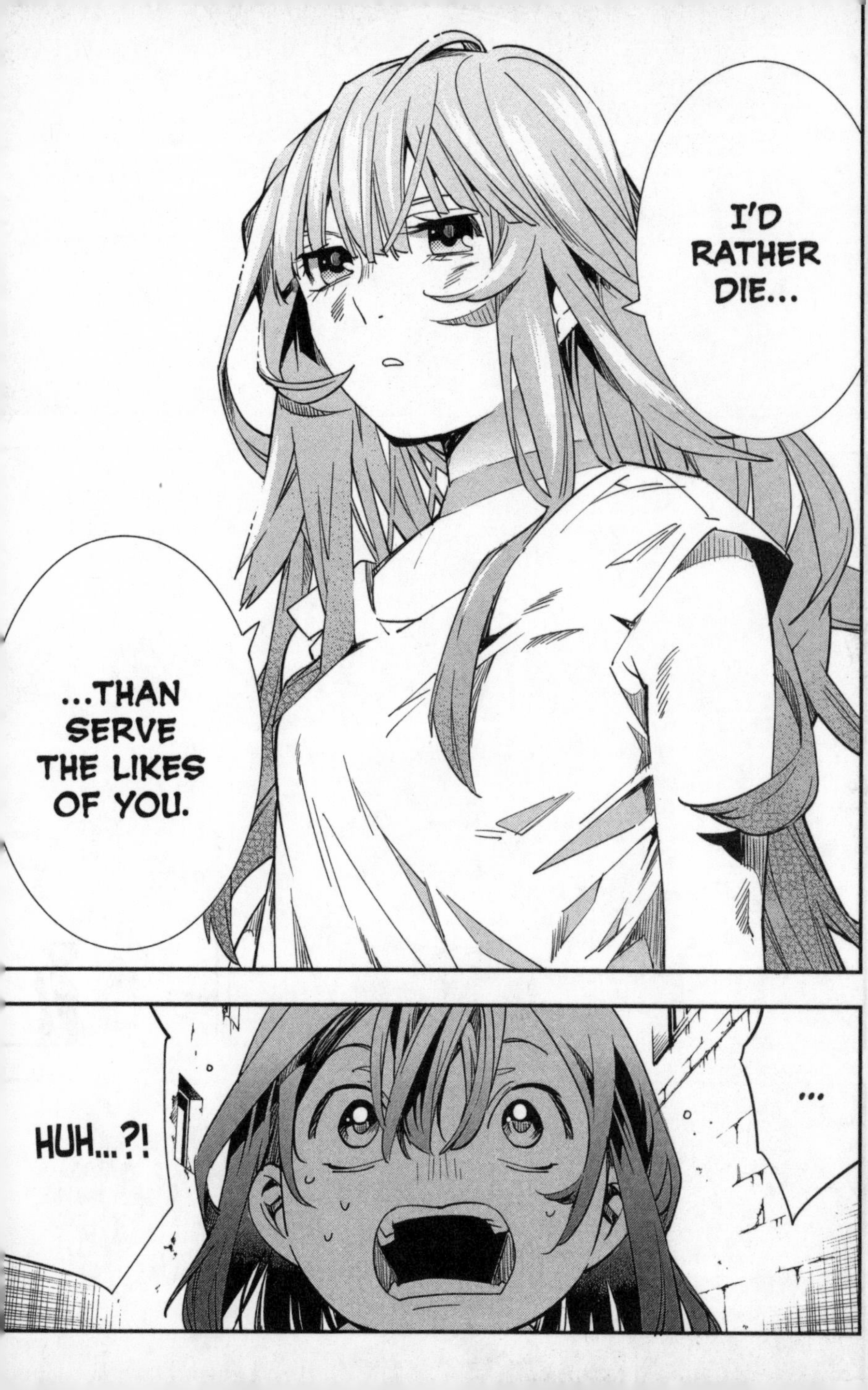
I'D RATHER DIE...
...THAN SERVE THE LIKES OF YOU.
...
HUH...?!

As a Reincarnated
ARISTOCRAT,
I'll Use My Appraisal Skill to
Rise in the World

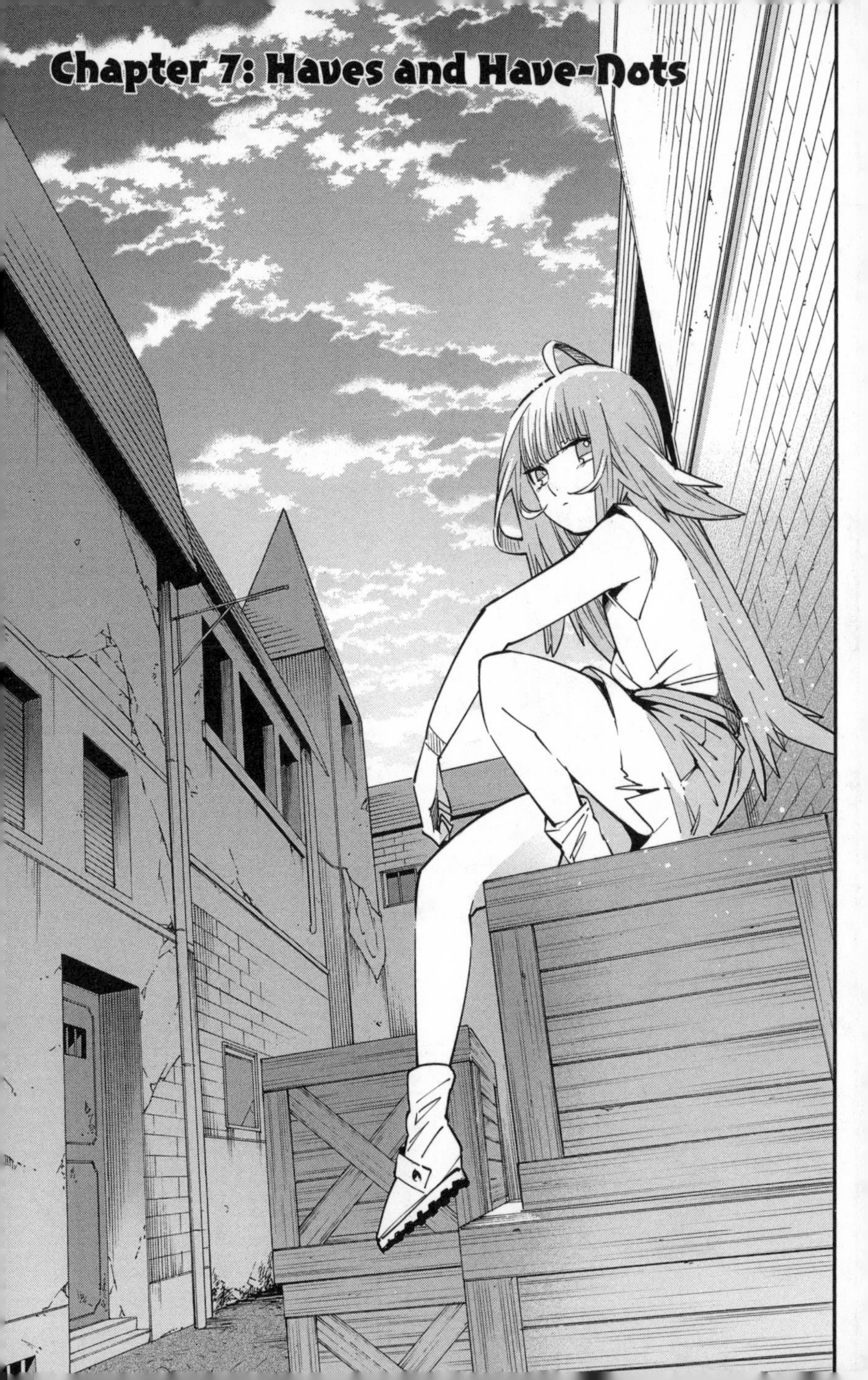
Chapter 7: Haves and Have-Nots

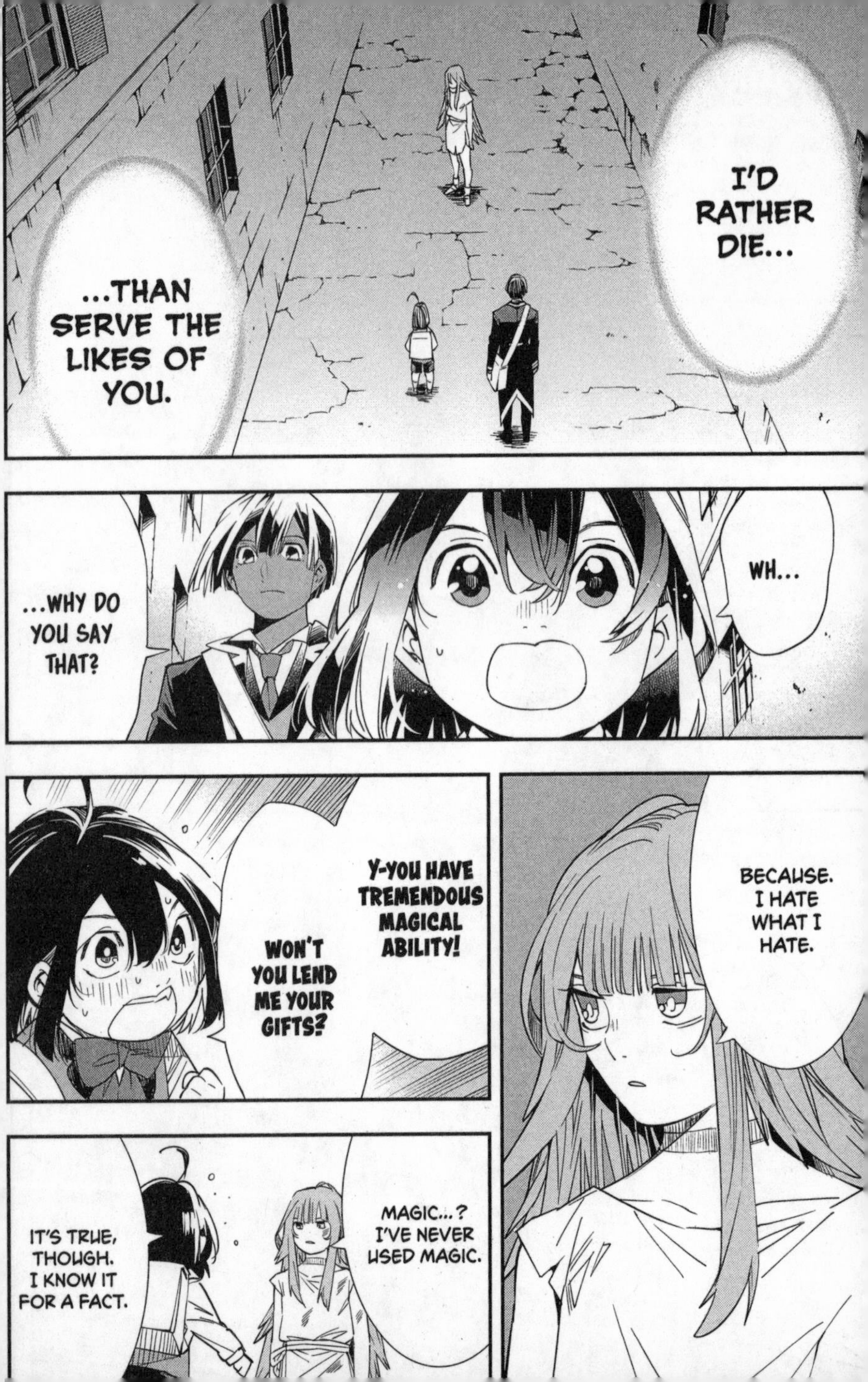
I'D RATHER DIE...
...THAN SERVE THE LIKES OF YOU.
WH...
...WHY DO YOU SAY THAT?
BECAUSE. I HATE WHAT I HATE.
Y-YOU HAVE TREMENDOUS MAGICAL ABILITY!
WON'T YOU LEND ME YOUR GIFTS?
MAGIC...? I'VE NEVER USED MAGIC.
IT'S TRUE, THOUGH. I KNOW IT FOR A FACT.

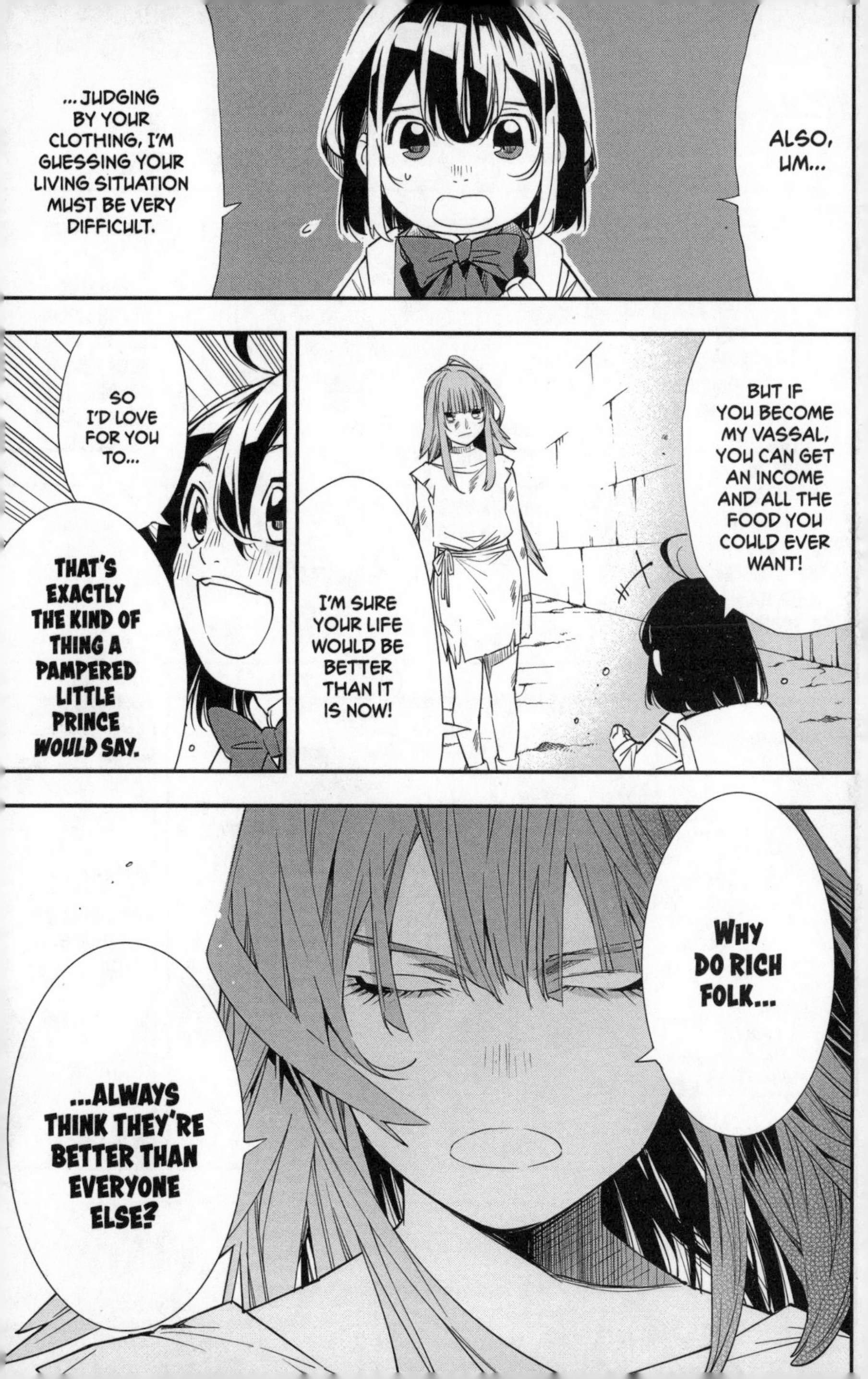
ALSO, UM...
...JUDGING BY YOUR CLOTHING, I'M GUESSING YOUR LIVING SITUATION MUST BE VERY DIFFICULT.
BUT IF YOU BECOME MY VASSAL, YOU CAN GET AN INCOME AND ALL THE FOOD YOU COULD EVER WANT!
I'M SURE YOUR LIFE WOULD BE BETTER THAN IT IS NOW!
SO I'D LOVE FOR YOU TO...
THAT'S EXACTLY THE KIND OF THING A PAMPERED LITTLE PRINCE WOULD SAY.
WHY DO RICH FOLK...
...ALWAYS THINK THEY'RE BETTER THAN EVERYONE ELSE?

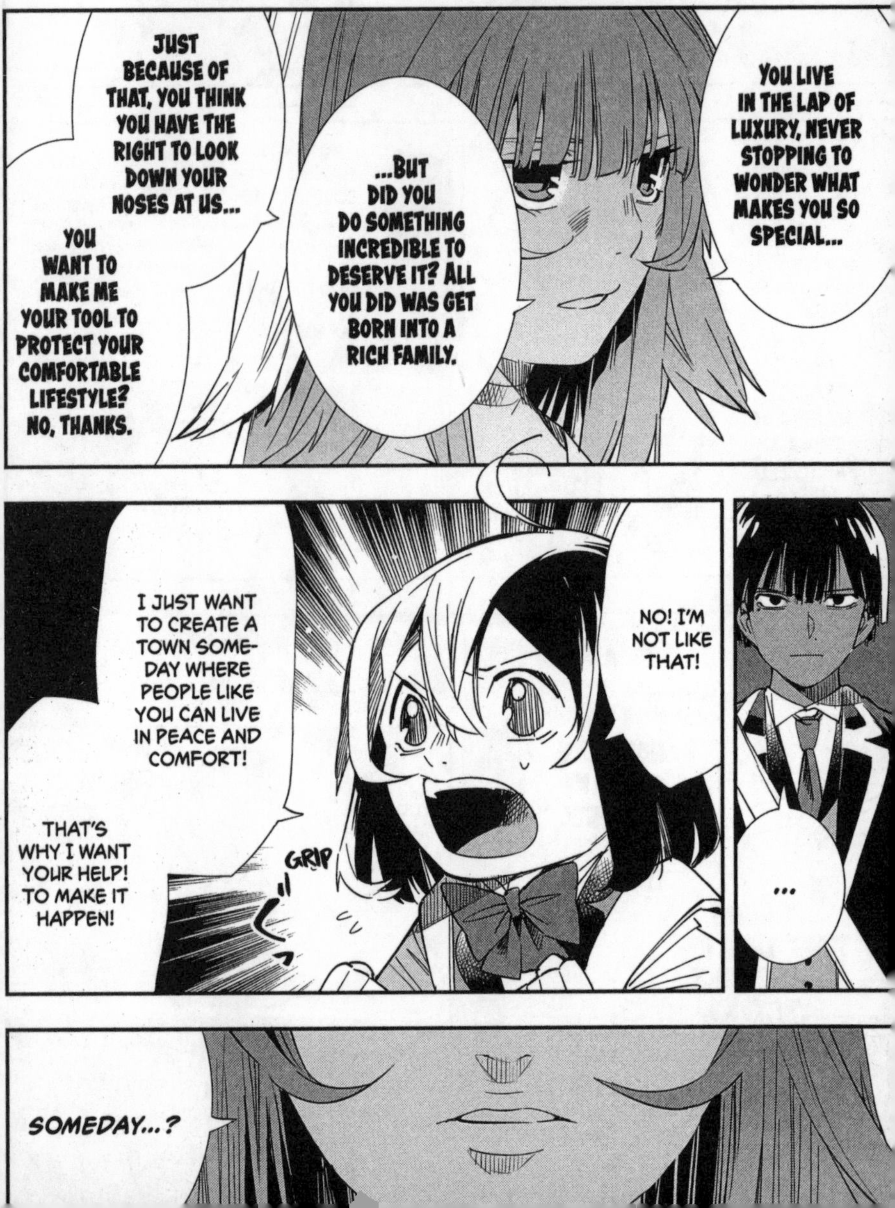
YOU LIVE IN THE LAP OF LUXURY, NEVER STOPPING TO WONDER WHAT MAKES YOU SO SPECIAL...
...BUT DID YOU DO SOMETHING INCREDIBLE TO DESERVE IT? ALL YOU DID WAS GET BORN INTO A RICH FAMILY.
JUST BECAUSE OF THAT, YOU THINK YOU HAVE THE RIGHT TO LOOK DOWN YOUR NOSES AT US...
YOU WANT TO MAKE ME YOUR TOOL TO PROTECT YOUR COMFORTABLE LIFESTYLE? NO, THANKS.
...
NO! I'M NOT LIKE THAT!
I JUST WANT TO CREATE A TOWN SOMEDAY WHERE PEOPLE LIKE YOU CAN LIVE IN PEACE AND COMFORT!
GRIP
THAT'S WHY I WANT YOUR HELP! TO MAKE IT HAPPEN!
SOMEDAY...?

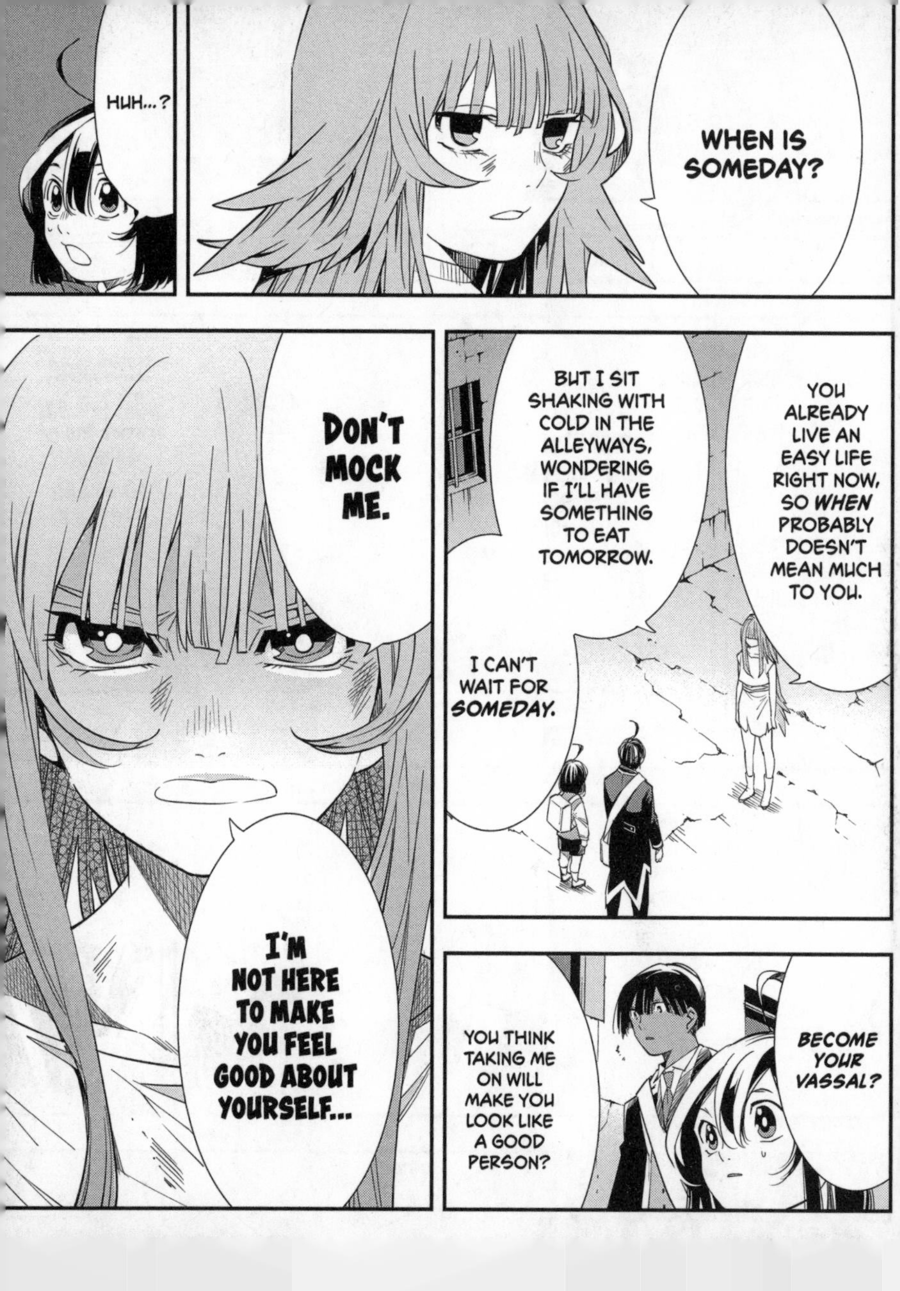
WHEN IS SOMEDAY?
HUH...?
YOU ALREADY LIVE AN EASY LIFE RIGHT NOW, SO *WHEN* PROBABLY DOESN'T MEAN MUCH TO YOU.
BUT I SIT SHAKING WITH COLD IN THE ALLEYWAYS, WONDERING IF I'LL HAVE SOMETHING TO EAT TOMORROW.
I CAN'T WAIT FOR *SOMEDAY*.
BECOME YOUR VASSAL?
YOU THINK TAKING ME ON WILL MAKE YOU LOOK LIKE A GOOD PERSON?
DON'T MOCK ME.
I'M NOT HERE TO MAKE YOU FEEL GOOD ABOUT YOURSELF...

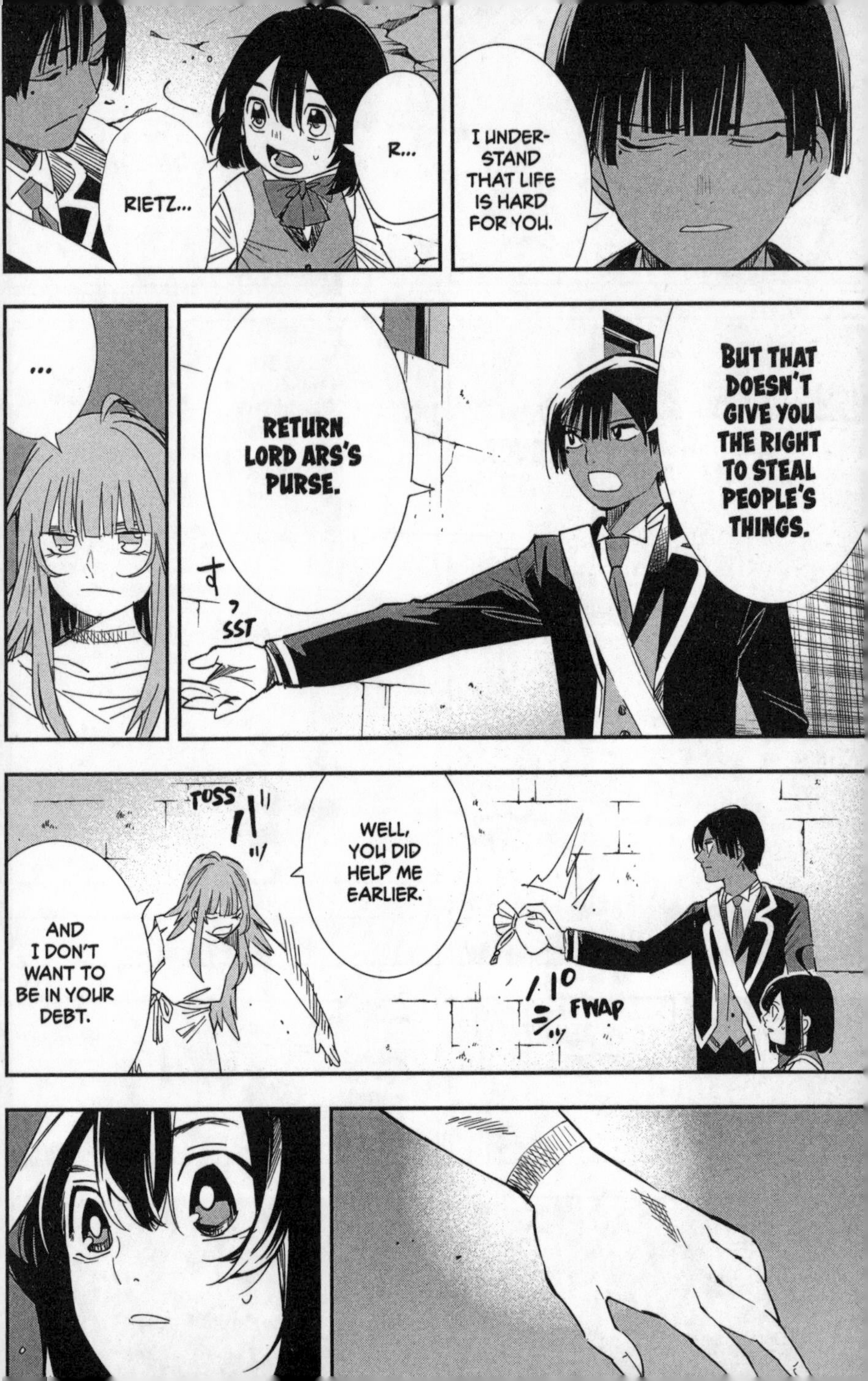
I UNDER-STAND THAT LIFE IS HARD FOR YOU.
R...
RIETZ...
BUT THAT DOESN'T GIVE YOU THE RIGHT TO STEAL PEOPLE'S THINGS.
RETURN LORD ARS'S PURSE.
す
SST
...
WELL, YOU DID HELP ME EARLIER.
FWAP
TOSS
AND I DON'T WANT TO BE IN YOUR DEBT.

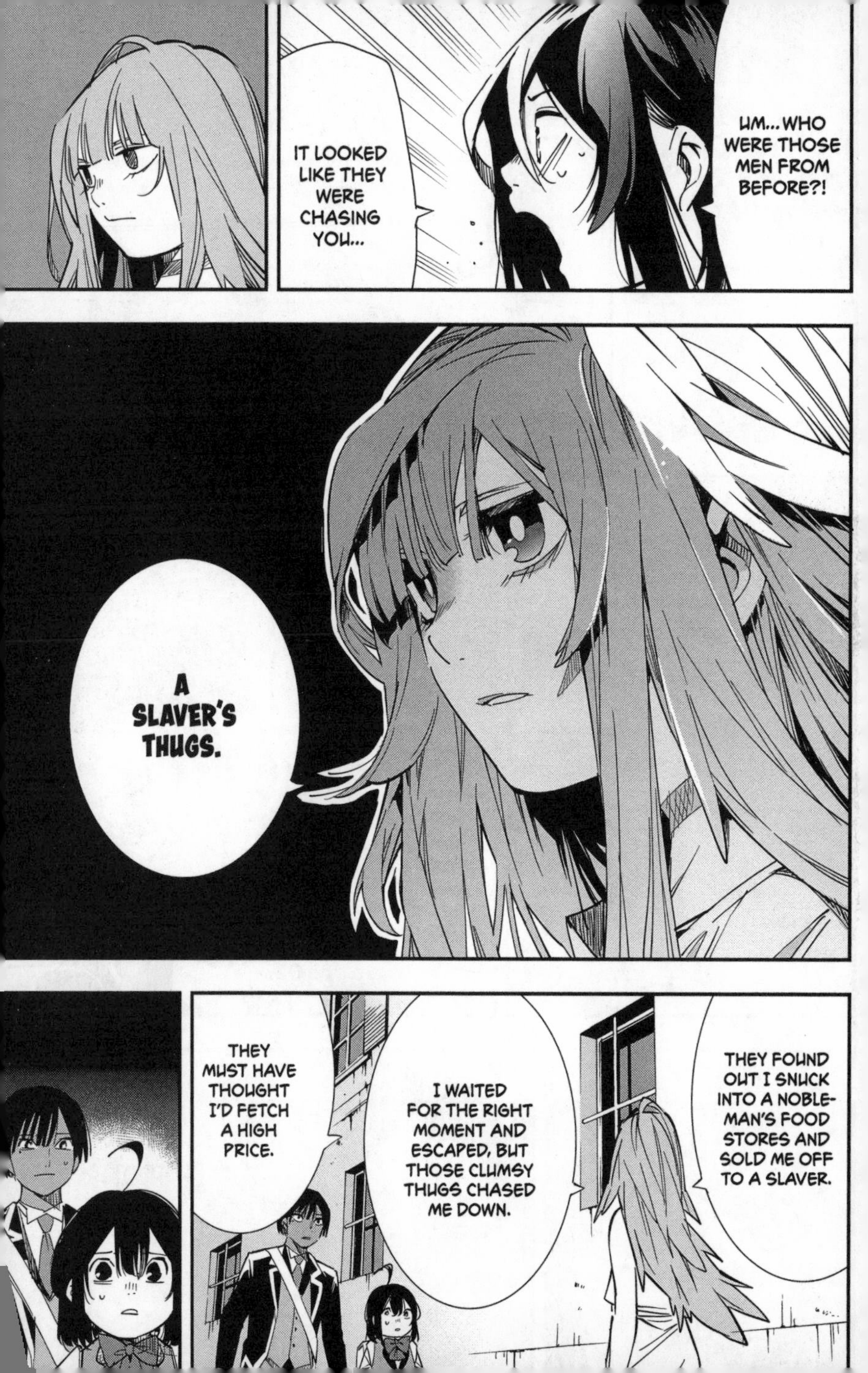
UM...WHO WERE THOSE MEN FROM BEFORE?!
IT LOOKED LIKE THEY WERE CHASING YOU...
A SLAVER'S THUGS.
THEY FOUND OUT I SNUCK INTO A NOBLE-MAN'S FOOD STORES AND SOLD ME OFF TO A SLAVER.
I WAITED FOR THE RIGHT MOMENT AND ESCAPED, BUT THOSE CLUMSY THUGS CHASED ME DOWN.
THEY MUST HAVE THOUGHT I'D FETCH A HIGH PRICE.

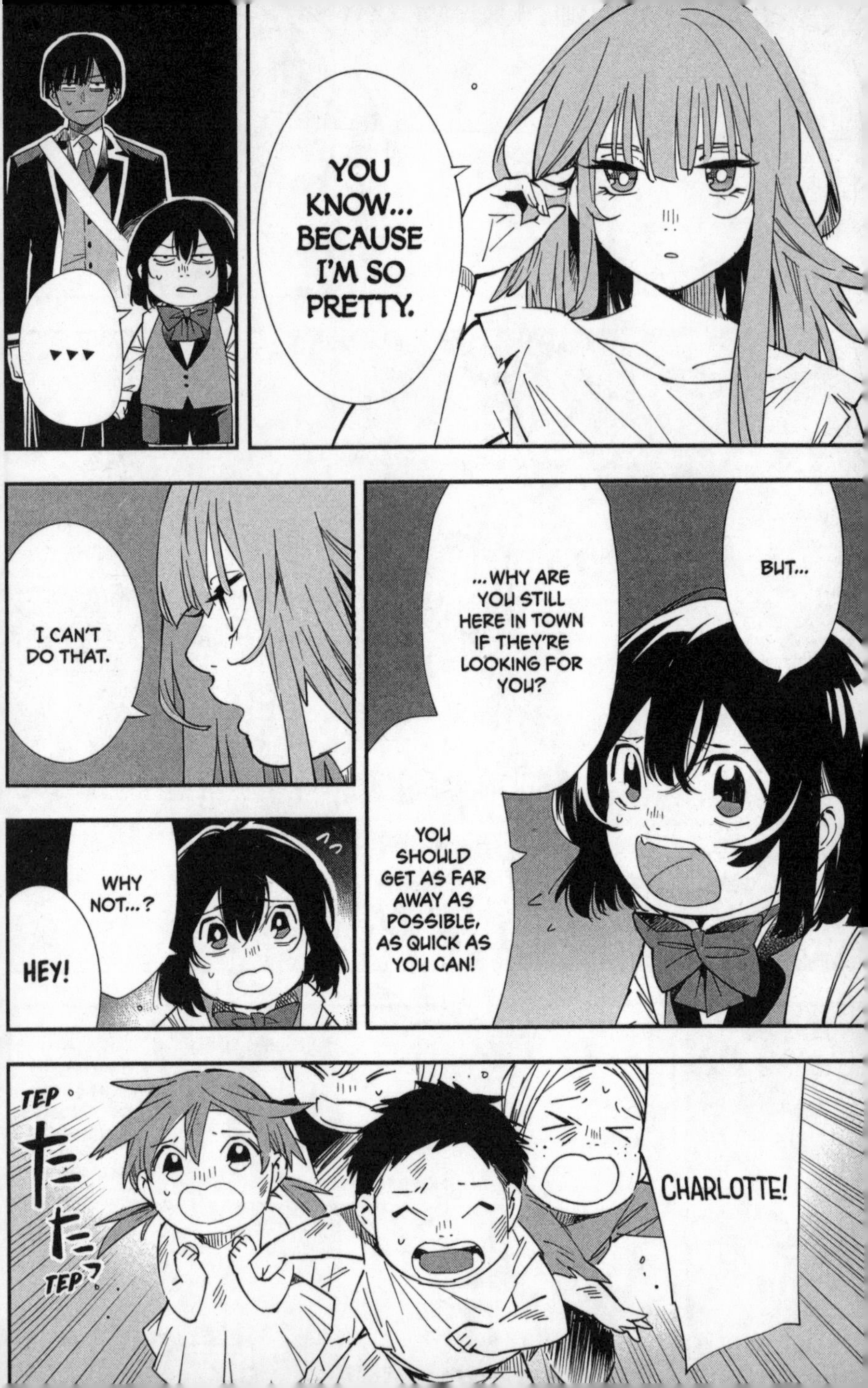
YOU KNOW... BECAUSE I'M SO PRETTY.
...
BUT...
...WHY ARE YOU STILL HERE IN TOWN IF THEY'RE LOOKING FOR YOU?
YOU SHOULD GET AS FAR AWAY AS POSSIBLE, AS QUICK AS YOU CAN!
I CAN'T DO THAT.
WHY NOT...?
HEY!
CHARLOTTE!
TEP
TEP

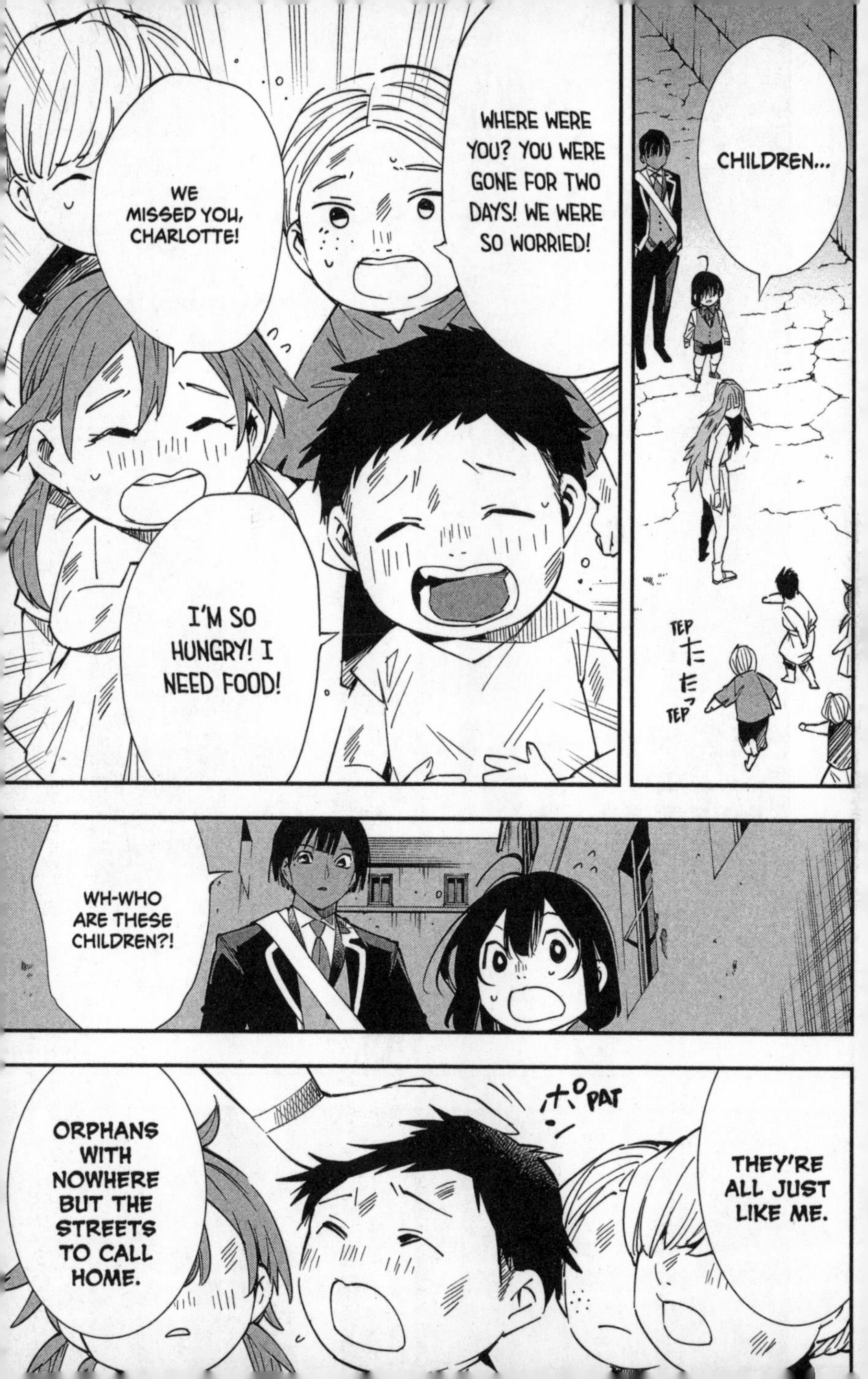
CHILDREN...
TEP TEP
WHERE WERE YOU? YOU WERE GONE FOR TWO DAYS! WE WERE SO WORRIED!
WE MISSED YOU, CHARLOTTE!
I'M SO HUNGRY! I NEED FOOD!
WH-WHO ARE THESE CHILDREN?!
THEY'RE ALL JUST LIKE ME.
PAT
ORPHANS WITH NOWHERE BUT THE STREETS TO CALL HOME.

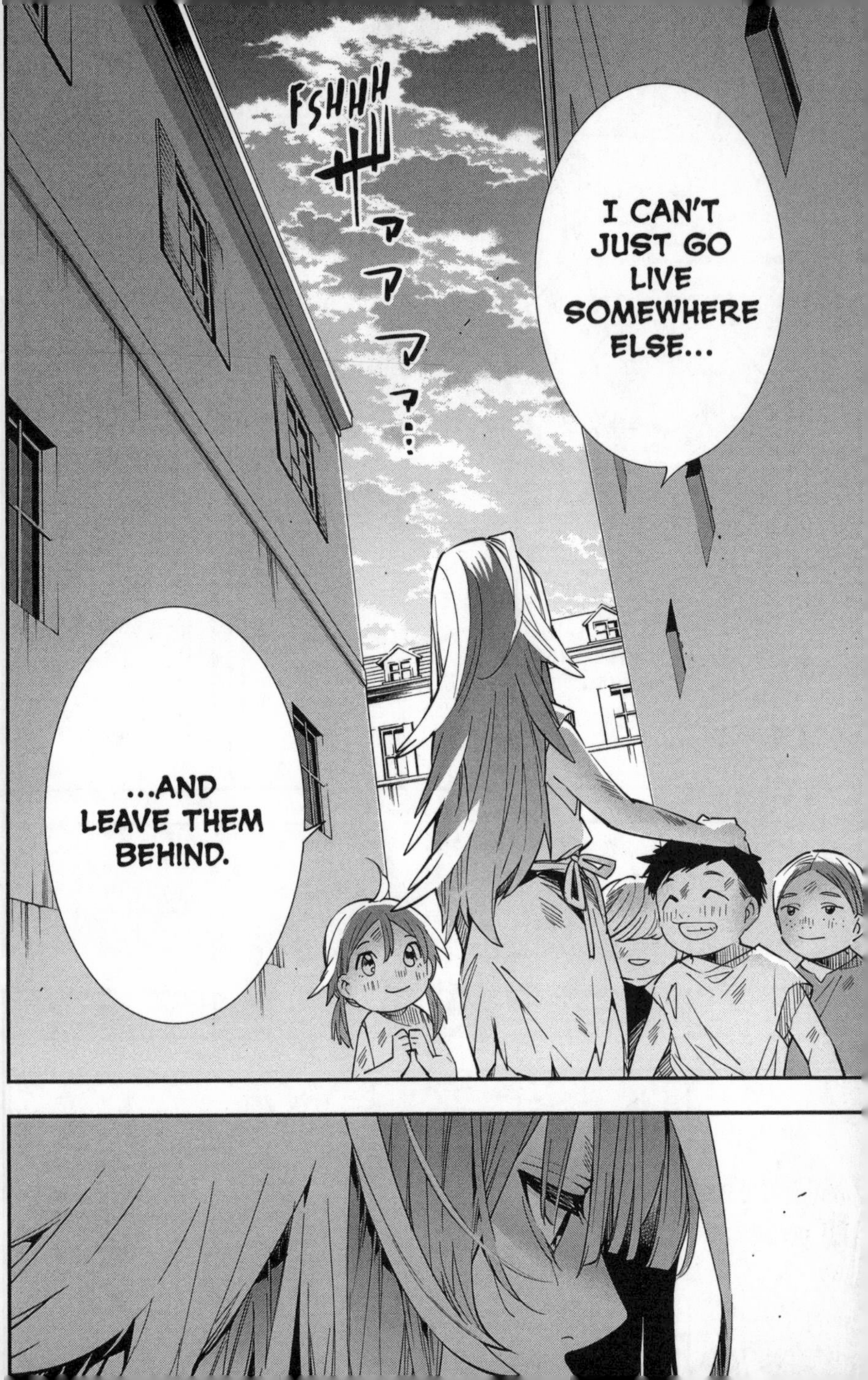
FSHHH
I CAN'T JUST GO LIVE SOMEWHERE ELSE...
...AND LEAVE THEM BEHIND.

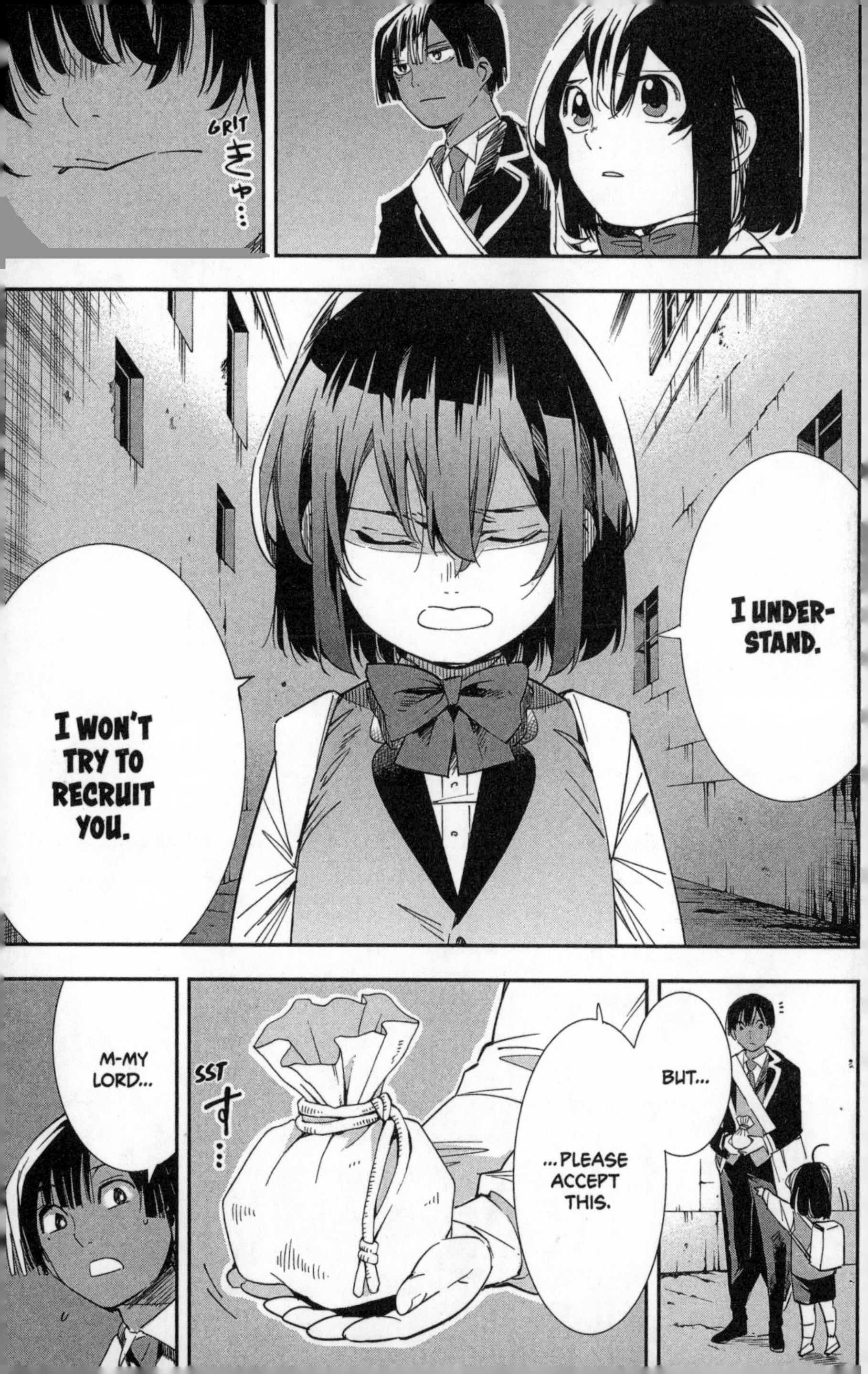
GRIT
きゅ…
I UNDER-STAND.
I WON'T TRY TO RECRUIT YOU.
BUT...
...PLEASE ACCEPT THIS.
SST
す…
M-MY LORD...

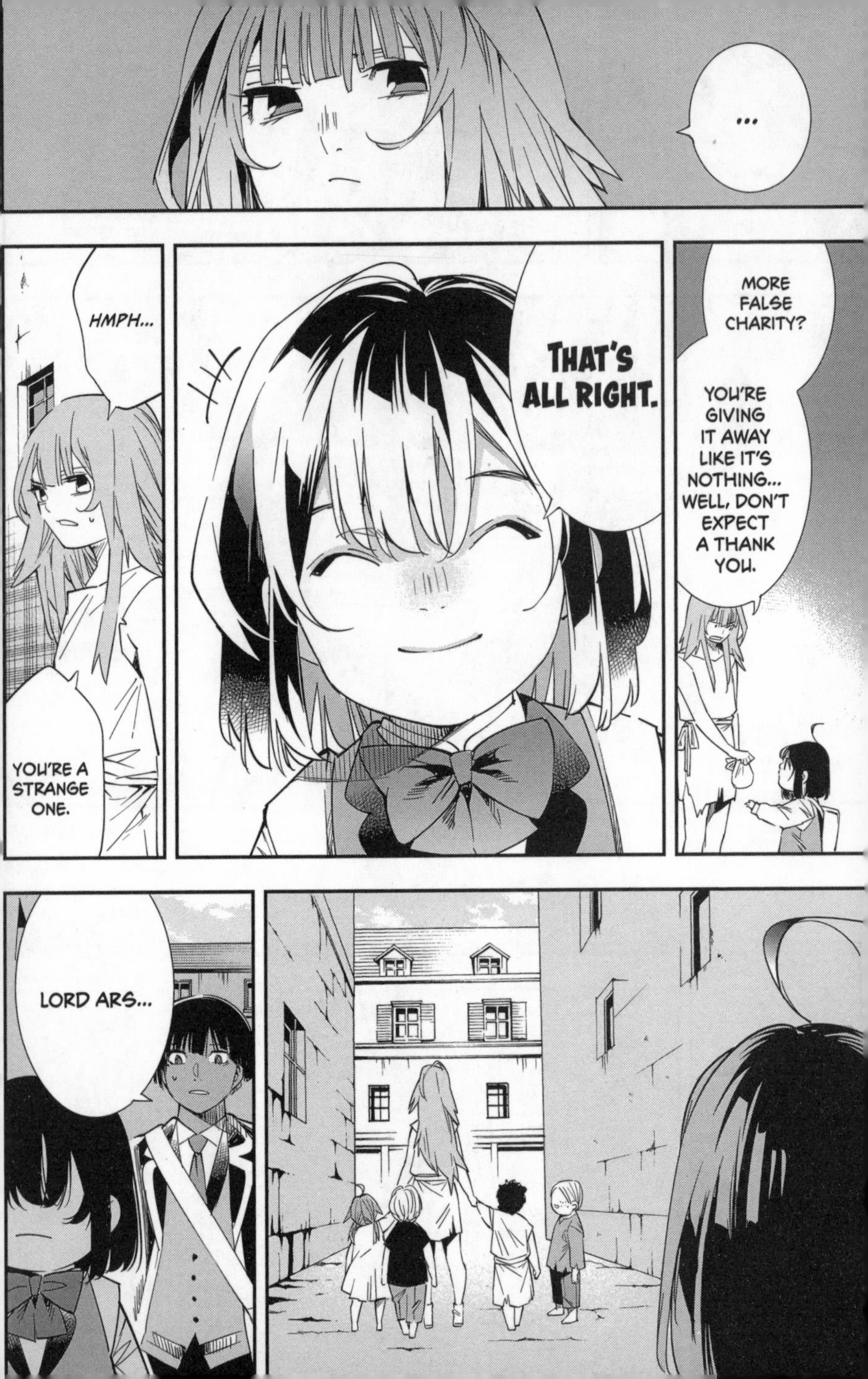
...
MORE FALSE CHARITY?
YOU'RE GIVING IT AWAY LIKE IT'S NOTHING... WELL, DON'T EXPECT A THANK YOU.
THAT'S ALL RIGHT.
HMPH...
YOU'RE A STRANGE ONE.
LORD ARS...

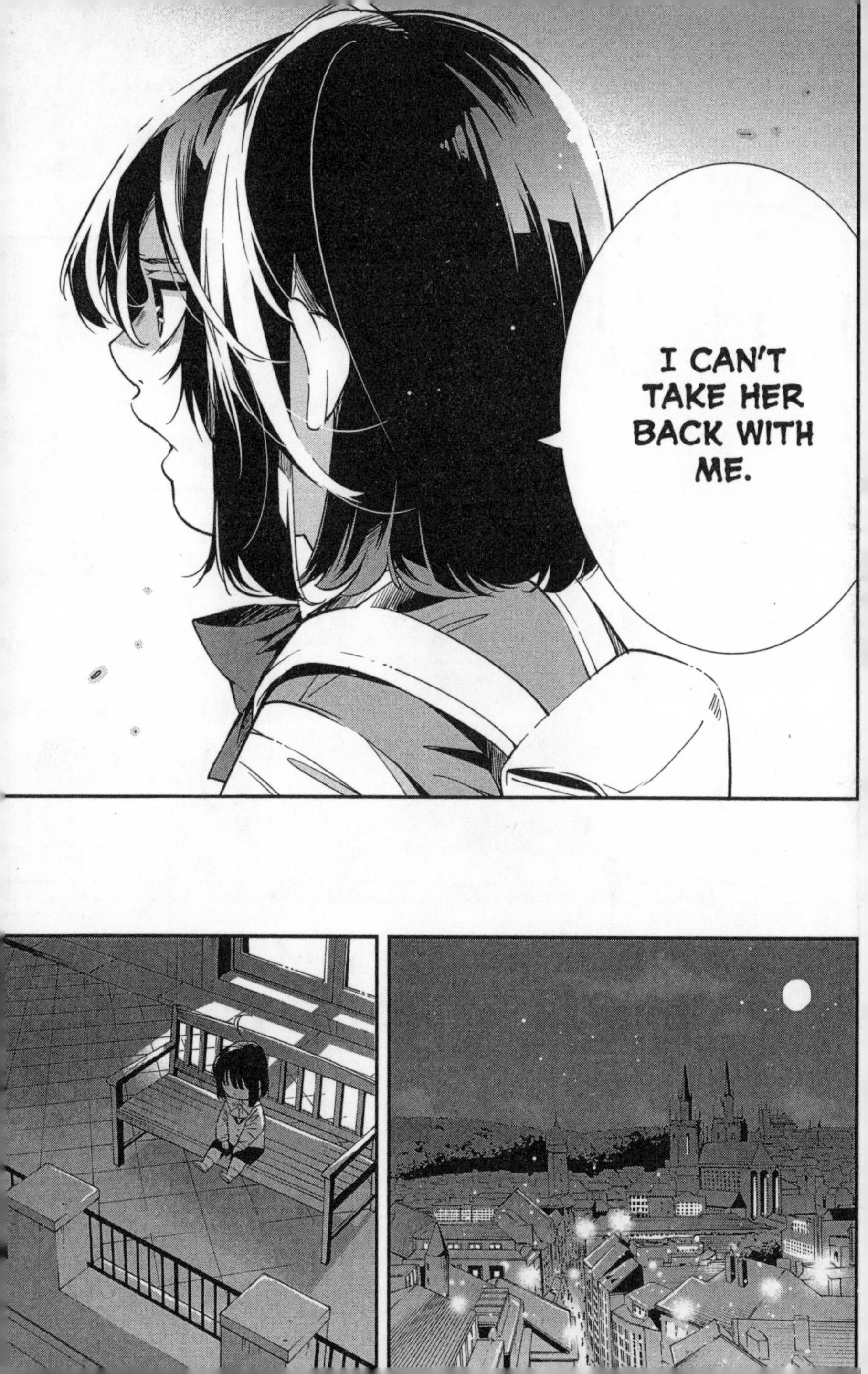
I CAN'T TAKE HER BACK WITH ME.

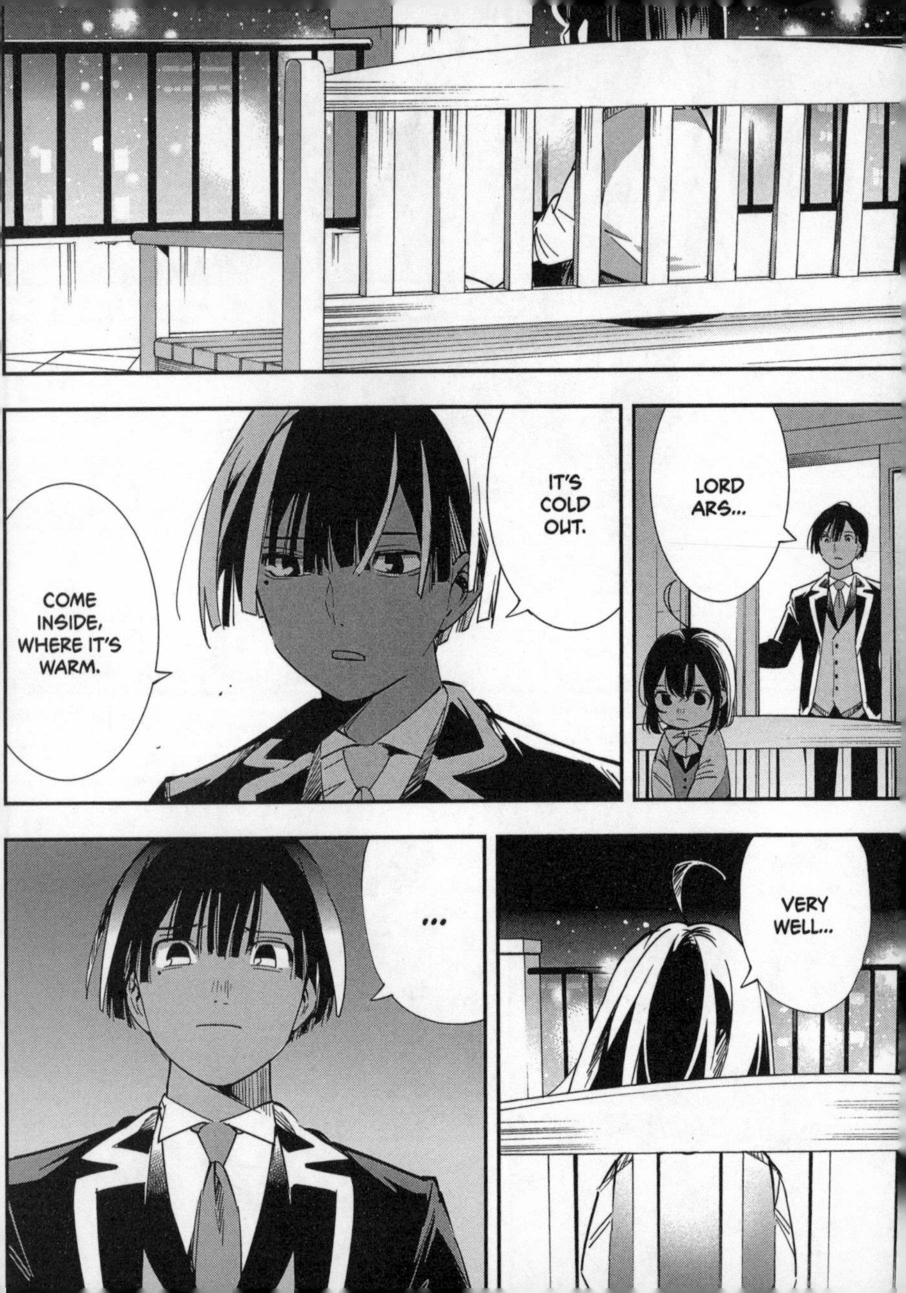
LORD ARS...
IT'S COLD OUT.
COME INSIDE, WHERE IT'S WARM.
VERY WELL...
...

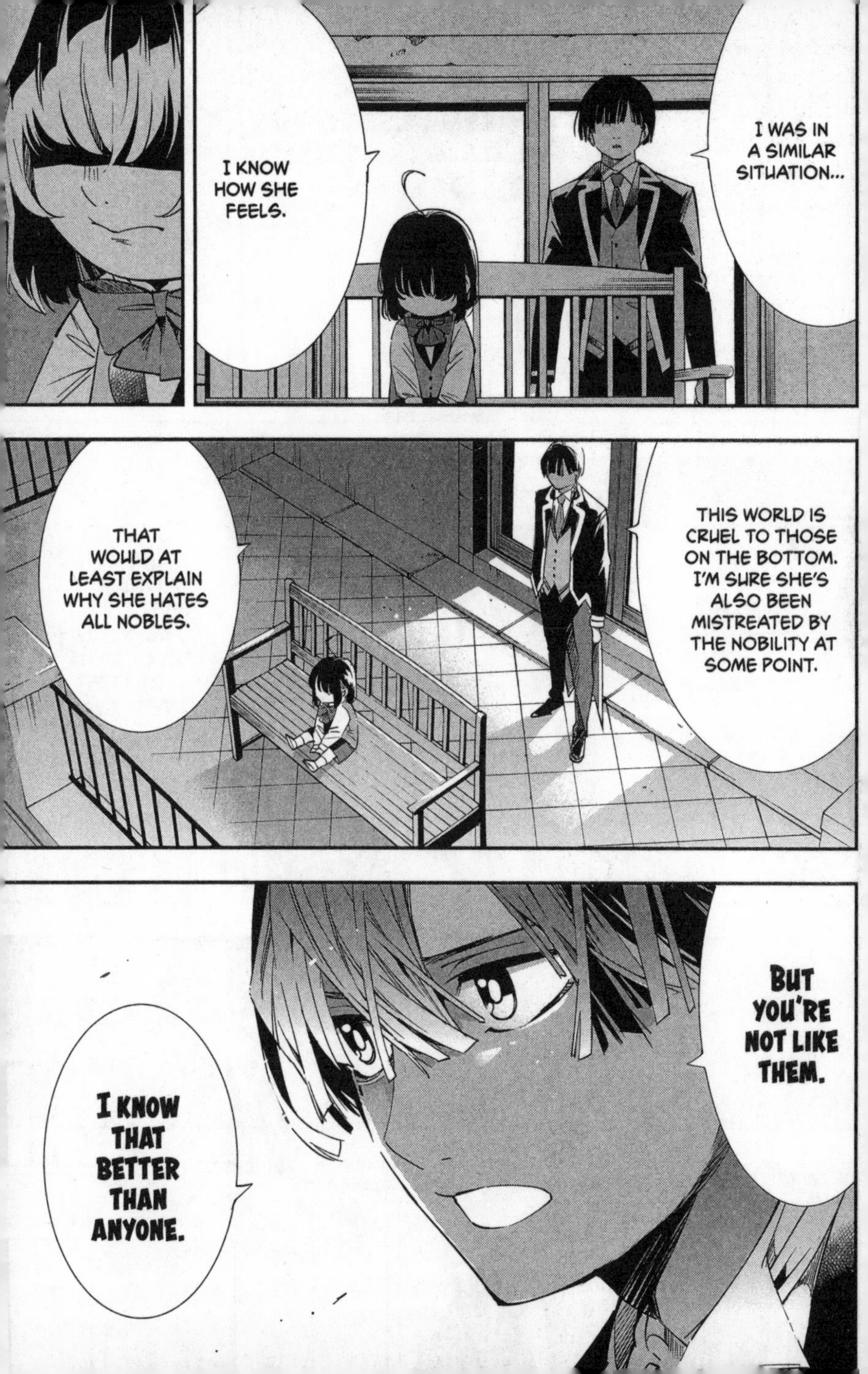
I WAS IN A SIMILAR SITUATION...
I KNOW HOW SHE FEELS.
THIS WORLD IS CRUEL TO THOSE ON THE BOTTOM. I'M SURE SHE'S ALSO BEEN MISTREATED BY THE NOBILITY AT SOME POINT.
THAT WOULD AT LEAST EXPLAIN WHY SHE HATES ALL NOBLES.
BUT YOU'RE NOT LIKE THEM.
I KNOW THAT BETTER THAN ANYONE.

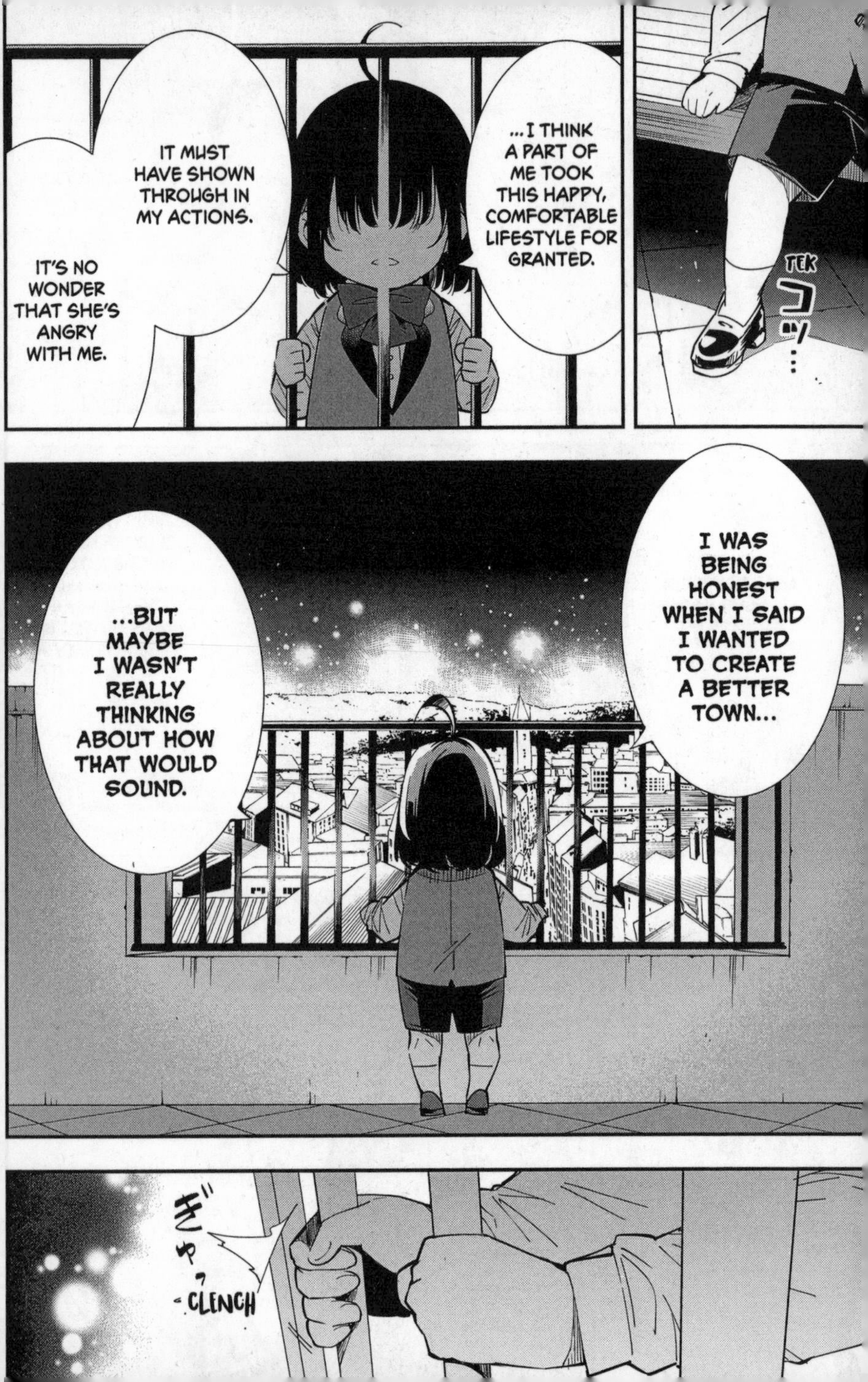
TEK
コツ…
...I THINK A PART OF ME TOOK THIS HAPPY, COMFORTABLE LIFESTYLE FOR GRANTED.
IT MUST HAVE SHOWN THROUGH IN MY ACTIONS.
IT'S NO WONDER THAT SHE'S ANGRY WITH ME.
I WAS BEING HONEST WHEN I SAID I WANTED TO CREATE A BETTER TOWN...
...BUT MAYBE I WASN'T REALLY THINKING ABOUT HOW THAT WOULD SOUND.
ぎゅっ
CLENCH

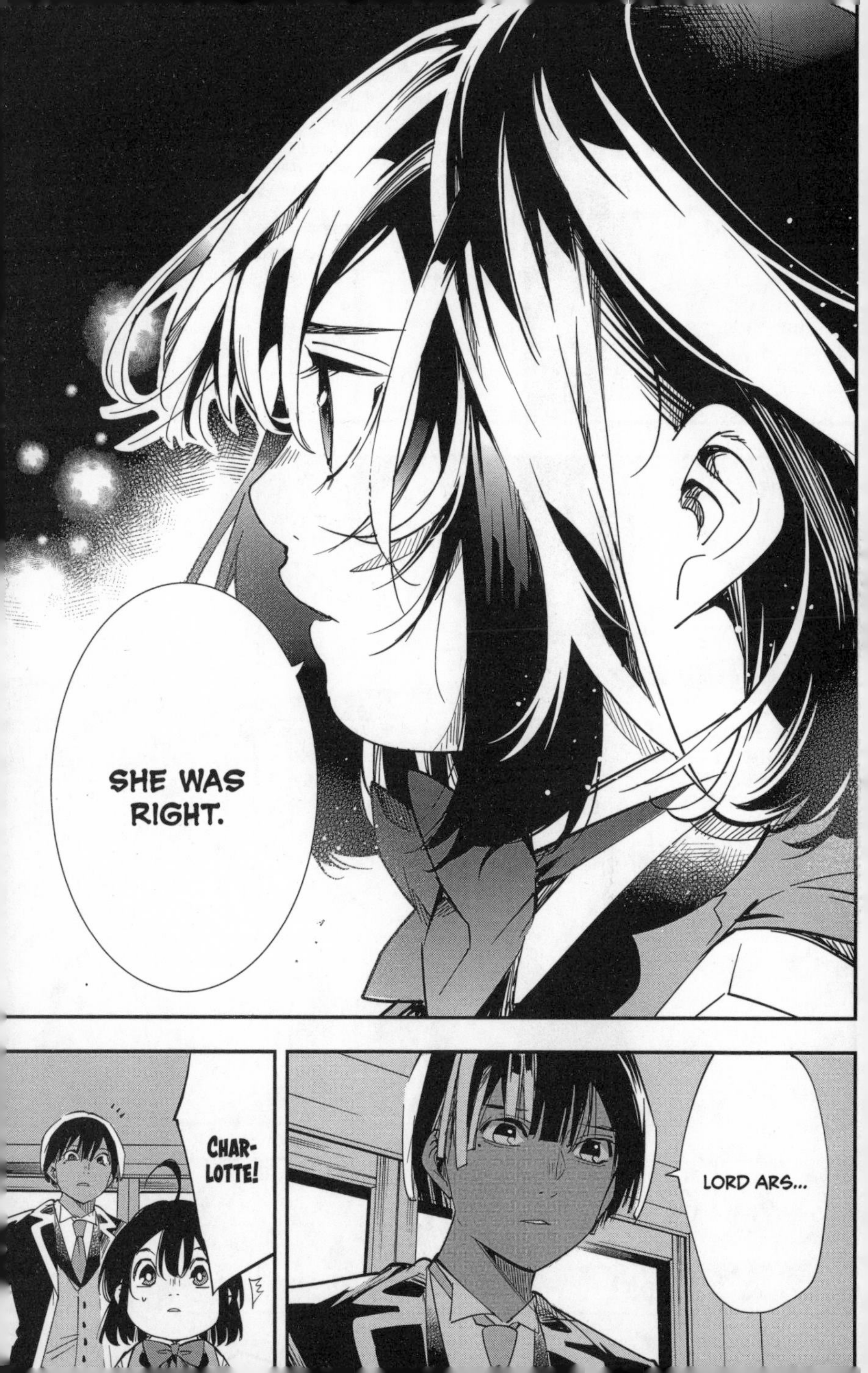
SHE WAS RIGHT.
LORD ARS...
CHAR-LOTTE!

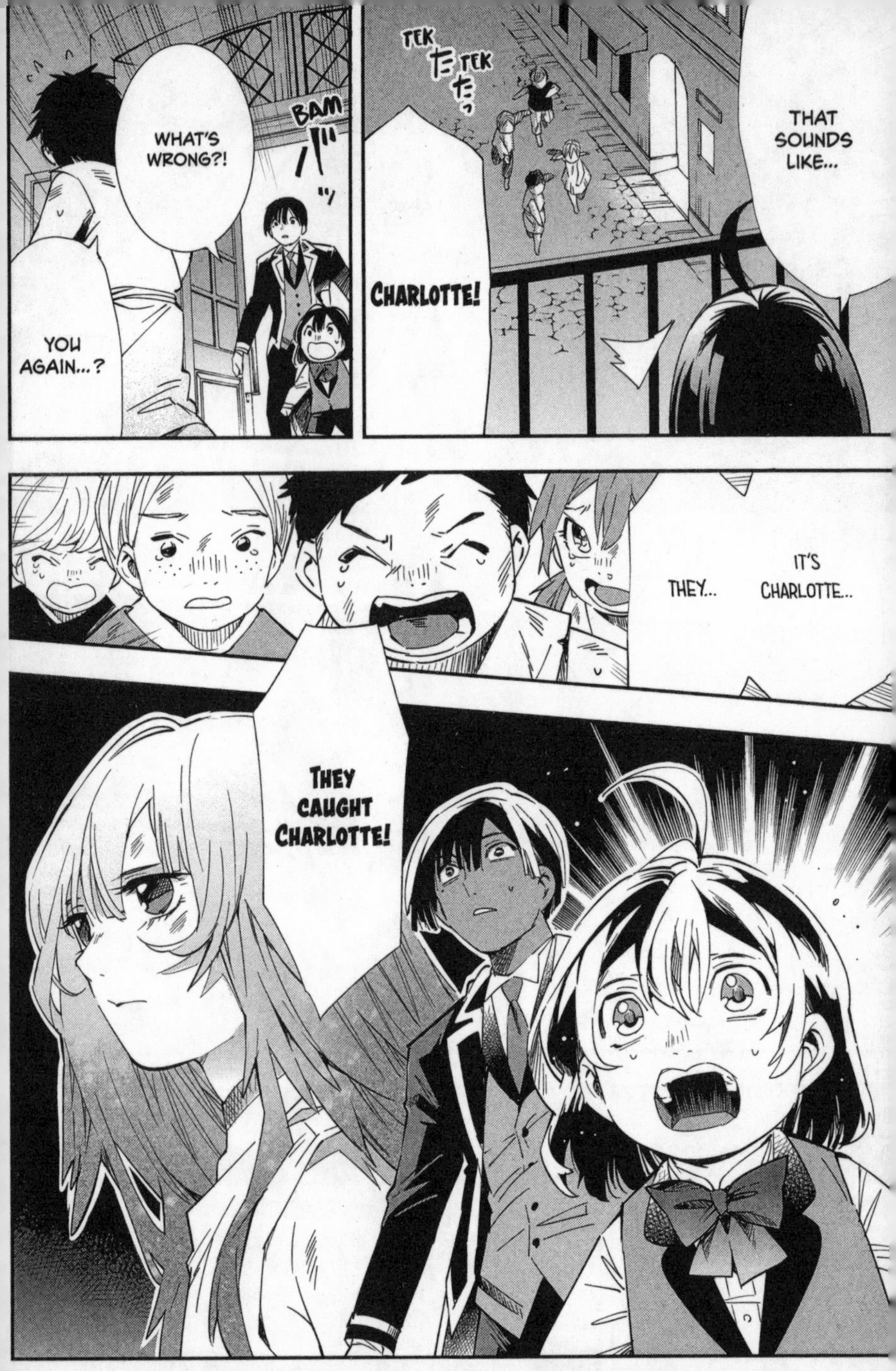
THAT SOUNDS LIKE...
TEK TEK
CHARLOTTE!
BAM
WHAT'S WRONG?!
YOU AGAIN...?
IT'S CHARLOTTE...
THEY...
THEY CAUGHT CHARLOTTE!

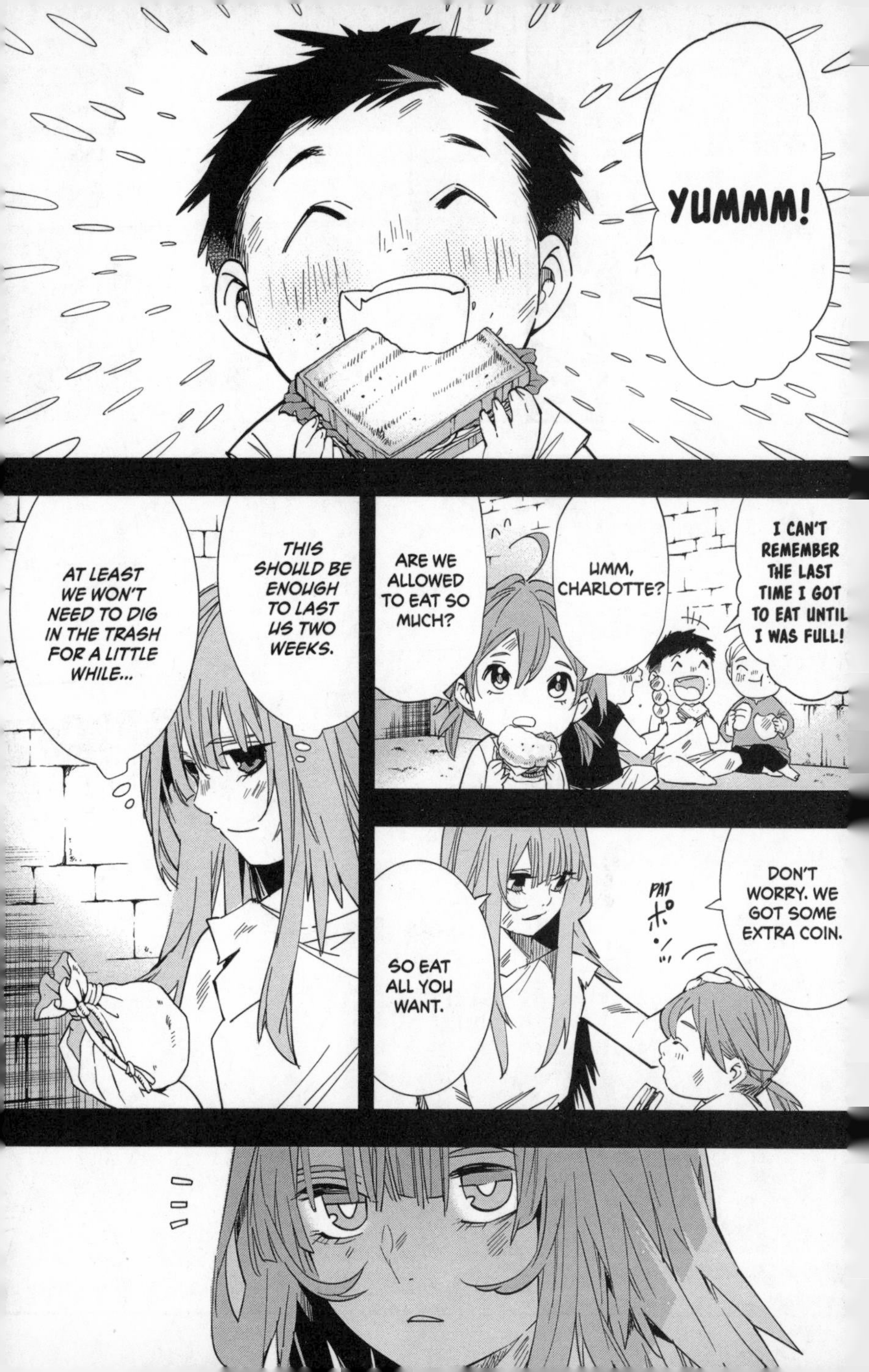
YUMMM!
I CAN'T REMEMBER THE LAST TIME I GOT TO EAT UNTIL I WAS FULL!
UMM, CHARLOTTE?
ARE WE ALLOWED TO EAT SO MUCH?
DON'T WORRY. WE GOT SOME EXTRA COIN.
PAT
ポ
SO EAT ALL YOU WANT.
THIS SHOULD BE ENOUGH TO LAST US TWO WEEKS.
AT LEAST WE WON'T NEED TO DIG IN THE TRASH FOR A LITTLE WHILE...

Chapter 8: Anger

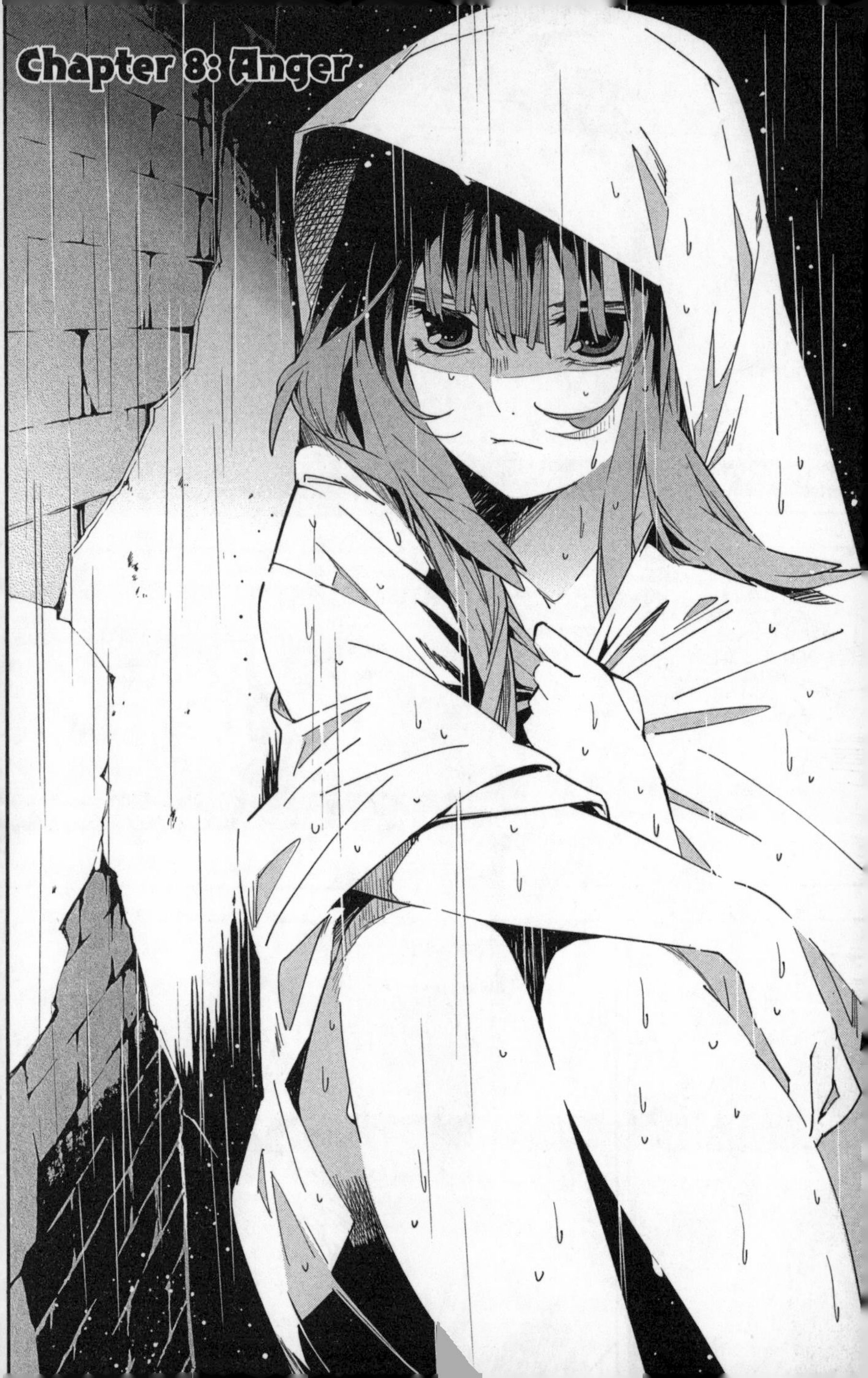

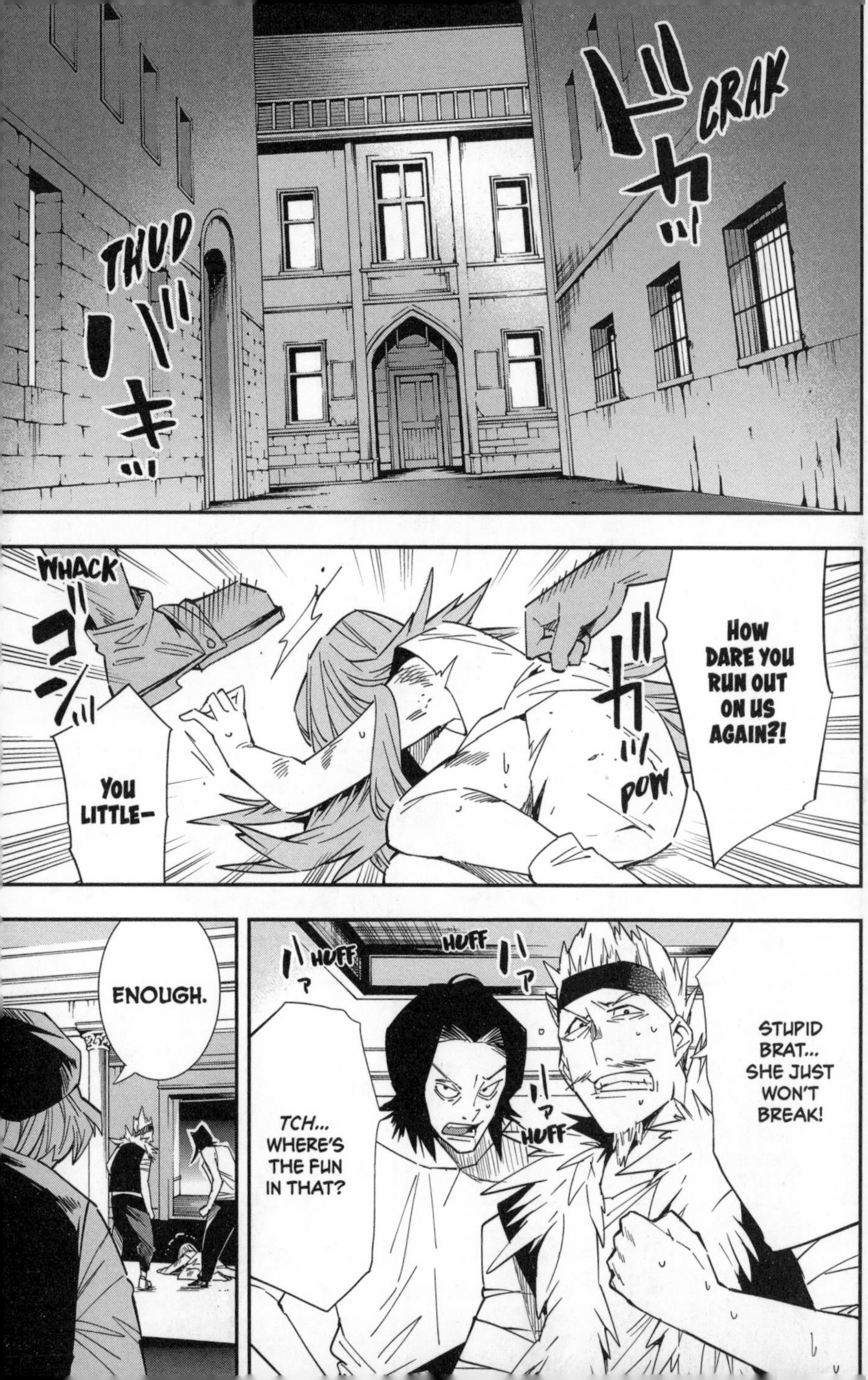
CRAK
THUD
HOW DARE YOU RUN OUT ON US AGAIN?!
POW
WHACK
YOU LITTLE-
HUFF
STUPID BRAT... SHE JUST WON'T BREAK!
HUFF
HUFF
TCH... WHERE'S THE FUN IN THAT?
ENOUGH.

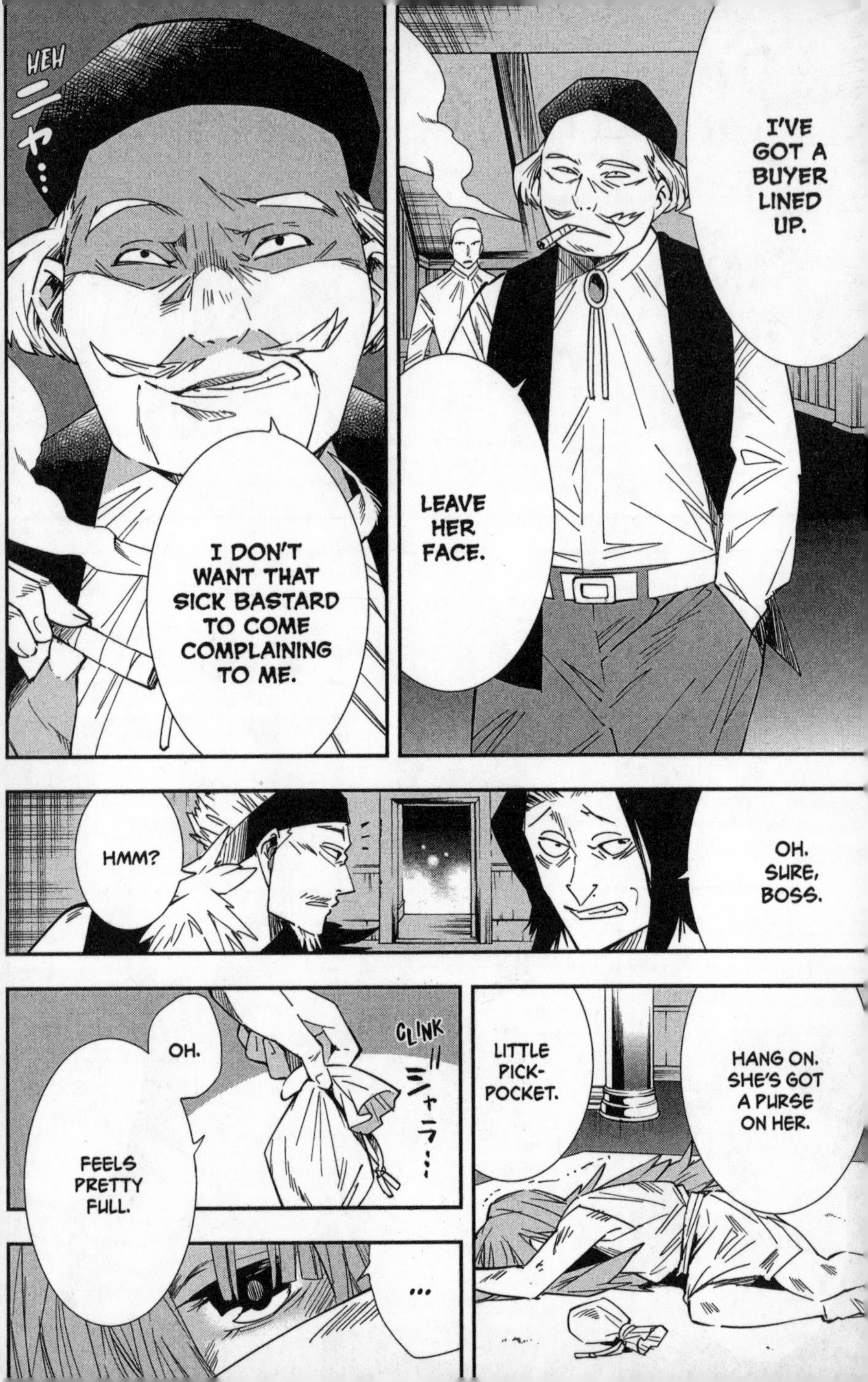
I'VE GOT A BUYER LINED UP.
LEAVE HER FACE.
HEH
ニヤ…
I DON'T WANT THAT SICK BASTARD TO COME COMPLAINING TO ME.
OH. SURE, BOSS.
HMM?
HANG ON. SHE'S GOT A PURSE ON HER.
LITTLE PICK-POCKET.
CLINK
ジャラ…
OH.
FEELS PRETTY FULL.
…

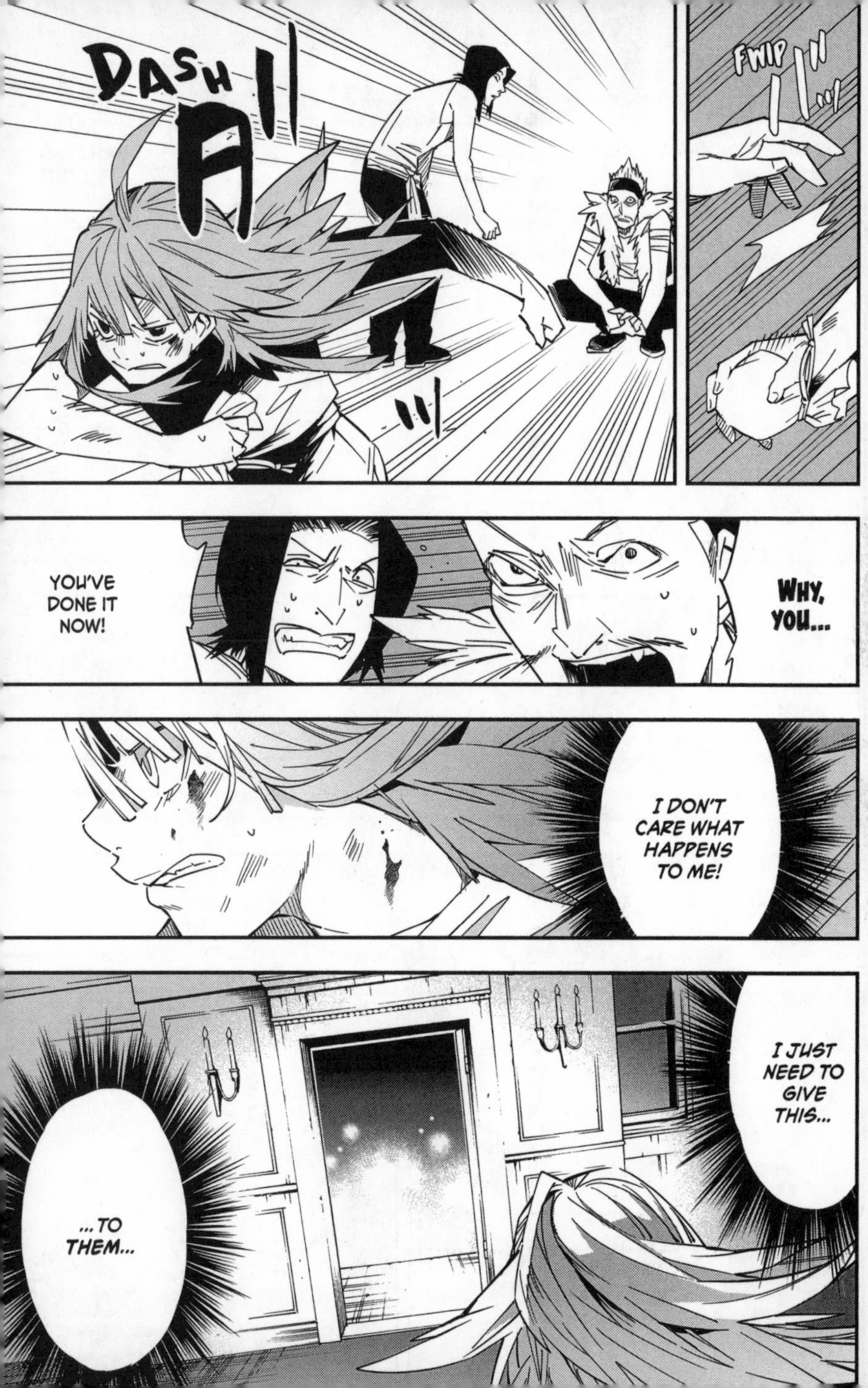
FWIP
DASH
WHY, YOU...
YOU'VE DONE IT NOW!
I DON'T CARE WHAT HAPPENS TO ME!
I JUST NEED TO GIVE THIS...
...TO THEM...

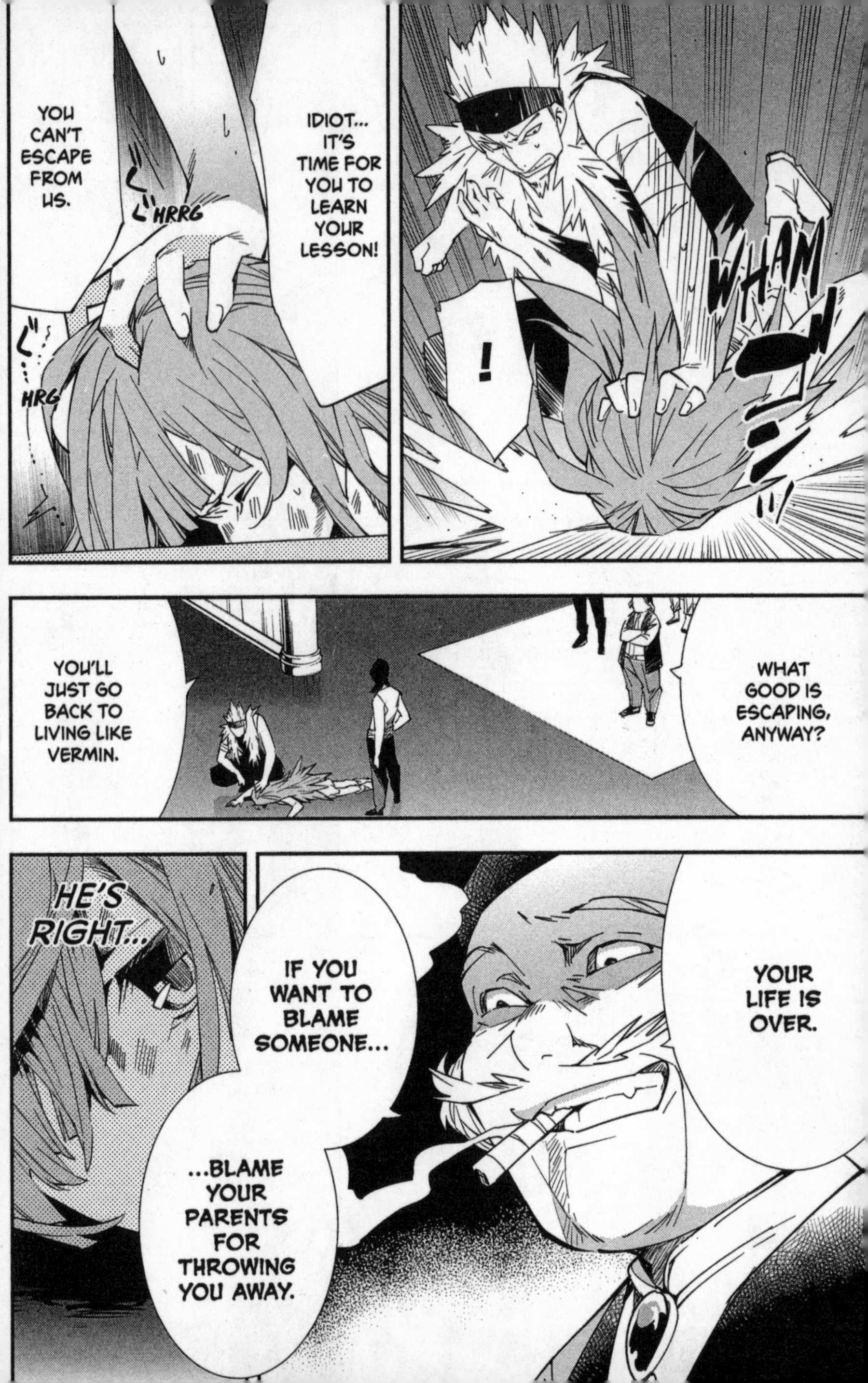
WHAM
!
IDIOT... IT'S TIME FOR YOU TO LEARN YOUR LESSON!
YOU CAN'T ESCAPE FROM US.
HRRG
HRG
WHAT GOOD IS ESCAPING, ANYWAY?
YOU'LL JUST GO BACK TO LIVING LIKE VERMIN.
YOUR LIFE IS OVER.
IF YOU WANT TO BLAME SOMEONE...
...BLAME YOUR PARENTS FOR THROWING YOU AWAY.
HE'S RIGHT...

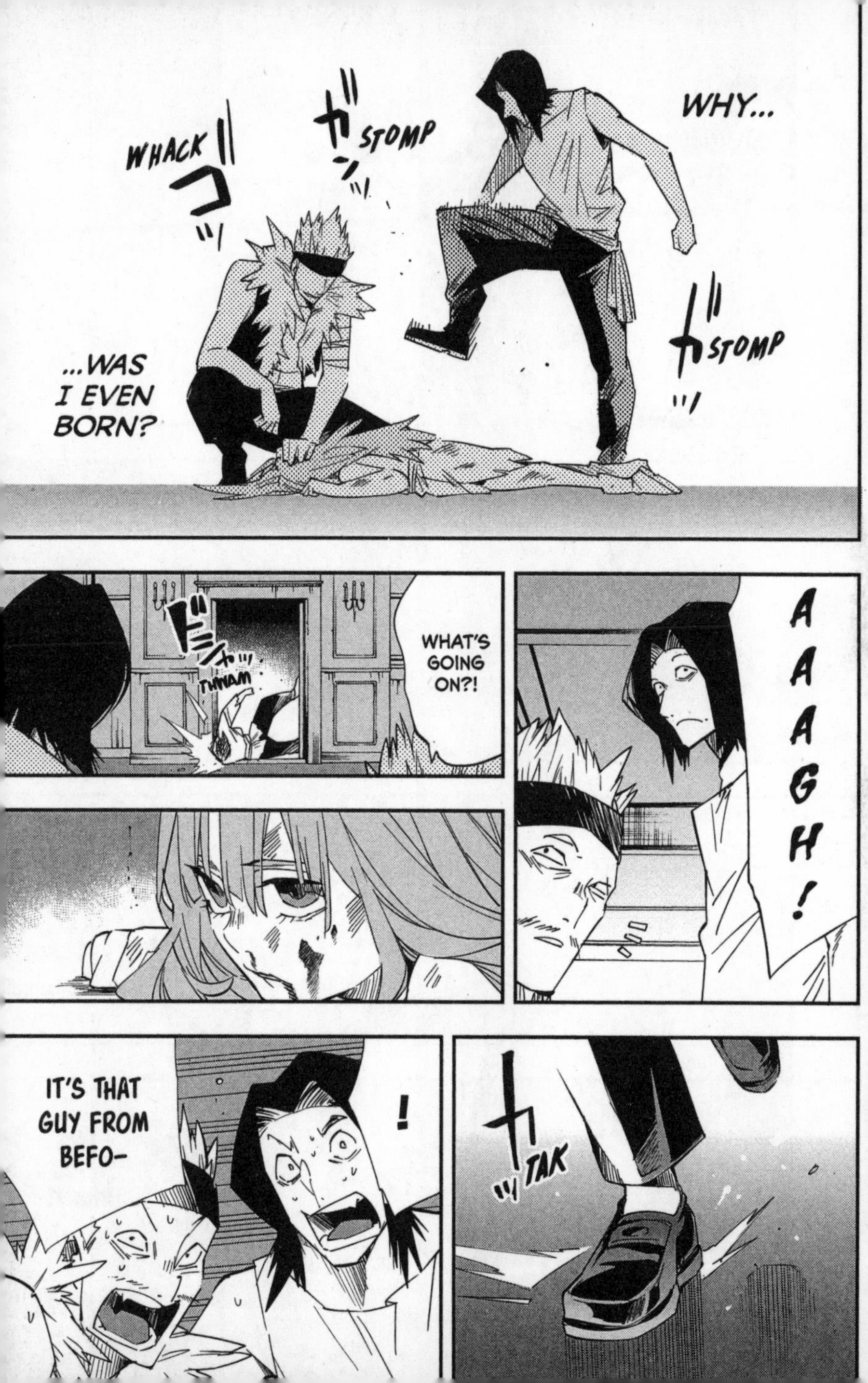
WHY...
STOMP
WHACK
STOMP
...WAS I EVEN BORN?
AAAAGH!
WHAT'S GOING ON?!
THWAM
TAK
!
IT'S THAT GUY FROM BEFO-

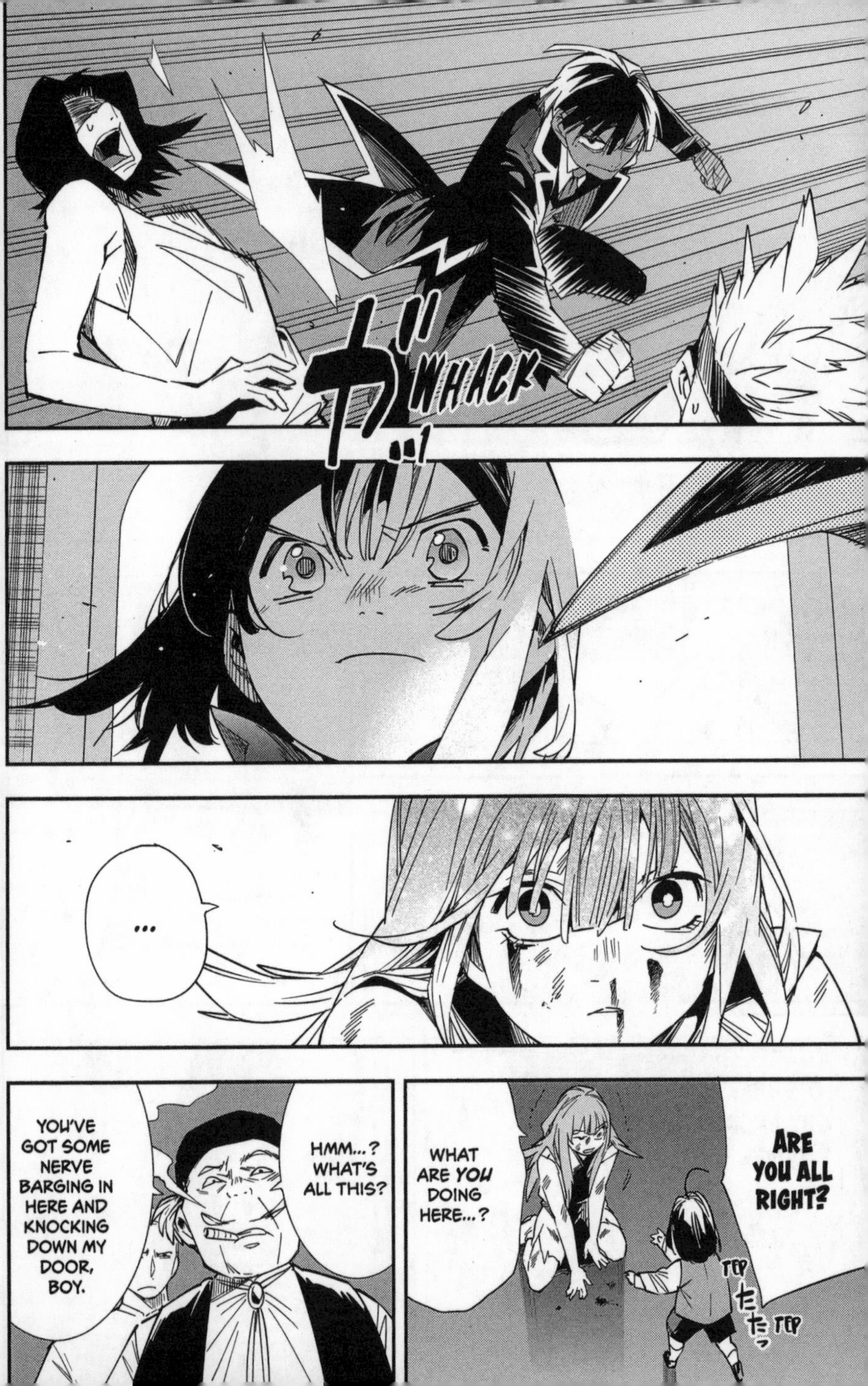
ガッ
WHACK
...!
...
ARE YOU ALL RIGHT?
WHAT ARE YOU DOING HERE...?
TEP
たたっ
TEP
HMM...? WHAT'S ALL THIS?
YOU'VE GOT SOME NERVE BARGING IN HERE AND KNOCKING DOWN MY DOOR, BOY.

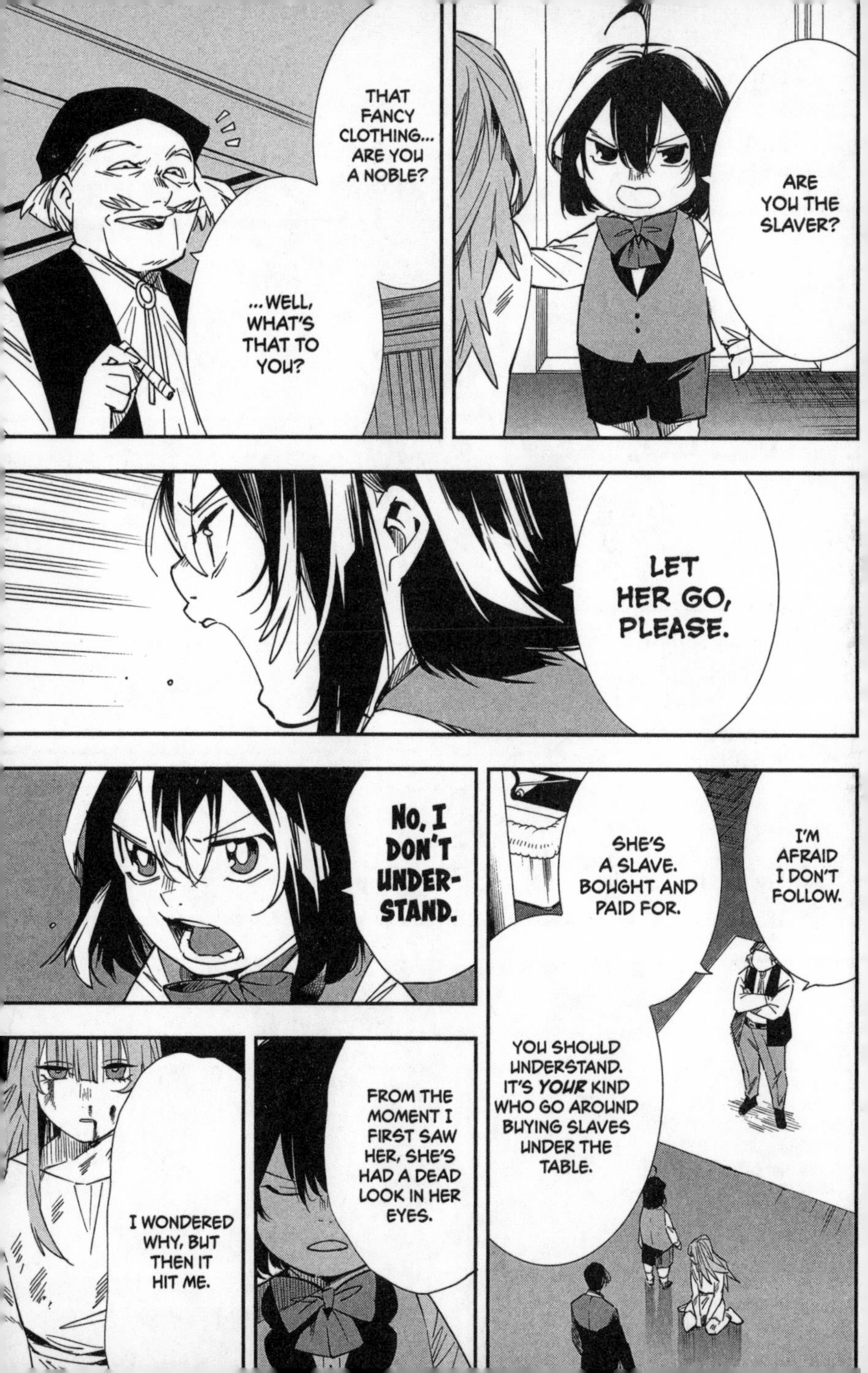
ARE YOU THE SLAVER?
THAT FANCY CLOTHING... ARE YOU A NOBLE?
...WELL, WHAT'S THAT TO YOU?
LET HER GO, PLEASE.
I'M AFRAID I DON'T FOLLOW.
SHE'S A SLAVE. BOUGHT AND PAID FOR.
YOU SHOULD UNDERSTAND. IT'S *YOUR* KIND WHO GO AROUND BUYING SLAVES UNDER THE TABLE.
No, I DON'T UNDER-STAND.
FROM THE MOMENT I FIRST SAW HER, SHE'S HAD A DEAD LOOK IN HER EYES.
I WONDERED WHY, BUT THEN IT HIT ME.

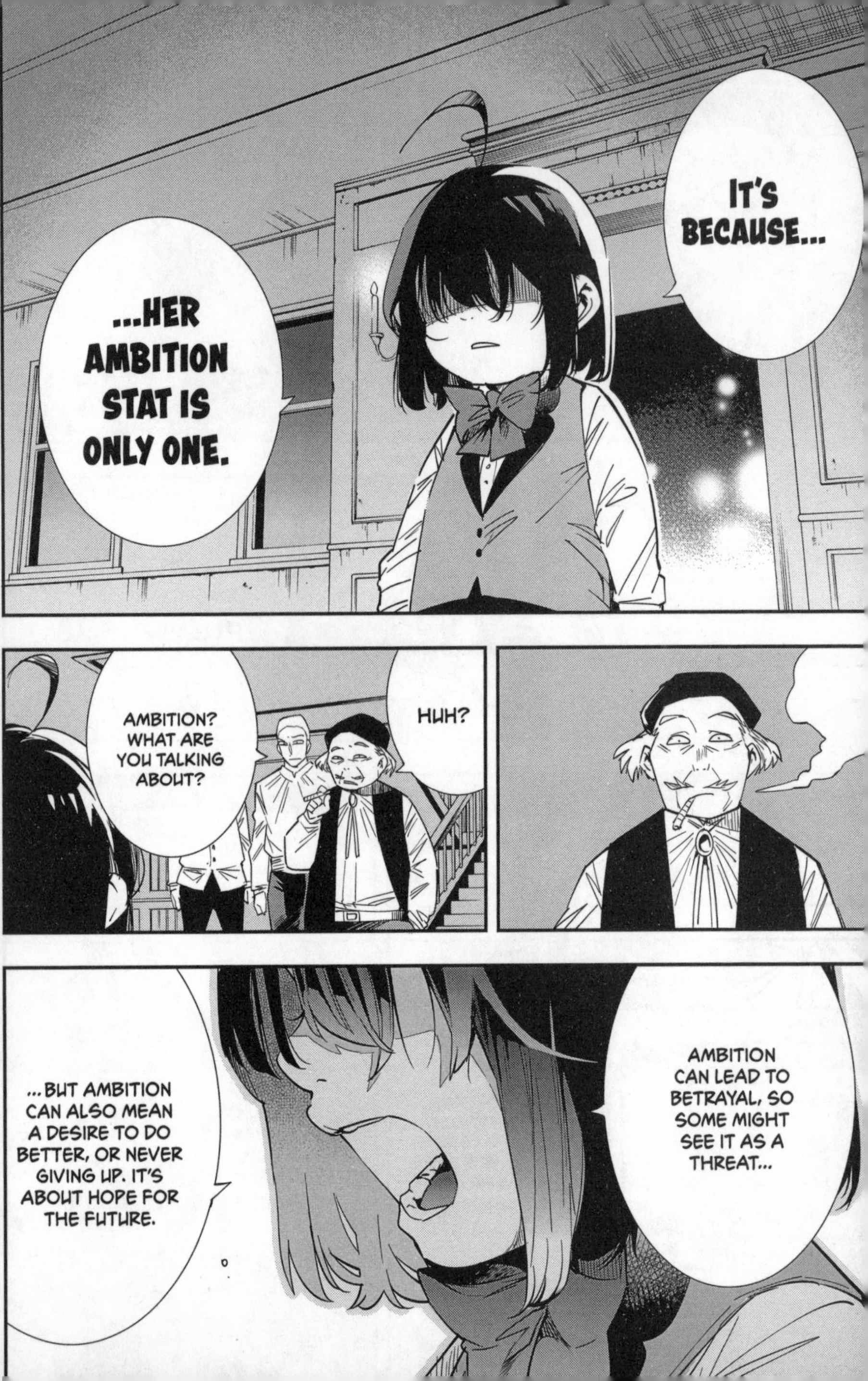
IT'S BECAUSE...
...HER AMBITION STAT IS ONLY ONE.
HUH?
AMBITION? WHAT ARE YOU TALKING ABOUT?
AMBITION CAN LEAD TO BETRAYAL, SO SOME MIGHT SEE IT AS A THREAT...
...BUT AMBITION CAN ALSO MEAN A DESIRE TO DO BETTER, OR NEVER GIVING UP. IT'S ABOUT HOPE FOR THE FUTURE.

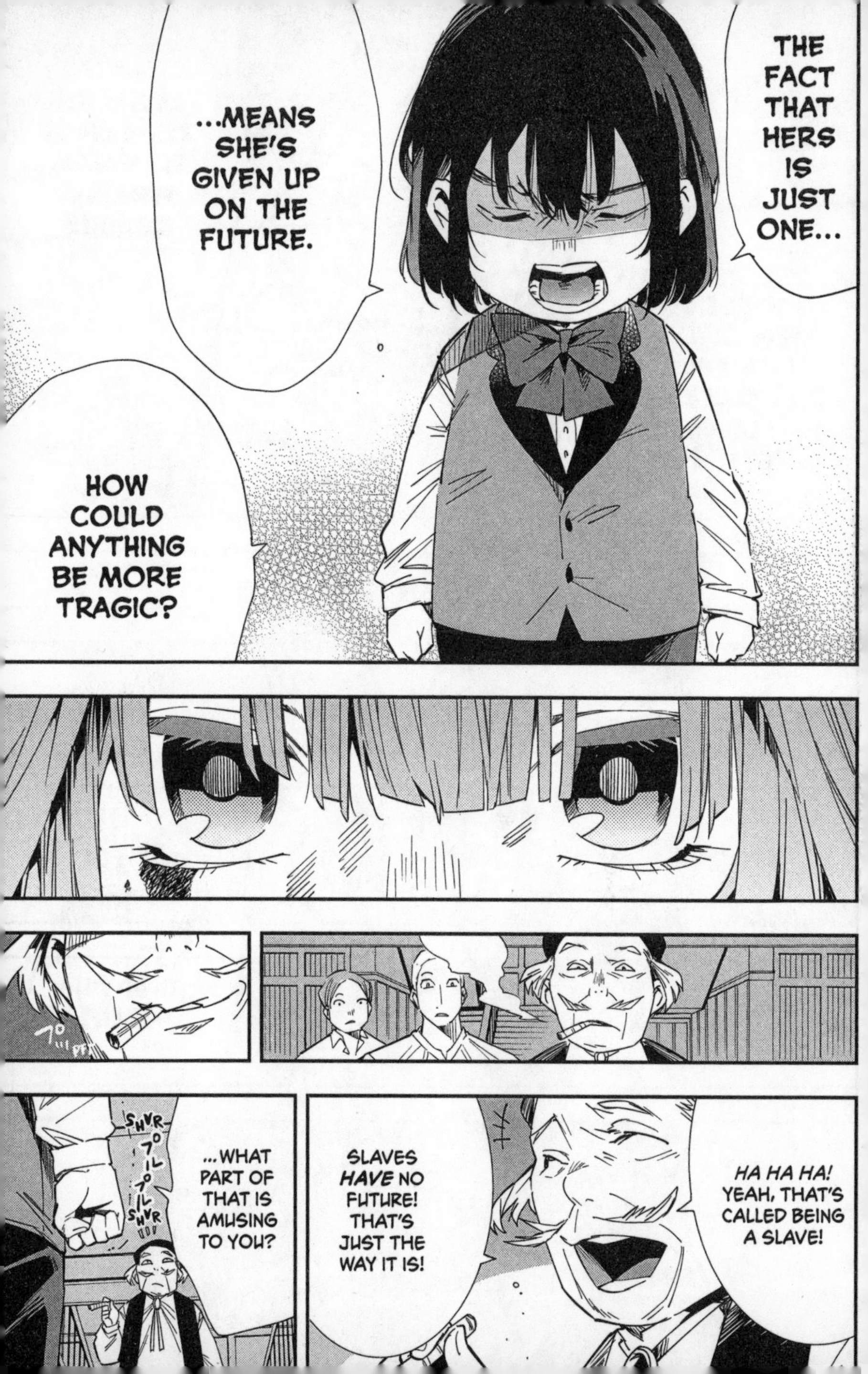
THE FACT THAT HERS IS JUST ONE...
...MEANS SHE'S GIVEN UP ON THE FUTURE.
HOW COULD ANYTHING BE MORE TRAGIC?
PFT
HA HA HA! YEAH, THAT'S CALLED BEING A SLAVE!
SLAVES *HAVE* NO FUTURE! THAT'S JUST THE WAY IT IS!
...WHAT PART OF THAT IS AMUSING TO YOU?
SHVR
SHVR

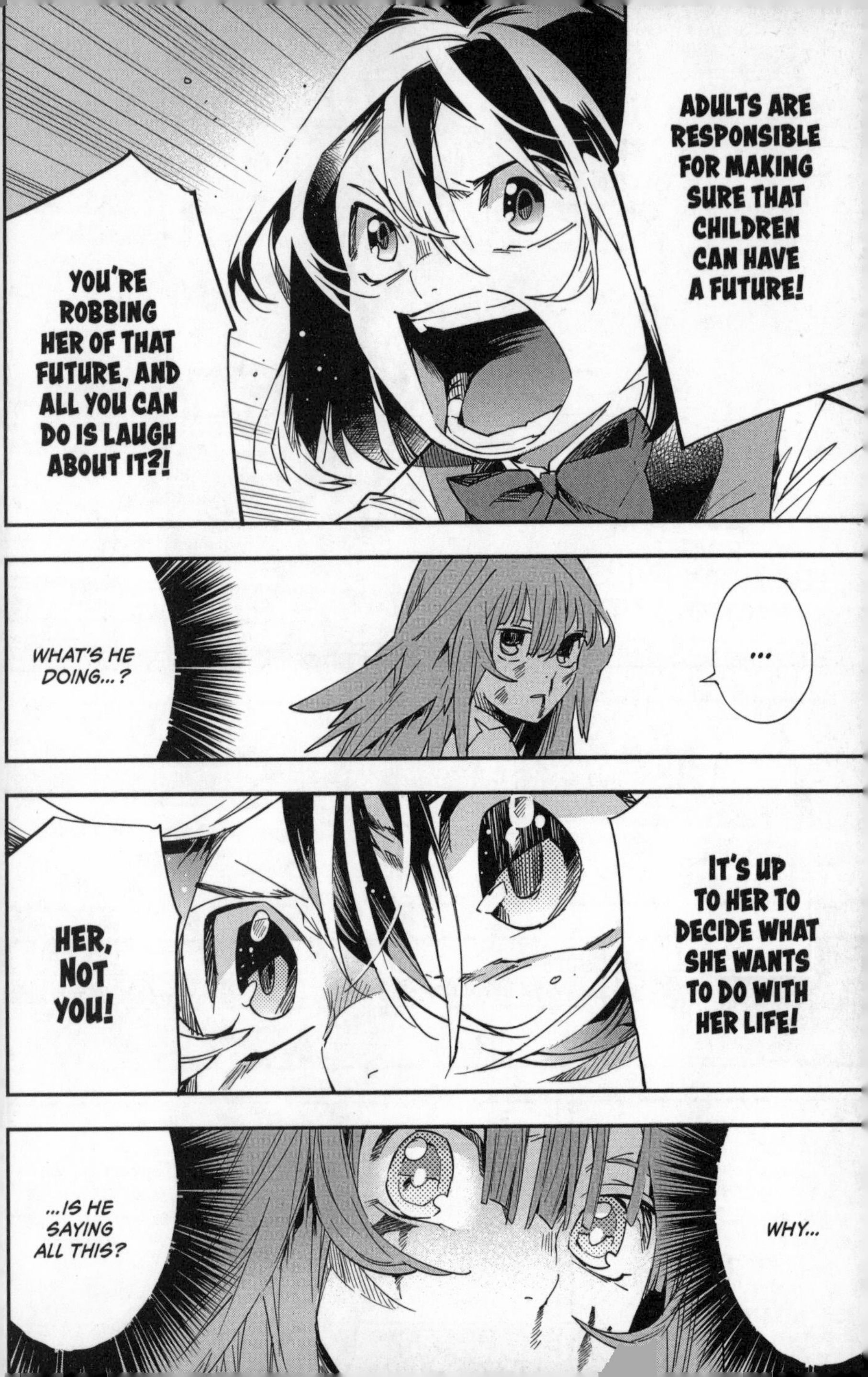
ADULTS ARE RESPONSIBLE FOR MAKING SURE THAT CHILDREN CAN HAVE A FUTURE!
YOU'RE ROBBING HER OF THAT FUTURE, AND ALL YOU CAN DO IS LAUGH ABOUT IT?!
...
WHAT'S HE DOING...?
IT'S UP TO HER TO DECIDE WHAT SHE WANTS TO DO WITH HER LIFE!
HER, NOT YOU!
WHY...
...IS HE SAYING ALL THIS?

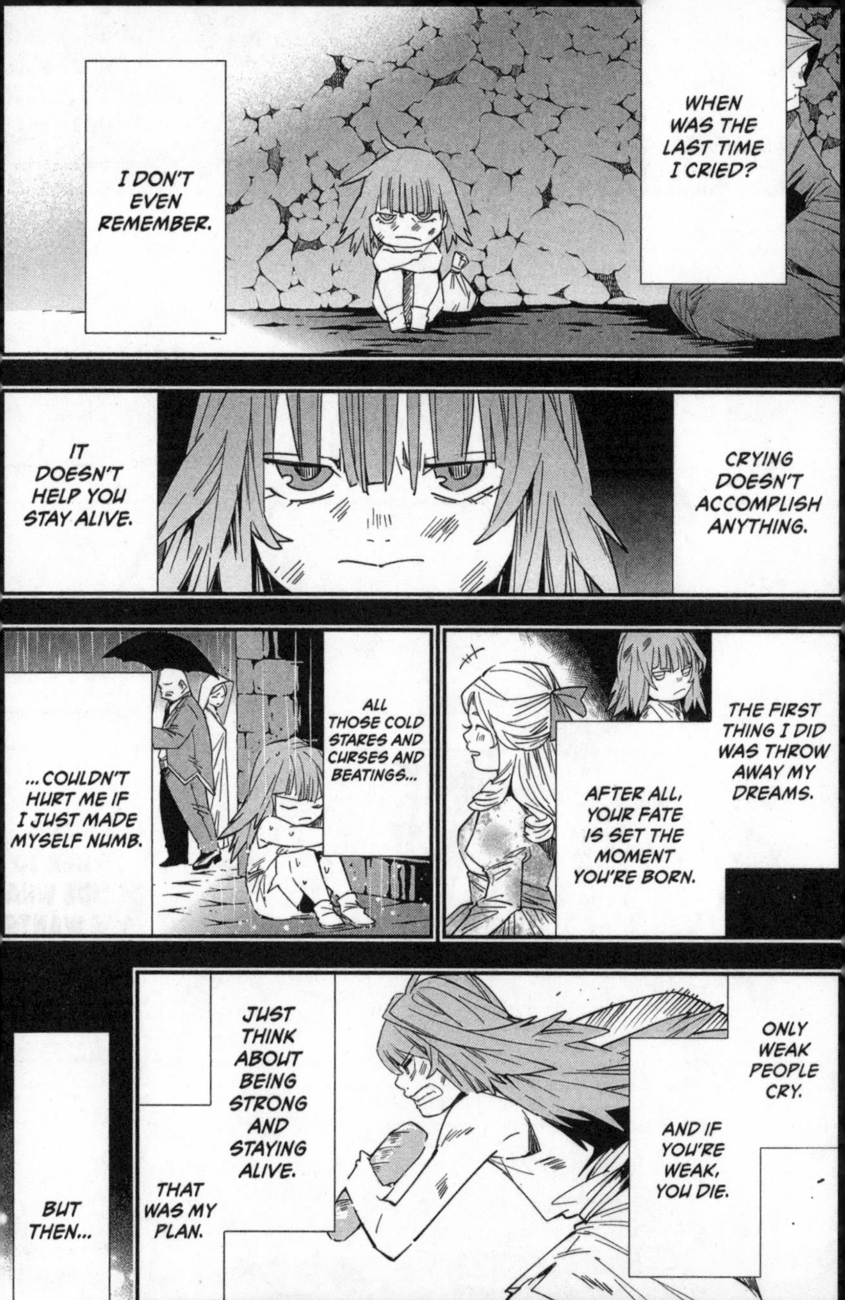
WHEN WAS THE LAST TIME I CRIED?
I DON'T EVEN REMEMBER.
CRYING DOESN'T ACCOMPLISH ANYTHING.
IT DOESN'T HELP YOU STAY ALIVE.
THE FIRST THING I DID WAS THROW AWAY MY DREAMS.
AFTER ALL, YOUR FATE IS SET THE MOMENT YOU'RE BORN.
ALL THOSE COLD STARES AND CURSES AND BEATINGS...
...COULDN'T HURT ME IF I JUST MADE MYSELF NUMB.
ONLY WEAK PEOPLE CRY.
AND IF YOU'RE WEAK, YOU DIE.
JUST THINK ABOUT BEING STRONG AND STAYING ALIVE.
THAT WAS MY PLAN.
BUT THEN...

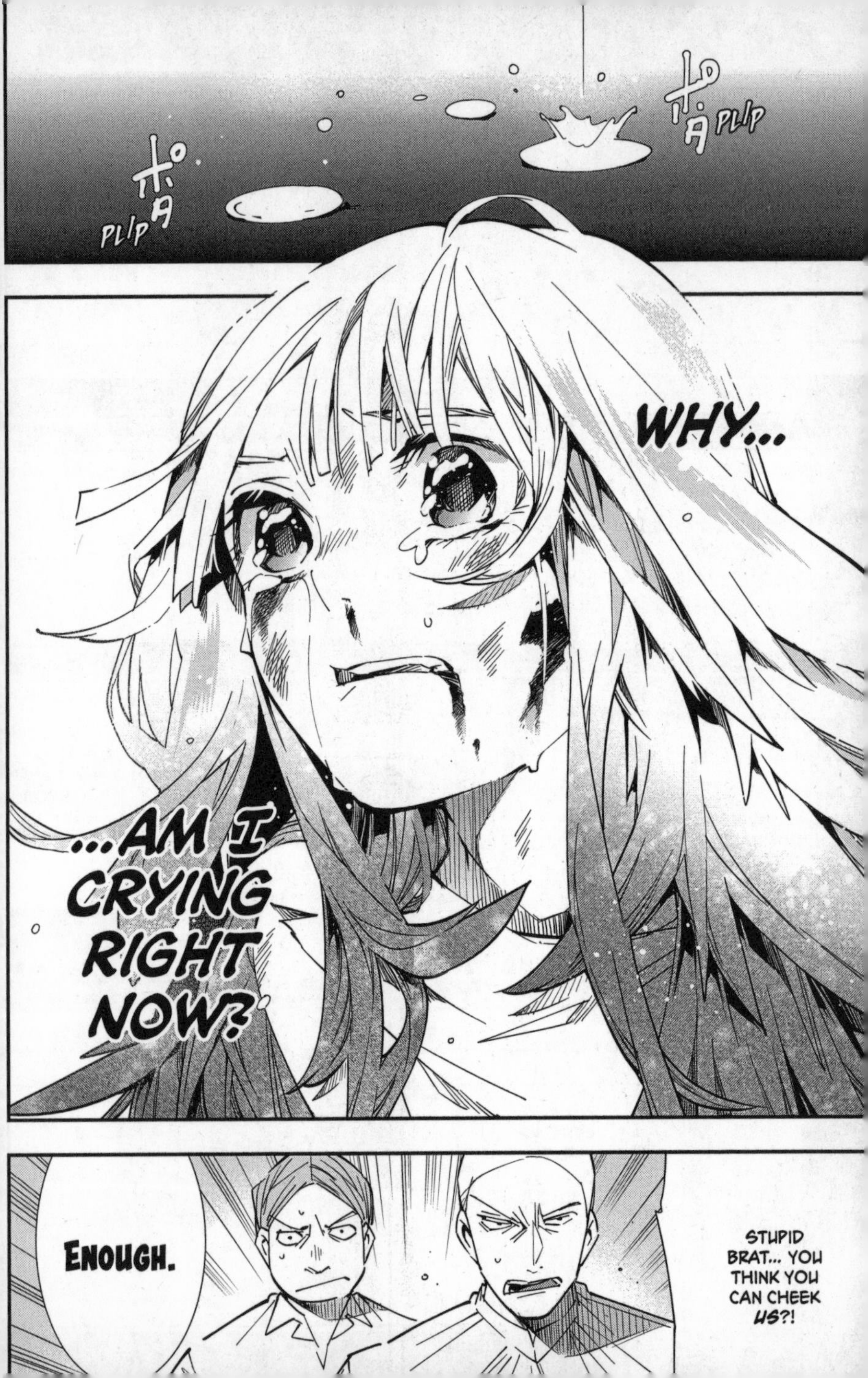
ポタ PLIP
ポタ PLIP
WHY...
...AM I CRYING RIGHT NOW?
STUPID BRAT... YOU THINK YOU CAN CHEEK US?!
ENOUGH.

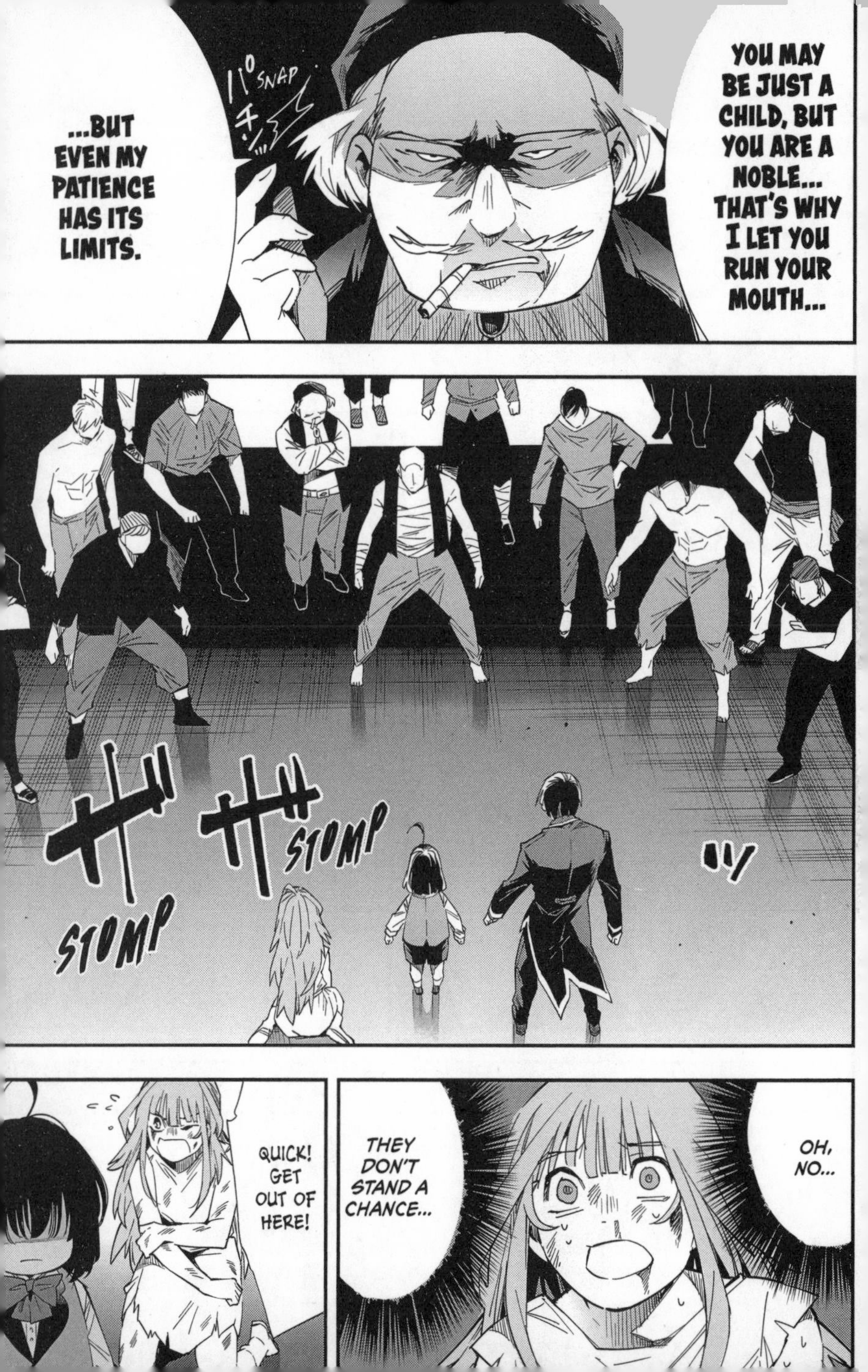
YOU MAY BE JUST A CHILD, BUT YOU ARE A NOBLE... THAT'S WHY I LET YOU RUN YOUR MOUTH...
SNAP
...BUT EVEN MY PATIENCE HAS ITS LIMITS.
STOMP
STOMP
OH, NO...
THEY DON'T STAND A CHANCE...
QUICK! GET OUT OF HERE!

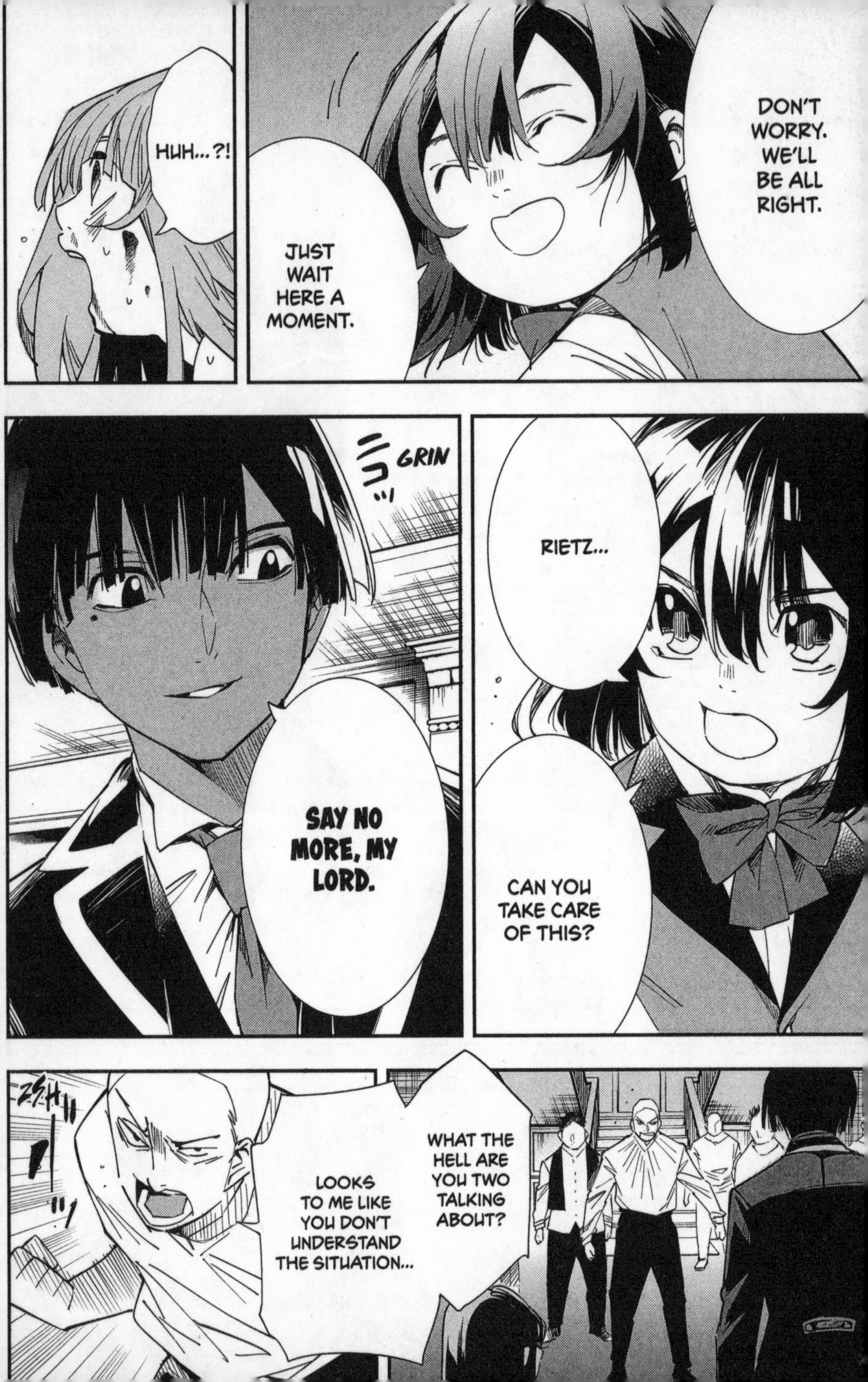
DON'T WORRY. WE'LL BE ALL RIGHT.
JUST WAIT HERE A MOMENT.
HUH...?!
RIETZ...
CAN YOU TAKE CARE OF THIS?
GRIN
SAY NO MORE, MY LORD.
WHAT THE HELL ARE YOU TWO TALKING ABOUT?
LOOKS TO ME LIKE YOU DON'T UNDERSTAND THE SITUATION...

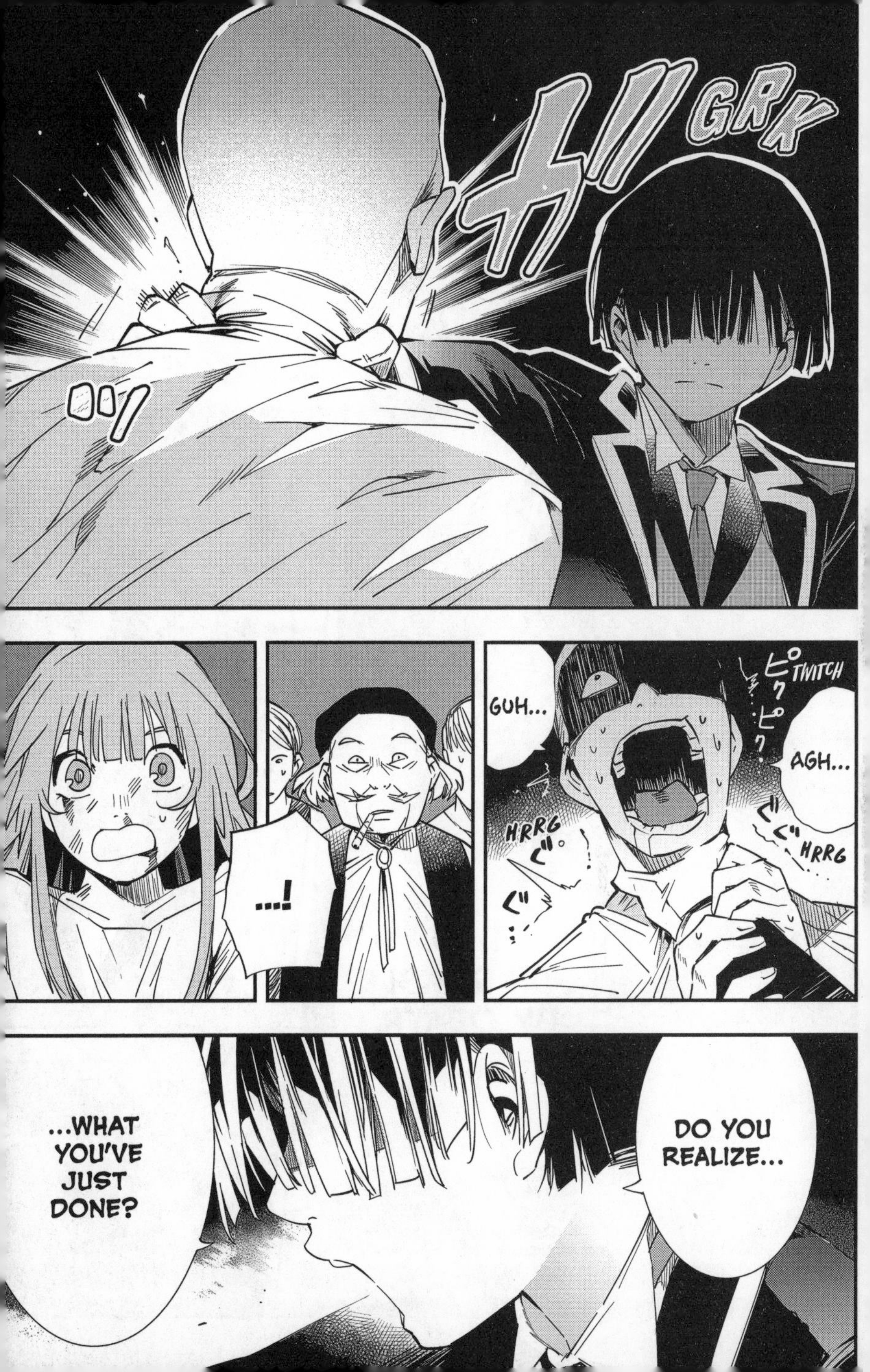
GRK
TWITCH
GUH...
AGH...
HRRG
HRRG
...!
DO YOU REALIZE...
...WHAT YOU'VE JUST DONE?

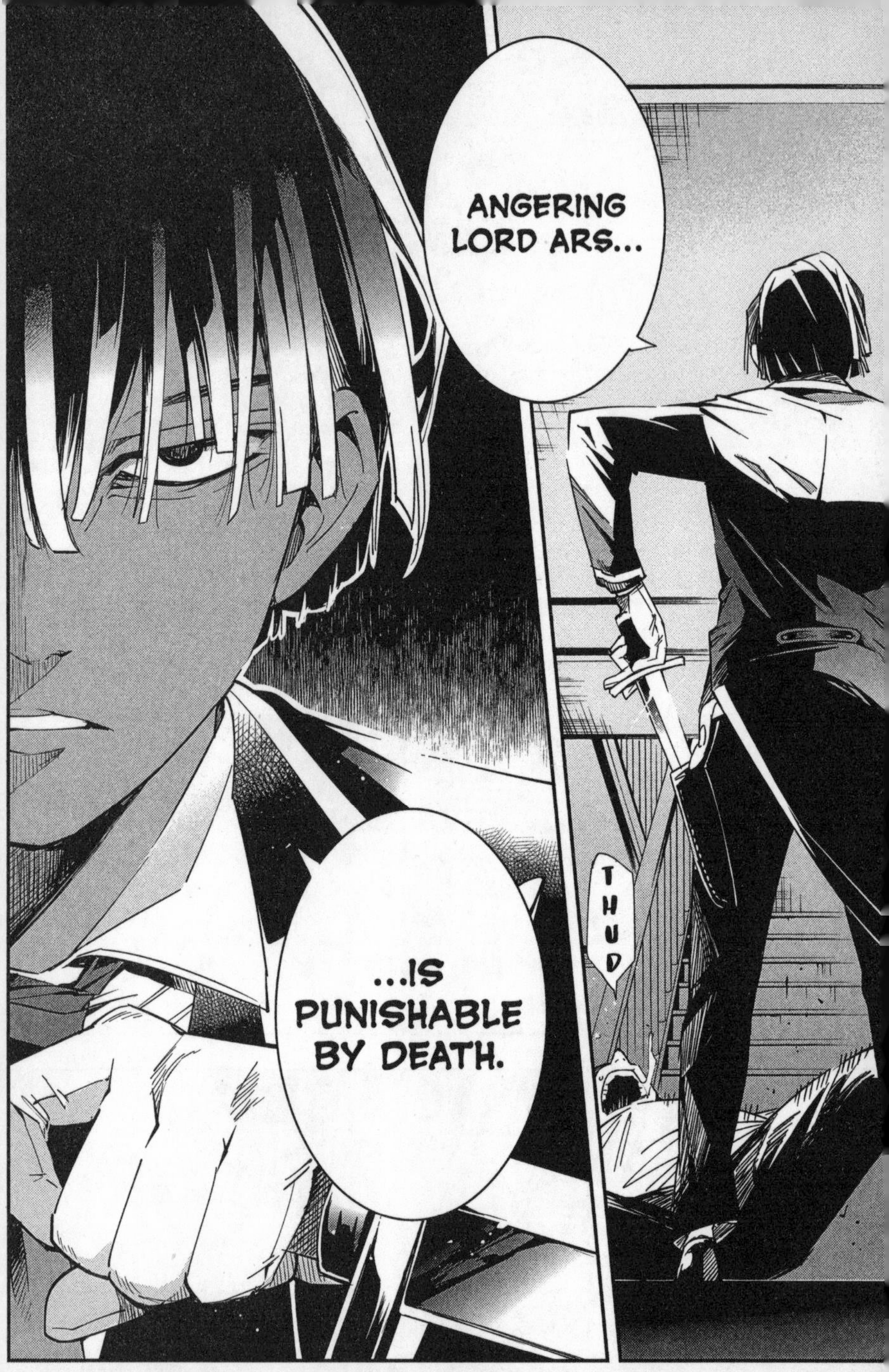
ANGERING LORD ARS...
THUD
...IS PUNISHABLE BY DEATH.

[Story] Miraijin A

Hello. I'm Miraijin A, the author of this work. Thank you so much for purchasing this book. "As a Reincarnated Aristocrat, I'll Use My Appraisal Skill to Rise in the World" was originally a light novel. I'm sure it can't be easy to turn a book into a manga, given that they're so different, but Natsumi Inoue-sensei really brought out 120% of the original story's charm through her artwork. I can't thank everyone enough.

While Ars doesn't achieve any great deeds in the first volume, he does demonstrate the key point of this story by using his appraisal skill to recruit excellent vassals. He's sure to find many more, and there are countless exciting developments in store for him. I hope you'll stick around and join us for that.

[Character Design] jimmy

Congratulations on volume one of the manga!

Rietz looks really cool!

jimmy

TRANSLATION NOTES

pg. 21
Ambition of the Three Kingdoms

Possibly a playful mashup of two famous military strategy games: *Nobunaga's Ambition,* about Oda Nobunaga's attempt to take over all of Japan, and *Romance of the Three Kingdoms,* about the war of the three Chinese kingdoms as depicted in the book of the same name.

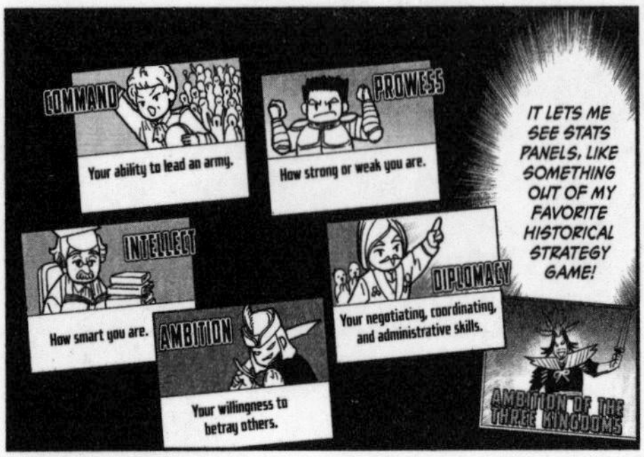

IT LETS ME SEE STATS PANELS, LIKE SOMETHING OUT OF MY FAVORITE HISTORICAL STRATEGY GAME!
PROWESS
How strong or weak you are.
COMMAND
Your ability to lead an army.
DIPLOMACY
Your negotiating, coordinating, and administrative skills.
INTELLECT
How smart you are.
AMBITION OF THE THREE KINGDOMS
AMBITION
Your willingness to betray others.

Rietz Muses – Age 14

Stats

	CURRENT	MAX
Command	87	99
Prowess	78	90
Intellect	89	99
Diplomacy	80	100
Ambition	21	

Aptitude

Fighter	A	Cavalier	S	Archer	A
Mage	C	Engineer	S	Armorer	A
Mariner	D	Pilot	C	Tactician	S

As a Reincarnated Aristocrat, I'll Use My Appraisal Skill to Rise in the World 1 is a work of fiction. Names, characters, places, and incidents are the products of the author's imagination or are used fictitiously. Any resemblance to actual events, locales, or persons, living or dead, is entirely coincidental.

A Kodansha Trade Paperback Original

Published in the United States by
Kodansha USA Publishing, LLC, New York.

Publication rights for this English edition arranged through
Kodansha Ltd., Tokyo.

First published in Japan in 2020 by Kodansha Ltd., Tokyo
as *Tensei kizoku, kantei sukiru de nariagaru,* volume 1.

ISBN 978-1-64651-512-7

Printed in the United States of America.

9 8 7 6 5 4 3 2 1

Translation: Stephen Paul
Lettering: Nicole Roderick
Editing: Andres Oliver
Kodansha USA Publishing edition cover design by Pekka Luhtala

Publisher: Kiichiro Sugawara

Director of Publishing Services: Ben Applegate
Director of Publishing Operations: Dave Barrett
Associate Director of Operations: Stephen Pakula
Publishing Services Managing Editors: Alanna Ruse, Madison Salters

KODANSHA.US

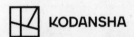

KODANSHA